The Comforts of Home in Western Europe

The Comforts of Home in Western Europe

1700–1900

Edited by Jon Stobart

BLOOMSBURY ACADEMIC
LONDON • NEW YORK • OXFORD • NEW DELHI • SYDNEY

BLOOMSBURY ACADEMIC
Bloomsbury Publishing Plc
50 Bedford Square, London, WC1B 3DP, UK
1385 Broadway, New York, NY 10018, USA
29 Earlsfort Terrace, Dublin 2, Ireland

BLOOMSBURY, BLOOMSBURY ACADEMIC and the Diana logo are trademarks of
Bloomsbury Publishing Plc

First published in Great Britain 2020
Paperback edition published 2021

Copyright © Jon Stobart, 2020

Jon Stobart has asserted his right under the Copyright, Designs and
Patents Act, 1988, to be identified as Editor of this work.

Cover design by Tjaša Krivec

Cover image: Frank and Fred Sarg in the drawing room, Worms / Watercolor
and gouache over pencil on paper
(© Mary Ellen Best / Artmedia / Alamy Stock Photo)

All rights reserved. No part of this publication may be reproduced or transmitted
in any form or by any means, electronic or mechanical, including photocopying,
recording, or any information storage or retrieval system, without prior
permission in writing from the publishers.

Bloomsbury Publishing Plc does not have any control over, or responsibility for, any
third-party websites referred to or in this book. All internet addresses given in this
book were correct at the time of going to press. The author and publisher regret any
inconvenience caused if addresses have changed or sites have ceased to exist,
but can accept no responsibility for any such changes.

A catalogue record for this book is available from the British Library.

A catalog record for this book is available from the Library of Congress.

ISBN: HB: 978-1-3500-9295-2
PB: 978-1-3502-4675-1
ePDF: 978-1-3500-9296-9
eBook: 978-1-3500-9297-6

Typeset by Deanta Global Publishing Services, Chennai, India

To find out more about our authors and books visit www.bloomsbury.com and
sign up for our newsletters.

In memory of Rosie MacArthur, 1981–2018

Contents

List of illustrations ix
Notes on contributors xi

Introduction: Comfort, the home and home comforts *Jon Stobart* 1

Part One The convenient house: Architectural ideals and practicalities 17

1 Convenience, utility and comfort in British domestic architecture of the long eighteenth century *Dale Townshend* 19

People in focus 1: Masters and servants: Parallel worlds in Blondel's *maisons de plaisance* *Aurélien Davrius* 39

2 Northern comfort and discomfort: Spaces and objects in Swedish country houses, c.1740–1800 *Johanna Ilmakunnas* 45

Object in focus 1: Marketing the necessary comforts in Georgian Dublin *Conor Lucey* 67

3 The invention of thermal comfort in eighteenth-century France *Olivier Jandot* 73

Object in focus 2: The improved tiled stove: Sweden's contribution to defining comfort? *Cristina Prytz* 93

People in focus 2: Keeping warm with Sir John Soane *Diego Bocchini* 99

4 The spread of comfort in nineteenth-century Belgian homes *Britt Denis* 104

Part Two Home making: Objects and emotions 125

5 Home Making: Women, marriage and comfort in Victorian middle-class drawing rooms *Jane Hamlett* 127

Object in focus 3: The ideal home in 1732: The Uppark Dolls' House as a study in comfort *Patricia Ferguson* 149

Object in focus 4: Comfort compromised? The 'bachelor box' in Finland at the turn of the twentieth century *Laika Nevalainen* 155

6   Feeling at home abroad: Comfort, domesticity and social display on
    the Netherlandish Grand Tour, 1585–1815 *Gerrit Verhoeven*   160

People in focus 3: Moving house: Comfort disrupted in the domestic
    and emotional life of an eighteenth-century bachelor *Helen Metcalfe*   181

7   Home from home? Making life comfortable in the Victorian
    barracks *Rowena Willard-Wright*   187

Object in focus 5: A wallpaper sandwich: Comfort in the student room
    in nineteenth-century Cambridge *Serena Dyer*   208

8   Making a home: Family, memory and domestic objects in England,
    c.1750–1830 *Jon Stobart*   214

Object in focus 6: The comfort of animal 'things' in late-Victorian
    Britain *Julie-Marie Strange*   234

Afterthoughts: The comforts of home *Jon Stobart*   239

Bibliography   245
Index   259

Illustrations

1.1	John Wood, *A Series of Plans, for Cottages or Habitations of the Labourer*, 1788	29
1.2	Edward Gyfford, *Designs for Elegant Cottages and Small Villas*, 1806	34
1a.1	Jacques-François Blondel, *De la Distribution des maisons de plaisance et de la décoration des édifices en général*, 1737–8	41
2.1	Carl Wijnblad, *Ritningar på fyrtio våningshus*, 1755	47
2.2	Jean Erik Rehn, *Granhammar House, Façade and Plans*, 1749–59	51
2.3	Olof Fridsberg, *Countess Ulla Sparre in her Writing Cabinet*, 1760s	55
2.4	Lorentz Svensson Sparrgren, *Interior with Clas Julius Ekebland and his wife, Countess Brita Horn*, 1783	57
2.5	Pehr Hilleström, *The Wool Winder*, c. 1780–90	60
2a.1	Handbill of Pemberton & Co., 1811	70
3.1	The bedroom in the Duchess of Orleans' appartement at the Palais-Royal, 1876	75
3.2	James Gillray, *The Comforts of a Rumford Stove*, 1800	81
3a.1	Old Style Tile Stove and the Improved Model of Cronstedt and Wrede	95
3b.1	Plan of the basement rooms at Sir John Soane's house and museum, 1839	102
4.1	Presence of Heating Devices, 1834–5 and 1880	107
4.2	Lighting Devices by Fuel, 1834–5 and 1880	111
5.1	Dining Room, H. J. Jennings, *Our Homes, and How to Beautify Them*, 1902	136
5.2	Drawing Room, H. J. Jennings, *Our Homes, and How to Beautify Them*, 1902	137
5a.1	The Uppark Dolls' House, c. 1730	150
6.1	Punt Jan, *Sophia Strikes up a Conversation with the Innkeeper after Dinner has been Served*, 1749	166
6.2	John Pettit, *The Amorous Traveller*, 1789	171
6a.1	Charles Lamb, 1754	182
7.1	Bed spaces in Horfield Barracks, Gloucestershire Regiment, 1904	192

7.2	Barrack room of Lieutenant Edward Hovell Thurlow at Landguard Fort, 1856	199
7.3	The adjutant's idea, pencil sketch, c. 1872–90	201
7a.1	Wallpaper Sandwich, 1795	210
8.1	Great Hall, Audley End, mid-nineteenth century	218
8.2	Armchair, c. 1725	219
8.3	George Hargreaves, Portrait Miniature of Catherine Hughes, c. 1824	224
8a.1	Christmas Day with his Favourite Companions, *The Idler*, 1897	236

Contributors

Diego Bocchini is an engineer and independent researcher. He graduated in 2015 from the University of Bologna with a thesis on John Soane at the outset of the modern movement. His latest interests concern the history of heating systems and domestic architecture.

Aurélien Davrius is assistant professor at the École nationale supérieure d'architecture Paris-Malaquais. A specialist in the history of architecture in France in the seventeenth to nineteenth centuries, he has published a biography of Jacques-François Blondel (1708/9-1774) (Paris, 2018) and is currently writing a book about architecture and politic in France and Germany during the eighteenth and nineteenth century.

Britt Denis is part of the Centre for Urban History of the University of Antwerp. Her PhD research, 'Domesticity in practice. Material culture, home technologies and space in an age of transition (nineteenth-century Antwerp)', questions the lived experience of the domestic ideology based on an innovative empirical study of Antwerp probate inventories. By explicitly focusing on the material, technological and spatial dimensions of 'home', this research sets out to unravel previously unstudied practices of homemaking for a society in transition.

Serena Dyer is Early Career Academic Fellow at De Montfort University and Associate Fellow of the Institute of Advanced Studies at the University of Warwick. She was previously Curator of the Museum of Domestic Design and Architecture and has previously published works on material culture, consumption and childhood in the eighteenth century. Her book, *Material Lives: Women Makers and Consumer Culture in the Eighteenth Century*, is forthcoming with Bloomsbury.

Patricia Ferguson is a British Museum Project Curator of eighteenth-century European ceramics, and since 2011 has been the advisor on ceramics to the National Trust. Her research interests focus on ceramics and the country house. Recent publications include *Ceramics: 400 years of British Collecting in 100 Masterpieces* (London, 2017) and *Garnitures: Vase Sets from National Trust*

Houses (London, 2017). She is currently editing a British Museum research publication, *Pots, Prints and Politics: Ceramics with an Agenda*.

Jane Hamlett is a Professor of Modern British History at Royal Holloway, University of London. Her research interests include the home, family, domesticity and material culture and her current research project focuses on pets and family life in England and Wales in the nineteenth and twentieth century. Her books include *Material Relations: Middle-Class Families and Domestic Interiors in England, 1850-1910* (Manchester University Press, 2010) and *At Home in the Institution: Material Life in Asylums, Schools and Lodging Houses in Victorian and Edwardian England* (Palgrave, 2015).

Johanna Ilmakunnas is Associate Professor of Nordic History at Åbo Akademi University, Finland. Her research interests include material culture, gender, lifestyle and consumption in eighteenth-century and early-nineteenth-century Europe. Recently, she has focused on the cultural history of work, particularly handiwork and crafts. Recent publications include *A Taste for Luxury in Early Modern Europe: Display, Acquisition and Boundaries* (2017, co-edited with Jon Stobart) and *Early Professional Women in Northern Europe, c. 1650–1850* (2017, co-edited with Marjatta Rahikainen & Kirsi Vainio-Korhonen).

Olivier Jandot holds the Agrégation and a PhD in History from the University of Lyon. He teaches in a secondary school in Arras (Lycée Gambetta-Carnot) and at the University of Artois, where he is a member of the History research centre (EA 4027 CREHS). His research focuses on the intersection between the history of material culture, the history of the body and the history of sensibilities. He is the author of *Les délices du feu : l'homme, le chaud et le froid à l'époque moderne* (Ceyzérieu: Champ Vallon, 2017).

Conor Lucey is Assistant Professor of Architectural History at University College Dublin, and President of the Royal Society of Antiquaries of Ireland. His research interests include early modern urbanism, neoclassicism and print culture, and the contested relationship between architectural design and building production. His most recent book is *Building Reputations: Architecture and the Artisan, 1750–1830* (Manchester, 2018).

Helen Metcalfe was awarded her AHRC-funded doctorate by the University of Manchester in 2017, which explored the social experience of bachelorhood in late-Georgian England. She is a social, gender and family historian of Georgian

Britain specializing in the history of masculinities, the home and domestic material culture, and is currently a Teaching Fellow at the University of York. Helen continues to develop her research interests in the history of emotions and sensory history, and in her next research project seeks to evaluate the relationship between physical and emotional responses to, and experiences of, grief, loss and resilience in Georgian society.

Laika Nevalainen is an historian of everyday life, housing and single life. She received her PhD from the European University Institute (Florence, Italy) in 2018. Her PhD research examined the everyday life and homes of bachelors in late nineteenth- and early twentieth-century Finland.

Cristina Prytz is a historian of early modern Sweden, currently lecturing at the Swedish University of Agricultural Sciences in Uppsala. Her work has lately (and as a Marie S. Curie financed research fellow at Manchester Metropolitan University in 2015–17) focused on emotions and the idea of home comforts in eighteenth-century Sweden and England. Her research also includes studies on property rights, work and gender.

Jon Stobart is Professor of History at Manchester Metropolitan University. His research interests span a range of topics in retailing and consumption, chiefly in eighteenth-century England. Recent projects have focused on the country house, both as a site of consumption and a place with the capacity to offer physical and emotional comfort. His recent publications include *Consumption and the Country House* (Oxford, 2016) and *Travel and the British Country House* (Manchester, 2017). He is general editor for the forthcoming series A Cultural History of Shopping (Bloomsbury, 2020).

Julie-Marie Strange is Professor of Modern British History at Durham University. Her research interests are broad and publications range from *Death, Grief and Poverty, 1870-1914* (2005), *Fatherhood and the British Working Class, 1865-1914*(2015) to more recent collaborative works, *The Invention of the Modern Dog: Breed and Blood in Victorian Britain* (2018) and *The Charity Market, 1870-1914* (2018). She is currently working with Jane Hamlett on 'Pets and Family Life' and has a new project, 'Love in the Time of Capitalism: Emotion & the Making of the Working Class'.

Dale Townshend is Professor of Gothic Literature in the Manchester Centre for Gothic Studies, Manchester Metropolitan University. He has particular research interests in the relationship between Gothic architecture and Gothic writing (fiction; poetry; drama) in the late eighteenth and early nineteenth centuries. His recent publications include *Gothic Antiquity: History, Romance, and the Architectural Imagination, 1760–1840* (OUP, 2019) and, with Michael Carter and Peter N. Lindfield, *Writing Britain's Ruins* (British Library, 2017). With Angela Wright and Catherine Spooner, he is currently completing the three-volume *The Cambridge History of the Gothic* (CUP, 2020).

Gerrit Verhoeven lectures in cultural history at the University of Antwerp (Belgium). Early modern travel behaviour is one of his favourite research topics with a special interest in the material culture of travel. Recent publications include *Europe within reach. Netherlandish Travellers on the Grand Tour and Beyond* (Leiden 2015) and the co-edited volume *Beyond the Grand Tour. Northern Metropolises and Early Modern Travel Behaviour* (London 2017)

Rowena Willard-Wright studied art history at the Courtauld Institute of Art, then started her career at Osborne House and was the curator for the Osborne centenary project in the late 1990s. As senior curator for English Heritage in the South East, she worked with the interiors and collections associated with nineteenth-century barracks at such properties as Dover Castlend Fort Brockhurst. Now working as a curator for the National Trust, while undertaking a doctorate looking at the influence of empire on Cold War emergency planning, she is interested in the long shadow that colonialism of the nineteenth century has thrown over the processes and thinking of British Government.

Introduction:
Comfort, the home and home comforts

Jon Stobart

At the moment of her departure, good Mr Errold was severely afflicted, and he felt all his early love for this dear object of his warm affection recur forcibly to his recollection; but a very short time restored him, and he considered her death as no real deprivation of home comforts and happiness.[1]

According to the *OED*, this passage from the 1797 novel *Milistina; or The Double Interest* is the first time that the phrase 'home comfort' appeared in print. It describes the reaction of the clergyman Mr Errold to the sudden and unexpected death of his boorish wife. Subsequent developments in the story underline the nature and importance of such comforts. The recently widowed Mr Errold is kindly offered residence in the 'truly hospitable' surrounds of Trent Hall, Dorset, the home of Sir George, Lady Berrel, their son Henry and their daughter the eponymous heroine Milistina. There, he availed himself of the physical and spiritual, material and immaterial comforts of home. Other writers of the period attest to the fact that, by the early nineteenth century, 'home comforts' had entered into common parlance, serving as an idiomatic expression or rhetorical shorthand that referred to both the physical and spiritual sense of refreshment and sustenance, consolation and relief that the domestic sphere, at its best, was capable of offering. This was dependent upon semantic changes that occurred to the term 'comfort' itself – a shift that requires some exploration if its full meanings and nuances are to be understood.

My object in this introductory essay is to explore these changes of meaning – of both comfort and home – and reflect upon their material and human dimensions. This forms an important presage to the wider ambitions of the volume: to offer a wide-ranging and pan-European exploration of the ways in which notions of comfort and home served to shape the domestic environment during the eighteenth and nineteenth centuries. My focus here is primarily on Britain, and more specifically

England, as this is where the word 'comfort' took hold and first developed some of its modern connotations. However, I also explore more briefly how those meanings spread across Europe in the late eighteenth and early nineteenth century.

Comfort

In early modern times, comfort was firmly associated with emotional well-being, a feeling of being comfortable and offering comfort (or consolation) to others. John Kersey's *New English Dictionary* (1713), for instance, defined it as a noun that meant 'help, ease or relief in distress'; in its verbal form, 'comfort' meant 'to afford comfort, to encourage'.[2] It is in this sense that Daniel Defoe used the word most frequently. In *Moll Flanders* (1722), the eponymous heroine worries that 'in this distress I had no assistant, no friend to comfort or advise me' or again that 'the good minister ... did what he could to comfort me with the same arguments'.[3] Little had changed by the time that Samuel Johnson compiled his *Dictionary of the English Language* (1755), though he added nuance to both noun and verb, offering three definitions: 1. Support; assistance; countenance; 2. Consolation; support under calamity or danger; 3. That which gives consolation or support.[4] Contemporary authors used the term in similar senses, with Samuel Richardson having his eponymous heroine in *Pamela* (1740) proclaim: 'You know sir ... that a father and mother's comfort is the dearest thing to a good child that can be.' There is a hint of materiality in Pamela's rejection of material possessions, especially fine clothes: 'I have no comfort in them, or anything else', she claims. But even here, comfort is emotional rather than physical, deriving, as it does, from the clothes as signifiers of status and not through her bodily experience of them.

Johnson, however, was himself clearly aware that comfort carried other meanings too. In his *History of Rasselas* (1759), he compares the situation of Europeans and Africans from the perspective of a fictional African traveller who observes that 'in enumerating the particular comforts of life, we shall find many advantages on the side of the Europeans'; such advantages, it soon becomes clear, include medical care, transport and houses.[5] There is a certain materiality to these to notions of 'creature comforts' that was already current in the mid-seventeenth century: the Westminster divine John Arrowsmith wrote in his *Chain of Principles* (1659) that 'the Scripture useth diminishing terms when it speaks of creature comforts', referring here to material things such as food, clothing and accommodation.[6]

Johnson was looking forward as well as back and presaged a change in the meaning of comfort that, as John Crowley argues, placed increasing emphasis on physical ease and thus on the corporeal body. This set of changes was also mapped by John Cornforth in his study of country house interiors, which he explicitly saw as a quest for comfort in a physical sense.[7] For Crowley, this 'invention of comfort' was manifest in changing attitudes among householders and in a related set of changes in domestic material culture: technological developments aimed at making the house warmer, lighter and better ventilated (through the use of lamps, stoves and chimneys); an array of different and especially upholstered furniture (most notably easy chairs and sofas), and shifts in the organization and setting of the house, with a growing emphasis on privacy.[8] Such changes were by no means culturally specific, as Joan DeJean has demonstrated in her study of late seventeenth- and early eighteenth-century Paris, where she also touches on water closets, bedrooms and the like.[9] Indeed, these two contexts can be seen as part of a longer trajectory of change in domestic environments, changes which, for some, reached their zenith in the cosy parlour of Victorian Britain, crammed as it was with upholstered furniture (see the chapter by Jane Hamlett).[10] For other scholars, such tendencies have continued well into the twentieth century, with its proliferation of labour-saving domestic devices such as vacuum cleaners and electric fires.[11]

Lexicographers were slow to recognize these developments, or at least to incorporate them into their dictionaries. By the end of the eighteenth century, James Barclay in his *Complete and Universal English Dictionary* (1792) was still defining comfort in the older sense of consolation: to comfort was, among other things, 'to make a person grow cheerful that is in sorrow, by advice and arguments', while 'comfortable' meant that which was able to be comforted or capable of receiving comfort. Even by 1839, Charles Richardson in his *New Dictionary of the English Language* stuck firmly with notions of solace, cheering up and strengthening.[12] Only in Noah Webster's *American Dictionary of the English Language*, originally published in 1828 but revised and expanded in 1839, do we see some variation. Among nine definitions of comfort, most of which remain fixed on ideas of support, strength, consolation and cheer, he offers the following: 'that which gives security from want, and furnishes moderate enjoyment'.[13] In this sense, comfort is something that lifts the individual out of absolute necessity and offers some cheer – ideas that are reflected in Elizabeth Gaskell's first novel, *Mary Barton* (1848), where the eponymous heroine notes that a home is dingy and comfortless without a fire and later makes some 'purchases necessary for her father's comfort'.[14]

Comfort as improvement applied to society as well as to the individual. Growing physical comfort signalled material and societal progress, and helped to defuse moral debates about luxury by offering a more morally neutral language of comfort and convenience.[15] Indeed, Marie-Odile Bernez suggests that comfort in the eighteenth century allowed contemporaries to critique foreign and especially French luxury, along with its overtones of waste, excess and inequality, with virtuous English comfort, available to all as a consequence of economic and social development.[16] Crowley goes further, arguing that there was a fundamental shift in mindset as comfort became a key goal for elite and middling householders by the closing decades of the eighteenth century: for the first time, bodily comfort was being prioritized over considerations of fashion, taste or gentility.[17] Despite DeJean's assertion of the origins of comfort in early-eighteenth-century Paris, writers in the early nineteenth century saw domestic comfort as something that was new and noteworthy. In *Ivanhoe* (1819), Walter Scott gave expression to the opinions of many when he claimed that domestic comfort was a thoroughly modern construct, tellingly interrupting his description of the visually sumptuous chamber of the twelfth-century Saxon Princess Rowena with the following claim: 'Yet let not modern beauty envy the magnificence of a Saxon princess. ... Magnificence there was, with some rude attempt at taste, but of comfort there was little, and, being unknown, it was unmissed.'[18]

Scott's view of the past and present is somewhat teleological, but the importance of material comfort rapidly worked its way into romantic-era literature. Jane Austen frequently invoked notions of comfort in the modern sense, exploring them in her early *Northanger Abbey* (1798–9) and developing them more fully in her later novels. Speaking of Colonel Brandon's home in *Sense and Sensibility* (1811), for example, Mrs Jennings observes that Delaford Parsonage 'is a nice place, I can tell you; exactly what I call a nice old fashioned place, full of comforts and conveniences'.[19] This pairing of comfort and convenience is telling: the two went hand in hand for Mrs Jennings, making the parsonage a physical comfortable home and also one that was suited to current modes of living. In *Pride and Prejudice* (1813), Mr Collins claims that a parish rector, having prepared his sermons and secured his parishioners' agreement on tithes, ought to attend to 'the care and improvement of his dwelling, which he cannot be excused from making as comfortable as possible'.[20] Receptive to the idea of marrying Mr Collins, Charlotte Lucas, in time, appropriately remarks to Elizabeth Bennet, 'I am not romantic, you know; I never was. I ask only a comfortable home'.[21]

The comfort that Charlotte seeks out in her marital home was likely predicated on the provision of warming fires, soft furnishings, ample lighting and the convenient arrangement of rooms – the hallmarks of the new domestic environment described by Crowley, DeJean and others, and no doubt in the mind of Mrs Jennings as well.[22] But it would also have involved arranging rooms and furniture in a manner that was in keeping with the increasingly informal modes of living found in well-to-do households from the later decades of the eighteenth century onwards and which was developed further in the bourgeois Victorian homes discussed by Jane Hamlett in this volume. Lady Louisa Stuart caught the mood well when writing to her sister about Archerfield, where she was visiting in the winter of 1799. It is, she noted,

> a most excellent [house] … all is new and nicely furnished in the most fashionable manner. It wants nothing but more furniture for the middle of rooms. I mean all is set out in order, no comfortable tables to write or read at; it looks like a fine London house prepared for company; quite a contrast to the delightful gallery at Dalkeith, where you can settle yourself in any corner.[23]

Dalkeith offered comfort that was absent in the stiff and formal environment at Archerfield which was rather behind the times in its continued emphasis on fashion. In his pioneering study of the English country house, Mark Girouard styled the period 1770–1830 as the 'arrival of informality'. This was a time, he argues, when country houses increasingly escaped from the formalities of earlier times – a shift that Cornforth has explored through the growing plethora of interior domestic paintings produced from the 1810s onwards.[24] For both, the English country house became more a place to live, the ideal of the Great House being replaced by that of the villa in terms of scale, organization of rooms, and arrangements of furniture. This linking of informality and physical comfort has a longer history, with DeJean finding abundant evidence of relaxed seating and clothing in early-eighteenth-century Paris.[25] In England, it was idealized in the early nineteenth century in the genteel and picturesque cottage. Thus, in Austen's *Sense and Sensibility*, Robert Ferrars declares: 'I am excessively fond of a cottage; there is always so much comfort, so much elegance about them'.[26] This was not merely a sentimental appropriation of the picturesque and rustic. Ferrars continues: 'If I had money to spare, I should buy a little land and build myself within a short distance of London, where I might drive myself down at any time and collect a few friends about me and be happy.' In other words, this would be an escape and a place of privacy and intimacy – qualities that coupled with informality to shape domestic settings that *felt* comfortable.

This domestic ideal was central to foreign perceptions and appreciation of 'English comfort': a combination of convenience, informality and good cheer captured by Prince Puckler-Muskau. Visiting England in the 1820s in search of a wife, he stopped briefly at Guy's Cliffe House near to Leamington Spa. He was much taken with the place, writing in his published journal that the outside:

> is very picturesque and the interior is furnished with in a manner that is equally tasteful and appealing ... in the [drawing] room itself burnt a comfortable fire; exquisite pictures adorned the walls, and many sofas of different shapes as well as tables covered with curiosities and furniture standing about in agreeable disorder made everything appear homely and charming.[27]

Puckler-Muskau's enthusiasm for the comfortable fire, inviting sofas and agreeable disorder is quite apparent. In this passage, he uses *ansprechend* (appealing) and *behagliche* (comfortable), but elsewhere in his letters he employs the English word 'comfort', taken into German around this time. A generation earlier, this option would likely not have been available to him. In an English–German dictionary from 1784, comfort as a noun is translated as 'trost, bergnügen' and as a verb it is 'trösten, stärken', both signifying consolation. Around the same time, the French word 'confort' was translated as 'solace' and was described as being old and no longer in use.[28] To describe feelings of physical ease, Puckler-Muskau might have opted for *bequemlichkeit* instead of *behagliche*. The former was often used in the *Journal des Luxus und der Moden*; for example in October 1788 readers were told of the importance of building according to the rules as well as with comfort and elegance [*Regelmäsighkeit, Bequemlichkeit und Eleg*anz].[29] The Swedes used the very similar word *bekvämlighet*, which carried the same connotations, while notions of discomfort were generally expressed as *obekväm* or *unbequem*. Thus, the writer Johan Oxenstierna noted in his diary that 'Sahlman arrived here from Regensburg, and as he stays here, I invited him to share my chamber. I am now paying for this hasty courtesy with my inconvenience and discomfort [*besvar ock obeqvamlighet*]'.[30]

When it first appeared in France, Germany, Sweden and elsewhere, comfort was often seen as an English term to describe an English ideal. For example, rather than rely on *bekvämlighet* (convenience, commodiousness or ease[31]), the Swedish author, Erik Gustaf Geijer (1783–1847), wrote during a visit to England in 1809 that 'an English country house, in its velvet-green settings and with white sandy paths winding along under lush trees, gives the most pleasant image of English Comfort [*Engelsk Comfort*]'.[32] Having re-introduced the term from England in the early nineteenth century, the French deployed *confort* in ways that were very different from its traditional meaning of consolation and soothing, and it obviously communicated something different to *aise* and *agréments*. Bernez argues that in France comfort took on connotations of luxury, but elsewhere in Europe it meant something simpler – the kind of relaxed informality that struck Puckler-Muskau so forcibly.[33]

While comfort came to signify this array of new meanings across Europe, it is important to remember that its older meanings were by no means lost. Austen may have written about the comfort and elegance of a cottage, but she most often used comfort to refer to emotions and expectations rather than physical attributes, as did Elizabeth Gaskell in the middle decades of the nineteenth century.[34] Even as it came to signify material and physical ease, comfort also meant consolation received in times of trouble, the enjoyment of social interaction, emotional support of family and friends, and, most especially, a contented marriage. Robert Sayer's satirical print *Comforts of Matrimony – A Smoky House and Scolding Wife* (1790) makes as much of the emotional as the physical discomfort of the situation.[35] Comfort could thus derive from people as well as goods, and the two could be combined in the sentimental attachment held by particular objects within the home.

Home

The distinction between house and home has long been a tricky thing to put into words.[36] Edward Phillips, in his *New World of Words* (1706), was guilty of understandable tautology in defining Home as 'house, or place of abode', and House as 'Home, Place of Abode'. In the following decade, however, John Kersey was able to differentiate between the two, suggesting that a house was a 'building to live or dwell in', while home remained an abode.[37] Samuel Johnson added notions of privacy and possession, defining home as (among other things) 'his own house; the private dwelling' – an association that was repeated in other dictionaries through the later decades of the eighteenth century. It was not until the early nineteenth century, however, that the affective nature of home is explicitly identified. In his 1839 *New Dictionary of the English Language*, Charles Richardson offered two possibilities. The first retained the earlier focus on home as a place of dwelling, residence or abode, but the second recognized home as the locus of 'our feeling or affections; our own hearts, our interests or concerns, our pursuits or aims'.[38]

While home as a place of sentiment, feelings of belonging and comfort can be traced back to John Heywood's *A dialogue conteinyng the nomber in effect of all the prouerbes in the Englishe tongue* (1546),[39] it is apparent that such associations crystallized in the late eighteenth and early nineteenth century – just as comfort was taking on its new connotations.[40] This emphasis on the sentimental associations of home is apparent in Hannah Moore's moral tale *Mr Bragwell and his two daughters* (1796). Whereas writers from Daniel Defoe to Fanny Burney had mostly used home to denote a place of abode, Moore characterized it as a place of virtue that could afford comfort and happiness. She contrasts Mr Worthy's 'neat and pleasant dwelling' with that of Mr Bragwell: 'it had not so many ornaments, but it had more comforts', including a 'good old-fashioned chair in a warm corner'.[41] Invited to stay for a meal, Bragwell notes the 'plain but neat and good dinner' prepared by his friend's wife and is duly made to reflect on his own domestic circumstances. His daughters, we are told, are 'too genteel to do any thing so very useful' because they view such work as 'extremely vulgar and unbecoming'. He quickly concludes that 'his late experience of the little comfort he found at home, inclined him now still more strongly to suspect that things were not so right as he had been made to suppose'.[42]

Moore's story, with its contrasting characters and domestic circumstances, is rather heavy-handed, but her emphasis on the home as a place of material and spiritual or social comfort was very much in keeping with her times. At the end of *Sense and Sensibility*, Austen has the narrator assure her readers of the fate of the rakish Willoughby that 'he lived to exert, and frequently to enjoy himself. His wife was not always out of humour, nor his home always uncomfortable'.[43] There are echoes here of the *Comforts of Matrimony*, Willoughby's home being rendered more or less comfortable and welcoming by the humour of his wife. More positively, Austen has Mrs Elton quipping in *Emma* (1816), 'Ah! There is nothing like staying at home, for real comfort.' She lauds home as an alternative to being out in the glare of society; it formed an escape from the world, with all its concerns and worries, and all its pretensions and pressures. But Mrs Elton continues: 'Nobody can be more devoted to home than I am. I was quite a proverb for it at Maple Grove.'[44] Home is not only a desirable place to be; it is also an extension of her character and virtue.

Such sentiments align closely with the ways in which historians have sought to understand home as both a social and material construct and a lived experience. Amanda Vickery has explored the 'nest of comforts' wrought by women's active engagement in the domestic production of artefacts and in the construction of homes that had emotional resonance.[45] In a similar vein, Judith Lewis and Helen Metcalfe have shown how emotional attachment to specific objects, often old or with particular familial associations, was central in the ways that women, but also men, made houses into homes by providing them with sentimental meaning for their occupants. For Harvey, it is these emotional, imaginative and representational dimensions that distinguished home from house.[46] Such studies pick up on older arguments, advanced by Witold Rybcynski and others, concerning the ways in which home was a place of emotional well-being and belonging; it was associated with family, intimacy and personal attachment, all of which could be symbolized, cemented and memorialized through material objects.[47] This process of remembering and memorializing is developed more fully by Gaston Bachelard who wrote an extended account of the ways in which people's relationship with things and collections of things are central both to their construction of home and their construction of self, both individually and socially.[48]

Material objects and material comforts were thus central in making the home, but so too were relationship with people. As Thomas Malthus noted in his *Essay on the Principle of Population* (1803), 'the evening meal, the warm house, and the comfortable fireside, would lose half their interest, if we were to exclude the idea of some object of affection, with whom they were to be shared'.[49] By this, of course, he meant husbands, wives and children, and it is notable that Rowlandson's contemporaneous view of the *Comforts of Matrimony* features a very similar assemblage of objects and people: the warming fire, a meal being prepared and a comfortable seat, plus the companionship of the marital partner and a contented group of children.[50] This contented brood will, no doubt, prove a comfort to their parents, unlike Mr Bragwell's daughters whose heads are too full of fashion and similar vanities to offer their father any spiritual or physical ease.

Rowlandson's craft realized a rather different perspective on the human and relational aspects of home in his paired images 'At Home and Abroad' and 'Abroad and at Home'.[51] In the first, the man is at home with his large and ugly wife, yet he is not connected with her or his surroundings. She is engaged in trying to prepare some food on a smoking fire, balancing awkwardly on the edge of the bed; he is asleep in his chair, a broken pipe and dropped book on the floor beside him. He is quite clearly not 'at home' in any meaningful sense. In the second image, the man is away from home, sitting in front of a warm fire on a large sofa that he shares with his lover; they lounge together and gaze into each other's eyes. He is making himself very much at home. What makes the difference is not the location but the relationship between the two people and the ways in which this intimacy is reflected in their material surroundings. For some, at least, the twin identities of home as the place of abode and the centre of feelings and affections were split between different locations and different human relationships.

More typically, people who were abroad – that is, away from home – expressed their feelings of anxiety and ennui at being removed from familiar places and people. Many boys sent to boarding school no doubt coped perfectly well with their new surroundings, but others wrote to their parents, expressing their worries at being away from home. The young Richard Huddleston, for instance, complained about his cold and dirty room, which lacked a fire, but also 'the morose and sullen temper' of his tutor.[52] In short, he lacked the physical and emotional comforts of home. Parents often recognized this, but saw it as a necessary part of their sons becoming independent and resilient. In February 1800, Juliana Mary Buxton wrote to her son that his complaint about the cold at his school in Middlesex 'is rather a proof that too much tenderness at home is a bad thing as it makes school seem the more hard'.[53] She thus problematized the comforts of home, tenderness here referring both to the physical and emotional distinction between home and school. Much the same was true of young men travelling on the Grand Tour, who, as Sarah Goldsmith makes clear, often expressed feelings of homesickness. They missed both the physical comforts of home and the familiarity of domestic routines and the emotional comfort of family. For Grand Tourists, there was the additional layer of home country, with its familiar norms and customs.[54] In this context, small reminders of home and family were extremely important; William Fitzgerald, for instance, treasured a miniature of his mother, noting the comfort it afforded 'to think I have you in my pocket'.[55]

Home, then, was much more than the built structure of the house; it was also more than the physical comforts of warm rooms, easy chairs and familiar objects. People as well as things made a house into a home. Returning to Mr Errold in *Milistina*, his rediscovery of 'home comforts' came as much from his burgeoning relationship with the family at Trent Hall as it did from the material surroundings of the house; it was also predicated on his growing awareness of the lack of comfort and homeliness that had been offered by his now-dead wife. Home was a place of emotional connection that afforded comfort and brought a sense of belonging.

Home comforts

Comfort and the comforts of home are clearly preoccupations that increasingly exercised householders and writers from the late eighteenth century onwards. Historians have reflected these concerns, yet they remain underdeveloped ideas with great potential as powerful explanatory tools to help us understand more fully the complex and changing nature of house and home.

This volume takes comfort as its defining theme and explores this in a variety of manifestations to address two broad issues. First is the transformative impact that comfort had on the domestic environment through the eighteenth and nineteenth centuries: to what extent were these changes and the conceptions of comfort that they reflect universal – or at least Europe-wide – and what were the key periods of transformation? It is too easy to see comfort in progressive, almost teleological terms, and there is a need to think also about alternative approaches and attitudes. Second is the way in which home comforts were forged by the complex interplay of the material and emotional, things and people, body and mind. To what extent were relationships, objects and emotions transferable across space and time; was home fixed or mobile?

These questions are addressed here through a combination of longer chapters that explore general themes from the literature and shorter case studies that focus on particular things and people to further illustrate these broader ideas. The former open up big questions about the nature, construction and experience of comfort, convenience and home; the latter drill down to discover more about how these played out in specific contexts, often lying towards the periphery of our usual field of vision: water closets, for example, or baby houses or pets. They are organized into two broad sections. In the first, *The convenient house: architectural ideals and practicalities*, contributions focus on treatises, technologies and spaces, and explore the ways in which comfort was linked to notions of convenience within the home. As we have already seen, contemporaries often used these words in conjunction with each other and the ways in which convenience underpinned the comforts of home become apparent in the contributions of Dale Townshend, Aurélien Davrius, Johanna Ilmakunnas and Conor Lucey in particular. Townshend explores how houses were conceived and constructed as to serve the (changing) needs of their owners, both practical and representational. This involved a re-conception of domestic space and a shift in the mindset of architects, firstly to notions of convenience and thence to considerations of comfort, both for the wealthy and the poor. It also meant thinking in practical terms, as Davrius highlights in his case study on Blondel's efforts to ensure separate spaces for masters and servants. These were planned ideals, but many householders had to work out ways of retrofitting corridors, backstairs and a growing number of water closets into existing buildings, the last of which provide the focus of Lucey's case study of Dublin homes. The ways in which these ideals were disseminated across Europe is explored by Johanna Ilmakunnas's account of the conflicts and compromises between taste and comfort. While we know a good deal about the new technologies introduced to make homes more comfortable, Olivier Jandot's chapter shows the tortuous ways in which new inventions made it into the home and why: in some cases, they failed to make much impression on householders wedded to existing technologies. He also reminds us that innovation was not always driven by a quest for comfort, but rather the need to save fuel – an important factor in the development of the tiled stove, as discussed in Cristina Prytz's case study. For poorer households, the uptake of new technologies and the enhancement of domestic comfort was piecemeal and ad hoc, as Britt Denis demonstrates in her analysis of nineteenth-century Belgian homes. Wealth allowed for greater experimentation and for Sir John Soane, who forms the focus of the case study by Diego Bocchini, the process of enhancing the warmth of the home was ongoing, almost obsessive.

The second section, *Home making: objects and emotions*, shifts the focus more firmly onto the home and examines how particular objects or assemblages were imbued with emotional meanings that served to construct ideas and ideals of home. Jane Hamlett examines the acme of domestic comfort: the Victorian middle-class home, exploring how emotional and physical comfort were brought together on the page of the prescriptive literature and in the materiality of people's drawing rooms. This was predicated on ideas of domesticity that were culturally specific yet remarkably mobile, as Hamlett herself demonstrates. Patricia Ferguson, in her case study, shows how they were manifest in scaled-down form in early-eighteenth-century baby houses which formed miniaturized versions of the 'ideal home'. Laika Nevalainen, meanwhile, makes clear how domestic comfort could also be achieved within the spatial confines of a Finnish bachelor flat – the subject of her case study – reminding us that comfort was not necessarily a female preserve. The centrality of particular aspects of domestic material culture to feelings of comfort becomes clearer still in Gerrit Verhoeven's analysis of the letters of Netherlandish Grand Tourists. They judged the comfort of their lodgings in terms of considerations such as privacy, cleanliness and company, showing how 'home comforts' were an amalgam of the material and emotional. Attempts by individuals to create some of the comforts of home when temporarily or more permanently dislocated are examined briefly by Serena Dyer and in more extended form by Rowena Willard-Wright. Some of the material aspects of this are revealed through the wallpapers pasted up by students in a Cambridge college and the specialized campaign furniture used by British officers. More telling in many ways are the emotionally charged personal objects with which ordinary soldiers decorated their barrack rooms in an attempt to keep alive memories of home and links to family. The importance of memory is examined more fully by Jon Stobart in his analysis of the ways in which domestic spaces and objects were used as reminders of family: he demonstrates how particular objects were linked to events that cemented familial relationships in space and time. The importance of personal relationships in making a home comes to the fore in Helen Metcalfe's case study of one bachelor and his unmarried sister who retained a sense of belonging despite frequent changes in residence. But comfort could also come from other animate beings, most notably pets – a point made by Julie-Marie Strange in her short piece on the many dogs of George Sims.

Read individually, these various chapters and case studies offer detailed insights into the mutuality of comfort and home in a wide range of domestic and institutional settings. Taken together, they offer much more: a complex tapestry in which the material and emotional are interwoven across time and space. Individual details thus form part of a bigger picture. Stand close and we can inspect in detail the rich variety of individual experience; stand back and we can view the broader interplay of comfort and home. From this it is apparent that comfort was bound up with both materiality and emotions; it was a state of mind as well as a physical experience. As such, comfort was an ideal shared across Europe without ever becoming a fixed end state: emphases shifted over time and space, as did the means to make a dwelling comfortable and homely. It was an aspiration as much as an end state.

Notes

1 *Milistina; or, The Double Interest: A Novel*, 2 vols (London: Sampson Low and C. Law, 1797), vol. 1, 5–6. I am grateful to Dale Townshend for supplying some of the literary material discussed in this chapter.

2. John Kersey, A *New English Dictionary* (London, 1713), n.p.
3. Daniel Defoe, *The Fortunes and Misfortunes of the Famous Moll Flanders* (1722).
4. Samuel Johnson, *A Dictionary of the English Language*, 2 vols (London, 1755–56), vol. 1, n.p.
5. Samuel Johnson, *The History of Rasselas, Prince of Abissinia* (1759; Oxford: Oxford University Press, 1988), 30.
6. John Arrowsmith, *Armilla Catechetica: A Chain of Principles* (Cambridge, 1659), 58.
7. John Crowley, *The Invention of Comfort: Sensibilities and Design in Early Modern Britain and Early America* (Baltimore: Johns Hopkins University Press, 2001); John Cornforth, *English Interiors, 1790-1848: The Quest for Comfort* (London: Barrie & Jenkins, 1978).
8. Crowley, *Invention of Comfort*; John Cornforth, *Early English Interiors* (New Haven: Yale University Press, 2004), 209–12; P. S. Barnwell and Marylin Palmer (eds), *Country House Technology* (Donington: Shaun Tyas, 2012); Marylin Palmer and Ian West (eds), *Technology in the Country House* (Swindon: Historic England, 2016); Mark Girouard, *Life in the English Country House* (New Haven: Yale University Press, 1978), 245–66; others
9. Joan DeJean, *The Age of Comfort: When Paris Discovered Casual and the Modern Home Began* (New York, 2009). See also Christine Adams, *A Taste for Comfort and Status: A Bourgeois Family in Eighteenth-Century France* (Philadelphia: Penn State University Press, 2000).
10. John Gloag, *Victorian Comfort: A Social History of Design from 1830-1900* (Basingstoke: Macmillan, 1961); Deborah Cohen, *Household Gods: The British and Their Possessions* (New Haven, CT: Yale University Press, 2006); Jane Hamlett, *Material Relations: Domestic Interiors and Middle-Class Families in England, 1850-1910* (Manchester: Manchester University Press, 2010).
11. Frank Trentmann, *Empire of Things* (London: Allen Lane, 2016), 222–71.
12. Charles Richardson, *A New Dictionary of the English Language* (London: William Pickering, 1839), n.p.
13. Noah Webster, *An American Dictionary of the English Language* (New York: N & J White, 1839).
14. Elizabeth Gaskell, *Mary Barton* (1848; Oxford: Oxford University Press, 2006), 342.
15. Paul Slack, *The Invention of Improvement* (Oxford: Oxford University Press, 2015), 215–28; Marie-Odile Bernez, 'Comfort, the acceptable face of luxury: An eighteenth-century etymology', *Journal for Early Modern Cultural Studies*, 14, no. 2 (2014): 3–21.
16. Bernez, 'Comfort, the acceptable face of luxury'.
17. Crowley, *Invention of Comfort*, 147.
18. Walter Scott, *Ivanhoe* (1820; Oxford: Oxford University Press, 1996), 73.

19 Jane Austen, *Sense and Sensibility* (1811; London: Penguin, 1995), 166, 322.
20 Jane Austen, *Pride and Prejudice* (1813; Oxford: Oxford University Press, 2004), 77.
21 Ibid., 96.
22 Crowley, *Invention of Comfort*; DeJean, *Age of Comfort*; Adams, *Taste for Comfort and Status*.
23 Alice Clark (ed.), *Caroline, Countess of Portarlington and Other Friends and Relatives* (Edinburgh, 1895), vol. 2, 281, letter from Lady Louisa Stuart to Lady Caroline Dawson, Countess of Portarlington, 2 November 1799.
24 Girouard, *Life in the English Country House*, 213–44; Cornforth, *English Interiors*. See also Charlotte Gere, *Nineteenth-Century Decoration: The Art of the Interior* (New York: Harry N Abrams, 1989).
25 DeJean, *Age of Comfort*, 102–30, 186–204.
26 Jane Austen, *Sense and Sensibility* (1811; Oxford: Oxford University Press, 1970), 219. For a fuller discussion of this idealisation of the cottage, see Adrian Tinniswood, *Life in the English Country Cottage* (London: Weidenfeld Nicholson, 1995), 104–33; John Crowley, 'From luxury to comfort and back again: Landscape architecture and the cottage in Britain and America', in Maxine Berg and Elizabeth Eger (eds) *Luxury in the Eighteenth Century: Debates, Desires and Delectable Goods* (Basingstoke: Palgrave Macmillan, 2003), 135–50.
27 Herman Pucklar-Muskau, *Briefe eines verstorbenen: Ein fragmentarisches Tagebuch aus England, Wales* (Halberger, 1831), 242–3. I am grateful to Daniel Menning for this translation, which lends the passage a rather different gloss from that given in Cornforth, *English Interiors*, 65.
    Quoted in Cornforth, *English Interiors*, 65.
28 Theodor Arnold, *A Compleat Vocabulary, English and German* (M. Johann Bartholomäus Rogler, Züllichau, 1784); Chretien F. Schwan, *Nouveau Dictionnaire de la Langue Francoise* (Mannheim, 1787).
29 *Journal des luxus und der Moden*; October 1788.
30 Gustaf Stiernström (ed.) *Dagboks-anteckningar åren 1769-1771* (Uppsala: Svenska Litteratursällskapet, 1881), 187. The translation is by Cristina Prytz who I would like to thank for her help in writing this section.
31 G. Widegren, *Ett Svenskt och Engelskt Lexicon, efter Kongl. Secreteraren Sahlstedts Svenska Ordbok*, Stocholm, John A. Carlbohm, (1788).
32 Erik Gustaf Geijer, *Minnen. Utrag ur bref och dagböcker* (1834); letter dated Sidmouth, 1 June 1810. Translation by Cristina Prytz.
33 Bernez, 'Comfort, the acceptable face of luxury', 16–19.
34 Kenneth Phillipps, *Jane Austen's English* (London: Duetsch, 1970), 74–5; Norman Page, *The Language of Jane Austen* (Oxford: Oxford University Press, 1972), 30, 38–9.
35 See Henry French and Mark Rothery, *Man's Estate: Landed Gentry Masculinities, 1660-1900* (Oxford: Oxford University Press, 2013), 191–5; Amanda Vickery,

Behind Closed Doors: At Home in Georgian England (New Haven: Yale University Press, 2009), 10, 193–222.

36 For a discussion of some of the difficulties, see Karen Harvey, *The Little Republic: Masculinity and Domestic Authority in Eighteenth-Century Britain* (Oxford: Oxford University Press, 2012), 8–13.
37 Edward Phillips, *The New World of Words or Universal English Dictionary* (London, 1706), n.p.; Kersey, *New English Dictionary* (1713), n.p.
38 Johnson, *Dictionary*, n.p.; Richardson, *New Dictionary*, n.p.
39 OED
40 Harvey, *Little Republic*, 10–12; Margaret Hunt, *The Middling Sort: Commerce, Gender and the Family in England, 1680-1780* (Berkeley: University of California Press, 1996), 193–215.
41 Hannah Moore, *Mr Bragwell and His Two Daughters* (1797), 11.
42 Ibid., 12
43 Austen, *Sense and Sensibility* (1995), 166, 322.
44 Jane Austen, *Emma* (1816; Oxford: Oxford University Press, 2003), 214.
45 Vickery, *Behind Closed Doors*, 207–30.
46 Judith Lewis, 'When a house is not a home: Elite English women and the eighteenth-century country house', *Journal of British Studies*, 48, no. 2 (2009): 336-63; Stephen Hauge, *The Gentleman's House in the British Atlantic World, 1680-1780* (Basingstoke: Palgrave Macmillan, 2016), 95–115; Helen Metcalfe, 'The social experience of bachelorhood in Late-Georgian England, c.1760-1830' (unpublished PhD thesis, University of Manchester, 2017), chapter 5; Harvey, *Little Republic*, 12. See also Hannah Chavasse, 'Material culture and the country house: Fashion, comfort and lineage' (unpublished PhD thesis, University of Northampton, 2015), chapter 4.
47 Witold Rybcynski, *Home: A Short History of an Idea* (New York: Viking, 1986).
48 Bachelard, *The Poetics of Space* (1958, trans. 1964).
49 Thomas Malthus, *Essay on the Principle of Population* (London, 1803), 91.
50 The family group is echoed in the cat and kitten lying by the fire.
51 See Karen Harvey, 'Men making home: Masculinity and domesticity in eighteenth-century Britain', *Gender and History*, 21, no. 3 (2009): 520–2.
52 Mark Rothery and Henry French, *Making Men: The Formation of Masculine Identities in England, c.1660-1900 – a Sourcebook* (Basingstoke: Macmillan, 2012).
53 Quoted in Ibid.
54 French and Rothery, *Man's Estate*, 67–74; Sarah Goldsmith, 'Nostalgia, homesickness and emotional formation on the eighteenth-century Grand Tour', *Cultural and Social History*, 15, no. 3 (2018): 333–60.
55 Letters dated 16 December 1766 and 3 February 1767, quoted in Goldsmith, 'Nostalgia', 345.

Part One

The convenient house: Architectural ideals and practicalities

1

Convenience, utility and comfort in British domestic architecture of the long eighteenth century

Dale Townshend

As scholars have often pointed out, British architects of the eighteenth century had very little to say about comfort in domestic architecture at all. To a certain extent, this was a consequence of the meanings mobilized by the term 'comfort' itself in the period: primarily signifying forms of moral support, spiritual solace and legal assistance, 'comfort' for much of the eighteenth century lacked the connotations of physical contentment, well-being and ease that the phrase 'home comforts' conjures up today.[1] Beyond this, and as John Archer has shown, eighteenth-century architects remained preoccupied by a number of weightier, far more abstract aesthetic concerns, including the authority of ancient Greek and Roman architecture and the desirability of emulating it in Britain; the proportions, meanings, associations, character, style and expression of a building; and the levels of creativity and 'original genius' that architects themselves brought to bear upon the task of architectural design.[2] This general disregard for the more practical considerations of physical comfort was no doubt compounded by the ways in which the period tended to conceptualize the role and identity of the architect himself. Through the emphasis that many aestheticians placed on the affiliations between architecture and the 'Sister Arts' of painting, sculpture, poetry and music, the architect was, first and foremost, an artist, one who was primarily concerned with the beauty and external aesthetic appeal of his designs, and one who thus tended to delegate the finer details of a building's interiors to the attendant upholsterer and furniture designer.

And yet, a key term to emerge in architectural theories of the early-to-mid-eighteenth century was 'convenience', a category, we might say, that served as a form of comfort *avant la lettre*, or at least the closet approach upon 'home comforts' that architects of the period would – or indeed, given the term's contemporary legal and moral meanings, *could* – make. As early as the 1690s, the lawyer-turned-architectural patron Roger North had paid considerable attention to the convenience of domestic architecture, a term that in his *On Planning a Country House* (c. 1696) and *Cursory Notes of Building* (1698) encompassed considerations of heating, light, privacy and the increasing specialization of internal rooms. Samuel Johnson's A *Dictionary of the English Language* (1755–6) provides some sense of the meanings with which 'convenience' was inflected in contemporary architectural discourse, several of which indicate that the term included within itself intimations physical ease that were more usually invoked in the phrase 'creature comforts': 1. Fitness and propriety; 2. Commodiousness, ease, freedom from difficulties; 3. Cause of ease; and 4. Fitness of time or place; in its adjectival form, 'convenient' signified 'fit; suitable; proper; well adapted; commodious'.[3] These are clearly the meanings that David Hume had drawn upon in *A Treatise of Human Nature* (1739–40) when, during his discussion of the role that sympathy played in the appreciation of beauty, he illustrated his claim through an important architectural example:

> A man, who shews us any house or building, takes particular care among other things to point out the convenience of the apartments, the advantages of their situation, and the little room loft in the stairs, anti-chambers and passages; and indeed 'tis evident, the chief part of the beauty consists in these particulars. The observation of convenience gives pleasure, since convenience is a beauty. But after what manner does it give pleasure? 'Tis certain our own interest is not in the least concern'd; and as this is a beauty of interest, not of form, so to speak, it must delight us merely by communication, and by our sympathizing with the proprietor of the lodging. We enter into his interest by the force of imagination, and feel the same satisfaction, that the objects naturally occasion in him.[4]

For Hume, architectural convenience, in itself, was a form of beauty, and the spectator received certain appreciation of a house's convenient aspects through entering into a sympathetic identification with those who inhabited it.

If Hume's account of convenience in *A Treatise of Human Nature* was subordinated to the larger task of describing the aesthetic workings of sympathy, 'convenience' would receive greater elaboration and enhanced practical application in the work of subsequent British architects. The argument in Isaac Ware's *A Complete Body of Architecture* (1756), for example, turned on a distinction between what he referred to as the 'convenience of the inhabitant' and 'the beauty and proportion of the fabrick'; the process of architectural design, he claimed, involved a careful negotiation of the requirements of these two somewhat opposed, even fundamentally incompatible elements.[5] As Ware argued, neither architectural convenience nor beauty was sufficient in its own right, and the emphasis that the architect afforded each principle was to be determined by the nature and intended function of the building at hand: while the homes of tradespeople required that 'principal attention' be shown to 'the article of convenience', the house of a 'person of fashion' demanded heightened attention to 'the beauty and proportional disposition of parts'.[6] Although Ware never paused to explain precisely what convenience in the realm of domestic architecture comprised, what eventually becomes clear in *A Complete Body of Architecture* is that the term mobilized meanings similar to those employed by North, Hume and Johnson, namely the size of the rooms in any given structure; their intended purpose, utility and general fitness for use; as well as such pragmatic and utilitarian concerns as the placement of water closets, the securing of appropriate heating through the inclusion of chimneys and fireplaces, a house's proximity to running water, the laying of adequate drains and sewers, and ways of ensuring within the home the circulation of fresh, salubrious air. Like Ware's distinctions between internal convenience and external beauty, such claims would play themselves out in architectural thought and practice well into the nineteenth century.

Like Colen Campbell in *Vitruvius Britannicus* (1715–25) before him, Ware was a firm proponent of Classical example and precedent, and, together with his earlier *The Four Books of Andrea Palladio's Architecture* (1738), *A Complete Body of Architecture* became a crucial handbook for the taste for Palladianism that so dominated eighteenth-century British architecture. While convenience thus remained, theoretically, one of Palladianism's most important architectural principles, Edward Denison and Guang Yu Ren have pointed out that, in practice, the style ultimately rendered the exterior form of a building far more important than its internal functions. Indeed, in such country houses as Chatsworth House, Blenheim Palace, Castle Howard, Burlington House and Houghton Hall, we consistently witness the sacrificing of what we would today term the 'domestic comforts' of their interiors to the symmetry, proportion and elegance of their Classical exteriors.[7] This was perhaps the inevitable consequence of Ware's insistence that, in distinction from the concern with convenience in the houses of the working classes, 'the beauty and proportional disposition of parts' should predominate over internal conveniences in the grand houses of the wealthy. Of course, and as scholarship in the field has shown, country houses were by no means devoid of comfort.[8] Nonetheless, there remains evidence of a prevailing assumption that comfort was not ordinarily to be found in such grand residences: as the Scottish writer Anne Grant put it in her popular *Letters from the Mountains* (1806), 'I believe there is no danger of my ever living in a great house, and I am not sorry for it. There is such a stately absence of all comfort; every thing that unsophisticated nature delights to cling to, is put so far away; and the owner seems somehow alone in the middle of his works, like Nebuchadnezzar, saying, "Behold now this great Babylon which I have made."'[9]

William Chambers continued in this Classicist vein in *A Treatise on Civil Architecture* (1759), arguing that the architect's primary function was to design and realize 'convenient habitations' that furnished their inhabitants with both 'ease of body' and 'vigour of mind', here too preempting the physical and sentimental components enshrined in the notion of home comfort that we see in the novels of Jane Austen and other literary texts of the period: 'Thus is appears that Architecture, by furnishing Men with convenient habitations, procures them that ease of body, and vigour of mind, which are necessary for inventing and improving Arts.'[10] If architecture was, first and foremost, the art of securing in a building states of mental and physical convenience, it followed that its practice was 'instrumental to the happiness of Men' and 'conducive to the wealth, fame, and security of kingdoms', a point that Chambers underscored by advancing a teleological history of architecture that was driven solely by convenience's ever-progressive requirements.[11] Alexander Gerard followed suit in *An Essay on Taste* (1759) of the same year, though substituting convenience for a notion of 'utility', a concept that he defined as 'the fitness of things for answering their ends', and an aspect of the broader category of beauty that bore particular implications for domestic architecture.[12] Gerard's ardent defence of the principle of architectural utility was bound up in a wry critique of the unfortunate 'inconveniences' imposed upon a building by the architect's over-zealous embrace of Classical regularity:

> *Utility*, or the *fitness* of things for answering their ends, constitutes another species of beauty, distinct from that of figure. It is of so great importance that, though *convenience* is sometimes in lesser instances sacrificed to *regularity*, yet a degree of inconvenience generally destroys all the pleasure, which should have arisen from the symmetry and proportion of the parts.[13]

Gerard's ideal building, then, combined elegant and regular exteriors with internal fitness and utility, a small concession to nascent notions of domestic 'comfort' in a tract that was otherwise preoccupied with the loftier architectural principles of novelty, sublimity, beauty, harmony, taste and judgment.

Henry Home, Lord Kames addressed the matter of architecture in volume three of *Elements of Criticism* (1762), asserting, like Gerard, the importance of utility to any architectural design. His argument also recalls the class-based distinctions that Isaac Ware had drawn between the 'convenient' houses of tradespeople and the 'beautiful' and proportional' facades of the fashionable: 'In palaces, and other buildings sufficiently extensive to admit a variety of useful contrivance', Kames writes, 'regularity justly takes the lead'; 'but in dwelling-houses that are too small for variety of contrivance', he reasons, 'utility ought to prevail; neglecting regularity so far as it stands in opposition to convenience.'[14] As in Ware, elegance becomes the prerogative of the gentry and aristocracy, and the more practical concerns of architectural utility the preserve of the middling and labouring classes. The differences between them was symptomatic of the broader tensions that Kames, like Ware, identifies between the principles of external regularity and internal convenience themselves:

> The unwearied propensity to make a house regular as well as convenient, forces the architect, in some articles, to sacrifice convenience to regularity, and in others, regularity to convenience. By this means the house, which turns out neither regular nor convenient, never fails to displease.[15]

Where Kames differs from Ware, though, is in his insistence upon the architect's prioritizing of utility in ordinary domestic architecture, to the extent that, as in earlier writers, utility comes to serve for him as a nascent yet still crude and unrefined notion of home comfort. As he reasons, the proportions of a domestic door ought to correspond with the size of the human body; the size of the windows must be proportionate to that of the room that they provide with light; and with respect to a home's internal division, 'utility requires that the rooms be rectangular; for otherwise void spaces will be left of no use'.[16] If he does not make use of the term 'comfort' in its physical sense, Kames is, at the very least, poignantly aware of the numerous physical 'inconveniences' inflicted upon the inhabitants of a house by an improper arrangement of internal space:

> The chief convenience of a great room, is unconfined motion. This directs us to the greatest length that can be obtained. But a square room of a great size is inconvenient, by removing far from the hand, chairs and tables, which, when unemploy'd, must be ranged along the sides of a room. Utility therefore requires a large room to be a parallelogram.[17]

Given the importance of use-value or spatial utility, Kames only reluctantly admits to architecture any aspect of ornamentation and embellishment that does not serve specific practical ends.

If Kames's prioritizing of internal utility over external elegance suggests a departure from the Classicism of his forebears, this is a note that will become more pronounced as his argument in *Elements of Criticism* unfolds. Ware, Gerard and Chambers had been united in their condemnation of the Gothic style as the epitome of 'inconvenient' architecture and bad architectural taste, and, indeed, their championing of the rules of external regularity was founded securely upon Classical precepts. Kames, however, reverses this hierarchical ordering by questioning the suitability of ancient Italian and Greek architecture to the cold and inclement climate of modern Britain:

> A colonnade along the front of a building, hath a fine effect in Greece and Italy, by producing coolness and obscurity, agreeable in warm and luminous climates. The cold climate of Britain is altogether averse to this ornament. A colonnade therefore, can never be proper in this country, unless when employ'd to communicate with a detached building.[18]

By contrast, 'The old Gothic form of building', he continues, 'seems well suited to the rough uncultivated regions where it was invented', particularly in those instances in which this vernacular British style has been reconciled to 'its new situation'.[19] According to this logic, Kames implicitly advocated the frequently maligned Gothic as the domestic architectural style most suited to late-eighteenth-century Britain, an assertion that did much to challenge the predominance of Classicism in the period.

As this suggests, notions of domestic convenience and utility – those forerunners to the modern conceptualization of the comfortable home – had been inscribed in what, in the nineteenth century, would be dubbed the battle of the styles, that often intemperate aesthetic controversy that raged over the perceived virtues and shortcomings of Classical and Gothic forms, and which would come to dominate and structure so much architectural thought and practice in the period. Countering Kames, for instance, William Gilpin, the period's greatest champion of the picturesque, held that convenience was a quality peculiar to country houses erected in the Grecian style, claiming that it was the sheer capaciousness of Gothic piles that rendered them 'incumbered [sic]', and, as such, unsuited to the requirements of modern living. 'We are amused with looking into these mansions of antiquity, as objects of curiosity', he wrote, 'but should never think of comparing them in point of convenience with the great houses of modern taste.'[20] Convenience, here, is firmly aligned with Classicism and the forces of modernity, Gothic with a benighted yet nonetheless picturesque past that was incapable of serving the domestic requirements of the present. Implicit in Gilpin's claim is the problem with which eighteenth-century architects and architectural aestheticians frequently grappled, namely, the difficulty of combining 'inconvenient' exteriors, be they either Classical or Gothic, with internal furnishings in a style thought to be better suited to convenient domestic habitation. Faced with the same dilemma, Richard Payne Knight resolved to combine a Gothic exterior with a more 'convenient' Grecian interior at his own Gothic country house at Downton Castle, Herefordshire, while Elizabeth Montagu insisted upon the coupling of James Wyatt's Gothic exteriors with neo-Classical interiors at Sandleford Priory, Berkshire.[21] As she wrote of Wyatt's work for Thomas Barrett at Lee Priory, Kent, in 1783,

> Where a part is to be extended beyond a first intention, the additions should be Gothick; for symmetry not being the object of the Gothick architects, irregularity is not considered an imperfection in their designs. Additions made to houses in any other taste destroy the intended proportions, and introduce confusion and deformity. I am more a friend to the Gothick on the outside than within; for, unless by great expense and care, the Gothick fitting-up is clumsy and gloomy.[22]

Elizabeth Montagu's long-time friend Horace Walpole approached the Gothic/Classical, internal/external divide with considerably greater gusto, choosing the Gothic style for both the exterior and much of the interior furnishings at his Gothic Revivalist home at Strawberry Hill, Twickenham. Registering so as to challenge the prevalent assumption that the Gothic style was not ideally suited to modern domestic life, he declared in the second edition of *A Description of the Villa of Mr Horace Walpole* in 1784, 'In truth, I did not mean to make my house so Gothic as to exclude convenience, and modern refinements in luxury. The designs of the inside and outside are strictly ancient, but the decorations are modern.'[23] Walpole's challenge at Strawberry Hill was to render Gothic interiors as convenient as their Classical and neo-Classical counterparts, even courting, as he did so, the century's condemnation of luxury as the sign of indolence and excess.[24]

'A warm comfortable plain room': Comfortable homes for the labouring poor

I have argued thus far that, lacking the connotations of physical consolation and ease only later assumed by the word 'comfort', architectural theorists and patrons of the period *c.* 1730–85 made recourse to the largely interchangeable terms 'convenience' and 'utility' as a way of addressing a building's suitability for modern domestic existence. Both concepts gauged the extent to which a home could furnish its inhabitants with a sense of physical ease, and both played an increasingly important role in the process of architectural design. Convenience and utility, the architectural principles respectively theorized by Ware and Chambers, Gerard and Kames, thus occupy an important place in the pre-history of home comfort in Britain in the latter part of the eighteenth century. John Crunden's *Convenient and Ornamental Architecture, Consisting of Original Designs, for Plans, Elevations, and Sections* (1767) is merely one example of how such principles were applied to practical architectural design.

It was in such a context that the word 'comfort', itself, first entered into the literature of British domestic architecture, but here, surprisingly, not in relation to the homes of the emergent middling classes, the class that scholars such as Rybczynski, Christine Adams and Joan DeJean have identified as comfort's primary vanguards, but in the series of tracts and architectural designs published from the mid-1770s onwards that were intended to ameliorate the living conditions of the labouring poor.[25] Nathaniel Kent's *Hints to Gentlemen of Landed Property* (1775) was particularly influential in this regard. Addressed to the owners of country estates across Britain, Kent's text was, at once, a passionate exposé of the squalid conditions in which rural labourers were forced to live and an articulation of a set of principles for the practical improvement of working-class domestic architecture: 'The shattered hovels which half of the poor of this kingdom are obliged to put up with, is truly affecting to a heart fraught with humanity. Those who condescend to visit these miserable tenements, can testify, that neither health nor decency, can be preserved in them.'[26] The full extent of Kent's concern becomes apparent as he enumerates the labouring class's numerous domestic afflictions. Exposed to the elements in their poorly heated homes, manual workers and their children are perpetually susceptible to illness; with a husband, his wife and as many as six children forced to share a single room, the couple have no privacy in which to enjoy the physical pleasures of marriage. 'Comfort' is the key term in his argument, to the extent that *Hints to Gentlemen of Landed Property* serves as one of the earliest applications of this category in its modern, physical sense to eighteenth-century domestic architecture:

> Estates being of no value without hands to cultivate them, the labourer is one of the most valuable members of society; without him the richest soil is not worth owning. His situation then should be considered, and made at least comfortable, if it were merely out of good policy.[27]

Kent's championing of workers' domestic comfort and ease, however, should not be construed as a dangerous promotion of luxury, and in such passages as the following, he is at pains to distinguish between what he calls 'a warm comfortable plain room' of a labourer's cottage and the expense and finery of a gentleman's country house:

> I am far from wishing to see the cottage improved, or augmented so as to make it fine, or expensive; no matter how plain it is, provided it be tight and convenient. All that is requisite, is a warm comfortable plain room, for the poor inhabitants to eat their morsel in, an oven to bake their bread, a little receptacle for their small beer and provision, and two wholesome lodging apartments, one for the man and his wife, and another for his children. It would perhaps be more decent, if the boys and girls could be separated; but this would make the building too expensive, and besides, is not so materially necessary; for the boys find employment in farm-houses at an early age.[28]

Occupying the middle ground between what Adam Smith one year later in *An Inquiry into the Nature and Causes of the Wealth of Nations* (1776) would polarize as 'necessaries' and 'luxuries', domestic comfort in Kent is figured as an experience of thrift, economy and moderateness. Extended here to the rural working classes, it is by no means an exclusively bourgeois or aristocratic phenomenon, for as Kent puts it, 'the poor are not less attached to domestic endearments than the rich'.[29] In practical terms, however, domestic comfort in this context is considerably different from the 'home comforts' of the middle and upper classes, for it is said to consist internally of such exigencies as ensuring the privacy of its inhabitants; the provision of adequate heating and warmth; and the inclusion of conveniences such as an oven and a space for the storage for food. Externally, it depended upon the landowner's provision of his workers with sufficient land to support a cow, a pig and a small kitchen garden; affordable rented ground for grazing; and proximity of the cottage to the labourer's place of employment. While it is tempting to think of Kent's programme as a philanthropic mission undertaken in the most humanitarian of sentiments, it is important to remember that what was ultimately at stake in his address to the landowners of England was a conviction that enhanced domestic comfort would bring greater economic productivity. Landed estates, he concludes, are only as remunerative 'in proportion to the comfortable, or miserable condition of the labourers who cultivate them'.[30]

Though returned to its most basic principles, the comfort of the home had nonetheless become in Kent an urgent political and economic concern.

John Wood realized Kent's theoretical principles through the act of practical architectural design, producing in *A Series of Plans, for Cottages or Habitations of the Labourer, Either in Husbandry, or the Mechanic Arts, Adapted as well to Towns, as to the Country* (1788) a selection of plans and elevations for 'comfortable' workers' homes. Although he uses the term interchangeably with 'convenience', domestic 'comfort' is, indeed, Wood's primary concern, having witnessed first-hand during a tour of the country ten years earlier the deplorable living conditions that urban and rural workers alike were forced to endure:

> It was discovered that these habitations of that useful and necessary rank of men, the LABOURERS, were become for the most part offensive both to decency and humanity; that the state of them and how far they might be rendered more comfortable to the poor inhabitants, was a matter worthy the attention of every man of property not only in the country, but in large villages, in towns, and in cities.[31]

'The greatest part of the cottages that fell within my observation', Wood, echoing Kent, emotively continues, 'I found to be shattered, dirty, inconvenient, miserable hovels, scarcely affording a shelter for beasts of the forest; much less were they proper habitations for the human species.'[32] Among their many inconveniences were their dampness, their cramped interiors, their coldness in Winter and their excessive heat in Summer. The seven principles of architectural improvement that he outlines are thus not only solutions to these problems, but also provide a clear sense of what working-class domestic comfort for Wood in the 1780s comprised. Cottages, he enumerates, should be '*dry* and *healthy*'; 'warm, chearful [sic], and comfortable'; 'convenient' in their internal arrangements of space; sufficiently wide in their execution; strongly constructed with sound materials; include sufficient ground for the establishment of a small garden; and ideally built in pairs. The published plans and elevations themselves arrange these comfortable habitations into classes, from the most simple (one room; 12 square feet; 7 ½ feet high, with a porch), to more elaborate structures of three and four internal rooms (Figure 1.1).

Although it was situated in the same architectural tradition, George Richardson's *New Designs in Architecture, Consisting of Plans, Elevations, and Sections for Various Buildings* (1792) perpetuated a version of the class-based stratifications that I have explored above, aligning physical 'comfort' exclusively with the 'comfortable habitations of gentlemen possessed of considerable fortunes' and 'convenience', its more exigent and utilitarian counterpart, with the labouring classes. At least two of these designs, he writes, are 'intended to

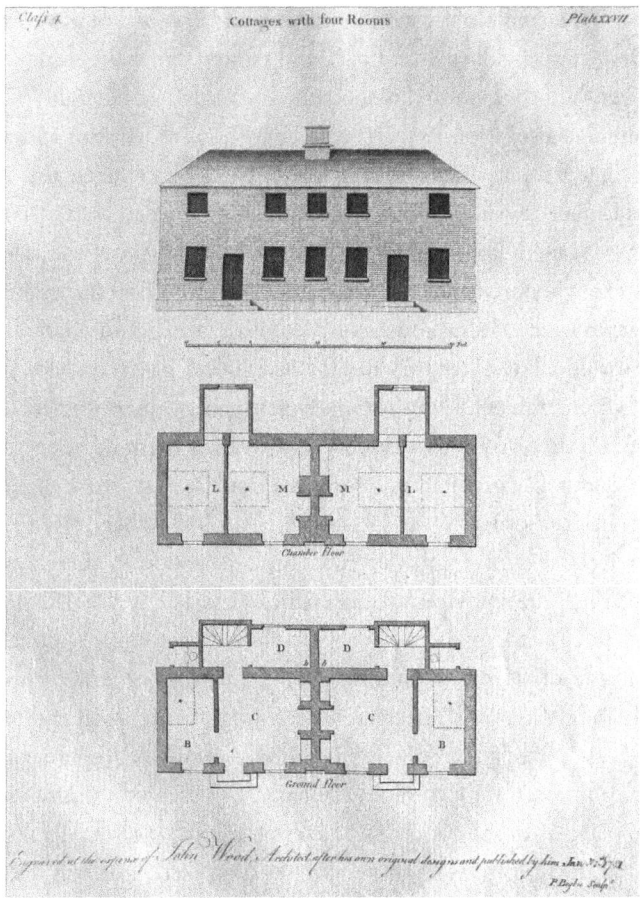

Figure 1.1 Plate XXVII, Elevation and Plans for Cottages with Four Rooms, from John Wood's *A Series of Plans, for Cottages or Habitations of the Labourer, Either in Husbandry, or the Mechanic Arts, Adapted as well to Towns, as to the Country* (1788). Courtesy of the Yale Center for British Art, Folio A 2009 30 Copy 1.

be erected in the fields of villages belonging to the estates of such gentlemen who take pleasure in building convenient dwellings for the families of their domestics of dependants'.[33] As in the earlier work of Kames and Ware, elegance is a property exclusive to the homes of the wealthy, the thatched cottages of the labourer aspiring to no more than simplicity and uniformity. John Soane, by contrast, reinvigorated the spirit of Nathaniel Kent in his *Sketches in Architecture: Containing Plans and Elevations of Cottages, Villas, and Other Useful Buildings, with Characteristic Scenery* (1793), including among his designs for country houses at least two plans for working-class houses, 'each consisting, on the ground-floor, of a small lobby for the warmth and comfort of a cottage, sitting-room 12 by 15, wash-house, a staircase and pantry under the same level, and a chamber over the sitting-room finished into the roof to gain height'.[34] These were clearly offered as a solution to the sordid conditions of working-class domestic habitation that he had identified at the outset: 'In cottages the rooms are unavoidably small, few in number, and frequently crowded with inhabitants'.[35]

By the 1790s, then, 'comfort', in all the modern, physical connotations of that word, had firmly entered into the literature of British domestic architecture, in some instances used coterminously with 'convenience', but in others replacing it entirely. It would fall to Humphry Repton, the successor to Lancelot 'Capability' Brown and the eighteenth century's last great landscape designer, the task of consolidating notions of home comfort and locating them more securely in the discourse of domestic architecture – though not, as in the work of Kent, Wood and Soane, in the homes of the labouring poor, but rather in the habitations of the upper classes. John Crowley has drawn attention to the ways in which the aesthetic of the picturesque, of which Uvedale Price, Richard Payne Knight and Repton themselves were the primary theoretical exponents, drove the programme of domestic comfort at the turn of the nineteenth century, particularly in relation to the design and building of functional and ornamental cottages.[36] Less appreciated, however, is the ways in which Repton, well beyond the example of picturesque cottage architecture, presented himself as comfort's veritable apostle, as home comfort's greatest and most pioneering advocate in a domestic architectural context, he implicitly suggested, that was characterized by great inconvenience and discomfort.

Having divided all contemporary architecture into 'Gothic' and 'Grecian' forms, Repton in *Sketches and Hints on Landscape Gardening* (1794) argued that Gothic-style interiors, unless improved by the innovations of 'modern comforts and convenience', were spectacularly unsuited to the ends of modern domestic life:

> I may here observe, that it is unnecessary to retain the Gothic character within the mansion, at least not farther than the hall, as it would subject such buildings to much inconvenience; for since modern improvement has added glass sashed windows to the ancient Grecian and Roman architecture, in like manner the inside of a Gothic building may, with the same propriety, avail itself of modern comforts and convenience.[37]

He would further develop and refine his interests in domestic comfort in *Observations on the Theory and Practice of Landscape Gardening* (1805), boldly declaring early on in the study that the prevailing taste for Classicism, with all its prioritizing of external 'symmetry', had resulted in the unfortunate neglect of interior comfort and convenience, domestic habitation's two primary 'requisites':

> Those who delight in depreciating the present by comparison with former times, may, perhaps, observe a decline of taste in many of the public arts; but surely in architecture and gardening, the present aera furnishes more examples of attention to comfort and convenience, than are to be found in the plans of Palladio, Vitruvius Britannicus, or Le Nôtre, where, in the display of useless symmetry, the requisites of habitation are often forgot. The leading feature in the good taste of modern times, is the just sense of GENERAL UTILITY.[38]

What is notable about this passage is the way in which, as in Repton's earlier study, comfort occupies the same semantic plane as the architectural 'convenience' of the eighteenth century. Barely distinguishable from one another, the two terms become interchangeable, and both are aligned with the 'just' principle of 'utility' that Repton invokes towards the end. With comfort, convenience and utility drawn together in this fashion, Repton addresses the concept of architectural 'fitness', including in this broad, portmanteau category 'the comfort, the convenience, the character, and every circumstance of a place, that renders it the desirable habitation of man, and adapts it to the uses of each individual proprietor'.[39] The crux of Repton's argument in *Observations on the Theory and Practice of Landscape Gardening* becomes clear in his subsequent claim that 'convenience and comfort should doubtless take the lead of every other consideration' when an architect sets about designing a house.[40] A clear riposte to the ways in which the 'useless symmetries' of the Classical style had compromised internal 'comfort and convenience', this comment also tacitly promoted, with a few qualifications, the Gothic as a suitable domestic style, a conviction that becomes more pronounced later on in the tract when Repton turns to reflect on the various forms of Gothic architecture. 'Castle Gothic', he claims, might only be used for domestic architecture if its original character is to some degree sacrificed to 'modern comfort'; 'Church Gothic', similarly, is 'seldom applicable to a house, without such violence and mutilation, as to destroy its general character'. What Repton terms 'House Gothic', however – the ancient medieval style blended with 'the elegance, the comfort, and the convenience of modern habitation', such as Walpole had achieved at Strawberry Hill – is mooted as a suitable, workable and appropriate alternative.[41] As earlier in the period, conceptualizations of the comfortable home were firmly bound up in the perceived differences between the Classical and the Gothic styles. Though Repton does not specify precisely what 'comfort' in the realm of domestic architecture comprised, it implicitly seems to consist of such factors as a country house's proximity to local supplies; 'uninterrupted communication' between a great house and its functional, more utilitarian 'offices'; and the internal subdivision of internal space into such function-specific rooms as a library, a music room, a billiard room and a conservatory.

Bourgeois home comforts

With their attendant emphases upon irregularity, Humphry Repton and Uvedale Price's theories of the picturesque both loosened the hold of Classicism and situated comfort at the heart of British domestic architecture. Comfort's purview here, however, was largely the country houses of the landed gentry and aristocracy. By the early nineteenth century, however, there is clear evidence of comfort having entered into the theory and practice of bourgeois domestic architecture. The point is best made through reference to the designs of two relatively obscure and undistinguished early-nineteenth-century architects: Edward Gyfford's *Designs for Elegant Cottages and Small Villas, Calculated for the Comfort and Convenience of Persons of Moderate and of Ample Fortune* (1806), and David Laing's *Hints for Dwellings: Consisting of Original Designs for Cottages, Farm-Houses, Villas, &c. Plain and Ornamental* (1800; reprinted in 1804; 1818; 1823; 1841). Both were London-based architects, and of the two, it is Laing who, largely through his early connections with John Soane, is best remembered today. In their very obscurity, though, they give some sense of how comfort was articulated in the homes of those who could not afford to commission designs by such better-known eighteenth-century architects as Nicholas Hawksmoor, Robert and James Adam and Soane himself. Their published design books of plans and elevations remain preoccupied with comfort in various ways, and, collectively, they attest to what we know to be the primary innovations in Georgian domestic architecture: the development of urban terraces; the construction of suburban villas for the moderately wealthy; and the movement towards increased architectural compactness, particularly as witnessed in the rise of the 'double-pile' structure (homes distributed over two levels, as compared with the sprawling single-pile constructions of earlier periods).[42]

The very title of Gyfford's *Designs for Elegant Cottages and Small Villas, Calculated for the Comfort and Convenience of Persons of Moderate and of Ample Fortune* indicates that, contemporary with its appearance in literary texts, comfort by the early nineteenth century had become an important architectural consideration, its locus now the middle classes of 'moderate fortune' as much as those of considerably larger resources. What is notable about the 26 plates and descriptions that accompany them is the pains that the architect takes to negotiate what, in the previous century, had been construed as the incompatible requirements of internal utility and external symmetry: emphatically, Gyfford claims, these are works of both 'utility and elegance'.[43] Equally, comfort is carefully distinguished from luxury insofar as it is the product of economic prudence and moderation, assumptions that become particularly discernible in the emphasis that the description of Plates I, II and III places upon spatial utility, functionality and lack of excessive ornamentation:

> Exhibits two views of a plain cottage, calculated to accommodate a small family, having a dining room, drawing room, with hall and kitchen, on the ground floor; three bed rooms and a water closet on [sic] the chamber; and the same on the attic floor. From the uniformity of this, as well as others in this selection of designs, they are applicable to any situation.[44]

The accompanying plate gives a clear sense of the house's functionality, its Classicism-inspired regularity and its distinct lack of ornamentation (Figure 1.2). If comfort resides in plainness and moderation, in a state that, though always in excess of the 'necessaries' of Adam Smith, is never surplus to requirements, it is also dependent for Gyfford upon the inclusion of water closets and certain other 'modern conveniences', that is, those amenities, appliances and fittings of a well-equipped, modern home that were first referred to as such in 1825 (*OED*).

Laing's *Hints for Dwellings* was equally driven by the need to combine the 'incompatible' demands of convenience, utility and elegance, presenting the pursuit of 'comfort' as the practicing architect's primary challenge:

> Of the Plans, I hope the distribution will be found to possess Convenience, Elegance, and Economy. This branch of the architect's profession is the most arduous; and to this point should all the powers of his mind be directed, united to all the intelligence which can be furnished by the employer; for within the house, those comforts and conveniencies [sic] will be sought, which shall compensate for all expense and trouble.[45]

Recalling David Hume's notion of sympathy and the role that it played in the appreciation of a house's inconveniences, Laing renders the architect's imagination as ultimately subordinate to the convenience of his client, his primary task here said to be the rendering of the home 'inviting to the master, and convenient to the family', for by a 'good distribution' much space is saved and applied to useful purposes.[46] Earlier notions of convenience, commodiousness and utility have been transformed here into a conceptualization of home comfort, the building

Figure 1.2 Plate I from Edward Gyfford, *Designs for Elegant Cottages and Small Villas, Calculated for the Comfort and Convenience of Persons of Moderate and of Ample Fortune* (1806).
Courtesy of the British Library Board, Wq1/6333 DSC.

itself no longer solely the expression of the architect's genius but a structure that is designed and erected primarily with the needs of the client in mind. Echoes of Roger North's earlier sense that convenience was the product of the inhabitants' lived experience rather than the architect's grand designs are never far away. For Laing, comfort's architectural realization greatly depends upon the principles of economy, compactness and regularity, each one enhancing the other through the adoption of a square groundplan:

> The nearer the plan of a building approaches to a Square, the greater are its conveniences, and the cost proportionately less. A square, equal in superficial extent to a parallelogram, requires less external walling, and consequently less internal furnishing. In the following Plans I have endeavoured to make the building as compact as possible, whereby convenience is produced and expense is saved: when the apartments are scattered, and lie wide from each other, with long passages, much unpleasantness must be experienced, and much expense ensue, by covering a larger space of ground than is absolutely necessary.[47]

As in Gwyfford, comfort is the product of moderate economy, its physical coordinates elaborated across the descriptions to the accompanying plans and elevations said to be dependent on heating; adequate water supply and the inclusion of such conveniences as water closets; the discreet placement and arrangement of the more functional rooms or 'offices'; and the devotion of particular interior rooms – kitchen; drawing rooms; bedrooms – to particular functions or 'utilities'.

By the time of the publication of Richard Brown's *Domestic Architecture* in 1841, home comfort had become somewhat discursively entrenched, albeit returned here to the country houses of the wealthy. Although Brown tends to conceive comfort as one particular element within that older and more encompassing concept of convenience – convenience itself, he argues, is the composite sum of comfort and utility – 'comfort' nonetheless emerges, alongside strength and beauty, as a primary architectural objective. 'Convenience', he writes, 'consists in the most *judicious distribution* and division of the apartments, and in their comfort and utility, as best suited to the purpose for which the building is destined.'[48] As Brown argues, comfort has been one of the primary drivers of change and innovation in British domestic architecture since its earliest times: 'Every change in the dwellings of mankind, from the rude cabin to the stately mansion, has been dictated by some principle of convenience, neatness, comfort, or magnificence.'[49] Architectural history in his estimation is thus not the story of ever-increasing levels of stylistic elegance so much as the British nation's progressive and continuous approach upon domestic comfort and convenience, one that, of necessity, abandoned the ecclesiastical forms of the Gothic in favour of neo-Classical styles. As in Gwyfford, home comfort for Brown is underpinned by a number of practical spatial considerations, among them the use of a square and symmetrical groundplan; ensuring that noxious effluvia from the kitchens do not penetrate the bed chambers; the provision of adequate water closets for the inhabitants; the availability of sufficient water nearby; the partial concealment of the offices; and provision for the discreet movements of the servants throughout the house. But comfort is also a function of the house's situation in the landscape, for 'the eye also turns with abhorrence from the cold and dreary situation, where no idea of comfort, fitness, or grandeur can be associated'.[50]

Conclusion

Thus it was that architects, architectural patrons and aestheticians of the long eighteenth century made their approach upon what, by the early nineteenth century, had become a commonplace notion of the comfortable home. As Mrs Elton would quip in Austen's *Emma* (1816), 'Ah! There is nothing like staying at home, for real comfort', before continuing that 'Nobody can be more devoted to home than I am. I was quite a proverb for it at Maple Grove.'[51] As this comment suggests, 'home comforts' by the second decade of the nineteenth century had become somewhat of an English proverb. Before this point, and working without the intimations of physical ease only later assumed by the term 'comfort', eighteenth-century architects made recourse to notions of utility and convenience as a way of addressing a building's suitability to modern life. Emerging initially in relation to the campaign for improved working-class habitation, comfort entered into architectural discourse rather late in the period, yet gained ever-increasing architectural and literary prominence and traction in the first three decades of the nineteenth century.

Notes

1. See Witold Rybczynzki, *Home: A Short History of an Idea* (London: William Heinemann, 1988), 20.
2. See John Archer, *The Literature of British Domestic Architecture, 1715–1842* (Cambridge, MA and London: MIT Press, 1985), 33–118.
3. Samuel Johnson, *A Dictionary of the English Language*, 2 vols (London: Printed by W. Strahan, for J. and P. Knapton; T. and T. Longman; C. Hitch and L. Hawes; A. Millar; and R. and J. Dodsley, 1755–56), vol. 1, n.p.
4. David Hume, *A Treatise of Human Nature: Being an Attempt to Introduce the Experimental Method of Reasoning into Moral Subjects*, 3 vols (London: Printed for John Noon, 1739–40), vol. 2, 154–5.
5. Isaac Ware, *A Complete Body of Architecture. Adorned with Plans and Elevations, from Original Designs*, re-issue of 1756 edition (London: Printed for J. Rivington, L. Davis and C. Reymers, R. Baldwin et al., 1768), 293.
6. Ibid., 293.
7. Edward Denison and Guand Yu Ren, *The Life of the British Home: An Architectural History* (Chichester: John Wiley and Sons, 2012), 184.
8. See John E. Crowley, *The Invention of Comfort: Sensibilities & Design in Early Modern Britain & Early America* (Baltimore: Johns Hopkins University Press, 2001); John Cornforth, *English Interiors 1790–1848: The Quest for Comfort* (London: Barrie and Jenkins, 1978), 209–12; and Jon Stobart and Cristina Prytz, 'Comfort in English and Swedish Country Houses, c. 1760–1820', *Social History*, 43, no. 2 (2018): 234–58.
9. Anne Grant, *Letters from the Mountains; Being the Real Correspondence of a Lady between the Years 1773 and 1807*, 4th edn, 3 vols (London: Printed for Longman, Hurst, Rees, & Orme, 1809), vol. 1, 30.

10 William Chambers, *A Treatise on Civil Architecture* (London: Printed for the Author, by J. Haberkorn, 1759), ii.
11 Ibid., ii.
12 Alexander Gerard, *An Essay on Taste* (London: Printed for A. Millar; Edinburgh: Printed for A. Kincaid and J. Bell, 1759), 38.
13 Ibid.
14 Henry Home, Lord Kames, *Elements of Criticism*, 3 vols (London: Printed for A. Millar; Edinburgh: Printed for A. Kincaid and J. Bell, 1762), vol. 3, 322.
15 Ibid., 326.
16 Ibid., 324.
17 Ibid., 325.
18 Ibid., 327.
19 Ibid., 349.
20 William Gilpin, *Observations on the Western Parts of England, Relative Chiefly to Picturesque Beauty* (London: Printed for T. Cadell and W. Davies, 1798), 127.
21 Peter N. Lindfield, *Georgian Gothic: Medievalist Architecture, Furniture and Interiors, 1730–1840* (Woodbridge: Boydell, 2016), 144–5.
22 This letter is extracted and published in John Doran, *A Lady of the Last Century (Mrs Elizabeth Montagu)* (London: Richard Bentley and Son, 1873), 318.
23 Horace Walpole, *A Description of the Villa of Mr Horace Walpole, Youngest Son of Sir Robert Walpole Earl of Orford, at Strawberry Hill near Twickenham, Middlesex* (Strawberry Hill: Printed by Thomas Kirgate, 1784), iii.
24 For studies of luxury in the period, see Christopher J. Berry, *The Idea of Luxury: A Conceptual and Historical Investigation* (Cambridge: Cambridge University Press, 1994); Maxine Berg, *Luxury and Pleasure in Eighteenth-Century Britain* (Oxford: Oxford University Press, 2005); and Maxine Berg and Elizabeth Eger (eds), *Luxury in the Eighteenth Century: Debates, Desires and Delectable Goods* (Basingstoke: Palgrave Macmillan, 2003).
25 For a detailed account of this tradition, see Archer, *The Literature of British Domestic Architecture*, 77–87. On the bourgeois underpinnings of comfort in the eighteenth century, see Rybczynzki, *Home*; Christine Adams, *A Taste for Comfort and Status: A Bourgeois Family in Eighteenth-Century France* (University Park: Pennsylvania University Press, 2000); and Joan DeJean, *The Age of Comfort: When Paris Discovered Casual – and the Modern Home Began* (New York: Bloomsbury, 2009).
26 Nathaniel Kent, *Hints to Gentlemen of Landed Property* (London: Printed for J. Dodsley, 1775), 229.
27 Ibid., 228.
28 Ibid., 232.
29 Ibid., 268.
30 Ibid., 265.

31 John Wood, *A Series of Plans, for Cottages or Habitations of the Labourer, Either in Husbandry, or the Mechanic Arts, Adapted as well to Towns, as to the Country* (Bath: Printed by Hooper and Keenes, 1788), 1.
32 Ibid., 2.
33 George Richardson, *New Designs in Architecture, Consisting of Plans, Elevations, and Sections for Various Buildings* (London: Printed for the Author, 1792), ii, i.
34 John Soane, *Sketches in Architecture: Containing Plans and Elevations of Cottages, Villas, and Other Useful Buildings, with Characteristic Scenery* (London: Taylor, 1793), i.
35 Ibid., n.p.
36 Crowley, *The Invention of Comfort*, 203–29.
37 Humphry Repton, *Sketches and Hints on Landscape Gardening* (London: Printed for W. Bulmer and Co., 1794), 15.
38 Humphry Repton, *Observations on the Theory and Practice of Landscape Gardening*, reprint of 1803 edition (London: Printed by T. Bensley for J. Taylor, 1805), 11.
39 Ibid., 2.
40 Ibid., 140.
41 Ibid., 190–208.
42 See Denison and Yu Ren, *The Life of the British Home*, 165–219.
43 Edward Gyfford, *Designs for Elegant Cottages and Small Villas, Calculated for the Comfort and Convenience of Persons of Moderate and of Ample Fortune* (London: Published by J. Taylor, 1806), vi.
44 Ibid., 1.
45 David Laing, *Hints for Dwellings: Consisting of Original Designs for Cottages, Farm-Houses, Villas, &c. Plain and Ornamental; with Plans to Each: In which Strict Attention is Paid to Unite Convenience and Elegance with Economy*, new edn (London: Printed for J. Taylor, 1818), 7.
46 Ibid.
47 Ibid., 8.
48 Richard Brown, *Domestic Architecture: Containing a History of the Science, and the Principles of Public Buildings, Private Dwelling-Houses, Country Mansions, and Suburban Villas* (London: George Virtue, 1841), 81.
49 Ibid., vii.
50 Ibid., 309.
51 Jane Austen, *Emma*, edited by James Kinsley, intro. and notes by Adela Pinch (1816; Oxford: Oxford University Press, 2003), 214.

People in focus 1:
Masters and servants: Parallel worlds in Blondel's *maisons de plaisance*

Aurélien Davrius

Even before the end of the reign of Louis XIV, the French nobility had grown tired of the immense rooms impossible to heat, and with servants at each door. The great king had set the example by constructing the castle of Marly between 1679 and 1696, where he received only a privileged few. Versailles was for the Court, Trianon for the family, and Marly for friends. Intended for the aristocracy, but increasingly also for the bourgeoisie, these urban hotels housed the owner and his family, allowing the master of the house to receive visitors for his business and to lead a social life fitting to his rank. They found their counterpart in rural cottages. This type of construction proliferated between 1720 and 1730, both around Paris and in the provinces, and even abroad. Architects wrote comprehensive treatises exclusively on this new type of dwelling, both its decor and spatial layout. It is this category of habitation, the *maisons de plaisance*, that will hold our attention here. Because of their specific function, for *otium* and pleasure, the question of domestic comfort, both physical and emotional, seems fundamental. Comfort means both the tranquillity of family life, separated from the bustle of the wider domestic realm, and the refinement of interior spaces, through distribution or decor, which provided the pleasant living environment sought by the occupants. For the owner and his family, private happiness and the place of children became increasingly important parts of domesticity, displacing – to some extent at least – displays of rank and status. This case study focuses on spatial separations within the home, between homeowners and the wider household, particularly as it is developed in the work of Jacques-François Blondel.

The typology of country houses had changed profoundly since the sixteenth century, when the Bolognese Sebastiano Serlio theorized in his sixth book on *la casa del povero contadino* and *la casa del ricco cittadino*. In 1727–38, Jean Mariette published in three volumes an *Architecture françoise* which gave pride of place to private mansions and country houses, with detailed plans, cross sections and elevations. Jacques-François Blondel, the famous royal architect, took his first steps alongside his uncle with this publication. It was he who first highlighted the necessity of bringing particular comfort to this type of dwelling by publishing in 1737–8 the treatise *De la distribution des maisons de plaisance*, which bears the subtitle *Traité d'architecture dans le goût moderne*. As the name suggests, the publication focused on the distribution of houses in the countryside. Far from the city and intended for the owner's relaxation, the architect designing such houses had to efface all the technical and physical constraints which could disturb the quietude of the master of house.

To design a rural or urban dwelling in the eighteenth century was to think of all the contingencies to which life required: to place the stables away from the house; to separate the kitchens in order to avoid the spread of smells without making them so distant that food arrived cold at the table; to locate water closets for comfort and convenience. But in the houses of the nobility and even of well-to-do bourgeois, these activities had to occupy a separate world, one that ran in parallel with that of the owner and his family.

In his models of a *maison de plaisance*, Blondel proposes new solutions to facilitate the work of servants, but also to conceal them from the sight of the masters. In the first model, which shows the plan of the kitchens, we see the spatial hierarchy which divides the *communs*, the *secrétaires*, the kitchen staff and the servants. A small house is even assigned to the chief gardener, from where he can direct his helpers and another lodging is reserved for the concierge, with two spacious rooms, wardrobes and *chambre en niche*. The *officiers de bouche*, and the chef, sommelier and *maître d'hôtel*, who were so important in the eighteenth century, had their own apartments and dined separately from the livery servants who took their meals in a common room.

Inside the main building, Blondel continues to combine the separation of ranks with the efficiency of domestic service (see Figure 1a.1). While the *intendants* of the house dine comfortably and separated from their subordinates in the Officers Antechamber (on the left of Figure 1a.1), spiral staircases on either side of the *Grand Salon à l'Italienne* allow the servants to move between floors while preserving the cleanliness and status of the grand staircase. Passages constructed between the walls are connected to stairs rising to the servants' rooms and descending to the cellars, thus facilitating a relatively direct and discrete marginal circulation. For the sake of convenience, the valve for the water closet located next to the Small Room in the Niche

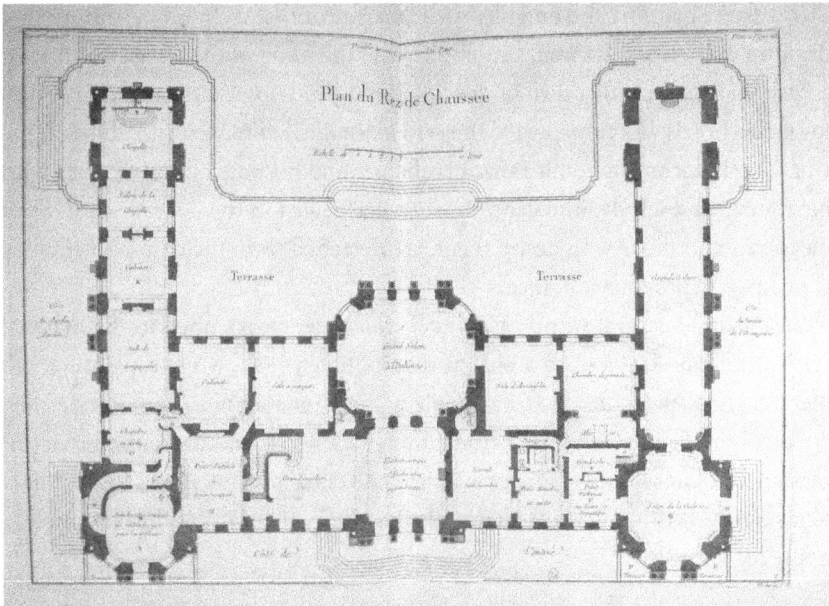

Figure 1a.1 Jacques-François Blondel, *De la Distribution des maisons de plaisance et de la décoration des édifices en général*, Paris, C.-A. Jombert, 1737-1738, t. I, plan 2, Plan du rez de Chaussée.

would be emptied from the rear passage. Blondel explains to us that these valves 'are very suitable to be placed next to the great apartments, because they never give a bad odour'.[1] They are nicely decorated and the architect specifies that

> we used to enclose the seat in a bench of marquetry or carpentry, which is placed in a niche in the form of Alcove, on both sides of which are small doors, one of which serves as a clearing to enter the wardrobe behind, and the other can serve as a wardrobe for preparing fragrant waters.[2]

Even utilitarian rooms and technologies were embellished and aestheticized as part of 'machine à habiter', which was conceived not only as a machine, but also as a work of art.

Blondel presupposes a rich and well-born clientele, receiving guests of at least equal rank. They are Catholics who attend the services in private chapels, scholars and collectors with their own libraries and galleries. They follow fashion, play billiards, drink coffee and grow plants in a greenhouse. They take long meals and refined baths, and their guests arrive with their own servants.

They service comfort and amenity with an array of new technology: pumps that draw up water from the well, kettles that heat the water of the baths, toilets with a flush that works with a turn of the tap. Blondel did not reserve these amenities for urban hotels, but transported them to *maisons de plaisance*, islands of escape where each 'according to his rank, his charges and his possibility, will taste with his friends and family, innocent pleasure that reigns in the countryside'[3]. Such pleasures, and those who desire them, are detached from the common country gentlemen of provincial France.

In the architectural world of Blondel, convenience extended to the master-servant relationship and to a spatial distribution which, while separating and hierarchizing, promotes and harmonizes their interactions. For Blondel, the architect can facilitate the daily functioning of a house and make the service of masters by their servants more convenient and efficient. This allows the architect to lay out everything that affects the client, as he explains in his third example, a house for a marquis:

> We must always be careful that the Domestics cannot be troubled in their different functions, nor embarrass each other [...] many people have to be applied to various work. In order to avoid confusion in this respect, care must be taken to ascertain the number of Domestics, and to provide for all that is necessary for this purpose; and for the work to be done easily. It is not enough in the country that the Master's lodging is of an elegant layout, and that it is richly ornamented; utility must accompany the agreeable, and even be preferred to it.[4]

This is the first time this aspect of layout had been theorized. Blondel considered the hierarchy of the servants as much as that of the masters when arranging the common rooms. The *intendants* of the property of the house dine and rest among their peers and separate from their subordinates. The cooks, the *intendant* and the concierge not only have sleeping quarters, but whole apartments. Blondel lodges the servants near their work, usually in the mezzanines above the large bedrooms, but sometimes in a bed – not on straw mattresses – in the closets near the master bedrooms and within reach of those they serve (vol. 1, pl. 23, 24, 32, 33).

This reflection finds its origin in the Versaillan model of the seventeenth century, but *Les Maisons de plaisance* allows Blondel the opportunity to develop an idea still insufficiently explored in architectural theory, that of the convenient organization of the house. Without neglecting the exterior aspects, the architect does not want to restrict himself to the architectural orders of the facades, which previously subordinated the arrangements of interior space, or to the placement of fireplaces and staircases. Blondel's book establishes a real harmony and a relation between internal organization and external appearance. Moreover, it seeks to establish general construction laws, even if they remain diffuse and not clearly explained.[5] One law, however, predominates this work : that of convenience, in all its different aspects. In all his writings, Blondel insists on the importance attached to it in his tripartite system of convenience, solidity and charm (*agrément*).

The idea of dedicating a book on the organization of this type of housing forces us to think first about the functioning of a house, composed of the family and the servants who are at its service. At the beginning of the eighteenth century, the common euphemism for domestic servants was the domestic enemies. There could be up to fifty servants in a house of this type. Of these, the greater number was in the service of the master and the others served the lady of the house. Most were men, liveried servants who spent the greater part of their time standing, two by two, in the doorways where they provided ceremonial access to private quarters and functioned as public demonstrations of the rank of their master at the top of the social hierarchy. Dressed and fed, they were sometimes paid irregularly. Moreover, the necessity of service forced them to live in precarious housing conditions, such as sleeping on straw mattresses in locker rooms, where they would be constantly available to their masters. This type of hierarchy, of partitioning servants from masters, was amplified in the nineteenth century with Haussmann buildings. There, between the noble floor and the maid's room and between ceremonial and service staircases, the separation of these two worlds is manifest. It finds its origins in the art of domestic organization born at the beginning of the eighteenth century.

The ever-increasing search for domestic comfort and family well-being which made the constant presence of several domestic servants so undesirable logically led architects to find discrete, but effective solutions. These parallel worlds reflect French society in the *Ancien Régime*, in which the nobility and clergy did not mix with the Tiers-État. At the level of the State, Louis XIV had taken his capital from Paris to Versailles, where he lived in a parallel world, rarely mixing with his subjects; in the eighteenth century, the same desire for separation was to be found, with the development of *maisons de plaisance* in the country, and the separation of two parallel worlds, that of the master and that of the servants.

Notes

1. Jacques-François Blondel, *De la distribution des maisons de plaisance* (Paris, 1737–38), vol. 1, 29.
2. Ibid., vol. 1, 29.
3. Ibid., vol. 1, 7.
4. Ibid., vol. 1, 121.
5. Ibid., vol. 1, 2.

2

Northern comfort and discomfort: Spaces and objects in Swedish country houses, c.1740–1800

Johanna Ilmakunnas

Throughout Europe, a house and an estate were valuable economic, socio political and cultural resources for landowning elites from the early modern period to the Second World War, and even beyond. A house represented the status and values of the elites, whether belonging to the nobility or aristocracy, or aspiring to social elevation. Furthermore, the house was often a home for the owner family and it offered its inhabitants both bodily and mental comfort. Recent research on European country houses has stressed the complex role the house and estate had locally, nationally and globally.[1] For Sweden, scholarship on eighteenth-century country houses has explored the architecture of and representational spaces at country houses, the house and estate as economic and social unifications, or country house and the everyday life, among other topics.[2] Moreover, the history of Swedish country houses and manor houses is not limited to the present-day boundaries of Sweden. To understand country house culture in Northern Europe, it is important to remember that large parts of today's Finland were integral to the Swedish realm from the twelfth century until 1809. Thus, when referring in this chapter to Sweden and Swedish country houses, I denote eighteenth-century Sweden, including present-day Finland.

In their comparative paper on comfort in English and Swedish eighteenth-century country houses, Jon Stobart and Christina Prytz have analysed comfort as a concept and the use of the word 'comfort' (*bekvämlighet* in Swedish). In their analysis, comfort is essentially well-being, both physical and mental, and is strongly linked to warmth and airiness, but also to social relations.[3] Their analysis draws on the work of John Crowley who discusses comfort as physical well-being and as access to warmth and light, arguing that towards the end of the eighteenth-century physical comfort became more important than aspects of appearance, fashion or taste.[4] Similarly, Joan DeJean suggests that the period of 1670–1765 was in Paris an 'age of comfort', linking modern comfort to the rise of urban aristocratic culture and informality in late-seventeenth-century Paris and to the emergence of a consumer culture, innovations and the availability of consumer goods that added physical comfort.[5] Since the Swedish aristocracy had close connections to France, the new ideas of comfort were rapidly imported and in many ways also adapted to Swedish context.[6] Marie-Odile Bernez links comfort and a comfortable lifestyle to material well-being and a critique of luxury, arguing that, in Britain especially, material comfort was morally superior to (French) luxury.[7] In Sweden too, public discussion of luxury and necessity affected how country houses were built and decorated.[8]

In this chapter, I will analyse how country houses were constructed as comfortable and convenient homes, and how comfort was created in Northern European context, focusing especially on architecture, space and the display of objects in houses. Comfort is here understood as an analytical tool, since it was seldom used explicitly in my sources. My analysis draws on comfort defined by Crowley, DeJean, and Stobart and Prytz as physical and mental well-being linked to furniture, space and thermal conditions, but also to human relations at home. First, I will explore how new ideas about architecture influenced the distribution of spaces in country houses and how ideals were accommodated to practicalities. Second, I will examine objects such as armchairs, movable desks or quilted textiles that enabled new comfortable lifestyle, and how these objects were displayed and used in the house. Third, I will discuss how comfort and discomfort were pictured in text and image. Finally, as a conclusion, I will discuss how, or, indeed, whether, country houses were experienced as homes in eighteenth-century Sweden and in what ways technology, architecture and spaces, objects and things influenced feelings of home.

Architecture, technology and comfort

From the early eighteenth century onwards, European country house architecture was deeply influenced by novel ideals of architecture and display of rooms, presented by the French architects Charles Étienne Briseux (1680–1754) and Jacques-François Blondel (1705–74) in their influential treatises on the architecture of country and town houses. As Aurélien Davrius argues in his contribution to this collection and elsewhere, the innovations in spatial distribution of French eighteenth-century country houses shaped comforts and conveniences of the habitants of country houses.⁹ These ideals were imported into Sweden mainly by Baron Carl Hårleman (1700–53), an architect educated in Rome and Paris. Hårleman was an architect of royal and aristocratic houses, and his influence on religious and secular architecture was incontestable. Hårleman's designs were engraved and printed as model drawings for different types of buildings.[10] In 1755, Captain Carl Wijnblad (1705–68) published in Swedish a collection of architectural plans of country houses in a number of sizes, forms and spatial arrangements. Wijnblad's designs were strongly influenced by the work of Hårleman, Blondel and Briseaux, and introduced to a larger audience architectural novelties such as small rooms with specific use, passageways, staircases and servants' quarters, as well as dining rooms. Yet Wijnblad did not slavishly follow French precedents, situating the principal rooms on the first floor, whereas Blondel placed them on the ground floor (Figure 2.1).[11] Since Wijnblad's model book included both extravagant palaces and modest one-floor houses with an attic, the plans were widely followed and influenced dwellings across social strata.[12]

Carl Hårleman and most of his clients belonged to the Swedish aristocracy that spent years in France, where they had opportunities to acquaint themselves with aristocratic houses and new, more comfortable living standards that appeared from the mid-seventeenth century onwards.[13] In Sweden, Hårleman's

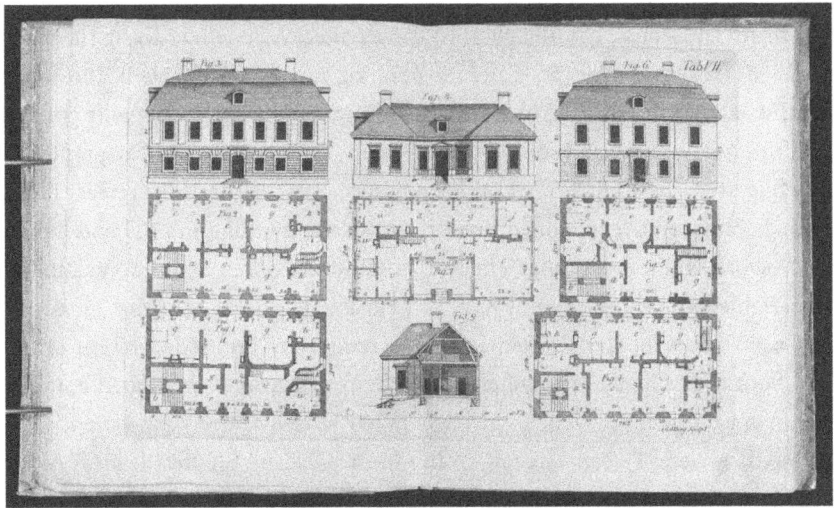

Figure 2.1 Plate VII from Carl Wijnblad's *Ritningar på fyrtio våningshus*, printed in Stockholm 1755.

Photo: Lund University Library. CC PD.

clients wished to build modern country houses that replaced vast and cold seventeenth-century palaces or to renovate old houses. From 1630 to 1680, the Swedish aristocracy engaged in a frenetic episode of building lavish country houses that displayed the political and economic power of their family.[14] These baroque houses were influenced by Dutch, French and Italian architecture, priority being given to the outer appearance of a house, to communicate the status and wealth of the owner, while thermal comfort or the usability of space were less significant.[15] Whether they were houses rather than homes when erected would be another research question; arguably, they became homes in the eighteenth century when refurnished, redesigned and remodelled according to the needs and wants of those who lived at the house and according to technological and architectural innovations that offered more effective heating and lightning. Moreover, for many aristocrats who owned a baroque country house, it was more realistic to improve the old house instead of building a new house.[16]

These changes and improvements are illustrated by two different works by Carl Hårleman: the renovation of a seventeenth-century house called Mälsåker and a plan for a new house, Granhammar. Both were country estates relatively close to Stockholm owned and occupied by aristocratic families linked to each other through marriage, military service and political ambitions.

Mälsåker was built by the enormously rich Baron Gustaf Soop (1624–79) who wanted a country house for his wife and daughter that would also display his wealth and status. The first plans by the architect Nicodemus Tessin the older (1615–81) date from the 1660s and the building was finished in 1680. The house comprised of more than fifty rooms, including a seventeen-metre-wide gallery. The interior was lavishly decorated between 1674 and 1677 in a grandiose baroque style with gilt leather wall hangings, large decorative fireplaces and ceilings of decoratively painted linen cloth (in the dwelling rooms) and Italian stuccowork (in the great gallery, main staircase and a dozen other rooms). In the mid-eighteenth century, Count Axel von Fersen (1719–94), the great-grandson of Gustaf Soop, let Carl Hårleman plan a renovation and redecoration of the first floor of the house. The gallery and other extravagantly decorated baroque rooms on the second floor, in Sweden called festivity floor (*festvåning*), were left as they were. Fersen was one of the most powerful political leaders of his time and a strong advocate of political power of the aristocracy instead of that of the sovereign and monarchy. For him, Mälsåker embodied the aristocratic ideals of seventeenth-century Sweden, the era that in the eighteenth century was regarded as the golden age of the nobility and aristocracy in Sweden.[17] At the same time, Mälsåker was a vast stone building with large rooms that did not meet the mid-eighteenth-century ideals of comfortable living.

In creating thermal comfort and a pleasant indoor climate in Northern Europe, warm and smoke-free rooms were key factors, as Gulhild Eriksdotter and Mattias Legnér have stressed. They argue that scholars of domestic material culture tend to overlook the importance of these factors in shaping the spatiality, interior decoration and furniture of house. Furthermore, they remind us that, to better contextualize and understand technological changes and alterations in interior designs, it is crucial to consider also broader influences such as climate.[18] In the early modern period, from the 1500s to the mid-nineteenth century, Northern Europe went through a cooling period known as the Little Ice Age, with extremely severe winters and cold, wet summers, which led to frequent crop failures, famines and exceedingly high mortality.[19] However, as Eriksdotter argues, the Little Ice Age was also a period of transition and adaptation during which buildings 'demonstrate various creative solutions in order to become both more energy efficient and comfortable, which might have led to altered living conditions and new social practices'.[20] Adaptations to climatic effects, new technological inventions and new ideals of home and comfort are all apparent in how Fersen and Hårleman, arguably together, refurbished Mälsåker to make it into a comfortable eighteenth-century home.

The renovations that made Mälsåker more comfortable to live involved a reorganization of space according to novel way to use rooms, and more efficient heating and insulation. Before his death in 1753, Hårleman designed a number of new rooms on the first floor that was the main dwelling floor. A drawing room (*förmak*), dining room and small rooms that presumably were used as bedrooms or closets were created out of the original large, multipurpose rooms. The walls of these rooms were lined with wooden panels and open fireplaces were replaced by tiled stoves; the large windows were changed or renovated and several mirrors were affixed to panels.[21] These renovations considerably enhanced the warmth and lightness of these rooms: regular smoke-free warmth – created by the tiled stoves and accentuated by wooden panelling, shutters and floors, as well as ceilings of cloth – produced a level of thermal comfort that arguably made Mälsåker comfortably warm to live in. However, while tiled stoves gave even and long-term heat and economized considerably on firewood because they needed to be lit only once in a day, they gave only little or no light.[22] Large windows and mirrors reflecting either daylight or artificial light were thus crucial in adding to the convenience and comfort of the rooms. In Northern Europe, the fluctuations of light conditions according to the season are conspicuous, autumn and winter being extremely dark without artificial light. Thus, technological improvements in mirror-making technique also influenced the experience of light and comfort in the home. The large and even surfaces of eighteenth-century mirrors reflected the light more efficiently than older mirrors and the importance of multiplying light was one of the reasons why mirrors became so fashionable in interiors. Added to this, they were essential also for conveniently watching what was happening in the room without needing to move from a comfortable chair by the fire.[23]

It is noteworthy, however, that not all architectural solutions that enhanced the comfort of a house were eighteenth-century innovations.[24] The main living and representative rooms were situated in the first floor at Mälsåker and other seventeenth-century houses. This was in keeping with the fashion of the time, but it also raised these rooms well above the cold and dampness of the ground floor. In addition, the floors were made of wood and the ceilings of main living rooms were covered with cloth, both warmer than the stone or stucco that were used in halls, the main staircase and the gallery. Significantly, while the eighteenth-century French architectural ideals introduced by Blondel and Briseux in France, and adapted in Sweden by Hårleman and his successors, placed key rooms on the ground floor, in Northern Europe, the ground floor was seldom convenient in terms of thermal comfort. For instance at Åkerö, the country house that Hårleman designed for his close friend, Count Carl Gustaf Tessin (1695–1770), the ground floor was so damp and uncomfortable that Tessin moved his rooms from there to the first floor of a wing. At Övedskloster, designed for the enormously wealthy Baron Hans Ramel (1724–99), Hårleman placed the main building in a slope, making possible an entrance to ground floor, under which is situated an underground floor that no doubt allowed the principal rooms to stay dry and warm, unlike at Åkerö.[25]

In addition to these grand houses, Hårleman also designed a number of less prominent houses and planned several schemes for modernizing seventeenth-century houses.[26] While Mälsåker represents an example of the latter, Granhammar, designed for Baron Jacob Albrect von Lantingshausen (1699–1769), is an example of the former.

Granhammar is worth a closer analysis because it represents a less well-known house that was designed for an individual commissioner instead of being outlined for a certain administrative position as were, for instance, the drawings for model houses for high officers and civil servants (Figure 2.2). However, the drawings of Granhammar were engraved as a sole example of a country house in the collection *Plans et Élevations des Bâtiments de Suède* in which Hårleman

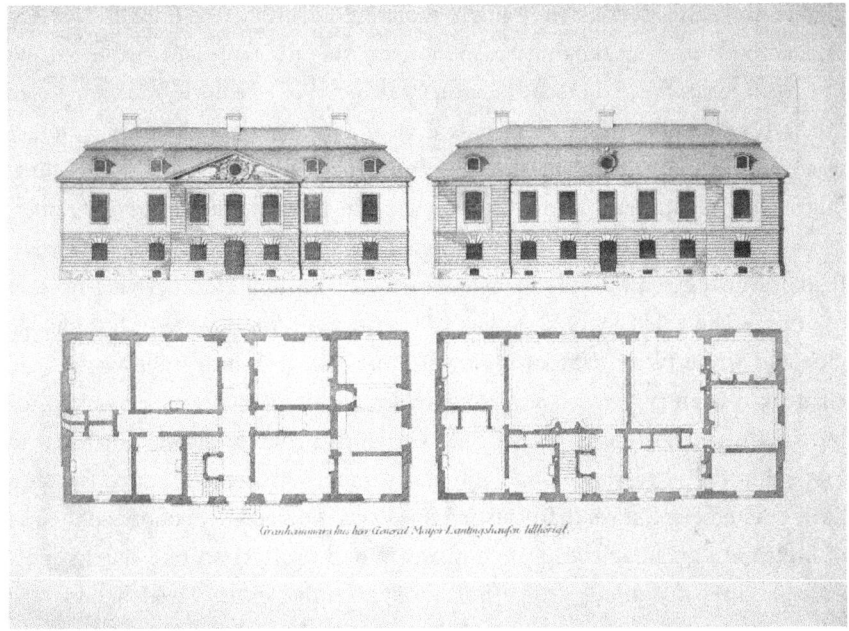

Figure 2.2 Jean Erik Rehn, after Carl Hårleman, *Granhammar house, façade and plans*, between 1749 and 1759.
Photo: Erik Cornelius, Nationalmuseum, Stockholm. CC PD.

amassed engravings of his drawings on key buildings, some private but mostly public.[27]

The plans of Granhammar show that the first floor was designed for both representation and habitation, whereas the ground floor was intended for household functions and for guests or children. The importance of the first floor is clear from the drawings of the elevations: the windows are larger and there is a prominent avant-corps on the main façade. In addition, the side risalits on the garden façade emphasize the first floor, while the ground floor with small windows remains less important. Even though the names of rooms are not included on the drawings, it is clear the suites of rooms are divided to the feminine and masculine. The suite of rooms occupied by the mistress of the house comprise of five rooms, including a large drawing room, whereas the rooms of the master of the house comprise three rooms on the opposite side of the building. In between the two suites is a large room, probably a drawing room or a dining room, although the latter may well have been on the ground floor.[28] Situating kitchen and other household functions to the ground floor had a significant impact on thermal comfort because the stoves and ovens in the kitchen were almost constantly alight, radiating warmth to the floor above. That said, comfort was not the only reason for situating the representative rooms on the first floor in the seventeenth-century manner. For one thing, the views from the first floor were usually more expansive and at Granhammar the new house was built on the remains of an older one which, according to Gösta Selling, might have encouraged the architect to place the *piano nobile* on the first floor.[29]

Granhammar also had wooden panelling and niches with tiled stoves.[30] In the drawing room, a tiled stove decorated with von Lantingshausen's coat of arms was erected in 1752. Other stoves on both floors were of fashionable blue and white tiles.[31] One of the most important technical improvements in eighteenth-century Sweden was a novel design for tiled stoves, presented for the Swedish government in 1767.[32] As Christina Prytz discusses in her text in this volume, the reason behind the government's assignment to construct a more fuel-efficient stove than existing ones was the need to economize the use of firewood that was needed for iron works and production of Sweden's most valuable imported goods, iron. Thus, in eighteenth-century Sweden, concerns for national economics were behind the technological innovation that perhaps most influenced on the comfort of homes through more efficient heating systems. Tiled stoves were often designed by the architects as part of decorative schemes and commissioned from skilful master-craftsmen in towns. From the second half of the eighteenth century onwards, there were also a number of factories making tiled stoves. Moreover, the stoves could be dismantled and reassembled when needed, for instance in the case of selling of a house.[33] Tiled stoves were the principal heating system at Swedish country houses, even though in the representative rooms there were also open fireplaces in marble or limestone. For instance at Ljung, built for Axel von Fersen in the 1770s and 1780s, the tiled stoves and open fireplaces were situated in the opposite ends of rooms, supplying thus both warmth and light, as well as being indispensable decorative elements.[34]

Comfort-related technical innovations, such as more efficient heating systems, were not exclusively reserved to house owners and their guests.[35] In the course of the eighteenth century, thermal comfort was democratized in grand houses, because tiled stoves were often installed in servants' rooms and sometimes in between rooms and passageways, where warmth given by a tiled stove radiated both in the room and in the passageway. Tiled stoves in servants' quarters at Ljung, for example, were technologically similar to those in representative room, but they differed in style and decoration, as well as in price.[36] While we do not know how often the tiled stoves in the servants' rooms actually were used, it is likely that they were heated at least occasionally to keep the rooms in a liveable condition during the winter frost. Architectural and technological innovations thus had a key impact on thermal comfort during the eighteenth century. Small rooms and floor plans that permitted the separation of spaces according to need made it easier to keep them warm – coupled with double glazing, shutters, wall panels, wooden floors and more efficient tiled stoves in several or perhaps even every room; this inflected the experience of comfort and discomfort in a house.

Comfortable home seen through objects

How were daily comfort and feelings of home created through objects and the display of interiors in a house? Which objects, both furniture such as beds or tables to smaller items such as tea and coffee sets or bed linen, were essential for a comfortable home in eighteenth-century Sweden and how can we interpret the comfortability of an item? In contrast to England or a number of Swedish townhouses, large sets of receipted bills are rare for eighteenth-century country houses in Sweden.[37] Probate and household inventories are thus the key source for exploring how homes were decorated, what furniture and objects were owned, and how they were displayed in different spaces. These lists and object descriptions can be supplemented by paintings, drawings and other visual material, sources which are especially rich in telling us how objects were displayed spatially and how sentiments of comfort and homeliness were constructed.

In the late seventeenth and early eighteenth century, furniture went through a transformation from rigid to comfortable, even though representativeness and display of political power retained their significance.[38] A similar transformation is visible in Sweden, where homes were strongly influenced by continental fashions in interior decoration and furniture. According to Gösta Selling, furniture still had a representative function in eighteenth-century Sweden, despite augmented emphasis on the 'user experience' and the functionality of materials and design. This duality to be representative and comfortable is distinct in easy sitting furniture such as tabourets, stools, chairs, armchairs and sofas. Chairs were the most common sitting furniture and they are far more numerous in probate inventories than sofas and armchairs. In dining rooms, galleries and sometimes also in drawing rooms, chairs were situated by the walls and the upholstery was protected with dust covers when not in use.[39] In the second half of the eighteenth century, comfortable armchairs such as thickly padded bergères, sofas and divans became indispensable furniture at any fashionable country house. For instance, at Mälsåker, one of Axel von Fersen's favourite houses, there were a dozen chairs upholstered in gilded leather in every drawing room and salon, whereas in bedrooms there were comfortable, upholstered armchairs, sofas with cushions and canopy beds with wool and straw mattresses, bolsters and pillows filled with down, quilted blankets and bedsheets in linen.[40]

Axel von Fersen's 749-page probate inventory, completed a year after his death in 1794, gives a detailed picture of interiors in late-eighteenth-century town and country houses. Fersen owned a palace in Stockholm and a number of estates and houses in Sweden and present-day Finland. The most carefully furnished were also those where Fersen spent most of his time – first with his wife and children, two daughters and two sons, and later with his wife, their married daughters and their respective children. The Fersen palace in Stockholm and the country houses Mälsåker, Löfstad and Ljung were all comparably furnished and lived by the Fersens, while the family seldom, if ever, stayed overnight at the houses at other estates.[41] Display of objects at Mälsåker, Löfstad and Ljung were similar to the display, furniture and decorations at other Swedish country houses. At Mälsåker and Löfstad, both erected in the seventeenth century and rebuilt in the 1750s and 1760s, interiors were a combination of old and new. Baroque tapestries, wall hangings and chairs were reminders of ancestry, while beds, sofas and armchairs in daily use were of eighteenth-century fashion.[42] Ljung was built to architect Jean Eric Rehn's (1717–93) drawings of the 1770s and 1780s for entertaining and socializing, and the floor plan and interiors were essentially modern. However, comfortable living at all three houses was characterized by the importance of bedrooms as social space with soft sitting furniture and beds to lounge in, chandeliers and candlesticks to give artificial light and mirrors above fireplaces and console tables to reflect and thus multiply the effect of light, plus a tiled stove to sustain thermal comfort. The fashionable and versatile small tables that were mostly used by women for handiwork, letter writing and reading were light and easily moved near windows for better light or near fireplaces for more warmth according to the requirements of the work at hand. Furthermore, a representative house and comfortable home was created through the display and use of objects in daily life. Access and use of clean bed linen, cutlery, coffee and teacups or porcelain decorated with coats of arms assured physical comfort, but had also reflected continued concern for social propriety.

Inventories, catalogues and estate inventory deeds are irreplaceable sources to material culture and consumption,[43] but they seldom include all objects in a certain room or describe in detail how they were displayed. Drawings, paintings or engraving may give us a better understanding on how a room was used and how a comfortable everyday life was experienced.

In the 1750s and 1760s, painter Olof Fridsberg (1728–95) realized several decorative *trompe l'œil* paintings at Carl Gustaf Tessin's Åkerö. He also depicted Tessin's wife, Countess Ulla Sparre (1711–68), at her cabinet.⁴⁴ The bright-coloured watercolour (Figure 2.3) is a rare example of an interior in mid-eighteenth-century Sweden. Compared to other eighteenth-century Swedish interiors, the cabinet of Ulla Sparre is striking in its vivid colours and astonishingly full of stuff. The walls are covered with floral cloth, the curtains that are mirrored from one of the cupboard's doors, are simple green cloth, probably taffeta, and the floor is of plain wooden planks. The small space is furnished with a cupboard and a large

Figure 2.3 Olof Fridsberg, *Countess Ulla Sparre in her writing cabinet*, 1760s. *Photo:* Cecilia Heisser. Nationalmuseum, Stockholm. CC PD.

French writing desk, richly decorated with gilded fittings. There is also a simple wooden table, a small sewing table and plain grey painted bookshelves, portraits in gilded frames, including a portrait of her husband, a clock, large porcelain pot, small statues, porcelain dogs, stationery and large volumes on the writing desk. The room, situated on the ground floor, was almost four metres high; to keep it warm there is a colourful carpet on the floor and an open marble fireplace, visible only partially on the left hand side. The most conspicuous piece of furniture is the Chinese cabinet in the right-hand corner of the room. The red lacquered cupboard on which sits a small figure clad in striped costume, is actually a simple wooden cupboard in *trompe l'œil*. In reality, the cupboard stretched from floor to ceiling and comprised not only the Chinese cupboard, but also the shells, figures and teapots on the shelf below, two Chinese figures only partially visible behind the countess's chair, and the opening with a green curtain and a putto near the ceiling.[45] The watercolour thus combines the richness of fashionable rococo objects such as the porcelain figures, the clock and the cupboard in *trompe l'œil* with functional furniture such as the writing desk with a shelving unit that allowed the countess to organize her correspondence and reading, and objects enhancing physical comfort, like the fireplace and carpet.

Two decades later, in 1783, an aquarelle (Figure 2.4) by Lorentz Svensson Sparrgren (1763–1828) depicts Count Clas Julius Ekeblad (1742–1808) and his wife Countess Brita Horn (1745–1791) in the countess's bedroom at Stola, the Ekeblads' country house.[46] Contrary to Ulla Sparre's cabinet, Brita Horn's bedchamber is decorated with pale colours. Even though colour palette of fashionable interior decorations in the second half of the eighteenth century was diverged from bright palette of early rococo, the contrast is strong in terms of both colours, objects displayed and the clothing of portrayed figures. The bedroom at Stola is decorated in a similar manner to bedrooms in many other eighteenth-century Swedish country houses. The walls are split by painted simple dados above which a number of paintings are hung, covering the wall up to the ceiling. Among them are family portraits, placed at eye level; above these are landscapes and higher still are nude studies and engravings of famous men and women. The furniture in the room is sparse, consisting of a canopy bed, a table, a gilded console table and a light armchair. The upholstery of the armchair in which Clas Julius Ekeblad sits is protected from dirt and sunlight by a dustcover made in simple chequered cloth. The bed on which Brita Horn lounges is representative with a canopy decorated with ostrich feathers and gilded wooden sections. The countess has raised her feet on the bed and she reclines comfortably to two large pillows behind her back. She is reading, presumably aloud, while the count is

Figure 2.4 Lorentz Svensson Sparrgren, *Interior with Clas Julius Ekebland and his wife, Countess Brita Horn*, 1783.
Photo: Alexis Daflos. Nationalmuseum, Stockholm. CC PD.

mending a fishing net. The watercolour portrays a harmonious and comfortable looking life that was in many ways also a reality for Clas Julius Ekeblad and Brita Horn. Despite financial anxieties, which prevented the Ekeblads from redecorating Stola more comfortably, they took great mental comfort in their relationship and spending time together. Thus for the Ekeblads, comfort meant both living in a comfortable home and having the spouse as a friend and solace.[47]

Comfort and discomfort pictured

How was the comfort and discomfort of daily life at houses and homes pictured in visual and verbal interpretations in eighteenth-century Sweden? As argued before, comfort and discomfort were linked by the contemporaries both to physical and mental well-being. In this section, I will analyse how the comforts of home created by architecture, technology and objects was visualized in paintings and private writing, such as letters and diaries. My aim is to show that comfort was pictured both visually and verbally in eighteenth-century Sweden, and that visual interpretations in particular augmented the comfort and 'homeliness' or feeling of a home in spaces where they were hung.

For eighteenth-century aristocracy, the lack of certain furniture, decoration or objects could create uncomfortable or awkward situations at home. Even the highest-ranking families did not necessarily possess enough stylish, comfortable or convenient furniture for entertainments considered necessary for their lifestyle. For instance, Count Johan Gabriel Oxenstierna (1750–1818) describes in his diary in summer 1805 the perturbation of his mother, Countess Sara Gyllenborg (1726–1824), when unexpected guests arrived at Gyllenborg's country house Skenäs at dinnertime. As the hostess and mistress of the house, she had to place the unanticipated guests at the table and ensure that there were enough food for everyone. After the diner, Countess Gyllenborg revealed her concerns to her son and reflected that luckily, she had ten matching chairs and ten similar spoons.[48] Gyllenborg and Oxenstierna were both wealthy and powerful families, but comfort at a country house was relative and mundane.

Swedish country houses were mainly modest compared to British or continental houses. This meant small spaces easy to warm and illuminate, but also cramped rooms without enough space for comfortable living in unusual circumstances such as when guests had to be accommodated. In early autumn 1766, the then sixteen-year-old Johan Gabriel Oxenstierna had to give up his bed for his relative Count Carl Johan Gyllenborg (1741–1811) when the latter visited Oxenstierna's parents at their country house Skenäs. Oxenstierna writes in his diary that he did not have anything against sleeping on the floor, which apparently was not uncomfortable. However, he found sleeping in a small space somewhat difficult, because when turning in his sleep, Oxenstierna was constantly about to knock over a chair or set his hand in the chamber pot. The latter did happen on one occasion, as Oxenstierna remarks with his dry humour.[49] For a young aristocrat, sleeping on the floor and giving up his bed for a relative was a slightly amusing rather than an extraordinary or objectionable event. However, Oxenstierna's bright attitude towards these apparent discomforts is probably due, at least in part, to his age and positive character. For an older person, whether a member of the host family or a guest, a similar situation would probably have been far more unpleasant and uncomfortable.

Another example of the relative nature of comfortable circumstances is weather and its effects on daily life. In August 1779, Countess Hedvig De la Gardie (1732–1800), the wife of Axel von Fersen, wrote from Ljung to her daughter that her rooms, into which the sun shone from morning to evening, were so hot and airless, that it was almost impossible to stay in them.[50] Only rarely did large trees shelter eighteenth-century houses, which were thus subject to the extremes of wind and sun. Despite the effects of the Little Ice Age, there were also warm days during summer and sunshine impacted significantly on the indoor climate. Large windows might make rooms comfortable warm spring and autumn, but in summer could become overheated, as Hedvig De la Gardie's letter makes clear. The discomfort of hot and airless rooms could, of course, be altered quickly by opening a window.[51] However, the house at Ljung about which Hedvig De la Gardie complained was not the modern brick house designed by Jean Eric Rehn, but an older and remarkably small timber house where the Fersens' stayed occasionally during the construction and decoration of the new house.[52] The small timber house heated up much faster than large houses built of brick and stone and might have also lacked the facility to open windows to create a cooling breeze through the rooms.

Eighteenth-century genre painting gives us another perspective on the comforts and discomforts of home and country house. Pehr Hilleström (1732–1816) was a key figure in creating the visual image of homely comfort in late eighteenth- and early nineteenth-century Sweden. Hilleström had studied in France and Holland and had knowledge of both contemporary genre paintings and the tradition of genre paintings with interiors picturing affluent households. Furthermore, he succeeded in establishing a style, which attracted art collectors who wished to hang on their walls Hilleström's harmonious paintings, depicting aristocratic and bourgeoisie interiors.[53] Recurrent subjects of Hilleström's extraordinarily versatile paintings are cosy chairs, soft textiles and warming fires. In a number of his paintings, women are raising their skirts in front of a fire, either in an open fireplace or a tiled stove, in order to get warm under the thick layer of skirts and underskirts.[54] Naturally, the topic also appealed to his wealthy clientele and was a common theme in genre painting. Nonetheless, Hilleström's scenes give a realistic impression of thermal comfort in eighteenth-century Swedish country houses.[55]

While tiled stoves radiate warmth relatively evenly, open fireplaces, still fashionable in representative rooms, are warming only when someone is very close to the fire, and then only on one side. Quilted petticoats or banyans, caps, shawls and fur-trimmed cloaks were used at home to keep warm in cold weather. Everyday garments were habitually plainer and less ornate in cloth, cut and decoration than formal dresses, adding to daily comfort through ease of movement and adaptation of clothing to thermal conditions accord to the season. This is visible in a number of Hilleström's paintings where women wear undecorated, monochrome dresses, jackets, shawls and caps, and are working or socializing in country house interiors. In the painting called *The Wool Winder*, executed in the 1780s–1790s, a young gentlewoman has fallen asleep in the middle of her chore of textile work (Figure 2.5). Typically for late-eighteenth-century Sweden, furniture is scarce, consisting of two upholstered chairs, an upholstered stool, an ornamental clock on the wall and a simple wooden table on which there is a warp reel and a basket full of balls of wool. Natural light from a large window casts over the women fallen asleep on her monotonous and

Figure 2.5 Pehr Hilleström, *The Wool Winder*, c. 1780–90.
Photo: Nationalmuseum, Stockholm. CC PD.

everyday work of reeling up.⁵⁶ Despite the uncharacteristically large window and sparse furniture for a Swedish country house, Hillström's painting accurately depicts daily comfort at an upper-class home, experienced through good lighting conditions, a soft chair to sit on, loose-fitting clothes and the possibility to doze off for a short while. All the furniture pictured is easy to move within and between rooms when required.

Sleeping figures on a sofa epitomize an eighteenth-century image of comfort. Pehr Hillström was far from unique in his interest on capturing sleepers in a passing moment. Architect and engraver Jean Eric Rehn, whose work on housing and the use of novel solutions for planning and distribution of spaces was vital in creating comfortable living, has visualized the comforts of home and everyday life in a number of drawings of sleeping people and animals. A drawing depicts a cat and two dogs asleep on a simple sofa with a mattress.⁵⁷ Here a comfortable home is pictured in modest and somewhat shabby furniture, unpretentious paintings on the wall and a bare chest of drawers. A sense of home and comfort is attached to animals and the obviously well-used sofa.

Conclusion: Creating a comfortable home in a northern climate

In the course of the eighteenth-century, ideals of country house architecture changed in Sweden. Following French examples, architects created new arrangements of rooms including small bedchambers, dining rooms and passageways. This resulted in the greater separation of spaces for masters and servants and added privacy for the former in particular. The new spatial order also enhanced thermal comfort because small rooms were easier to heat and rooms could be closed up depending on the need for warmth. In any country house, there was at least a couple of representative rooms that were heated only occasionally, closed doors preventing the cold from spreading out. At the same time, technological innovations such as energy-efficient tiled stoves and double-glazed windows added extra thermal comfort, large windows allowing also daylight to better enter and illuminate spaces.

Comfortable, easy armchairs and sofas emerged alongside the upright chairs that had been the most important representative furniture during the seventeenth century. Canopy beds, with curtains that could be drawn against the cold in winter, light in summer and for privacy, became the norm and bedrooms formed an important space for comfortable socializing, reading, writing, working or contemplating. According to eighteenth-century ideals, the apartment of the mistress of the house was larger than that of the master, and included the key social spaces such as drawing rooms and dressing rooms, all furnished with easy seating, light and movable tables, and mirrors to reflect light and enlarge the space. Alongside these changes in space and furniture, smaller objects such as comfortable and warm clothing, tea sets and books were also essential for comfortable lifestyle.

Bodily and mental comfort and discomfort were described in letters and diaries, and depicted in paintings that were hung on country house walls, amplifying the idea of comfortable home in the eyes of inhabitants and guests alike. Clearly, for those who owned and lived in several country houses, some held greater emotional resonance than others. However, the importance to the family of making a house into a comfortable home is tangible in letters and diaries that describe the everyday events at home with family and friends. Johan Gabriel Oxenstierna's diaries and Hedvig De la Gardie's letters are windows on daily life but also lay bare the importance of physical and mental comfort.

Notes

1 See, for example, Anna-Sophia von Celsing and Rebecka Millhagen Adelsvärd, ed., *Biby: Ett fideikommiss berättar* (Stockholm: Bokförlaget Langenskiöld, 2014); Michel Figeac, *La douceur des Lumières: Noblesse et art de vivre en Guyenne au XVIIIe siècle* (Bordeaux: Mollat Éditions, 2001); Margot Finn and Kate Smith, ed., *The East India Company at Home, 1757–1857* (London: UCL Press, 2018); Judith S. Lewis, 'When a house is not a home: Elite English women and the eighteenth-century country house', *Journal for British Studies* 48, no. 2, Special Issue on Material Culture (2009): 366–3; Jon Stobart and Mark Rothery, *Consumption and the Country House* (Oxford: Oxford University Press, 2016); Joachim Eibach and Inken Schmidt-Voges, ed., *Das Haus in der Geschichte Europas: Ein Handbuch* (Oldenburg: De Gruyter, 2015).

2 Göran Alm et al., *Carl Hårleman: Människan och verket* (Stockholm: Byggförlaget, 2000); Gösta Selling, *Svenska herrgårdshem under 1700-talet: Arkitektur och inredning 1700–1780* (Stockholm: Albert Bonniers förlag, 1937); Anna-Maria Åström, '*Sockenboarne*': *Herrgårdskultur i Savolax 1790*–1850 (Helsingfors: Svenska litteratursällskapet i Finland, 1993); Olle Sirén, *Malmgård: Grevliga ätten Creutz' stamgods* (Helsingfors: Svenska litteratursällskapet i Finland, 1984); Olle Sirén, *Sarvlaks: Gårdshushållningen och gårdssamhället från 1600-talet till 1900-talet* (Helsingfors: Svenska litteratursällskapet i Finland, 1980); Göran Ulväng, *Herrgårdarnas historia: Arbete, liv och bebyggelse på uppländska herrgårdar*

(Hedemora: Hallgren & Björklund Förlag, 2008); Göran Ulväng, *Hus och gård i förändring: Uppländska herrgårdar, boställen och bondgårdar under 1700- och 1800-talens agrara revolution* (Hedemora: Gidlund, 2004); Johanna Ilmakunnas, *Ett ståndsmässigt liv: Familjen von Fersens livsstil på 1700-talet* (Helsingfors and Stockholm: Svenska litteratursällskapet i Finland and Atlantis, 2012); Henrika Tandefelt, ed., *Sarvlax: Herrgårdshistoria under 600 år* (Helsingfors: Svenska litteratursällskapet i Finland, 2010).

3 Jon Stobart and Christina Prytz, 'Comfort in English and Swedish country houses', *Social History* 43, no. 2 (2018): 234–58.

4 John E. Crowley, *The Invention of Comfort: Sensibilities and Design in Early Modern Britain and Early America* (Baltimore: Johns Hopkins University Press, 2001).

5 Joan DeJean, *The Age of Comfort: When Paris Discovered Casual – and the Modern Home Began* (New York: Bloomsbury, 2009).

6 Johanna Ilmakunnas, 'Aristocratic Townhouse as Urban Space: The Fersen Palace in Eighteenth-Century Stockholm', in Elaine Chalus and Marjo Kaartinen (eds), *Gendering Spaces in European Towns, 1500–1914* (New York and London: Routledge, 2019), 15–31; Johanna Ilmakunnas, 'French Fashions: Aspects of Elite Lifestyle in Eighteenth-Century', in Johanna Ilmakunnas and Jon Stobart (eds), *A Taste for Luxury in Early Modern Europe: Display, Acquisition and Boundaries* (London: Bloomsbury Academic, 2017), 243–63; Charlotta Wolff, *Vänskap och makt: Den svenska politiska eliten och upplysningstidens Frankrike* (Helsingfors and Stockholm: Svenska litteratursällskapet i Finland and Atlantis, 2005); see also DeJean, *The Age of Comfort*, passim.

7 Marie-Odile Bernez, 'Comfort, the acceptable face for luxury: An eighteenth-century cultural etymology', *Journal for Early Modern Cultural Studies*, 14, no. 3 (2014): 3–21.

8 See, for example, Ilmakunnas, *Ett ståndsmässigt liv*; see also Leif Runefelt, *Att hasta mot undergången: Anspråk, flyktighet, förställning i debatten om konsumtion i Sverige 1730–1830* (Lund: Nordic Academic Press, 2015).

9 Aurélien Davrius, *Jacques-François Blondel, architecte des Lumières* (Paris: Classiques Garnier, 2018).

10 Göran Alm, *Carl Hårleman och den svenska rokokon* (Lund: Bokförlaget Signum, 1993), 79–85, 120–21; Johan Mårtelius, 'Mönsterbildaren', in Göran Alm and al., *Carl Hårleman och den svenska rokokon* (Lund: Bokförlaget Signum, 1993), 285–99.

11 Carl Wijnblad, *Ritningar på fyratio våningshus af sten, och trettio af träd, samt åtskilliga lusthus ...* (Stockholm, 1755); Carl Wijnblad, *Ytterligare tilökning af ritningar på våningshus, sextio af sten och tiugu af träd, samt hwarjehanda flygel-byggnader och pavillons ...* (Stockholm, 1756); see also Carl Wijnblad, *Tilökning af General-planer til tio sätesgårdar, förestälte uti 11 kopparstycken med deras förklaring* (Stockholm, 1765).

12 See Johannes Daun and Christer Ahlberger, ed., *Bondeherrgårdar: Den nyrika bondeklassens gårdar 1750–1850* (Lund: Nordic Academic Press 2018) on how wealthy farmers' houses (*bondgård*) resembled manor houses (*herrgård*).

13 On the novel standards for aristocratic living in seventeenth-century France, see, for example, DeJean, *The Age of Comfort* and Nina Lewallen, 'Architecture and Performance at the Hôtel du Maine in Eighteenth-Century Paris', *Studies in the Decorative Arts*, 17, no. 1 (Fall–Winter 2009–2010): 2–32.
14 Fredric Bedoire, *Guldålder: Slott och politik i 1600-talets Sverige* (Stockholm: Bonnier, 2001).
15 On Dutch influences in Sweden, see Badeloch Vera Noldus, *Town Houses and Country Estates: Dutch Architecture in Sweden* (Stockholm: Embassy of the Kingdom of the Netherlands in Stockholm, 2013).
16 See Stobart and Prytz, 'Comfort in English and Swedish country houses', 247.
17 Probate inventory after Axel von Fersen. Axel von Fersen d.ä.:s arkiv, vol. 34, Stafsundsarkivet, Swedish National Archives, Stockholm; Bedoire, *Guldålder*, 243–45; Ilmakunnas, *Ett ståndsmässigt liv*, 278–80. On Fersen's other building projects, see Johanna Ilmakunnas, 'To build according to one's status: A country house in late 18th-century Sweden', in Jon Stobart and Andrew Hann (eds), *The Country House: Material Culture and Consumption* (Swindon: English Heritage, 2016), 33–41. On Fersen and politics, see also Göran Norrby, *Maktens rivaler: Drottning Lovisa Ulrika, Gustav III, Axel von Fersen och Carl Fredrik Pecklin, 1755–1792* (Stockholm. Carlssons, 2018).
18 Gunhild Eriksdotter and Mattias Legnér, 'Indoor climate and thermal comfort from a long-term perspective: Burmeister house in Visby, c. 1650–1900', *Home Cultures*, 12, no. 1 (2015): 29–53.
19 Gunhild Eriksdotter, 'Did the little ice age affect indoor climate and comfort? Re-theorizing climate history and architecture from the Early Modern Period', *The Journal for Early Modern Cultural Studies*, 13, no. 2 (2013): 24–42; see also Brian M. Fagan, *The Little Ice Age: How Climate Made History 1300–1850* (New York: Basic Books, 2000).
20 Eriksdotter, 'Little ice age', 28.
21 Probate inventory after Axel von Fersen. Axel von Fersen d.ä.:s arkiv, vol. 34, Stafsundsarkivet, Swedish National Archives, Stockholm; Ilmakunnas, *Ett ståndsmässigt liv*, 279–80.
22 See Susanna Scherman, *Den svenska kakelungnen: 1700-talets tillverkning från Marieberg och Rörstrand* (Stockholm: Wahlström & Wistrand, 2007); Britt and Ingemar Tunander, *Svenska kakelugnar* (Stockholm: Nordiska museets förlag, 1999).
23 See DeJean, *The Age for Comfort*, 94–5.
24 Eriksdotter, 'Little ice age'.
25 Selling, *Svenska herrgårdshem*, 95–7, 106–8, 111–6, 125, 216–23; see also Johanna Ilmakunnas, 'Högadeln bor i staden: Fersenska palatset som urbant mikrokosmos i Stockholm ca 1740–1795', *Bebyggelsehistorisk tidskrift*, 68 (2014): 11–2.
26 Alm, *Carl Hårleman och den svenska rokokon*; Göran Alm & al., *Carl Hårleman: Människan och verket* (Stockholm: Byggförlaget, 2000).

27 Mårtelius, 'Mönsterbildaren', 285-98.
28 Jean Erik Rehn, after Carl Hårleman, *Granhammars hus, fasader och planer*, between 1749 and 1759, engraving on paper, 28.5 × 46 cm. NMG 921/1890, Nationalmuseum, Stockholm.
29 Selling, *Svenska herrgårdshem*, 203-4.
30 Carl Hårleman, 'Ritning till vägg med kakelugn i bred nisch, elevation', between 1745 and 1753, drawing on paper, 36.6 × 5.1 cm. NMH CC 3245, Nationalmuseum, Stockholm.
31 Lars Sjöberg, 'Inredningar', in Göran Alm & al., *Carl Hårleman: Människan och verket* (Stockholm: Byggförlaget, 2000), 225-8.
32 Carl Johan Cronstedt, *Beskrifning på Ny Inrättning af Kakelugnar Til Weds Besparing* (Stockholm: 1767); Carl Johan Cronstedt, *Samling af beskrivningar på Åtskilliga Eldstäder, Inrättande til besparing af wed* (Stockholm: 1775); see also Stobart and Prytz, 'Comfort in English and Swedish country houses', 241-3.
33 Scherman, *Den svenska kakelungnen*; Tunander, *Svenska kakelugnar*.
34 Ilmakunnas, 'To build according to one's status'.
35 See Eriksdotter, 'Little ice age', 36; see also Scherman, *Den svenska kakelungnen*.
36 Ilmakunnas, *Ett ståndsmässigt liv*, 294-5; Ilmakunnas, 'To build according to one's status'.
37 See Stobart and Rother, *Consumption and the Country House*; see also Ilmakunnas, *Ett ståndsmässigt liv*, 251-98.
38 DeJean, *The Age of Comfort*, 102-30; see also Leora Auslander, *Taste and Power: Furnishing Modern France* (Berkeley: University of California Press, 1996) and Dena Goodman and Kathryn Nordberg, ed., *Furnishing the Eighteenth Century: What Furniture Can Tell Us about the European and American Past* (New York and London: Routledge, 2007).
39 Selling, *Svenska herrgårdshem*, 336-42.
40 Probate inventory after Axel von Fersen. Axel von Fersen d.ä.:s arkiv, vol. 34, Stafsundsarkivet, Swedish National Archives, Stockholm.
41 On the Fersens' lifestyle and property, see Ilmakunnas, *Ett ståndsmässigt liv*.
42 Probate inventory after Axel von Fersen. Axel von Fersen d.ä.:s arkiv, vol. 34, Stafsundsarkivet, Swedish National Archives, Stockholm.
43 See, for example, Annick Pardailhé-Galabrun, *La naissance de l'intime: 3 000 foyers parisiens, XVIIe-XVIIIe siècles* (Paris: Presses Universitaires de France, 1988) and David M. Mitchell, '"My purple will be too sad for that melancholy room": Furnishings for Interiors in London and Paris, 1660-1735', *Textile History*, 40, no. 1 (2009): 3-28.
44 Olof Fridsberg, *Grevinnan Ulla Tessin i sin skrivkammare*. Watercolour on paper, 16.5 × 12.3 cm. NMH 145/1960. Nationalmuseum, Stockholm.
45 Selling, *Svenska herrgårdshem*, 127; Sjöberg, 'Inredningar', 214-17.

46 Lorentz Svensson Sparrgren, *Interiör med landshövding greve Clas Ekeblad och hans maka Brita, f. Horn*, 1783. Watercolour, pencil and ink on paper, 38.5 × 33 cm. NMB 1402. Nationalmuseum, Stockholm.
47 Stobart and Prytz, 'Comfort in English and Swedish country houses'.
48 Johan Gabriel Oxenstierna, *Journal: Skenäs 1805* (Stockholm: Bokvännerna, 1964), 79.
49 29 August 1766, 1 September 1766. Johan Gabriel Oxenstiernas journal 1766–1768. Tosterupsamlingen, vol. 108, Swedish National Archives, Stockholm.
50 Hedvig De la Gardie to Sophie von Fersen 12 August 1779. B XXV a:14, Regional State Archives in Vadstena, Sweden.
51 See Eriksdotter, 'Little ice age', 28.
52 Ilmakunnas, 'To build according to one's status', 41.
53 Mikael Ahlund, 'Att se vardagen: 1700-talet genom Pehr Hilleströms ögon', ed. Kirsti Eskelinen and Reetta Kuojärvi-Närhi, *Pehr Hilleström: 1700-talet i blickpunkten* (Helsingfors: Konstmuseet Sinebrychoff, 2014).
54 See, for example, Gerda Cederblom, *Pehr Hilleström som kulturskildrare*, vol. I (Uppsala: Nordiska museet, 1927), fig. 32, fig. 64, fig. 88.
55 On verisimilitude in Hilleström's paintings, see Ahlund, 'Att se vardagen', 56, 60 and Gösta Selling, 'Schablon och realitet i Pehr Hilleströms måleri', in *Gustavianskt: Studier kring den gustavianska tidens kulturhistoria tillägnade Sigurd Wallin på hans femtioårsdag* (Stockholm, 1932), 130–4.
56 Pehr Hilleström, *Nysterska*, ca 1780–1790. Oil on wood, 39.5 × 31.5 cm. NM 2453. Nationalmuseum, Stockholm.
57 Jean Eric Rehn, *En katt och två hundar sovande i en sofa*. Drawing on paper, 42 × 55 cm. NMH 559/1995. Nationalmuseum, Stockholm.

Object in focus 1:
Marketing the necessary comforts in Georgian Dublin

Conor Lucey

Historians of the domestic interior have long argued that the eighteenth century represented a period when the 'formal' house evolved into the 'social' house; when a concern with ceremony and magnificence gave way to the 'quest for comfort'.[1] Related to this emerging demand for comfort and informality was the development of closets; private rooms of intimate scale and diverse purpose, described in 1734 as 'one great improvement in modern architecture'.[2] Curiously, this did not inevitably extend to the *smallest room* in the house. In fact, of those indispensable conveniences associated with modern habitation, the water closet (or lavatory) was not customarily regarded as a prerequisite to refined living. While French architects had published designs for *appartements des bains* with *lieux à soupape* ('toilets with a valve') as early as the 1730s, such spaces remained a rarity in even the grandest British and Irish homes.[3] In his *A Complete Body of Architecture*, first published in 1756, Isaac Ware opined that the first floor of a 'large house' should comprise an anti-chamber, saloon, drawing room, bedchamber and dressing room. The provision of a water closet, at some distance from the principal reception rooms and connected by a passage, was described as 'a useful addition', but evidently not a necessary one.[4] Descriptions of water closets are indeed rare in eighteenth-century architectural treatises and builders' handbooks generally: the *beau monde* continued to rely on chamber pots, often discreetly concealed within 'pot-cupboards' and 'night tables', while the outdoor 'bog house' (or 'privy' or 'necessary house'), routinely cleaned by 'nightmen', served the needs of the remainder of the household.[5] Plan drawings prepared in 1769 for the town house of William Gore, Bishop of Elphin, in Dublin's fashionable Sackville Street intimate such an arrangement, with the 'necessary house' located in the basement area at the rear of the dwelling, adjacent to the servant's hall and the coal vaults.[6] By the end of the century, however, a burgeoning upper-middle class created the impetus for new standards in sanitary amenities. In 1794, describing a property then erecting in St Stephen's Green, bricklayer and speculative builder William Pemberton observed that water closets and powdering rooms (for storing and dressing wigs) were 'generally considered indispensable' in a genteel house.[7] Drawing on newspaper advertisements in the decades either side of 1800, and sensible of an emerging early nineteenth-century understanding of the word 'comfort' (and 'comfortable') to mean a state of physical and material contentment, this case study considers the correspondence between domestic convenience and domestic comfort in late-Georgian Dublin, focusing in particular on the water closet.[8]

A water closet in eighteenth-century parlance described a lavatory pan that could be flushed directly from a cistern (and only very rarely from a water pipe).[9] English innovations such as the 'S-bend' and valve closet, developed in 1775 by Alexander Cumming and refined by Joseph Bramah in 1778, were quickly available to Irish consumers.[10] By 1781, demand for Bramah's improved apparatus had encouraged the appointment of a Dublin agent: having discovered the means to prevent the escape of 'unwholesome Smells', these devices were advertised as being 'so constructed that they may be fixed in a Bed-chamber or Dressing-room without a possibility of being in the least Degree offensive'.[11] This is especially significant, being contrary to Isaac Ware's advice and indicating instead a desirable spatial proximity between water closets and bedrooms, dressing rooms and powdering rooms. Their location in architect Robert Adam's town houses was certainly convenient, often situated in a discrete space adjacent to a private bedroom suite and service staircase, as at 20 St James's Square, London, designed in 1771–5 for Sir Watkin Williams Wynn. Correspondence between Lady Louisa Conolly, chatelaine of Castletown House in county Kildare, and her sister Emily, Dowager Duchess of Leinster, on the fitting out of Frescati House in the Dublin suburb of Blackrock during the course of 1776, confirms that a bedchamber with an adjoining water closet and 'warm bath' constituted 'the most complete apartment' of domestic comfort and convenience.[12]

Here we need to exercise some caution. While the 'water closet' in a house in Eustace Street in 1772 boasted 'a leaden Reservoir to supply it with water', during the eighteenth century the phrase signified either an apparatus or an architectural space.[13] A 1762 inventory of 45 Kildare Street, designed in 1747–53 for Hayes St Leger, Viscount Doneraile, itemizes the sanitary fixtures in 'closets' throughout the property: that on the ground floor adjacent to 'My Lord's Dressing Room', for example, contained a 'necessary stool and cover pan', a 'mahogany bidet', a 'large chamber pot' and two 'white basins'; the closet adjacent to the bed chamber on the first floor accommodated a 'mahogany necessary stool, cover and pan', a 'white basin' and three 'chamber pots'.[14] While neither of these closets boasted a flushing mechanism, it is significant that their relationship to dressing rooms and bedrooms was the same configuration recommended to the Dowager Duchess of Leinster. Elsewhere, form followed function: at a house in Cavendish Street in 1770, the 'water closet' was located 'up 2 pair [of] stairs' and contained a 'mahogany commode', so clearly referring to a designated space for ablutions;[15] accounts relating to the building of 12 Merrion Square in 1764–6 include a payment for 'white tiles' for the water closet at that house, suggesting a room conceived with a decidedly hygienic aesthetic.[16] Nevertheless, Dublin's limited mains supply of water continued to adversely affect sanitary engineering citywide, and the proper integration of household lavatories and bathrooms into this infrastructure was an achievement of the Victorian age.[17]

In a period when real estate advertising customarily focused on location, degrees of architectural elegance and social exclusivity, it remains to be considered how modern solutions to the problems of waste disposal were marketed to polite audiences.[18] Indeed, although sporadic before 1800, occasional references in newspapers confirm the emerging consumer appetite for indoor sanitary utilities.[19] A notice in 1794 announcing the leasehold of the present number 63 Merrion Square places unusual emphasis on modern amenities, the description of the interior apartments being confined to the identification of a dressing room, powdering room and water closet alone;[20] the following year, a large house in Buckingham Street was 'finished in the most superb stile of the present fashion', and equipped with 'conveniences such as are not to be met with in many houses in this city, such as a bathing house, complete water-closets, cisterns'.[21] The particular distinction accorded to these intimate rooms is noteworthy. In the first instance, it reflects a desire to live more agreeably: Bramah supplied 6,000 London homes with water closets between 1778 and 1797,[22] and by 1822, architect Richard Elsam counselled that 'no good house [was] without one or more' (Figure 2a.1).[23] More importantly, it demonstrates the perspicacity of the construction industry: operating at their own capital risk, house-builders customarily embraced innovations in both fashion and technology to augment the increasingly standardized form of the urban dwelling. In 1814, water closets (plural) were among the foremost items described in an upcoming sale of a house in Sackville Street; three years later, in 1817, 'one of the best houses' in Belvedere Place numbered a water closet among its principal selling points (representing 'every convenience a house can require').[24] And given the general unpleasantness associated with the removal of waste-water generally, a 'well built and permanent

Figure 2a.1 Handbill of Pemberton & Co., 1811.

house' in Synnott Place, advertised for auction in June 1808, boasted a water closet with a 'forcing pump'.[25]

Another factor in the appearance of water closets in property advertising around 1800 relates to changing patterns of tenancy and owner-occupancy: by the close of the eighteenth century, elite real estate in Dublin, as in London, was increasingly designed to attract (and accommodate) the rising upper-middle classes.[26] This almost certainly affected the location of the powdering room and water closet in the 'attached offices' at 63 Merrion Square (described above). Indeed, the only other contemporary reference to a powdering room in a Dublin property advertisement concerns the sale of a house in Gloucester Street in 1793: here it was described as a 'neat detached office' in the 'passage to the lower apartments'; the dressing room, on the other hand, was on the same floor as the principal bed chambers.[27] Dressing rooms, of course, often served as social spaces in patrician homes, typically associated with the entertainment of companies of female intimates. Something of this ostensibly 'public' character is discerned in the spatial arrangement at 27 Mountjoy Square, advertised in 1818 as a 'capital town residence': distinguished by being 'fitted up in a very superior style', it boasted an extension from the first-floor landing that comprised 'a large Conservatory, Boudoir and Water Closet'.[28] However, the location of the dressing room in 63 Merrion Square (in the 'attached offices'), and in the house on Gloucester Street (adjacent to the bed chambers above the drawing room storey), suggests a private rather than public function, devoted to the performance of daily ablutions as opposed to the performance of social identities. A similarly discreet location is observed in the description of a 'remarkably fine' house in Upper Fitzwilliam Street in 1824: attached to the principal bedroom was 'a Dressing-room, having a Water Closet in it'.[29]

References to water closets and (to a lesser extent) bath rooms and powdering rooms in urban real estate advertising during the late-Georgian era suggest two things: first is the technological advances that improved sanitary wares and so made them a more attractive proposition for containment within the interior space of the home; and second, and arguably more significant, is the changing social demographic for elite housing. Traditional forms of indoor lavatory such as commodes and close stools required a retinue of servants, characteristic of a more aristocratic way of life; a bourgeois family typically managed a less ample staff in general, and so demanded a different solution to the management of 'night soil'.

Notes

1. For the origin of these longstanding tropes see Mark Girouard, *Life in the English Country House: A Social and Architectural History* (New Haven and London: Yale University Press, 1978); John Cornforth, *The Quest for Comfort: English Interiors 1790–1848* (London: Barrie and Jenkins, 1978).
2. Definition of 'Closet' in *The Builder's Dictionary: Or, Gentleman and Architect's Companion*, 2 vols (London: Printed for A. Bettesworth and C. Hitch, 1734), vol. 1, n.p.
3. Peter Thornton, *Authentic Décor: The Domestic Interior 1620–1920* (1984; London: Seven Dials, Cassell & Co., 2000), 97, 150.
4. Isaac Ware, *A Complete Body of Architecture* (London: T. Osborne & J. Shipton, 1756), 328.
5. Patricia McCarthy, *Life in the Country House in Georgian Ireland* (New Haven and London: Yale University Press, 2016), 201–5.
6. National Library of Ireland, Killadoon papers, 36,013.
7. Dublin City Archives, Minutes of the Wide Streets Commissioners, XII (August 1793–December 1794), 115.
8. See historic definition of 'comfort' in www.oed.com.ucd.idm.oclc.org/view/Entry/36890.

9 Dan Cruickshank and Neil Burton, *Life in the Georgian City* (London: Viking, 1990), 96.
10 Lawrence Wright, *Clean and Decent: The Fascinating History of the Bathroom and the Water Closet* (London: Routledge and Kegan Paul, 1960), 107.
11 *Saunders's News-Letter*, 8 June 1781, 6 December 1781, 18 January 1782. Bramah appointed Richard Mallett of Little Britain Street as his sole Dublin agent. *Dublin Evening Post*, 5 February and 5 March 1782.
12 Brian FitzGerald (ed.), *The Correspondence of Emily, Duchess of Leinster 1731–1814*, 3 vols (Irish Manuscripts Commission: Dublin, 1957), vol. 3, 213.
13 *Dublin Journal*, 12 May 1772.
14 David Griffin, 'The building and furnishing of a Dublin townhouse in the 18th Century', *Bulletin of the Irish Georgian Society*, 37 (1996/7): 24–39.
15 British Library, Cockburn Papers, MS Add. 48134.
16 Public Record Office of Northern Ireland, Brownlow Papers, D1928/H/2.
17 Diarmuid Ó Gráda, *Georgian Dublin: The Forces that Shaped the City* (Cork: Cork University Press, 2015), 254, 258; Susan Galavan, *Dublin's Bourgeois Homes: Building the Victorian Suburbs, 1850–1901* (London and New York: Routledge, 2017), 158. As late as 1816, 'prestigious Sackville (O'Connell) Street had operational cesspools'. Michael Corcoran, *Our Good Health: A History of Dublin's Water and Drainage* (Dublin: Dublin City Council, 2005), 27.
18 Rachel Stewart, *The Town House in Georgian London* (New Haven and London: Yale University Press, 2009), 76–89.
19 Lee Jackson, *Dirty Old London: The Victorian Fight against Filth* (New Haven and London: Yale University Press, 2014), 46–51.
20 *Saunders's News-Letter*, 28 February 1794.
21 *Dublin Evening Post*, 13 June 1795.
22 Wright, *Clean and Decent*, 107.
23 Stefan Muthesius, *The English Terraced House* (New Haven: Yale University Press, 1982), 58.
24 *Freeman's Journal*, 2 December 1814; *The Dublin Journal*, 16 October 1817.
25 *Freeman's Journal*, 17 June 1808.
26 David Dickson, 'Death of a Capital? Dublin and the Consequences of Union', in Peter Clark and Raymond Gillespie (eds), *Two Capitals: London and Dublin, 1500–1840* (Oxford: Oxford University Press, 2001), 124–5.
27 *Saunders's News-letter*, 22 March 1793.
28 *Dublin Evening Post*, 21 November 1818. On the ground floor the corresponding sequence of rooms comprised of 'a Study, Dressing-Room, and a second Water-Closet'.
29 *Dublin Evening Post*, 12 October 1824.

3

The invention of thermal comfort in eighteenth-century France

Olivier Jandot

The time of the impossible fight against the cold

For centuries the French people suffered the slings and arrows of winter with a resignation that still astounds us today. Stories about harsh winters, anecdotes found in memoirs on the effects of the cold, diaries, letters, clerics' comments in the margins of parish registers, testimonies from scientists and from the first meteorologists from the eighteenth century onwards, clinical studies from physicians about the effects of cold on the body all enable us to reconstruct our forebears' relationship with cold and heat, which was very different from ours today.

During each rigorous winter (statistically one winter out of four or five during the Early Modern period),[1] frost invaded homes. Those who wrote, who generally did not belong to the poorest social classes, noted that ink froze at the tip of their quill. During the winter of 1695, the famous marquise de Sévigné, for example, writes in one of her letters that her inkwell is frozen and that she has difficulty driving her quill correctly on paper because she is chilled to the bone and her fingers are numb with the cold.[2] The writings of physicians who corresponded with the Royal Society of Medicine, founded in 1778, are filled with anecdotes about the lack of comfort in old dwellings, and the illusory aspect of the protection houses supplied against cold. One of them, for example, recounted the variations of the cold spell during the winter of 1789 by measuring the thickness of the ice in a jug filled with water which was placed in his bedroom for his ablutions.[3] Another one noted that most of his patient's houses, built in 'earth or mortar', with dirt floors and poorly isolated roofs, prevented 'neither abundant dew nor frost from penetrating the best-locked wardrobes.'[4] Therefore the dwellings of the poor, as those of the rich, become thermal colanders during the wintertime. In the winter of 1776, a physician wrote that the cold weather was responsible for the death of many newborns whose limbs froze while they were lying in their cribs. They would die of the effects of gangrene.[5]

This situation resulted from the incapacity of fireplaces to heat properly the rooms in which they were placed. All the testimonies highlight the inadequacy of this heating system, to which the French were nevertheless deeply attached. Fireplaces did not heat effectively and they produced a lot of smoke. To improve the evacuation of the smoke, people usually left the door open (at least slightly) to ease the combustion and to create an ascending draught; this, of course, ruined any attempt to heat the room. As noted not long before 1800 by Dr Macquart, 'fireplaces appear to be fitter for the tenements' decoration rather than truly heating. Indeed, it has to be admitted that there are no colder places than countries where fireplaces are used, unless a tremendous amount of wood is consumed; people usually roast at their front and freeze at the back.'[6] Therefore, the traditional fireplace hardly managed to raise the ambient air temperature and the heat released by the fire never went further than the closest proximity to the fireplace. Consequently, it was necessary to be near the fireplace and to use multiple other strategies to fight the attacks of the numbing air. These included the use of easily transportable heating sources such as foot and hand warmers, which were carried under women's petticoats, specific interior clothing for those who had to remain motionless for hours (for example the dressing-gowns that writers wore, or the bearskin bags into which they slipped their legs), or the invention of smaller, better isolated and/or heated spaces in the house, where one could take shelter, waiting for better days. Alcoves, closed beds, canopied beds closed by more or less thick curtains (according to the social rank), screens, and large winged-armchairs closing off draughts from either side. To be less cold and to avoid the freezing draughts, some aristocrats even spent winters locked inside their sedan chairs, in the middle of their drawing room.[7]

What might the temperatures inside the houses have been? It must be said that such a question is in fact anachronistic. At the time, nobody cared about measuring indoor temperatures. For a long time, the thermometer (invented in the early seventeenth century) remained an expensive and uncommon instrument. When it did become more generally available in the second half of the eighteenth century, when modern meteorological science was being invented, it was nevertheless mainly used to measure outdoor temperatures. Therefore, indoor temperature data are scarce and fragmentary. Yet, it is possible to give a rough picture of the main characteristics of indoor climates. First, there was a considerable difference between the temperature next to the fireplace and that at the far end of the room. In the 1940s, measurements made by ethnologists in old cottages dating from the late eighteenth century made it possible to clarify matters. At an outside temperature of −5°C, the fire sparkling in the hearth released a heat of 18 to 25°C within a radius of one metre around the fireplace. But as soon as one moved away from the fire, the room temperature dropped to around 10°C.[8] There was an even greater difference in temperature between the rooms which were heated and those which were not: bedrooms for example, in which freezing temperatures were common on very cold days (see Figure 3.1 for an illustration of the inadequacy of bedroom fireplaces). In the drawing room, the temperature would generally be between 12 and 15°C, an indoor temperature of 14°C being considered as 'very sweet warmth'[9], whereas one of 19 or 20°C was deemed physically unbearable.[10]

This is made particularly visible in the comments of travellers or French soldiers who visited Germany, even those districts immediately at the eastern border of France. This cultural border divides Europe schematically in two halves. In the West, the fireplace prevails, occupying almost every house. In those of the peasants or humble people, there was one fire, mainly used for cooking meals

Figure 3.1 The bedroom in the Duchess of Orleans' appartement at the Palais-Royal (Paris).
Source: Paul Lacroix, *The 18th Century. Its Institutions, Customs, and Costumes. France, 1700-1789* (London: Chapman and Hall, 1876).

and the rooms were warmed slightly by the heat of a fire lit to make the pot boil. Wood or other combustible material (peat, dry cowpat, bark, etc.) was constantly sought out and saved. In wealthy people's homes, fireplaces are more numerous. Yet, as we have already seen, they barely prevented the cold from penetrating the house, despite all the combustible material burnt in them. On the other hand, in Eastern Europe, where continental winters are harsher, another means of heating was used: the tiled stove. French people who experienced the interior climate of Swiss or Alsatian houses never failed to mention their surprise at this sweet yet invisible heat emanating from this huge mass. Yet, though some emphasized the undeniable qualities ('equal, constant and universal heat' wrote Montaigne in his *Essays*, from his *Travel Diaries*;[11] heat that penetrates 'even the areas of the room farthest to the stove' as another traveller wrote[12]), many denounced its use for the exact same reasons. For them, the heat was excessive and uncomfortable. French soldiers accommodated in Alsace during the winter 1674–5 kept opening the windows to lower the temperature of the rooms in which they lived, to the despair of their German hosts, sensitive to cold.[13] The officers accommodated in Strasbourg even asked for the stoves in their quarters to be dismantled and replaced by fireplaces.[14] These two anecdotes show that one person's comfort can be different from another's. But they also show that the notion of comfort is not to be dissociated from its historical, geographical, social and cultural context. It is of prime importance to keep this fact in mind, for lack of which we might look at the past with a gaze corrupted by anachronism: 'sin of all sins – the one that is the most unforgivable of all' as written in a catchphrase Lucien Febvre, the famous historian.[15] The definition of what is comfortable (and what is not) is the result of a complex construction in which multiple factors combine: the technical skills of society and an individual's economic resources, but also the importance granted (or not) to the matter and the rhetoric around it (moral or medical, for example). Combined, these contribute to the construction of tolerance thresholds, likely to evolve with time.

Scientific and technical reflections on domestic heating in the eighteenth century

This characterization of how, for centuries, the French attempted to resist the harshness of winter illustrates their habituation to cold and discomfort. The course of their daily lives was regularly disrupted by the cold: huddled around their fireplaces, surrounded by icy draughts, their eyes stung by smoke, people were able to put up with very low indoor temperatures, the simple mention of which makes us shiver. To describe this way of living as 'uncomfortable' is to use an analytical concept which did not exist at that time. The discomfort described here is the obverse of comfort, but there was no comfort for anyone at that time; indeed, the word 'comfort' itself did not exist in its current sense of a state of physical ease end freedom from pain or constraint, partly because the possibility of living in a house really protected from the consequences of seasonal temperature variations did not exist. Discomfort thus characterized the daily life of the entire population. The king and aristocrats in their castles, the merchants in their shops, the craftsmen in their workshops, the students in their colleges, the peasant in their cottages – all had to suffer the inconveniences of winter. It was only during the eighteenth century that this secular situation slowly began to change. Progress in the fight against the cold made it possible to soften living conditions. By gradually making it possible to spend the winter locked indoors, with the body effectively protected from the bite of the cold, in a gentle and even thermal environment, a series of technical advances allowed the gradual emergence of a new situation and a new concept: thermal comfort. This historical turn is precisely what requires further study. One must try to understand how and when the change from one form of sensitivity to another occurred. To study the arrival of thermal comfort in eighteenth-century France is to look at the numerous factors that triggered the end of the old *status quo*, but also at the way this evolution was perceived at the time. Far from being accepted as a form of progress, this slow and cumulative conquest of heat faced numerous detractors who used many an argument to condemn it.

At the origin of this evolution was a book. In 1713, an obscure physicist, but nevertheless eminent reader and popularizer of Newton's theories, Nicolas Gauger, published *La Mécanique du Feu* (The Mechanics of Fire) in Paris.[16] For the first time, a scientific and technical essay addressed the way in which combustion occurs in a fireplace and the way in which its heat propagates across the room. The book offered a series of theoretical considerations on the various heating systems, along with technical propositions to improve the thermal effectiveness of traditional fireplaces without too much difficulty. Gauger's reflection is one of the multiple consequences of the birth of modern science in seventeenth-century Europe. The creation of the thermometer permitted the quantification of temperature for the first time, though the instruments of the time were still flawed and lacked precision. Physicists began to think about the nature and effects of fire and to question Aristotle's ancient theory.[17] Furthermore, Newton's work on optics and refractibility of light fed Gauger's reflections which applied the concept of refractibility of heat (as well as light) emanating from fire. Gauger's work can therefore be characterized by the use of different means of analysis based on the latest scientific progress of the time, which he was capable of combining for a new subject of study: domestic heat. Thus he contributed to the autonomization of a scientific and technical reflection upon heat. The fireplace and other heating instruments gradually stopped being the concern of architects (who are more interested in its harmonious integration to rooms) and increasingly became the specialty of scientists, technicians and inventors of all kinds, as well as educated amateurs, who were more interested in heating performance. The innovative aspect of the book gave it an immediate international reputation. In 1715, Gauger's work was translated into English by John Theophilus Desaguliers, under the title: *Fires improved: being a new method of building chimneys, so as to prevent their smoking: in which a small fire, shall warm a room better than a much larger made the common way. With the manner of altering such chimneys as are already built, so that they shall perform the same effects.*[18] The publication of the book was the milestone of a new science: caminology (science dealing with fireplaces), which would develop in France and in the Anglo-Saxon world during the second half of the eighteenth century.

Although a Frenchman initiated this major redirection in the history of domestic comfort, it was an American citizen who took over from him. The influence of Gauger's book on Benjamin Franklin has been noted by historians of well-being.[19] His work on the creation of efficient and economical heating devices from the 1737–8 winter onwards is well known.[20] Less familiar, however, is the intellectual energy that was deployed in France in the second half of the eighteenth century to improve the heating of homes. Indeed, following in Gauger's footsteps, academic circles and science amateurs avidly participated in the debate which was part of a more general interest in physics. Following the re-publication of Gauger's book in 1749,[21] began half a century of abundant publication tackling the question of perfecting fireplaces. Not all books are equal, but this publishing inflation reflects a new focus on solving problems that had not previously received such attention. In 1756, la *Caminologie, ou Traité des cheminées* (Caminology, or Treaty of Fireplaces) was published in Dijon by the Benedictine monk Pierre Hébrard.[22] Three years later, in 1759, Léopold de Genneté published a book resulting from the presentation of his work at the Royal Academy of Sciences in Paris.[23] Both mainly focus on providing solutions to prevent fireplaces from smoking. Completely absent from Genneté's work, Gauger's teachings were only partially reproduced in Hébrard's work, which was a compilation work that retained only the least innovative aspect of Gauger's work. The issue of the hearth's heating performance was not a concern for either of them.

At exactly the same time, however, two articles published in the *Journal œconomique* show a renewed interest in the matter. In its June 1758 issue, one can read an anonymous article entitled 'Means to increase the heat of the fire in a room without putting more wood in the hearth'[24]. In the January 1759 issue, the title 'New methods to heat up rooms economically and without inconvenience' appeared.[25] This sudden fondness for the matter can be understood better by reading the March 1758 issue of the same periodical 'Dissertation over the rarity and high cost of heating woods in Champagne, and how to substitute them' by Dupré d'Aulnay.[26] The author deplores the tripling of the price of wood in thirty years, according to him due to the combination of three factors: the growing rarity of wood, the monger's greed, and 'Man's taste for luxury, which has increased the consumption of wood to a point that will lead to total destruction'. He added in a catchphrase both reflecting reality and judgment: 'Our fathers, humbler than us, used to heat themselves with the same fire for the whole family; now fires have multiplied so much in every house, that a single person consumes as much fire as a family used to.' This type of assertion, which is repeated like a mantra in the writings of lettered men during the second half of the eighteenth century, sheds light on the profound cause of this sudden upturn in research and essays dealing with improving the efficiency of heating devices. These respond to a real social demand that made fuel economy a priority. Physicists and technicians therefore faced a challenge that had to be addressed: to ensure that fires produce more heat, due to a higher social requirement for well-being, while consuming less fuel, the price of which was constantly increasing. The technical reflection that really began then developed on several levels: that of theoretical and practical treaties which were then published by real specialists; that of simple pamphlets or articles published in scientific journals that were the result of empirical research. Finally, there are the mémoires generated by the academic prize contests.

The three levels of the technical reflection

The path that gradually led to improvement in the thermal comfort of homes was therefore first of all quite clearly marked by some major publications. These were always cited by the authors of technical treaties that proliferated in the nineteenth century; they recognized both the contribution of their predecessors to solving the problem of the fight against the cold and the intellectual debt owed to them. Almost all of the authors of these works gravitated in the orbit of the Royal Academy of Sciences in Paris. It is for example the case of Marquis of Montalembert, a French officer who had served with the Swedish and Russian troops during the Seven Years' War. Thanks to his personal experience, he was able to witness the efficiency of ceramic stoves used in Eastern Europe to face the torment of continental winters. Yet, conscious of the French love for fireplaces, he came up with a solution that was a synthesis of both heating methods, through a modification of the fireplace to improve its thermal efficiency without removing its traditional assets. In allowing the owner to still be able to enjoy the sight of the flames, it was a more discrete way of introducing the stove into the apartment. In 1763, he therefore presented before the Academy his essay (mémoire) on the ways to transform a fireplace into a stove.[27] But the proposed process did not gain support, in part because of the complete reconfiguration of the chimney flue required for its installation and in part because loss of the visual pleasure afforded by the sight of the fire itself. Ten years later, the Franklin stove, also known as the 'Pennsylvania fireplace', engineered in the 1740s by the American scholar reached France thanks to the translation of his major works.[28]

It is worth pausing here and noting that the rather banal issue of domestic heating interested the best minds of the time in part because it also resonated with a more theoretical but ever-increasing interest shown by physics and especially chemistry in the nature of fire and heat. From the mid-1770s onwards, Lavoisier's numerous works, including the *Memoirs of the Royal Academy of Sciences* which reflect the steady progress made, helped to challenge the phlogistic theory inherited from Stahl that permeated all scientific thought in the eighteenth century. We can then witness the progressive emergence of a new branch of science, thermodynamics,[29] which would truly develop only at the very beginning of the nineteenth century, thanks to Jean-Baptiste Joseph Fourier's among others.[30] It is also from 1778 that Rumford developed his work on heat, in an approach that combined both a theoretical approach and practical experiments that aimed to allow the immediate application of his discoveries.[31] In 1799, he published in his *Political, Economic and Philosophical Essays* the results of his experiments to improve the heating efficiency of fireplaces.[32] Inconvenienced like so many others by the 'penetrating winds that make one part of the body shiver while the other is roasted by the fire of the fireplaces',[33] he had been working to correct defects in existing fireplaces to ensure that they better distributed the heat from the fireplace. The modifications he proposed were much simpler than the technical systems invented by Gauger or Franklin. They could be carried out by any mason to whom the procedure had been explained and required only a few bricks and a little mortar. These modifications consisted of reducing the size of the existing fireplace by lining it with bricks arranged on the jambs in such a way that they formed an angle of 135°, which is more heat-refracting than the right angle usually formed by the jambs arranged parallel to each other on either side of the hearth.[34] Reduced in width, the fireplace was also reduced in height and depth; now located further forward, the fire would thus diffuse its heat into the room more easily. The fumes would no longer rise vertically, but be evacuated by an oblique duct that joined the original vertical duct thus eliminating the usual draught that causes unpleasant stream of cold air in the room. Rumford, who claimed to have rectified the defective construction of five hundred fireplaces in this way, considered that this modification made it possible to reduce fuel consumption by 50 per cent or even two-thirds (see Figure 3.2).[35] The 'Paris savant' (Knowledgeable Paris)[36] of the second half of

Figure 3.2 James Gillray, *The Comforts of a Rumford Stove* (London: Hannah Humphrey, 1800).

the eighteenth century is therefore the crossroads of technological innovation in heating systems: after Franklin, we meet again an American scientist who, after living in Bavaria, ended his life in France where he died in 1814 after marrying Lavoisier's widow.[37] The circle is complete.

Attempts to improve thermal comfort were also developing at a lower level, far from the prestigious academic circles and scientists. We too easily overlook the work of enlightened amateurs, do-it-yourselfers and inventors of all kinds, who experimented with innovative technical solutions and published the fruit of their labours in the scientific periodicals that proliferated at the time. For example, we see an Italian count who, having read Franklin's book, boasts of having developed a fireplace of a new design.[38] Or the canon who announced the realization of an economic fireplace for the benefit of the prior of the abbey of Saint-Lô in Rouen. Inspired by the Montalembert stovepipe, this was equipped with sliding sheet metal slabs at the front and back of the fireplace and could be used to heat two adjacent rooms (one bedroom and one cabinet). The plate used as a counter-heat radiates its heat into the room at the back of the fireplace. The two parts can alternatively enjoy the spectacle of the flame depending on whether one decides to lower one or the other of the plates, or even at the same time if the two plates are lifted simultaneously. By lowering both slabs at the same time, this fireplace can even become a stove.[39] Here again, it is an Abbot who reads a memoir on an economic stove at the Brussels Academy.[40]

The third level at which this intellectual energy mobilized around the issue of domestic heating is deployed was that of academic prize contests.[41] Even if the prizes proposed for the competition were not always awarded, due to an insufficient number of participants or because the organizers considered the quality of the submissions insufficient, the choice of such competition topics is testimony to an interest of the great minds of the time in a subject that went beyond the banal to become a real societal issue at the crossroads of multiple issues. The ephemeral Société libre d'émulation (Free Society of Emulation) (1776–81) founded by the Abbot Baudeau,[42] which aimed to stimulate technological innovation, devoted one of the sixteen prizes it awarded in its short existence to a competition on 'the most advantageous ways of providing heating for the poor and the people, other than those they currently use.'[43] This competition, like many others, was a failure: the £900 and £300 prizes that were to be awarded in June 1778 were never made. Only a £24 bonus was awarded to one of the few candidates who had entered the competition.[44] In the same spirit, the Société royale d'Agriculture de Lyon (Royal Agricultural Society of Lyon) proposed in 1784 a prize of £600 to be awarded in 1786: the objective was to find a way to increase 'by about a third the heat of an apartment produced by a fireplace or stove, using only the same quantity of wood'.[45] Rather than the originality of the competitors' proposals, which generally summarized the technical literature available at the time, it is their profile that is interesting: we find a Norman Benedictine who admits to being involved for a long time out of a taste for caminology, a former soldier, two lawyers in Parliament, two architects, and so on.[46] From the last quarter of the eighteenth century onwards, the improvement of thermal comfort therefore seems to have been a widely shared concern within French society.

The invention of thermal comfort: Progress and reluctance to change

This sudden popularity in studying thermal comfort marked a major civilizational watershed. For centuries people had tolerated low indoor temperatures and only architects were interested in fireplaces – and even then they were actually only preoccupied with aesthetics – focusing on its position, size, decoration and occasionally on how to avoid the house being smoked out. Yet progressively in the eighteenth century, the fireplace became a subject of interest and research. In this evolution of sensitivity, complex interactions are at stake. Technical research was not only fuelled by the quest for better thermal comfort. It also originated from the awareness of the fireplace's poor calorific output: most of the heat was basically lost up the chimney or, as the French saying goes, 'to warm the little birds'. It was the increasing price of the wood during the entire eighteenth century and also the relative scarcity of this fundamental resource due to its growing use in industry that led scientists and technicians to look for technical solutions which would produce the same quantity of heat – or even more and better-quality heat – while using less wood. The concern about energy efficiency was, as much as the research of comfort, a driving force behind those technical evolutions (see also Interlude 4).

The rising price of the wood was itself due to an increase in domestic demand. Numerous clues indicate a growing social requirement for heat all through the eighteenth century. The permanent increase in demand for firewood driven by demographic growth was accentuated by a change in individual behaviour and habits that was constantly highlighted and denounced by forest specialists. As early as 1725, a specialist in forest law pointed to the inexorable and worrying decline in the forested areas of France. For him, this was accentuated by the fact that 'men have become more voluptuous in all things, warming themselves more than our Fathers did in the past'.[47] When the provincial Academies chose as the subject of their competition a question relating to good forest management or the comparative advantages of different fuels – which was quite common in the second half of the century, when a collective reflection on the need for an energy transition begins[48] – competitors responded with their own expressions of concern about this sudden frenzy of heat. A candidate for a contest organized in 1771 by the Besançon Academy, for example, wrote that the worrying increase in the price of wood 'has its source in the general slope of all orders of citizens towards the commodities of life',[49] which leads to the reckless multiplication of fireplaces in homes, proof that people are starting to heat rooms that were not previously heated. It is precisely this evolution towards a permanent search for material well-being that Louis-Sébastien Mercier ironically emphasized in a passage from his famous *Tableau de Paris* (Picture of Paris):

> More economical and more seasoned against cold, our fathers almost never heated themselves. [...] They also braved the coldest and hottest weather, and the ignorance of the Royal Academy of Architecture. What does it matter what luxury of ornaments, and the symmetry and sequence of apartments, if we are forced to blow in our fingers, or to live there smoked like foxes? Since luxury, introduced by finance, had perverted everything among us, it has lit inextinguishable fires in every corner of our homes, and carried the tireless axe through all our forests, which soon became insufficient.[50]

This constant quest for warmth is typical of a new taste for 'conveniences' as they were called at the time; that is, for comfort. If the word 'confort' then existed in the French language, it did not yet have its modern meaning of material well-being. It was not until 1842 that this new meaning of the old word that previously meant spiritual comfort was confirmed in a dictionary of the French language. It was often still written 'comfort', as in the English language, proof of the pioneering nature of the Anglo-Saxon world in this evolution towards milder living conditions.[51] In the field of thermal comfort, there are many small signs to confirm what lawyers, scientists or moralists emphasized at will.

The number of fireplaces in households progressively increased, people started planning to warm up rooms which, until then, were not generally heated; and for the first time people started to care about heating places such as prisons, guardhouses or monks' bedrooms. In the countryside, the agricultural growth enabled farmers to improve the quality of the curtains that enclosed their beds or to buy woollen blankets, warmer than those they had previously woven themselves. Another remarkable fact was the progressive introduction of ceramic and iron stoves inside houses. Although the calorific superiority of the system had been recognized since the sixteenth century, the French only started to adopt the stove during the eighteenth century, overcoming their traditional reluctance towards this heating instrument, accused of being contrary to French good taste because it spoiled the alignments and the effects of perspective in the rooms where they were situated. During the eighteenth century, stoves started to be used in public places such as the Parisian cafés, and the anterooms of some private mansions. Yet, in reception rooms, people remained attached to the fireplace, which had the advantage of offering the visual and familiar entertainment of the fire. In the working classes or in the few regions where coal started to be used, small stoves made of sheet metal also allowed the inhabitants to save fuel while trying to be less cold.

Therefore the dynamic of change was fuelled by this double concern: trying to save fuel and looking for comfort. To these two inseparable and complementary driving forces of change, one must add the progress in physics, which gave inventors new conceptual tools to measure heat and to understand the logics of its propagation in a space. In that sense, the true watershed occurred when all these factors were assembled, that is to say around 1750. It is important to underline that Gauger's pioneering book, published for the first time in 1713, still only contributed to the theoretical and technical reflection when its second edition was published in 1749, when the forest crisis became a matter of growing concern.

However, the diffusion of this technical innovation did answer a social demand for thermal comfort. Some inventors understood this. With their peculiar skill to grasp the fashion of the day and to imagine the commercial possibilities, they became enthusiastic promoters of their own inventions, publishing works and booklets, the purpose of which was clearly promotional. A case in point is the architect Charles-François Désarnod, of Lyon, who designed in 1783 the fireplace 'à la Désarnod', largely inspired by Franklin's Pennsylvanian fireplace.[52] It appears to be the first heating system to have been mass produced in France and comprised slabs and pieces of cast iron, sold in kit form so it could be brought home and built inside the fireplace. Released in 1789, the commercialization of this new type of fireplace presupposed the existence of a market to supply. It was also to answer the social demand for heat and comfort that the architect François Cointeraux published in the 1790s several opuscules dealing with ways to properly heat a house or a flat, without having excessive expenses for wood.[53]

As the industrial and technical nineteenth century got under way, the first works dedicated to the question of domestic heat were published in the 1820s, offering truly innovative technical solutions, often coming from England.[54] It was during these years that thermal comfort began to spread slowly in the interiors of the Parisian bourgeoisie.[55] While the key turning point thus came at the start of the nineteenth century, these advances in home heating were the result of research and the overwhelming intellectual energy devoted to this subject over the previous half-century. To remain warm in winter was no longer an odd demand and scientific and technical progresses made it increasingly possible to satisfy this social craving for heat. The nineteenth and twentieth centuries were marked by a slow and progressive dissemination of thermal comfort, which then tended to become a 'social norm', to quote sociologist Olivier le Goff's expression.[56] In that sense, the eighteenth century truly was a key moment, carrying the remnants of a past still very present (people literally and metaphorically froze to death during the winters of 1776, 1784 and 1789) and the seeds of a future which was being born, that of a society where the contrasts between seasons were far less pronounced and where the house become a sweet shelter against the pangs of winter's cold.

What must finally be underlined is that this evolution, of which the contemporaries themselves were conscious, was far from being uniformly perceived as a positive change. Though it may seem surprising to us, many voices made themselves heard to condemn this softening of manners. The writings of physicians, moralists or philosophers often took the very opposite stand to that for which the majority of people yearned. The writings of eighteenth-century physicians never ceased to praise the virtues of the cold, which tightened the veins, increased body tone and strengthened the body; heat, by contrast, was considered as debilitating. Montesquieu, and then Gibbons, would also claim that one of the causes of the decline and fall of the Roman Empire was the Romans' unreasonable taste for complacency which made them forget their ancestors' frugal and manly way of life. With them, moralists of all sorts also endlessly condemned this new taste for material well-being and for warmth that would inexorably result in the destruction of the forests of the kingdom. For all these authors, this desire for thermal comfort led society along a dangerous slope and was not the result of the necessary fulfilment of a physical need but of a superfluous one, a useless luxury. This reluctance for thermal comfort also existed in more or less explicit ways in the hygienist and prescriptive discourse which was starting to be structured. It is precisely because of the unusual heat they generate that physicians condemn the new use of stoves. As an obscure provincial doctor from Calais noted: 'the cold, when it is not outraged, is less harmful than the heat of the stoves which only tends to soften' and which makes people sensitive to cold.[57] In his *Dictionary of Human Conservation* published in 1798, the physician Louis-Charles-Henri Macquart, synthesizing the majority of medical writings of the time, considered that any accessories that offered some form of thermal comfort (warming pans, skullcaps, quilted cardigans and heating pads for example) were only good for the elderly and for women.[58] More discriminating than Rousseau, he nonetheless advised parents to toughen children from the age of five or six against cold by keeping them away from the fire, the proximity of which would make them cowardly and lazy. He also encouraged them to warm up by practising a salutary physical activity. Toughened in this way, the children would be, according to him, more resistant to winter diseases, colds and fluxions. He even wrote that a difference in temperature of more than 10°R (12.5°C), between indoors and outdoors was dangerous for health, which amounts to advising an indoor temperature of below 10°C during the coldest months of winter. Even if these are only prescriptions (it is unlikely that someone who can afford to heat himself voluntarily maintains such low temperatures at home), this shows that this new taste for thermal comfort was far from being unanimously accepted.

Conclusions: The complexities of improving thermal comfort

The example of the invention of thermal comfort in eighteenth-century France highlights the sinuous paths that led from an ancient way of life, that had not changed over many centuries, to ours today. If it enables us to pinpoint the elements which allowed for the development of the dynamics of innovation on one hand, it also leaves open many routes for further research. Among these, I would like to point out two. The first concerns the conditions and temporalities of the social diffusion of thermal comfort, which can only be conducted through quantitative investigations in all the layers of society. We would witness, without doubt, a very slow diffusion of thermal comfort from cities to the countryside, and from the wealthiest classes of society to the poorest, a diffusion that did not end in France before the 1950s and 1960s. Until the middle of the twentieth century, the fireplace, despite its defects, was still sometimes the only source of heat in traditional farms. And when it was replaced by a cast-iron kitchen stove, the other rooms in the house were not heated, especially the bedrooms. Ethnological surveys conducted since the 1940s show that the French countryside is still an astonishing conservatory of ancient lifestyles, lifestyles of 'the world we have lost'.[59] One only has to read on this subject the setbacks of the American sociologist Laurence Wylie, who came to live for a year with his family in a village in the south of France in 1950, to understand that the requirement to obtain a temperature of 20°C in the rooms of the house is then considered, by his French landlord, as a request as crazy as it is surprising.[60]

The second path that could be taken by research on thermal comfort would be a comparative approach between the different European countries. In a continent summarily divided between the fireplace's supporters (in the west), who for a very long time suffered from the incapacity of the open fireplace to heat their houses sufficiently, and the stove's supporters (in the east) who benefited from the unparalleled performance of the enclosed hearth or stove from the Middle Ages onwards, there are two different sensitivities to cold and heat, two different ways to live winter, two different ways also to conceive home. This study would certainly show that the design of thermal comfort differs according to time but also according to location. It would be interesting to see when and how these different conceptions converged to lead (if this is really the case) to our current conception of comfort which tends to eliminate completely the contrasts of the seasons and to the creation of artificial indoor climates perfectly homeothermic by the combined effects of modern heating and cooling techniques. Living at home, working in an office or travelling in a car in a thermal environment perpetually set at 20°C, this would undoubtedly surprise our ancestors and also reflect a form of globalization and standardization: that of sensibilities and our body's relationship to our environment.

Notes

1 Olivier Jandot, *Les délices du feu: l'homme, le chaud et le froid à l'époque moderne* (Ceyzérieu: Champ Vallon, 2017), 80.
2 Madame de Sévigné, *Lettres (1648-1696)*, ed. Emile Gérard-Gailly (Paris: Gallimard, 1953–1957), vol. 3, 877.

3 Bibliothèque de l'Académie nationale de médecine (Paris), Archives de la Société royale de médecine (hereafter SRM), SRM 158/12/6.
4 SRM 176/1/3.
5 SRM 169/1/1.
6 Louis-Charles-Henri Macquart, *Dictionnaire de la conservation de l'homme* … (Paris: Bidault, an VII [1798]), vol. 1, 263.
7 Gaston de Lévis, *Souvenirs-portraits* (1813; Paris: Mercure de France, 1993), 102–3.
8 Archives du Musée National des Arts et Traditions Populaires (Paris, 1937–2005), Enquête d'Architecture Rurale 1425, Seine-et-Oise, Monographie 833/3.
9 François Cointeraux, *L'économie des ménages* … (Paris: Impr. de Vezard et Le Normant, 1793), 34.
10 Jandot, *Les délices du feu*, chap. 7.
11 Montaigne, *Essais,* III, chap. 13, in Albert Thibaudet and Maurice Rat (eds), *Œuvres complètes* (1580–1595; Paris: Gallimard, 1962), 1058.
12 Lazare de La Salle de l'Hermine, *Mémoires de deux voyages et séjours en Alsace, 1674-1676 et 1681,* ed. Joseph Coudre (Mulhouse: Impr. Vve Bader, 1886), 189.
13 Ibid., 123.
14 Archives municipales de Strasbourg, AA 2140.
15 Lucien Febvre, *Le problème de l'incroyance au XVIe siècle: la religion de Rabelais* (1942; Paris: Albin Michel, 2003), 15.
16 Nicolas Gauger, *La mécanique du feu, ou l'art d'en augmenter les effets et d'en diminuer la dépense. Première partie, contenant le traité de nouvelles cheminées qui échauffent plus que les cheminées ordinaires et qui ne sont point sujettes à fumer, etc.* (Paris: Jacques Estienne, 1713).
17 Robert Locqueneux, *Sur la nature du feu aux siècles classiques: réflexion des physiciens et des chimistes* (Paris: L'Harmattan, 2014), 55–65.
18 Nicolas Gauger, *Fires improv'd: being a new method of building chimneys, so as to prevent their smoking …,* trad. John Theophilus Desaguliers (London: J. Senex and E. Curll, 1715).
19 Joan DeJean, *The Age of Comfort: When Paris Discovered Casual – and the Modern Home Began* (New York: Bloomsbury, 2009), 99; John E. Crowley, *The Invention of Comfort: Sensibilities & Design in Early Modern Britain and Early America* (Baltimore: Johns Hopkins University Press, 2001), 171–90.
20 Joseph A. Leo Lemay, *The Life of Benjamin Franklin, v. 2: Printer and Publisher (1730-1747)* (Philadelphia: University of Pennsylvania Press, 2006), 468.
21 Nicolas Gauger, *La Mécanique du feu …,* 2nd edn (Paris: C.-A. Jombert, 1749).
22 Pierre Hébrard (O.S.B.), *Caminologie ou Traité des cheminées* … (Dijon: F. Desventes, 1756).
23 Léopold de Genneté, *Nouvelle construction de cheminées* … (Paris: M. Lambert, 1759).

24 'Moyen d'augmenter la chaleur du feu dans une chambre sans mettre plus de bois dans la cheminée', *Journal œconomique* (Paris: A. Boudet, June 1758), 259–61.

25 'Nouvelle méthode pour échauffer les appartemens avec œconomie & sans inconvénient', *Journal œconomique* (Paris: A. Boudet, January 1759), 31–6.

26 Dupré d'Aulnay, 'Dissertation sur la rareté & la cherté des bois de chauffage dans la Champagne, & sur les moyens d'y suppléer', *Journal œconomique* (Paris: A. Boudet, March 1758), 104–6.

27 Marc-René de Montalembert, 'Mémoire sur une façon de changer les cheminées en poêles, sans leur faire perdre aucuns des agrémens qu'elles peuvent avoir comme cheminées', *Histoire de l'Académie royale des sciences ...* (Paris: Imprimerie royale, 1763), 335–46.

28 Benjamin Franklin, *Œuvres de M. Franklin,...* trad. Barbeu Dubourg (Paris: Quilleau, 1773).

29 Robert Locqueneux, *Préhistoire et histoire de la thermodynamique classique: une histoire de la chaleur* (Paris: Société Française d'Histoire des Sciences et des Techniques, 1996).

30 Jean-Baptiste Joseph Fourier, *Théorie analytique de la chaleur* (Paris: Firmin-Didot, 1822).

31 Benjamin Thompson, Comte de Rumford, *Mémoires sur la chaleur* (Paris: Firmin-Didot, 1804), VIII.

32 Benjamin Thompson, Comte de Rumford, 'Quatrième essai. Des cheminées & de leurs foyers. Différens moyens de les perfectionner pour épargner le combustible, rendre les maisons plus saines & plus agréables, & empêcher les cheminées de fumer', in *Essais politiques, économiques et philosophiques* (Genève: G. J. Manget, an VII[1799]), 309–86.

33 Ibid., 311–12.

34 Ibid., 331.

35 Ibid., 314.

36 Bruno Belhoste, *Paris Savant: Capital of Science in the Age of Enlightenment*, trad. Susan Emanuel (2012; trad., New York: Oxford University Press, 2018).

37 Lavoisier was guillotined in 1794.

38 M. le Comte de Cisalpin, 'Description d'une cheminée et étuve de nouvelle invention', *Observations sur la physique, sur l'histoire naturelle et sur les arts* (Paris: Ruault, 1777), January: 49–56.

39 J. Mongez, 'Description d'une nouvelle cheminée économique, et observations sur les causes qui font fumer les cheminées', *Observations sur la physique, sur l'histoire naturelle et sur les arts* (Paris: Ruault, 1777), March: 162–70.

40 Abbé de Witry, 'Extrait du mémoire lu à la Séance du 21 mai 1776 sur un Poêle économique plus propre à échauffer les appartemens que ceux inventés jusqu'ici',

Mémoires de l'Académie Impériale et Royale des Sciences et Belles-Lettres de Bruxelles (Bruxelles: Imprimerie académique, 1780), vol. 2, IV–IX.

41 Jeremy Caradonna, *The Enlightenment in Practice: Academic Prize Contests and Intellectual Culture in France, 1670-1794* (Ithaca: Cornell University Press, 2012).

42 Liliane Hilaire-Pérez, *L'invention technique au siècle des Lumières* (Paris: Albin Michel, 2000), 209–20.

43 *Observations sur la physique, sur l'histoire naturelle et sur les arts* (Paris: Ruault, 1777), Avril: 310–13.

44 Hilaire-Pérez, *L'invention technique au siècle des Lumières*, 219.

45 *Observations sur la physique, sur l'histoire naturelle et sur les arts* (Paris: Ruault, 1784), Août: 156–7.

46 Bibliothèque Municipale de Lyon, ms. 5568.

47 Gallon, *Conférence de l'ordonnance de Louis XIV du mois d'août 1669, sur le fait des eaux et forests …* (Paris: D. Mouchet, 1725), vol. 2, 40.

48 Reynald Abad, 'L'Ancien Régime à la recherche d'une transition énergétique ? La France du XVIIIe siècle face au bois', in Yves Bouvier and Léonard Laborie (eds), *L'Europe en transitions: Énergie, mobilité, communication XVIIIe-XIXe siècles* (Paris: Nouveau Monde éditions, 2016), 23–84.

49 Bibliothèque Municipale de Besançon, ms. Académie 36, Mémoire 8 (view 221/771).

50 Louis-Sébastien Mercier, *Tableau de Paris*, ed. Jean-Claude Bonnet (1781–1789; Paris: Mercure de France, 1994), vol. 2, 990.

51 Jean-Pierre Goubert, 'Le confort dans l'histoire: un objet de culte', in Jean-Pierre Goubert (ed.), *Du luxe au confort* (Paris: Belin, 1988), 21–9.

52 Joseph-François Désarnod, *Mémoire sur les foyers économiques et salubres de M. le Docteur Franklin et du Sieur Désarnod …* (Lyon/Paris: Dessenne & Gattey/Royer/Bailli, 1789).

53 François Cointeraux, *Le chauffage économique, ou Leçons élémentaires avec lesquelles chacun pourra chauffer à peu de frais l'intérieur de sa maison ou de son appartement* (Paris: Vezard et le Normant, 1792); *L'économie des ménages …* (Paris: Vezard et le Normant, 1793).

54 Thomas Tredgold, *Principes de l'art de chauffer …* (Paris: Bachelier, 1825); César Gardeton, *L'art d'économiser le bois de chauffage …* (Paris: L. Cordier/J. Janet/Gondar Roblot, 1827); Ph. Ardenni, *Manuel du poêlier-fumiste …* (Paris: Roret, 1828); P. Hamon, *Examen comparatif des différents modes de chauffage des habitations …* (Paris: Librairie scientifique et industrielle, 1829); P. Hamon, *Art de chauffer …* (Paris: Librairie scientifique et industrielle, 1829).

55 André Guillerme, 'Chaleur et chauffage: l'introduction du Confort à Paris sous la Restauration', *History of Technology* 14 (1992): 16–53.

56 Olivier Le Goff, *L'invention du confort: naissance d'une forme sociale* (Lyon: Presses universitaires de Lyon, 1994).
57 SRM 117/3.
58 Charles-Henri Macquart, *Dictionnaire de la conservation de l'homme.*
59 Peter Laslett, *The World We Have Lost* (London: Methuen, 1965). On this subject, see also: Eugen Weber, *Peasants into Frenchmen: The modernization of Rural France, 1870-1914* (London: Chatto and Windus, 1977).
60 Laurence Wylie, *Village in the Vaucluse* (Cambridge: Harvard University Press, 1957), chap. 6.

Object in focus 2:
The improved tiled stove: Sweden's contribution to defining comfort?

Cristina Prytz

In his travel account, written during a stay in Switzerland in the 1870s, a young Swedish poet called Verner von Heidenstam noted that 'a house where one cannot make oneself independent of the outdoor temperature cannot be called a home [...] and what provides this homeliness? The tiled stove and double glazing'.[1] As so often is the case with travel accounts, the author unabashedly shares his views of the world with the reader. Many of his points clearly derived from his experiences from home and what he himself must have found familiar or unfamiliar. Specifically, he links climate control not only with convenience, but also with emotions of homeliness or home comfort. When the book was published in 1888, the indoor climate in Swedish houses had generally been in the control of homeowners for almost half a century and the indoor temperature was relatively constant all year round. It can well be argued that emotions such as comfort, ease, homeliness and convenience can be perceived differently by individuals depending on their personal experience. By focusing on the technological inventions singled out by Heidenstam as responsible for indoor climate control, this case study will argue that ideas of comfort can be learned and altered over time, and can even become part of a national discourse.

As a technological invention, the tiled stove can be presented as part of a long-running dilemma in architecture: how to create warm rooms without risking uncontrolled fires or smoky interiors. It is a very old idea to store heat by channelling smoke and hot air through stone or bricks for as long as possible before letting it out. The Roman hypocaust and Turkish hamam are two early examples. Massive stone or brick stoves, such as the Russian or Austrian oven, were also early inventions for storing heat. By the fifteenth century, most Swedish houses had chimneys, usually centrally placed in the house rather than on a cold external wall. Most houses depended on open fireplaces, often placed in a corner, on which the firewood was placed vertically against the back for maximum light and heat radiation. For those who did let the fire die down a damper in the chimney helped keep the heat inside the house.² Larger brick stoves were also used on farms and estates in kitchens, as well as in smaller outbuildings, built for drying grain, or in bath houses, breweries and bakeries. A century later cast-iron stoves were more prevalent, especially in the south and west of Sweden. By the sixteenth century, tiled stoves had reached Sweden from central Europe; the ceramic tiles acted as insulation and helped to store heat more efficiently.³ However, it took time to heat up a tiled stove, much of the heat was lost up the chimney and massive amounts of firewood were needed.⁴

Since coal was scarce in Sweden, wood remained the main energy source well into the nineteenth century. By the mid-eighteenth century, the price of firewood was soaring for both private users and industry, with mining and metal production consuming a lot of energy (see also Chapter 3). The government initiated a number of projects aimed at improving the availability of fuel. This period saw new regulations aimed at reducing damage to growing trees, caused by grazing and slash-and-burn farming, and controlling the timber trade. A number of competitions were launched to encourage the development of more efficient domestic stoves. As a result, a new type of tiled stove was presented to the public in 1767, the efficiency of which quickly made it very popular.⁵ It is said to have changed how people used their homes and socialized in the northern winter.⁶ The inventors, Count Carl Johan Cronstedt (architect and later minister of finance) and Baron Fabian Casimir Wrede (a military general), had developed a stove approximately eight times more efficient than the existing masonry stoves.

In comparison with earlier models, the new stove had a smaller fireplace opening, thus reducing the risk of building fires that burned too hot which could damage the stove and cause smoke and ash damaging the room. Inside the stove, smoke was led through a masonry pipe system. These flue channels had been made more complex, winding vertically up and down. In effect, the stoves became denser and more compact. The idea of filling the inside of the stove with more bricks, thus increasing the storage capacity, was not new; but most of the earlier models had horizontal hinders for the smoke, making the smoke zigzag up through the stove. In Russia, though, experiments had been made with the same kind of vertical flues, which might have inspired Cronstedt and Wrede.⁷ Vertical flues made it quite easy to sweep the stove. Initially, a few bricks inside the fireplace could be removed; later hatches for sweeping the flues were added on the outside of the stove.⁸ Improvements were also made to refine control of the amount of air going in and out of the stove, thus increasing or decreasing the heat of the fire. In consequence their new model was presented as smoke-free, it could be made relatively small, and it was easily decorated to match any type of decorative scheme.[9] Even in mid-winter, it was enough to light a fire in the stove just twice a day. The heat radiated for a long time and at a fairly constant temperature, making stove-heated rooms into islands of warmth and comfort. In a few years, the new model spread all over the country and became a common feature in Swedish homes. In 1771, Cronstedt's son, Fredrik Adolf, presented the new stove at the *Académie royale d'architecture* in Paris and in 1787 a few Swedish tile stoves were installed at Versailles, where the queen Marie Antoinette enjoyed their warmth for a short period.[10] The technology of the Swedish stove spread to the colder areas in Europe where firewood was the main fuel for heating houses, but they never became very popular in Denmark or Norway, or in Great Britain.

A1 is the older model of tiled stove. The inside of the stove could be empty, just holding the heat and smoke for a little longer than an open fireplace. The fireplace opening is rather large. A2 shows a later development in which the smoke had to zigzag through stone or brick 'shelves' (thus making it very hard to sweep the inside) before it passed out into the chimney. B is the model constructed by Cronstedt and Wrede. The fireplace opening is much smaller. Inside, the smoke is channelled through vertical flues (making cleaning easier) and the air travels under the hearth

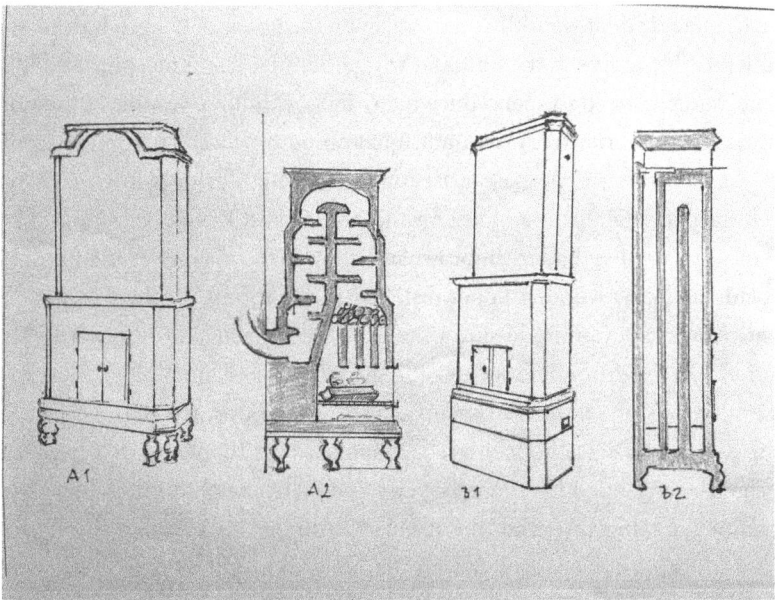

Figure 3a.1 Old style tile stove and the improved model of Cronstedt and Wrede (original drawing by author).

as well. A damper could close the way out into the chimney (usually placed high up on the side of the stove) and the air going into the stove could be controlled by the doors and through an extra air intake.

So why was it that the new type of tiled stove spread so quickly in Sweden, Russia and continental Europe, but not in the west? In the late eighteenth century, many authors presented a cultural explanation and argued that a fondness for good ventilation was in fact a national trait in Great Britain (see also Chapter 3).[11] However, there is also a technological explanation underpinning this cultural trait – coal fires need a better air supply than firewood in order to burn properly and to give off as much heat as possible. Accordingly, Lawrence Wright argues that British homes were generally too draughty for stoves to work properly.[12] Neither did the early stoves work very well in corridors, stairways or in very big rooms. Indeed, the tiled stove was dependent on other technical developments in order to work properly. The room where the stove was placed needed to be quite air tight, often requiring extensive changes to the house – as Clas Julius Ekeblad and his wife Brita Horn found out in 1775 when they set out to improve the indoor climate of their home. One of their first priorities after moving into the house at Stola was to install the new type of tiled stove. Stola, the ancestral home of the Ekeblad family, was a stone house built in the early 1710s and is situated close to the Lake Vänern in western Sweden. Most of the rooms had open fireplaces and it was difficult to warm up the house in winter; indeed, it was hardly possible to live in the house in winter because it was so cold. Clas Julius's parents had preferred to spend the winters in Stockholm or in one of their other houses. As an alternative, it was not uncommon for Swedish families to move in to a smaller house, perhaps a freestanding wing, during winter. Clas Julius and Brita placed their first stoves in the library and Brita's bedroom, but this also meant that they had to improve and control the airflow of the house. The Ekeblads had new wooden floors installed in the rooms on the first floor (the main living area) and made sure they were better insulated in order to lessen the draft. On the ground floor (housing the kitchen and amenities), most rooms had draft-free stone floors resting on a layer of sand over the house cellar. Most of the doors inside the house were also looked over to ensure that frames and thresholds overlapped the door properly and were as tight as possible.[13] We do not know for certain whether the Ekeblad's also installed double glazing in the eighteenth century, but many Swedish families did. In winter an extra window (where the glass was fixed with putty in a wooden frame) was put in place from the inside. Over the coming years the family at Stola went on to have several other stoves replaced with more efficient or fashionable models, and tiled stoves were also installed in the servant's quarters. The only room where an open fireplace was kept was in the formal dining room where it offered an impressive focal point.

For Brita and Clas Julius, the new heating system was well worth the time and effort it took to install and many of their contemporaries felt the same. In 1770, a Swedish diplomat living in Copenhagen had a tiled stove built in his Danish house and in the 1790s another diplomat, Gustaf Mauritz Armfelt, sent for drawings of a Swedish stove which he wanted for his house in Naples.[14] It is no wonder that Verner von Heidenstam enjoyed the Swiss tiled stoves a century later: a relatively high and even room temperature was something he was well acquainted with. He took one step further, however, arguing that, for the Swedes to feel *hemtrevnad* or the Swiss to be *zu House* (at home) meant something more than simply the opposite to being out or being undisturbed and private; for them, being at home meant physical well-being and an idyllic experience which was not possible without the tiled stove.[15] For von Heidenstam, comfort was defined and shaped by national expectations and norms that depended upon particular technologies.

Notes

1 Verner von Heidenstam, *Från Col di Tenda till Blocksberg* (Stockholm, 1888), 78. 'En bostad där man icke kan göra sig oberoende af temperature utomhus förtjenar ej namn av hem [...] och det som möjliggör denna huslighet är – kakelugnen och dubbelfönstret'. Heidenstam (1859–1940) was a Swedish poet, novelist and laureate of the Nobel Prize in Literature in 1916.
2 Joakim Hansson, *Komfort framför allt, men även till Nytta och Nöje: Teknik, Apparater och Redskap i Byggnader före andra Världskriget* (Helsinki, 2015).
3 Hansson, *Komfort framför allt*, 62–3.
4 Gösta Selling, 'Den Svenska Kakelugnens Tvåhundraårsjubileum', *Saga och Sed* (1967): 75–101.
5 Carl Johan Cronstedt, *Beskrifning på ny Inrättning af Kakelugnar til Weds besparning* [...] (Stockholm, 1767).
6 Hansson, *Komfort framför allt*.
7 Ibid., 70.
8 Selling , 'Den Svenska Kakelugnens', 100.
9 Margareta Cramér, *Den Verkliga Kakelugnen: Fabrikstillverkade Kakelugnar i Stockholm 1846–1926*, (Stockholm, 1991); Susanna Scherman, *Den Svenska Kakelugnen: 1700-talets Tillverkning från Marieberg till Rörstrand* (Stockholm, 2007).

10 Linnéa Rollenhagen Tilly, *Carl Johan Cronstedt, Arkitekt och Organisatör* (Stockholm, 2017); Jonas Nordin, *Versailles: Slottet, Parken, Livet* (Stockholm, 2013), 317–18.
11 Leonore Davidoff and Catherine Hall, *Family Fortunes: Men and Women of the English Middle Class 1780–1850* (Chicago, 1987), 383.
12 Lawrence Wright, *Home Fires Burning: The History of Domestic Heating and Cooking* (London, 1964).
13 Riksarkivet, Stockholm, Ekebladska samlingen E 3571, Letter from Brita Horn to Clas Julius Ekeblad, dated Stola 26/9 1777.
14 Selling, 'Den Svenska Kakelugnens', 92.
15 Heidenstam, *Från Col di Tenda till Blocksberg*, 78.

People in focus 2:
Keeping warm with Sir John Soane

Diego Bocchini

At its delicate moment of transition between the eighteenth and nineteenth centuries, British architecture found one of its leaders in Sir John Soane. He embodied all the elements typical of this transition era: a heavy heritage coming from the past and a strong push towards the future, a conscience leaning to romanticism but still tied to the Enlightenment, suspended between feelings and rationality. In his architecture, the essence of the modern movement, with his approach more definite and 'primitive': the use of innovative materials and technologies, the constant search for appropriate architectural languages and avant-garde technological devices and the desire for comfort with attention to the users of buildings and their well-being. In this context, the word comfort is interpreted as a series of circumstances aimed at making everyday life simpler and more convenient. These include material needs, organizational systems, installations and accessories used to induce positive feelings of well-being.

The analysis here focuses on one specific building: Soane's house-museum at 12, 13 and 14 Lincoln's Inn Fields, London. This is one of the few buildings that remains largely unaltered since Soane's death; it was the place where he spent most of his time and where he could allow himself more creative design, free from customers' requirements. Soane acquired the first part of the complex in 1796 and in the following years he carried out considerable extension and refurbishment adding number 14 to the group of buildings in 1824. Lincoln's Inn Fields soon became a reference point for Soane's family, his students and collaborators, and the committees with which he worked. As a result, the building was a perfect hybrid: a house, a museum, an office, a library and a catalogue.

The visitor today can find many characteristics of the building that still appear extremely modern. The main elements which can be related to the concept of comfort are essentially devices connected to technology designed to improve environmental well-being, such as the use of central heating systems, and plumbing and lighting systems. In a mental or emotional register, Soane's personal search for comfort is seen in the utilization of chimneys, the use of new materials, the desire for privacy and the design of furniture. While the fireplace has always been considered as the heart of the house and its presence is crucial for the regular development of the domestic life, the design of furniture started to evolve rapidly from the seventeenth century onwards as the needs of the 'modern man' changed. Attempts were made to create a sort of 'complicity, sensitive, gradual and intimate correspondence between objects and desires, material forms and psychology'.[1] With the industrial revolution, new materials were created such as artificial stone (Soane preferred the Coade stone[2]) and technological improvements permitted other developments, including the creation of bigger glass panels that led to the creation of bigger windows.

Heating big rooms in the eighteenth century was a challenge that required much attention and care. In his house-museum, Soane experimented with many different central heating systems. The last one of them was particularly efficient and was still in use until 1964. Soane focused mostly on the Office since it was the room where he and his *entourage* would spend most of their time, working for eleven or twelve hours a day and for six days a week. Initially, the whole building was heated only by stoves and fireplaces. Plans of the basement of the building also mark coal vaults, accessible directly from the kitchen, which were refilled by workers through a hole in the ceiling connected with the street above. In the same plan, there was also a stove positioned in a recess on the staircase whose flow was supposed to heat the whole floor of the building. The temperature in the house was also influenced by the thin external walls that offered little insulation; the situation was not helped by the big windows comprising thin glass panels. Together these meant that stoves and fireplaces were certainly insufficient. Charles James Richardson (1806–71) was a member of Soane's staff and wrote a treatise on the heating and ventilation of buildings, in which he also discussed the problem found in his personal experience. He noted that:

> The Soane Museum presents great difficulties to the procuring a circulation of warm air within it, as has been sufficiently proved by the repeated failures of the various systems which from time to time have been introduced there for that purpose, several of which are in my recollection. Among them was one of steam and one by the common method of heated water.[3]

The first phase of improvements to the Office took place between 1820 and 1822 when a Meckley steam system for central heating was first installed then removed a year later in favour of a hot air system. A second and more radical refurbishment came in 1824 when a hot air system was employed, originally heating just one room but later extended to warm all the professional spaces. Unfortunately, this system was again found to be inadequate.

There are plans and perspectives of the whole complex made by C. J. Richardson in 1825 showing the renewed building. Into this space, Soane installed further hot air systems and two hot water systems between 1825 and 1830. Heating seems to have become Soane's personal struggle, a sort of obsession that is recorded in a series of receipts for stoves and estimate quotes for these successive if not successful installations. In the following years, a man named Feetham had several connections with Soane.[4] The receipts show a series of works that he carried out: stoves and boilers, and new pipes and cylinders to try and heat each room in the house-museum, including the maids' and butler's rooms. Soane also took note of the temperature reached; in January, for example, he recorded figures of 53 or 54°F (11–12°C) in the museum. Later in 1831, Soane decided to replace the Feetham system with another one working with hot water by H. C. Price, allowing him to obtain a room temperature of 60°F (15.5°C) with an external temperature of 30°F (-1°C). Unfortunately, even this system did not work properly and Soane replaced it in 1832 with a pressurized hot water system produced and installed by A. M. Perkins. That was the ultimate and definitive system.

Of course, a room temperature of 13–15°C for us is rather cold, but at that time it was quite avant-garde (see also Jandot's chapter in this volume). This was achieved through central heating systems, but Soane thought that the psychological connotations of fireplaces should still be taken into consideration. That is why, in the residential portion of his building, he placed a fireplace in practically every room. Soane's fireplaces were quite different from the ones designed by his predecessors: they are flat rather than massive and have light and delicate ornaments so that they can be perfectly integrated with the walls. In some cases, in public rooms such as the library or in the dining room, the walls around the fireplace were totally covered with mirrors. This had multiple effects: they gave the impression that the walls were disappearing, enlarged the space and reflected lights (see also the chapter by Ilmakunnas).

A central heating system could not replace the warm sensation and the domestic feelings of seeing a burning flame or simply the joy of sitting in front of a fireplace to have a familiar chat. The merits of different heating systems were hotly debated and there were numerous treatises and papers written on the heating and ventilation of buildings, but almost everyone agreed on a peaceful cohabitation of the two heating systems. Following this argument, there was no

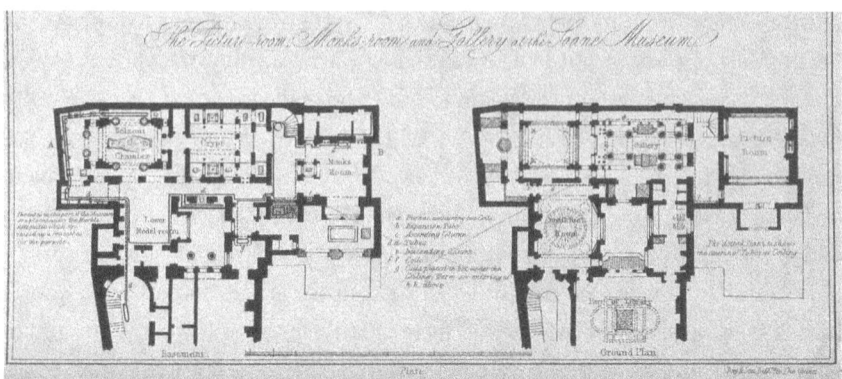

Figure 3b.1 Plan of the basement rooms at Sir John Soane's house and museum. Charles Richardson, *A popular treatise on the warming and ventilation of buildings* (John Weale, London, 1839)

need for fireplaces in non-residential buildings or in work rooms, confirming that the idea of a fireplace was (and still is, perhaps) strongly connected with the idea of domestic life.

The work of research was aimed at defining new comfort parameters and it was also helped by the analysis presented in Lecture number VIII, delivered at the Royal Academy by Soane in 1815. This lecture included some historical references to the orientation of buildings and on heating systems from authors such as Vitruvius, Plinius and Seneca, but it also had a more modern focus on comfort. Soane argued that 'fireplaces must all throw sufficient heat, the windows admit a due quantity of light, and the doors, passages and staircases must afford easy communication with every part of the structure'.[5] This forms the culmination of a radical change in the minds of architects and designers: the house had to adapt to the resident's needs and not *vice versa*. Soane refused to suffer the inconveniences of living and working in a damp and cold space and chose (or at least tried) to mould his house to his needs and wants:

> In the early decades of the nineteenth century the ideal of comfort provided values, consumption patterns, and behaviors crucial to the transformation of a middle class. The culture of comfort that developed in eighteenth-century British and Anglo-American society asserted its essential domesticity, its technological promise, and its universality: all people were entitled to physical comfort, and all people could be comfortable the same way.[6]

In conclusion, we can certainly say that Soane was a man of his time, and loved to experiment with new techniques and new materials at a time when technological change was starting to run fast. Undoubtedly the absolute new feature in Soane's architectural discourse is his right of primogeniture of integrated planning and he could be considered as a sort of unconscious pioneer of architectural organicism. He set priorities in designing his own space and the result was the definition of new parameters of comfort: a series of benefits mostly related to light and warmth. He studied ancient architecture closely and learnt from his predecessors, not imitating them, but analysing the ways in which some effects were obtained. Soane, at the intersection of converging disciplines and with his interest in physical and emotional well-being, masterfully summed the key questions related to the search for ease and comfort and through his work contributed to building and structuring the image of British comfort that was to become archetypical in the decades that followed.

Notes

1. Renzo Dubbini, *Nascita dell'idea di comfort*, in '*Storia del disegno industriale*', (Milan: Electa, 1989), vol. 1.
2. Mrs Eleanor Coade (1733–1821) created the artificial stone in 1770 in London. The main uses of the Coade stone were sculptural and architectonical. She ran the business from 1769 to 1833.
3. Charles Richardson, *A Popular Treatise on the Warming and Ventilation of Buildings* (London: John Weale, 1839), 51–2.
4. William Feetham: stove grate maker and furnishing ironmonger. He is credited with the world's first mechanical shower patent in 1767. His contraption consisted of a basin, where the bather stood, and an overhanging water tank. The bather used a hand pump to pump water from the basin to the tank, and then pulled a chain to dump all the water at the same time over his head. He improved the showering equipments with various patents in 1822. He was based in Ludgate Hill, London.
5. David Watkin, *Sir John Soane: Enlightenment, thought and the Royal Academy Lectures* (Cambridge: Cambridge University Press, 1996).
6. John Crowley, *The Invention of Comfort: Sensibilities & Design in Early Modern Britain & Early Modern America* (Baltimore & London: Johns Hopkins University Press, 2001).

4

The spread of comfort in nineteenth-century Belgian homes

Britt Denis

In the introduction of her book *Home Comfort*, Christina Hardyment states: 'It is easy to ignore the long history behind the facility with which we now make ourselves comfortable'.[1] This immediately puts her finger on the wound. And in the said long history, the nineteenth century played a pivotal role, as I will argue in this chapter. The large-scale breakthrough of domestic comfort in terms of lighting and heating is generally considered as one of the major achievements of this era, which according to Jan de Vries made 'all that went before appear as trivial, part of a seemingly motionless history'".[2] Whereas 'comfort' for centuries had remained the privilege of a happy few,[3] the nineteenth century witnessed the emergence of new or improved 'modern' amenities in an increasing number of homes. As a result, the home had never been so comfortable for so many people, 'inhabitants, as it were, of a totally different world'.[4] However, while it is arguably true that the flood of new technologies entering the home in the nineteenth century was truly revolutionary, surprisingly little scholarly attention has been given to these technologies. Consequently, their use, (social) spread and immense impact on the everyday practices of the household and on the relations within this unit and across the social scale is taken for granted rather than discussed. This neglect inevitably plays down the complexities at work within the domestic domain and ignores the meaningful diversity and fluidity of everyday practices, as I have argued elsewhere.[5]

With regards to domestic technologies themselves, the neglect is twofold. First, traditional narratives in the history of technology have predominantly dealt with the (male) inventors, rather than with users.[6] While this makes us well informed on the nuts and bolts of technological innovations, it remains unclear how these innovations were actually put to use in ordinary homes. Second, and more fundamental, domestic technology was usually not even seen as *proper* technology. In consequence, the home was invariably overlooked as a locus of industrialization, and more often even characterized as its antithesis.[7] Yet, by considering the technological changes in the home as insignificant, this 'form of cultural obfuscation', as Ruth Schwartz Cowan has called it, not only failed to recognize the revolutionary character of the changes, but disregarded the enormous and profound impact of these changes on the daily life of people, on various levels (socially, spatially, symbolically, practically).[8]

From the perspective of studies of the home, it is also baffling that the diffusion of comfort and domestic technologies has not been a hot topic of research, since the 'deeply felt appreciation of home as place of peace, seclusion and refuge would have meant little without certain standards of comfort, privacy and routine'.[9] Home technologies and the domestic ideal reinforced each other and as the disposable income for larger groups in society rose throughout the nineteenth century, more time and resources could be invested in the domestic environment and higher levels of comfort could be enjoyed.[10]

In this chapter, therefore, these domestic technologies take centre stage and more specifically those related to heating the homes and providing light, or the struggle with cold and darkness as Daniel Roche calls it.[11] These can be considered as closely intertwined, elementary amenities, without which comfort becomes inconceivable.[12] I study the diffusion of new heating and illumination technologies within a broad social and occupational group and assess its impact on day-to-day domestic practice, exploring the extent to which it made domestic life in Belgium in 1880 more comfortable than in the 1830s. Contemporary normative literature is used here to investigate the context in which these innovations found their way to the homes of (more or less) ordinary people.[13] At the same time, their presence in the advice literature signals that these new technologies caused anxieties, often described in contrasting terms of convenience/inconvenience, comfort/discomfort, ease/unease and so on. While symptomatic of the strong moral connotations of dark/light or hot/cold dichotomies, it also indicates that the impact on the household must have been immense.

And yet we know very little on how it affected them in reality.[14] How did heating and lighting technologies work, how and where were they fitted in the home, how did they transform daily routines, what were the implications for family members or across the social pyramid, and so on. To answer these questions and to qualify the discourse, I present a long-term empirical study of probate inventories, which gives us unique access to the homes in which domestic technologies were actually put to use (or even explicit non-use, as we will see), sometimes in unforeseen and unexpected ways. The probate inventories studied here cover the Belgian city of Antwerp for two sample periods, with 1834–5 sketching a picture of pre-industrial domestic practices: before the drastic transformations of modernization and the second period covering 1880, by which time we might expect these evolutions to be found in many homes, without having yet reached widespread acceptance.

Domestic comfort

With contemporary literature as guideline, comfort is perhaps best described as well-being in its broadest sense (physically, emotionally, socially). This well-being was malleable: it was possible to 'create an idealized domestic space *made* [original emphasis] comfortable' and, in the contemporary literature, we can identify three ways to do so.[15] First, and most obviously, through the use of a large variety range of consumer items or tools available to make homes more comfortable, such as furniture, stoves, lamps, window curtains, mattresses and so on.[16] While the struggle with cold and darkness essentially is the same for everyone, regardless of social position, the tools for conquering them were very different and socially determined. A second possibility was to create comfort via the spatial arrangement of the house, ideas that circulated already before the nineteenth century (see also the contributions of Townshend and Davrius).[17] It entailed a clear separation between the 'superior parts of the house' and the domestic offices, which was closely related to the third means for creating comfort, namely the practices of efficient household organization.[18]

In what follows, domestic comfort or convenience is seen predominantly in this more material sense, as expressed in/through the material culture, spatial organization and practices of the home. Probate inventories show evidence of the revolutionary technological progress in Belgian homes, with a widening range of items used for heating and lighting in an increasing number of households across the social scale. The growing demand for and the actual improvement of domestic comfort can be deduced from the growing implementation of heating and lighting technologies, as evident in the spread, quantity and diversity of related objects.

'The comfortable hearth'[19]

In the course of the nineteenth century, open fires would increasingly make way for closed iron (cooking) stoves and ranges that were able to spread warmth more evenly with less fuel and in a safer way.[20] The sample dates used here cover this crucial transition period.

In Antwerp, the more 'modern' and efficient types of heating are already prevalent in the 1830s homes (Figure 4.1).[21] In both sample periods, the most common type was the generic stove (*kachel/stoof/poêle*), which was fairly even spread socially, with only a slight inclination towards the upper groups. Hence, in contrast to the eighteenth century, the stove does not appear to be a luxury item, to be found only in wealthier households.[22] However, domestic heating does seem to be influenced by social factors, because in both periods, the ownership of both fixed and flexible heating devices clearly correlated with the overall material wealth of the households.[23] This allowed more rooms to be heated and enabled spatial differentiation, with each room having its appropriate, specialized device.[24] Poorer households, in contrast, usually only owned one stove in the main living room that served multiple purposes, such as heating, cooking and miscellaneous household tasks (providing warm water for washing and cleaning, heating irons and so on).

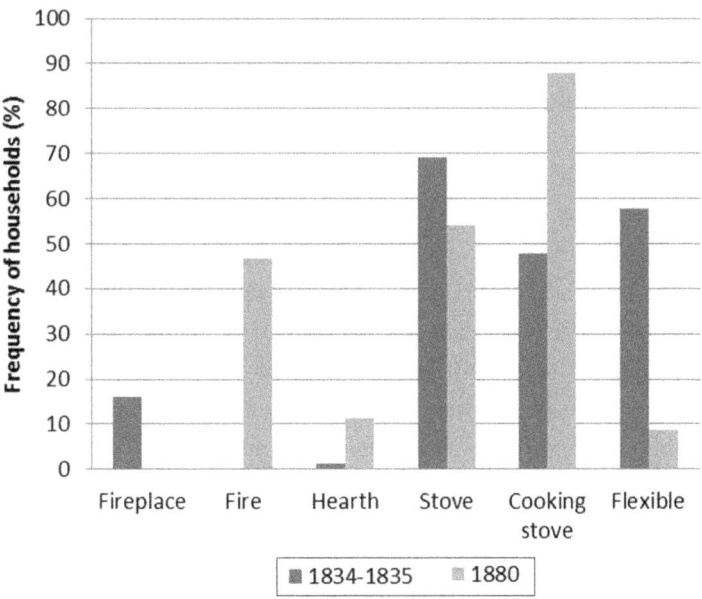

Figure 4.1 Presence of heating devices, 1834-1835 & 1880. (Graph 4.1 offers a first impression of heating technologies in Antwerp homes. The first three types represent older technologies (open, visible fire), while stove and cooking stove stand for the newer, more heat-efficient types of heating (enclosed fire). The flexible heating devices comprise smaller, transportable devices used for cooking, warming or heating water.)
Source: Database Probate Inventories.

By 1880, heating technologies appear to have been democratizing as social differences became less pronounced.[25] However, rather than becoming more widespread, the number of Antwerp households owning a stove actually decreased.[26] A plausible explanation is that this decline was compensated by the strong spread of specialized stoves for cooking or *cuisinières*, of which ownership more than doubled.[27] Perhaps it is also an indication that the heating devices had become more effective, making auxiliary heating superfluous. This hypothesis is backed up by the spectacular decrease of flexible heating devices (see Figure 4.1).[28]

Yet another curious observation is that a considerable amount of households apparently held on to the more 'archaic' heating technologies and (again) contrary to expectations, this number grew substantially in 1880.[29] A case in point was the column stove, a cast iron, cylinder shaped stove.[30] This type was quite popular in the first sample period, despite being known as a high-maintenance, ill-smelling, wasteful device.[31] Paradoxically, this type of stove was predominantly found in more representative rooms, such as the salon, dining room or rooms with a professional character.[32] Moreover, the majority of the column stoves were found in the wealthier households who often owned more than one piece. It appears that the column stove served as a status symbol, given that only these well-to-do households could rely on servants for lighting and maintaining the stove and there was no need for them to be economical. It also showed they had the necessary means to buy an additional device for cooking, which the column stove did not allow. Much the same was true of open fires. The nomenclature changed from fireplaces (*schouw/cheminée*) in the 1830s to the rather more vague fire ((*open*) *vuur/feu* (*ouvert*)), but it is uncertain whether this represented a change in technology.[33] Certainly, their shared characteristic was a visible fire. According to *An encyclopædia of domestic economy*, newer fireplaces were 'far more effective in warming our apartments, and have become more comfortable and elegant, as well as more economical in point of fuel'.[34] In reality, though, these types were deficient and frequently ridiculed.[35] Again, this kind of heating devices was almost entirely found in the upper echelons of society.

The persistence of old technology, notably in the more public areas of the home, like the front room, the salon and dining room, and the overall decline in stoves begs the question why the diffusion of new technologies was so slow and even backward, despite its unchallenged better thermal and economic efficiency.[36] While it is true that stoves became more readily available and affordable in the nineteenth century through improvements in the manufacturing process, the cost alone clearly does not tell the whole story.[37] It was not only a matter of improving one's physical comfort, and contemporary literature on the subject indicates that other more decisive considerations were made by advocates and opponents of both technologies.

At first sight, those advocating open fire technology were mainly concerned with hygiene and health. Contrary to the hearth, stoves were accused of producing too much heat, which created an oppressive atmosphere that 'boils your head and freezes your feet'.[38] Aesthetically, stoves were considered ugly devices that should be avoided.[39] This was connected to a certain sentimentality for the charming fire, which a closed stove lacked.[40] Yet, surprisingly, stoves were not banned from the whole house. For example, they were considered appropriate heating devices for dining rooms and consultation rooms, based on the same arguments of health and generally accepted habits.[41] Moreover, stoves were considered a good heating device for the lower social classes.[42] In domestic advice aiming at these groups, the stove was even proclaimed as the 'most beautiful adornment of the housewife'.[43] But for wealthier households, the practicality of the new technologies was not convincing. Lighting and maintaining a fire was an unenviable job, often carried out by servants or women, that required skilful hands.[44] Despite such efforts, the inefficiency of open fire technology must have been at least discomforting and according to some even unhealthy.[45] Moreover, especially when using coals, heating the home also meant living with the smell of carbon smoke and damaging soot and dust, leaving stained furniture, carpets and curtains desperately in need of proper cleaning.[46] As Robert Southey suggested, there might have been 'a pride in using the cleaner materials'[47], which confirms notions on cleanliness were often clearly linked to ideas about class or gender.[48]

Evidently, the transition towards closed and more efficient stoves (or the conscious rejection of such technologies) went far beyond simply changing one type of heating device for another. To understand why older technologies persisted in wealthier home, we need to acknowledge that the teleological success story of these novelties simply does not hold up and that 'different social groups ... have different ideas about material technologies'.[49] Do we see the same evolutions in lighting technologies?

When light conquers night

For centuries, the hearth had been the most important source of artificial light, only complemented with the flickering, weak light of candles and oil lamps. The latter had to be easily transportable, so people could take it with them to the room they wished to illuminate. Even though wealthier households had more and better-quality lighting devices, generating more light essentially required more candles or lamps.[50] This only changed at the end of the eighteenth century, with the invention of the improved oil lamp that was much more economical (hence cheaper), cleaner (less smoke) and provided a more intense and stable light.[51] In the inventories, these lamps are often referred to as *Quinquet* lamps. Its enormous impact can hardly be underestimated.[52] The technology was further improved with the *Carcel* lamp, that moved the oil reservoir under the lamp, instead of next to it and using a clock mechanism to bring the oil to the wick.[53] Of course, such lamps were quite expensive and most people could not afford them. If a candle did the trick, *Quinquets* remained a superfluous luxury.[54]

In the 1830s, households were still highly dependent on candles and oil lamps. Initially, these were mainly characterized by their transportability, but there was a general trend towards more fixed illumination. Compared to the 1830s, the hanging (suspension) lamps were widespread by 1880, when two new options had also appeared. The first novelty was gas lighting, found in about 20 per cent of the households and predominantly put to use in more public rooms of the house as well as in other very public spaces like shops or inns. Even though its unwelcome side effects (such as yellow light, excess heat, danger of fumes and fire) were widely discussed, it was undoubtedly a powerful epitome of financial strength, given the high cost of acquisition and use. The introduction of the petrol (paraffin) lamp in the 1860s offered a second, cheaper alternative and was supposedly affordable for more people. Petrol lamps pop up in the 1880 sample, but only in higher social layers. This seems odd, since they were technically not as refined as gas lighting, but they were a good alternative when gas distribution was still limited geographically.

Significantly, these new forms of lighting did not oust oil lamps and candles completely. Upon closer inspection, it appears these were predominantly used as decoration, given the lack of use of accessories such as candle snuffers or save-alls. Again, it appears these more traditional, labour-intensive technologies could be actively put to use as 'a conspicuous demonstration of affluence'.[55] Wolfgang Schivelbusch explained this resilience as 'a reaction to the industrialisation of lighting', against a centralized supply system.[56] To judge the modernization of lighting technologies, we therefore need to take into account how these evolutions affected the (perceived and/or experienced) comfort.[57]

According to J. H. Walsh, 'for the purpose of domestic comfort it is necessary to provide for the admission of the sun's rays without the accompaniment of rain,

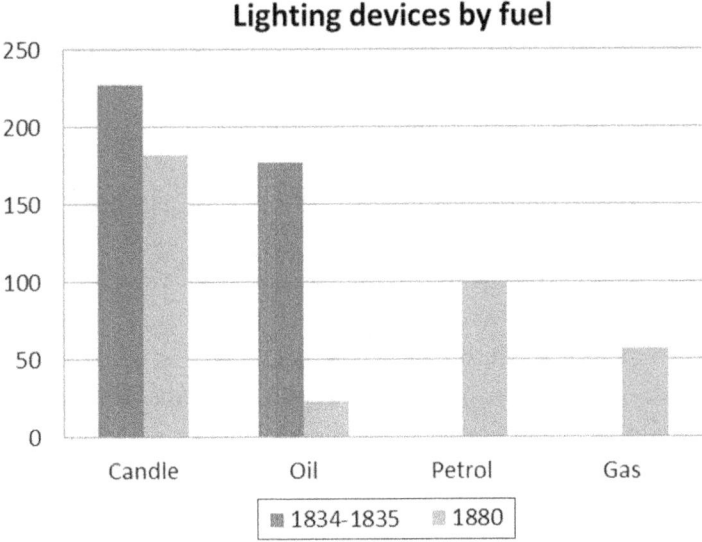

Figure 4.2 Lighting devices by fuel, 1834–5 & 1880.
Source: Database Probate Inventories.

snow, and wind; and besides this, to take care that in his absence a substitute shall be maintained by means of artificial light'.[58] However, the evolution in lighting the home appears to have been more contradictory, to say the least. On one hand, the improvement in the production of glazing enabled ever larger windows to draw in as more natural light as possible. For this purpose, numerous advice books dedicate pages to the ideal orientation of the house and certain rooms, the placement of windows and so on. On the other hand, the same books advise on how to regulate the natural light coming in, by filtering, manipulating, reflecting or even averting it, resulting in 'the oft-cited twilight atmosphere of the bourgeois interior'.[59] The reasons for this manipulation were obviously practical, given sunlight's corroding effect on furniture, carpets and so on. However, too much natural light entering the home was also considered uncomfortable, since it was seen as an invasion of private space and a form of social control, due to the 'prying eyes of the over-curious'.[60] Again, these ideas were not new, but in the nineteenth century there was growing awareness among an ever larger group.

It is clear that, just as with heating, the implications of new technologies went far beyond simply introducing new lighting devices in the home. Conversely, inventories indicate that not all people necessarily preferred the new (improved) technologies, or at least not in all rooms, and many held on to tried-and-tested ones. In order to understand this, it is useful to look further into the spaces in which the new technologies were (or were not) put to use and its effect on the use of space.

Spatial arrangements and household organization

Looking at elements of heating and lighting can give us an idea of the use of space. Due to the transitions described above, it became increasingly possible to warm and illuminate several rooms, making it no longer necessary to concentrate all domestic activities in a single space. However, whether diffused and more diverse heating and lighting meant that households enjoyed higher standards of domestic comfort is question of debate. It has been suggested for instance that smaller houses were actually warmer.[61] Nevertheless, the evolution towards more fixed heating and lighting technologies, at the expense of flexible, transportable devices indicates a transition towards a more clearly delineated use of space. This functional specialization of domestic space aligned with new (bourgeois) ideas on family life and (more importantly) the changing roles of men and women. As a result, more fixed devices (and thus predetermined room use) also meant decreasing scope to appropriate these ideas and discouraged the multiple use of rooms. It also led to an increasing separation of productive spaces, in which the tools used for creating comfort could be increasingly concealed.[62]

One of the consequences of technological progress was thus that 'productive' functions increasingly disappeared behind the scenes (and hence out of sight), since 'the comfortableness of a house indicates exemption from all such evils as draughts, smoky chimneys, kitchen smells, damp, vermin, noise and dust'.[63] However, the social consequences of this removal were severe since it was also propagated as a way to avoid contact with servants. Moreover, despite being promoted as the 'sanctuary of the mother', the secluded kitchen assigned women to the backstage, hereby facilitating the idealized gender roles and even actively contributing in consolidating these roles. The kitchen thus became a space exclusively for work and no longer the locus of family life. While these arguments and arrangements were seen before the nineteenth century, more and more homes show evidence of a growing separation of productive functions and thus increasing delineated roles for men and women.

Nowadays, all it takes is a turn of a dial or press a button to start warming our homes, begin cooking or turn on the light. It is hard to imagine that in the nineteenth century, despite these innovations of home technologies, domestic comfort still required a lot of work. It called for lighting the fire or candles, constant vigilance to make sure they were kept alight (by regularly adjusting or cutting the wick or adding fuel when necessary), hauling the fuel, daily cleaning of the devices and so on. Moreover, all devices had their own (sometimes considerable) drawbacks that had to be taken into account (fire hazard, soot that settled on furniture, unstable provision of gas and so on).

Comfort thus required domestic toil, which made the functional organization of domestic work crucial. According to Jan de Vries, 'the market could not yet offer alternatives to goods requiring extensive household labor to provide ready access to water, illumination, heat and hygiene'.[64] Above all, this was the job of the housewife (or servants if the household was wealthy enough) and contemporary advice books offered abundant practical tips in this matter, explaining the numerous duties of the housemaid upon which the comfort of the family depended. It comprised advice relating to cleanliness, order, neatness, hygiene and maintenance of technologies, among many others. The importance of the right handling and maintenance of devices cannot be underestimated, given the many dangers lurking in the (ill-)use of new technologies.

Moreover, as new technologies became widespread, not only the standard, but also the expectation of comfort rose. What was considered comfortable in the 1830s was no longer sufficient in the 1880s. Comfort was thus highly contingent and as Lesley Hoskins has argued, different people had different standards of suitable or comfortable amounts and arrangements of domestic space.[65] Therefore, another way of thinking about comfort is perhaps to question whose comfort exactly was at stake and in what way it added to their convenience. In the promotion of new technologies for domestic comfort, for example, arguments of labour-saving hardly mattered. In wealthy households, a preference existed for shiny, polished objects (glasswork, crystal items, silverware) and surfaces (parquet floors, polished furniture, mirrors) to capture, mediate and reflect light as much as possible. This must have been a nightmare for those who had to clean it all, not in the least due to the devices that were responsible for much of the dust and soot that themselves required a lot of maintenance. Clearly, it was not the servants' comfort in the balance, especially since contemporary literature suggests they were simply not meant not be comfortable. In their rooms, we hardly find objects related to heating or lighting, which shows that it was not supposed to be used during day time. Moreover, in *La future ménagère*, the readers are advised to give their servants, who were often sleeping directly under the roof, a duvet or a blanket. The author explicitly adds that it is to keep them warm, not to make them comfortable.[66]

Another case in point was the specialized kitchen stove, which spread through all social groups (see Figure 4.1). With its 'remarkable benefits', it led to a drastic transformation of cooking practices and diet.[67] But it did not necessarily relieve the workload. Cooking remained a dirty, time-consuming and labour-intensive job that required a lot more supervision of the process compared to cooking on an open fire.[68] Moreover, the ranges were designed in such a way that they gave out as little heat as possible to the surroundings. According to advice manuals, it mattered little that the housewife, or the servants who did the cooking, were freezing as a result. In case of servants, they simply had to work harder in order to keep warm.[69] So the (in this case strong) social spread of the technology did not lead to a parallel democratization in comfort.

Reasoned resilience

In terms of domestic comfort, the (in)ability to control the domestic atmosphere proved a vital problem to be tackled. In the nineteenth century, the technologies of heating and lighting experienced fundamental changes and improvements.[70] Based on the probate inventories, we can conclude that overall there was a widening range of home technologies for heating and lighting. Moreover, due to the fall in the relative price of heating and illumination in the period under investigation, these also became cheaper.[71] Combined with significant rising purchasing power for more households, domestic technologies became increasingly widespread, leading researchers to argue that their modernity lies in their social spread as much as their technical advances.[72]

Social differences were still very real, however. They help to explain why the technical efficiency or economy of new devices was often not paramount.[73] It seems that the wealthier households in the samples were marked by a certain conservatism, or what Olivier Le Goff has called 'sempiternel retard technique', evident in their taste for labour-intensive, inefficient and wasteful devices.[74] This seems particularly ironic 'in a period that considered and proliferated itself explicitly as modern'.[75] In fact, the inadequacy of the preferred devices was so striking that contemporaries frequently ridiculed these supposed 'modern' comforts of the home. But, while the critical voices tend to mislead us in disdaining these phenomena as a sign of backwardness, conspicuous consumption or anti-modernism, we need to acknowledge the various ways in which they also served as markers of modernity.[76] It confirms the paradox researchers have observed, in that 'what was "better" in technical terms was not necessarily "better" in consumption terms'.[77] The resilience of older technologies makes clear that the spread of innovations often was not a linear story of progress, but unravelling the rationale behind it is more complex than often assumed.[78]

First, in the light of a larger cultural crisis, holding on to familiar, more traditional technologies can be seen as a way to come to terms with and appropriate the drastic societal transformations of the age, in this case industrialization and commercialization that led to a certain homogenization.[79] At the same time, it offered a sophisticated way to distinguish oneself from the lower social strata and their lure for the new.

Second, it also fits in what Cieraad has referred to as the 'autarkic illusion', in which the bourgeoisie could uphold the self-sufficiency of the household thanks to servants. Needless to stress, lighting the fire was a labour-intensive, dirty job, which juxtaposed with ideals of idleness and cleanliness in these affluent circles, but, crucially, required servants to turn the heating on. Thus, objects and domestic technologies were chosen that needed to be worked and handled, and emphasized domestic labour, a crucial marker of a wealthy home.[80] Or as Olivier Le Goff argued, in a world of luxury and abundance, '[l]e summum du luxe est l'utilitaire inutilisé'.[81]

Third, motivations of comfort and convenience prevailed over economy, which led to fashion at the expense of physical comfort or what Judith Flanders had termed showy discomfort.[82] The almost obsessive attention for the hearth and its surroundings that speaks from advice literature proves that it was not so much a question of efficient heating, but a question of social distinction.[83] Especially in the second half of the nineteenth century, when growing purchasing power tremendously increased social mobility, the treasured private home was brought to the fore by the domestic ideology, which was essentially a bourgeois ideology. As a material epitome of (desired) status, the domestic interior had to be meticulously orchestrated to signal the appropriate ideas and values. At the same time it set the standard to rate other (inferior) social groups, such as the working class.[84] As such, for the bourgeoisie, the hearth became a sophisticated way to distinguish themselves from other social groups. The preference for the hearth aligned with the growing criticism of unsanitary, multifunctional dwellings in which cooking, living and sleeping all occurred in the same space.[85] This argument of social distinction was amplified by the powerful imaginary that was connected to the hearth. According to an important Dutch Dictionary from late nineteenth century, for example, the hearth was no less than the meeting point where family and friends would gather and hence, 'the focal point of domesticity, coziness and hospitality'.[86] Under the influence of the domestic ideology, the hearth was placed right at the centre of the ideal home and even came to signify it.[87] According to domestic manuals, the sitting arrangements for example had to be arranged 'vers la cheminée'.[88] Moreover, like it had been for centuries, its form and materials continued to signal hierarchical differences dynamically, where the distance to the hearth expressed the power relations in the household. Like Raffaella Sarti asserts, 'it was within each individual family that access to heat created hierarchies and inequalities'.[89] Clearly, material and spatial practices connected to the home actively created and amplified divergences, tensions and boundaries between urban social groups, men and women, ethnic groups, age categories, and between household members alike.

Conclusion: Technologies and identities

It is clear that no simple generalizations can be made about the breakthrough of comfort in nineteenth-century Belgian homes. First, the mere invention of modern technologies did not necessarily lead to their widespread use and we must be very cautious not to *a priori* accept a story of progress.[90] Even though the nineteenth century witnessed a lot of innovations in heating and lighting, these were not necessarily taken up everywhere at the same moment and a difference in pace can clearly be discerned.[91] To understand changes therein, their appropriation and implications for domestic life, it is also necessary to reconstruct both the social and mental frameworks of the people who adopted them.[92]

Second, not all innovations were available for all social groups or for all household members at the same time, nor were they sought after by all. It is clear that the often-used (albeit not explicit) argument that comfort and the tools for creating it were susceptible to a trickle down process in the nineteenth century, deserves nuance, since it implies the inherent superiority (and hence determined success) of new technologies, in enhancing comfort or improving living conditions.[93] Rather than the linear story of progress technological determinists would like us the believe, modernization was complicated and messy.[94] It could be sought after or imposed upon, one could be excluded from new commodities or resist alternatives spontaneously, old technologies could persevere against all odds, new technologies could be used in unintended ways or create unforeseen collateral effects.[95] The value that was placed on comfort and the way people experience comfort thus not only changed over time and place, it was also highly dynamic. Moreover, we should question the actual use of these technologies by different users and the 'differences in power relations among the actors involved'.[96] An improved stove for example might have provided comfort for the master of the house, but not for the servant who needed to light it every day. We therefore need to address explicitly these divergences between social groups and within the confines of the home, in terms of access to and/or control of the new technologies and regarding the changing requirements of what was considered a respectable and comfortable urban home.

Finally, we should be conscious of the active role of new heating and lighting technologies in creating identities, enforcing social and gender inequalities and shaping behaviour. As Willem Scheire suggests, far from passive objects, we should consider them important means for changed practices.[97] New domestic technologies for heating and illumination exerted a large impact on daily practices, domestic space and power relations between household members, especially when seen in terms of increased workload and changing expectations of what was considered comfortable. In this respect, it is interesting to see that domestic comfort was not a necessary condition or sought-after outcome for all and it served to make distinctions between social groups and household members alike. As well as providing domestic comfort, these technologies appear to have been used as vehicles for conspicuous consumption, and they played an active role in enforcing and consolidating unequal relations within the home.

Notes

1 Christina Hardyment, *Home Comfort: A History of Domestic Arrangements* (London: Viking and the National Trust, 1992), xi.
2 Jan de Vries, *The Industrious Revolution: Consumer Behavior and the Household Economy, 1650 to the Present* (New York: Cambridge University Press, 2008), 129.
3 'An old analysis, maintained long into the 19th century, allowed for luxury for the aristocracy, comfort for the bourgeoisie and mere necessity for the working class.' – Stefan Muthesius, *A Poetic Home: Designing the 19th-Century Domestic Interior* (New York: Thames & Hudson, 2009), 16.
4 Ruth Schwartz Cowan, *More Work for Mother: The Ironies of Household Technology from the Open Hearth to the Microwave* (New York: Basic Books, 1983), 3.
5 Britt Denis, 'In search of material practices: The nineteenth-century European domestic interior rehabilitated', *History of Retailing and Consumption*, 2, no. 2 (2016): 97–112.
6 Nelly Oudshoorn and Trevor Pinch (eds), *How Users Matter: The Co-construction of Users and Technology* (Cambridge: MIT Press, 2003), 4.
7 Judith Flanders, *The Making of Home: The 500-Year Story of How Our Houses became Homes* (London: Atlantic Books, 2014), 277.

8 This had been the central tenet of Ruth Schwartz Cowan's liminal study, claiming that home was and is as much a site of industrialized work as factories or assembly lines had been. – Cowan, *More Work for Mother*.
9 John Tosh, *A Man's Place: Masculinity and the Middle-Class Home in Victorian England* (Yale: Yale University Press, 1999) 13, 27; Amanda Girling-Budd, 'Comfort and gentility: Furnishings by Gillows, Lancaster, 1840 – 55', in Susie McKellar and Penny Sparke (eds), *Interior Design and Identity* (Manchester and New York: Manchester University Press, 2004), 40; Katherine C. Grier, *Culture and Comfort: Parlor Making and Middle-class Identity, 1850-1930* (Washington and London: Smithsonian Institution Press, 2010) 2.
10 Both product and process innovation (for example more effective heating devices, mechanization and standardization) made these devices cheaper and enabled production on a larger scale.
11 Daniel Roche (transl. Brian Pearce), *A History of Everyday Things: The Birth of Consumption in France, 1600-1800* (Cambridge : Cambridge University Press, 2000), 106.
12 Manuel Charpy, 'Le théâtre des objets. Espaces privés, culture matérielle et identité bourgeoise, Paris, 1830-1914' (Doctorat d'histoire contemporaine de l'Université François Rabelais de Tours, 2010), 143–6; John E. Crowley, *The invention of comfort. Sensibilities and design in early modern Britain and early America* (Baltimore: Johns Hopkins University Press, 2001), x.
13 Crowley, *The Invention of Comfort*; Mark H. Rose, *Cities of Light and Heat: Domesticating Gas and Electricity in Urban America* (University Park: Pennsylvania State University Press, 1995), 4.
14 Irene Cieraad, 'Van haardscherm tot beeldscherm. Over de relatie tussen meubelschikking, sociabiliteit en woontechniek', in Clara H. Mulder and Fenne M. Pinkster (eds), *Onderscheid in wonen. Het sociale van binnen en buiten* (Amsterdam: Amsterdam University Press, 2006) 27–8.
15 Cindy R. Lobel, *Urban Appetites: Food and Culture in Nineteenth-Century New York* (Chicago and London: The University of Chicago Press, 2014), 148.
16 Charpy, 'Le théâtre des objets', 21 ; Crowley, *The Invention of Comfort*, 290–1.
17 Clive Edwards, *Turning Houses into Homes: A History of the Retailing and Consumption of Domestic Furnishings* (Aldershot: Ashgate, 2005), 90.
18 Jan de Vries, *The Industrious Revolution*, 128.
19 Robert Kerr, *A Gentleman's House; Or: How to Plan English Residences, from the Parsonage to the Palace; with Tables of Accommodation and Cost, and a Series of Selected Plans* (London, 1865), 281.
20 Cowan, *More Work for Mother*, 58; H. W. Lintsen (ed.), *Geschiedenis van de techniek in Nederland. De wording van een moderne samenleving 1800-1890. Deel IV* (Zutphen: Walburg Pers, 1992), 30–1; Roche, *A History of Everyday Things*, 125; Anton J. Schuurman, *Materiële cultuur en levensstijl, Een onderzoek naar de taal der*

dingen op het Nederlandse platteland in de 19ᵉ eeuw: de Zaanstreek, Oost-Groningen, Oost-Brabant (Utrecht: HES Uitgevers, 1989).

21 In absolute numbers, the stove was undisputedly the predominant device used for heating, though often only found in the main living area of the home. For providing warmth in the other rooms of the house, people relied on transportable devices, such as foot stoves and braziers.

22 Roche, *A History of Everyday Things, 133;* Raffaella Sarti (transl. Allan Cameron), *Europe at Home: Family and Material Culture 1500-1800* (London and New Haven: Yale University Press, 2004), 93; J. J. Voskuil, 'Boedelsbeschrijvingen als bron voor groepsvorming en groepsgedrag', *Volkskundig Bulletin*, 13, no. 1 (1987): 30–58.

23 Ruth Schwartz Cowan, 'The consumption junction: A proposal for research strategies in the sociology of technology', in Wiebe E. Bijker and Trevor Pinch (eds), *The Social Construction of Technological Systems: New Directions in the Sociology and History of Technology* (Cambridge and London: The MIT Press, 1989) 264; Roche, *A History of Everyday Things*, 129.

24 W. M. Logeman, *Kachels* (Leiden: A.W. Sijthoff, 1872), 3–4.

25 As evident in the spread of items that were first the preserve of the wealthier households and in 1880 could be found across the social scale (f.e. *cuisiniere*).

26 H. Fois-Mie had argued by mid-century, asserting that nearly all hearths were replaced by stoves except 'un bien petit nombre que l'on a conservés à grands frais'. – H. Fois Mie, *Manuel du foyer domestique ou nouvel système de chauffage d'habitation* (Lyon: Couvat, 1853), 18.

27 Louis-Eugène Audot, *La cuisinière de la campagne et de la ville ou Nouvelle cuisine économique* (Paris: Audot, 1853), 34.

28 Their large number in 1834–5 clearly illustrates the deficiency of existing domestic heating, increasing the need for additional heat sources to fight the cold. Following this argument, the serious decline of flexible solutions in 1880 indicates that the heating devices have become more suitable and effective in heating the homes. It also suggests that as fixed heating devices became more widespread throughout the house, transportable heating devices became superfluous.

29 Manuel Charpy identifies the same resilience of older technologies. –Charpy, 'Le théâtre des objets', 226.

30 This type was especially in vogue in the first half of the century, as Meindert Stokroos indicates. In 1880, we encounter only two column stoves. – Meindert Stokroos, *Verwarmen en verlichten in de negentiende eeuw* (Zutphen: Walburg Pers, 2001), 13; Rijksarchief Antwerpen, *Notariaat*, 12125 (L.G. Steens), 252 (13/10/1880); 20391 (F. Brabants) 425 (26/01/1880).

31 Stokroos, *Verwarmen en verlichten*, 13–14; Logeman, *Kachels*, 18.

32 RAA, *Notariaat*, 7456 (X.A. Gheysens) 651 (20/05/1834) ; 506 (P.J. Demeester) 506 (30/10/1835); 7348 (J.F. Gellynck) 37 (26/02/1834); 1285 (C.J. Theunissens) 153 (01/08/1835); 140 (J. Blockx) 57 (28/04/1834).

33 Jozef Vuylsteke suggests that it was an iron stove, exclusively used for heating, with visible fire. – Jozef Vuylsteke, *Vak- & Kunstwoorden. Nr 2. Ambacht van den smid* (Gent: Siffer, 1895), 105.

34 Thomas Webster and Mrs. Parkes, *An Encyclopædia of Domestic Economy Comprising Subjects Connected with the Interests of Every Individual* (New York: Harper & Brothers, 1855), 93.

35 M. G. Beleze, *Le livre des ménages. Nouveau manuel d'économie domestique* (Paris: Hachette et Cie, 1860), 63; Crowley, *The Invention of Comfort*, 179; Louis Figuier, *De wonderen der wetenschap of de geschiedenis der voornaamste uitvindingen* (Den Haag: Gebr. Belinfante, 1869), 354–5; Logeman, *Kachels*, 21–5; John Henry Walsh, *A Manual of Domestic Economy Suited to Families Spending from £100 to £1000 a Year* (London and New York: G. Routledge & Co, 1857), 109.

36 B. Koning, *Noodig berigt voor den Nederlander wegens eene nieuwe verbeterde wijze van kunstverlichting, door middel van vlamvatbaar gas uit steenkolen* (Amsterdam: Johannes Van der Hey, 1816) 1.

37 According to Anton Schuurman, the price often even is not an explanatory variable. – Schuurman, *Materiële cultuur en levensstijl*, 170; M. N. Briavoinne, *De l'industrie en Belgique: causes de décadence et de prospérité. Sa situation actuelle*, Tome 2 (Bruxelles : Adolphe Wahlen et comp., 1839), 320.

38 Henry Havard, *L'art dans la maison (grammaire de l'ameublement)*, Troisième partie (Paris: Edouard Rouveyre, 1887), 374.

39 The inventories seldom inform us on the design of the stoves, even though its central location in a room made it hard to blend in. In the margin of Belgian industrial expositions, we learn that its design in the 1830s still left 'a lot to be desired'. Luckily, by mid-century huge progress is reported and stoves now heated *and* adorned the dwelling. – s.n., *Rapports du jury et documents de l'exposition de l'industrie Belge en 1847* (Bruxelles: M. Hayez, 1848), 164–5; M. Gachard, *Rapport du juri sur les produits de l'industrie Belge exposés à Bruxelles dans les mois de septembre et d'octobre 1835* (Bruxelles, 1836), 296.

40 s.n., 'At home. L'Anglais dans l'intimité', *Le home Anversois. Journal de la dame de maison, de la ménagère et de la famille / Blad voor de huismeesteres, de huishoudster en het huisgezin*, 1, no. 1 (Antwerpen, 1910), 2–3.

41 M. G. Beleze, *Handleiding tot de huishoudkunst. Eene vraagbaak voor huwbare meisjes en jonge vrouwen* (Gouda: G.B. Van Goor, 1862), 66.

42 Figuier, *De wonderen der wetenschap*, 278.

43 Van Gehuchten, *De gids der jonge huishoudster* (Lier: Joseph Van In & Co, 1893), 7.

44 Henry Brown, *De Nederlanden. Karakterschetsen, kleederdragten, houding en voorkomen van verschillende standen* ('s Gravenhage: De Nederlandse Maatschappij van Schoone Kunsten, 1841), 26–7; Figuier, *De wonderen der wetenschap*, 352; Vincent Heyman, 'Architecture et habitants: les intérieurs privés de la bourgeoisie à la fin du XIXe siècle: Bruxelles, quartier Léopold-extension nord-est' (Thèse de

doctorat, Université Libre de Bruxelles, Faculté de Philosophie et Lettres, 1994), 308; Sarti, *Europe at home*, caption figure 20.
45 Crowley, *The Invention of Comfort*, 179; Figuier, *De wonderen der wetenschap*, 354–5.
46 Stépanie-Félicité de Genlis Ducrest de Saint-Aubin, *Manuel de la jeune femme: contenant tout ce qu'il est utile de savoir pour diriger avec ordre, agrément et économie, l'intérieur d'un ménage* (Paris: Béchet, 1827), 117; Elsje Visser, *De bekwame huishoudster. Handleiding voor huisvrouwen en jonge dochters uit den aanzienlijken en den burgerstand om een huishouden overeenkomstig de eischen der tijds, net, doelmatig en goedkoop in te richten* (Leiden: D. Noothoven Van Goor, 1868), 69–70.
47 Robert Southey, *Journal of a tour in the Netherlands in the autumn of 1815* (London: William Heinemann, 1903), 97.
48 Victoria Kelley, *Soap and Water: Cleanliness, Dirt and the Working Classes in Victorian and Edwardian Britain* (London and New York: I.B. Tauris, 2010), 1.
49 Chris Otter, 'Locating Matter: The Place of Materiality in Urban History', in Tony Bennett and Patrick Joyce (eds), *Material Powers: Cultural Studies, History and the Material Turn* (New York: Routledge, 2013), 38–59.
50 Lintsen, *Geschiedenis van de techniek*, 93; Roche, *A History of Everyday Things*, 112.
51 Wolfgang Schivelbusch (transl. Angela Davies), *Disenchanted Night. The industrialization of light in the nineteenth century* (Berkeley, Los Angeles and London: The University of California Press, 1995), 9.
52 Roche, *A History of Everyday Things*, 115; Virginie Loveling, 'Herinneringen uit mijn kindertijd', *Groot Nederland*, 19, no. 5 (1921): 576–618.
53 Walsh, *A Manual of Domestic Economy*, 129.
54 Lintsen, *Geschiedenis van de techniek*, 101.
55 Marilyn Palmer and Ian West, 'Nineteenth-century technical innovations in British country houses and their estates', *Engineering History and Heritage*, 166, no. 1 (2013): 41.
56 Schivelbusch, *Disenchanted Night*, 160–2.
57 Alice Barnaby, 'Light Touches: Cultural practices of illumination, London 1780–1840' (PhD Thesis, University of Exeter, 2002) 19.
58 Walsh, *A Manual of Domestic Economy*, 119.
59 Schivelbusch, *Disenchanted Night*, 184.
60 Walsh, *A Manual of Domestic Economy*, 122; Schivelbusch, *Disenchanted Night*, 186.
61 Flanders, *The Making of Home*, 209.
62 Perversely, this also included the housewives and domestic servants who performed the work. Irene Cieraad, 'Van haardscherm tot beeldscherm', 28–30; Thomas Webster, Mrs. Parkes, *An Encyclopædia of Domestic Economy*; Anna Bergmans, Jan De Maeyer and Wim Denslagen en Wies van Leeuwen, 'Inleiding. Een pleidooi voor goede manieren', in Anna Bergmans, Jan De Maeyer and Wim Denslagen

en Wies van Leeuwen (eds), *Neostijlen in de negentiende eeuw. Zorg geboden? Handelingen van het twee Vlaams-Nederlands restauratiesymposium Enschede 3-4 september 1999* (Leuven: Universitaire Pers Leuven, 2002), 7–12.

63 Kerr, *A Gentleman's House*, 70.

64 de Vries, *The Industrious Revolution*, 128.

65 Lesley Hoskins, 'Reading the inventory: Household goods, domestic cultures and difference in England and Wales, 1841-81' (PhD Thesis, Queen Mary, University of London, 2011), 49. See also Martin J. Daunton, *House and Home in the Victorian City: Working-class Housing 1850-1914* (London: Edward Arnold, 1983), 279–82; Richard Dennis, *Cities in Modernity: Representations and Productions of Metropolitan Space, 1840-1930* (Cambridge: Cambridge University Press, 2008), 109–10.

66 Ernestine Wirth, *La future ménagère: lectures et leçons sur l'économie domestique, la science du ménage, l'hygiène, les qualités et les connaissances nécessaires à une maîtresse de maison: à l'usage des écoles et des pensionnats de demoiselles* (Paris : Hachette et co, 1887), 142.

67 Visser, *De bekwame huishoudster*, 22.

68 Marc Overton, Jane Whittle, Darron Dean and Andrew Hann, *Production and Consumption in English Households, 1600-1750* (London and New York: Routledge, 2004), 100–1. See in general: Inneke Baatsen, Bruno Blondé, Sofie De Caigny and Britt Denis, 'In de keuken', in Leen Beyers and Ilja Van Damme (eds), *Antwerpen à la carte: eten en de stad, van de Middeleeuwen tot vandaag* (Antwerpen: BAI, 2016), 98–127.

69 Mme Pariset, *Nouveau manuel complet de la maitresse de maison ou lettres sur l'économie domestique* (Paris: Librairie encyclopédique de Roret, 1852), 26.

70 Charpy, 'Le théâtre des objets', 143–6; Crowley, *The Invention of Comfort*, x, 176; Thad Logan, *The Victorian Parlour: A Cultural Study* (Cambridge: Cambridge University Press, 2006), 123.

71 Yves Segers, *Economische groei en levensstandaard. Particuliere consumptie en voedselverbruik in België, 1800-1913*, ICAG Studies (Leuven: Universitaire Pers Leuven, 2003), 369–75, 386; Visser, *De bekwame huishoudster*, 64.

72 'Perhaps the most obvious new reality with which middle class families can compete with one another is what I would call the democratization of comfort' – Peter Gay, *The Bourgeois Experience. Victoria to Freud. Volume One: Education of the Senses* (New York: Oxford University Press, 1984), 438; Tomas Maldonado (transl. John Cullars), 'The idea of comfort', *Design Issues*, 8, no. 1 (1991): 35–43.

73 Crowley, *The Invention of Comfort*, 291; Hester Dibbits, *Vertrouwd bezit, Materiële cultuur in Doesburg en Maassluis, 1650-1800* (Nijmegen: Uitgeverij SUN, 2001), 115; Schuurman, *Materiële cultuur en levensstijl*, 170.

74 The implementation of new technologies remained the exception rather than the rule until after the Second World War, in sharp contrast with the United States

where labour-saving devices were adopted and spread more widely during in the nineteenth century. It has been argued that the cheap domestic labour in Continental Europe provided few incentives to modernize the home - Sofie De Caigny, *Bouwen aan een nieuwe thuis. Wooncultuur in Vlaanderen tijdens het interbellum* (Leuven: Universitaire Pers Leuven, 2010), 20; Olivier Le Goff, *L'invention du confort. Naissance d'une forme sociale* (Lyon: Presses universitaires de Lyon, 1994), 40–2; Ileen Montijn, *Leven op stand 1890-1940* (Amsterdam: Thomas Rap, 1998), 55.

75 Deborah Cohen, *Household Gods: The British and Their Possessions* (New Haven, CT: Yale University Press, 2006), 146.
76 Bergmans et al., 'Inleiding. Een pleidooi voor goede manieren', 7–12.
77 Schwartz Cowan, 'The consumption junction', 273.
78 Charpy, 'Le théâtre des objets', 226.
79 Logan, *The Victorian Parlour*, 123; Schivelbusch, *Disenchanted Night*, 186.
80 Logan, *The Victorian Parlour*, 29.
81 « L'utilité d'un objet est la marque même de sa vulgarité, dans un monde défini par le luxe et le superflu. » – Le Goff, *L'invention du confort*, 40–1.
82 Flanders, *The Making of Home*, 209.
83 Charpy, 'Le théâtre des objets', 222–8.
84 Anton J. Schuurman, 'Aards Geluk. Consumptie en de moderne samenleving', in Anton J. Schuurman, Jan de Vries and Ad Van der Woude (eds), *Aards geluk. De Nederlanders en hun spullen, 1550-1850* (Amsterdam: Balans, 1997), 11–28, 19.
85 (Door een R. K. Priester), *Het boek voor moeder en dochter. Volledig onderricht in alles wat eene vrouw als huishoudster en moeder dient te weten* (Amsterdam: F.H.J. Bekker, 1907), 29.
86 Woordenboek der Nederlandse Taal, 1897.
87 Havard, *L'art dans la maison*, 311.
88 Wirth, *La future ménagère*, 132.
89 Sarti, *Europe at Home*, 118.
90 Vanessa Taylor and Frank Trentmann, 'Liquid politics: Water and the politics of everyday life in the modern city', *Past & Present*, 211, no. 1 (2011): 199–241, 201.
91 De Caigny, *Bouwen aan een nieuwe thuis*, 20; Montijn, *Leven op stand*, 55; Willem Scheire, 'Geschiedschrijving van het evidente: het verhaal van de koelkast', *Volkskunde*, 113, no. 2 (2012): 129–51.
92 Crowley, *The Invention of Comfort*, 171; 174; 291.
93 Otter, 'Locating Matter', 38–59; Oudshoorn and Pinch, *How Users Matter*, 1–25.
94 Graeme Gooday, *Domesticating Electricity: Technology, Uncertainty and Gender, 1880-1914* (London: Pickering & Chatto, 2008), 17.
95 Maldonado, 'The idea of comfort', 36.
96 Oudshoorn and Pinch, *How Users Matter*, 6.
97 Scheire, 'Geschiedschrijving van het evidente', 129–51.

Part Two

Home making: Objects and emotions

5

Home Making: Women, marriage and comfort in Victorian middle-class drawing rooms

Jane Hamlett

In 1873, Mrs Jane Ellen Panton published her first domestic advice book *From Kitchen to Garret*. In it, Panton gave detailed instructions for young middle-class newly-weds – explaining how to set up the home room by room. As well as giving practical information, and discussing decoration and furnishing, Panton also stressed the importance of using rooms and material objects in the right way – to create an appropriate atmosphere in the home. The arrangement of the drawing room was particularly important:

> It is on little things that our lives depend for comfort, and small habits, such as a changed dress for evening wear with a long skirt, to give the proper drawing-room air, the enforcement of the rule that slippers and cigars must never enter there, and a certain politeness maintained to each other in the best room, almost insensibly enforced by the very atmosphere of the chamber, will go a long way towards keeping up the mutual respect husband and wife should have for each other.[1]

Here Panton equates the correct arrangement of furniture and behaviour in the drawing room with long-term marital success. Both husband and wife have a stake in creating 'comfort' in the home, not just through an appropriate material space, the drawing room, but through a mutually agreed set of rules and behaviours. Being comfortable is an emotional state as much as a physical one, and is intimately related to marriage. Panton's manual also puts forward a gendered division of power in the home, in which the husband remained the patriarchal head with ultimate financial control, but the wife was given considerable licence in managing the home and setting its tone. The drawing room – and the restrained behaviour entry into this room required – set the stage for 'politeness' in marriage. In Panton's construction of the use of space in the home, women controlled not just decoration but atmosphere, behaviour and morality. By the second half of the nineteenth century, the drawing room was established as an important space within the middle-class home. Often crowded with upholstered furniture, heavily draped and decorated, these rooms were sometimes seen as the zenith of comfort, but were also criticized by contemporaries. This chapter explores the idea of comfort in relation to the Victorian drawing room, looking at how comfort was described and understood, who was responsible for creating it, and how it was realized through objects, practices and behaviours. In particular it considers the gendering of comfort – how its provision was seen as a female role and duty, but how it created an emotional world that involved both male and female participation and could sometimes allow female self-assertion in patriarchal domestic space.

The presence of comfort in the Victorian home has been a long-term preoccupation for design historians. John Gloag argues that 'the Victorians loved comfort without shame', and that the search for comfort constituted an overarching philosophy and mindset distinct to the nineteenth century.[2] This has been complicated by studies locating the emergence of comfort in early eighteenth-century Britain and late-seventeenth-century Paris respectively.[3] What we can say in relation to the nineteenth century is that this was a point at which larger numbers of people in the West, from a wider social range, had access to more material goods than before, which brought about greater potential for material comfort.[4] Understandings of the meanings of comfort were considerably advanced by Katherine Grier in her study of the nineteenth-century North American home. Importantly, Grier argued that there was no single notion of comfort – advice writers, furniture manufacturers and individual women and men used it in different ways, and its meaning changed over time.[5] Rather than seeing the search for comfort as a shared mindset realized through design, Grier looked at the relationship between people, domestic objects and social behaviours to explore how comfort was created and understood. Recent studies of the Victorian home have acknowledged the importance of comfort but have not analysed the use of the word in depth.[6] Lesley Hoskins' PhD thesis opens up a useful discussion of the term – showing how it was used by contemporaries in different ways, and calling for further exploration.[7] A few studies have drawn attention to the importance of gender in relation to comfort. In his study of comfort in early modern Britain and America, John Crowley argues that in mid-nineteenth-century America two distinct gendered versions of comfort emerged – one created by female advice writers that focused on the creation of domestic space as work, and another shaped by male architectural writers who saw the domestic sphere as a place for leisure.[8] More recently Judith Lewis has shown how aristocratic women in the eighteenth and early nineteenth century used the language of comfort to express the way in which they made themselves emotionally at ease in country houses, and how its use related to marital relationships.[9] In this chapter, I will take these ideas further – paying attention to how the language of comfort was used in association with women and the home in a range of different cultural registers, showing how it was understood in relation to gendered roles, but also how comfort was seen as an expression of relationships, and women's emotional independence and autonomy.

In the wider literature on the home that has emerged in recent decades, a great deal of ink has been spilt over the roles of men and women and their relationships with spaces and objects. The growth of women's history in the 1980s and 1990s led to an increased awareness of women's relationship with domesticity.[10] While in the case of Victorian women, the home was sometimes seen as a 'gilded cage' in which women were confined, domestic space has also been seen as a forum for female self-expression. The turn towards the study of masculinity has also been productive for home studies. Karen Harvey and Vickery have both shown the importance of men in eighteenth-century homemaking – and have explored how men and women had different 'terrains' of consumption in the home.[11] Deborah Cohen, meanwhile, has pointed to an important male investment in the mid-nineteenth-century home.[12] The emotional significance of domestic objects for women has also been highlighted. Amanda Vickery and Thad Logan on the eighteenth and nineteenth centuries respectively demonstrated how the domestic goods played a vital role in creating female emotional worlds.[13] Judith Lewis has shown how aristocratic women in the eighteenth and early nineteenth century formed powerful emotional attachments to country houses – using objects to transform space and create emotional bonds.[14] In my own work I have explored the significance of wedding gifts in Victorian homes, and the role of the drawing room and bedroom with dressing room attached in marital relationships.[15] In this essay I further explore the emotional meaning of the home for women – looking at the way in which the language of comfort was attached to spaces and objects. I will focus closely on the drawing room – usually seen as a pre-eminently female space – and consider how comfort was created there.

The source material for the essay revisits research conducted for my PhD thesis and first book – which used contemporary cultural sources to explore how domestic space was represented and idealized, but also looked at 'everyday' sources.[16] For the purposes of this survey, I defined the middle classes very broadly with the aim of showing social difference as much as cultural cohesion. At the bottom end, curates and clerks on around £100 a year were included in the selection – and at the higher end I also included the gentry – partly because they are very well documented but also because they provide an interesting contrast to the newly wealthy upper-middle classes. I have chosen to revisit this material because of this volume's wider project to rethink the meaning of comfort across time and across nations. But it is also a response to a shift in the wider historiography in the past decade that has placed a new emphasis on the history of the emotions.[17] This call to pay closer attention to the role of emotions in the past seems particularly relevant to understandings of comfort which, for the Victorians, had a strong emotional resonance. Finally, drawing new studies on middle-class homes across Europe I will reflect on how far the gendered notions of comfort explored in this essay were specifically English.

Women and comfort in the home

The words 'comfort' and 'comfortable' were widely used by the Victorians in different ways. As Jon Stobart shows in the introduction to this volume, the meaning of comfort changed between the early modern period and the nineteenth century – to become a complex term that encompassed both physical and emotional experience. Being comfortable was associated with a basic material standard – for example, in the early 1860s *Cassell's Household Guide* wrote of 'the bare necessaries of comfortable living'.[18] Comfort was thus linked to socio-economic standing, and the phrase 'the comfortable classes' was sometimes used.[19] The language of comfort frequently appeared in discussions of domestic space – and in considerations of how it should be laid out, arranged and decorated. According to the architect Robert Kerr, 'a comfortable home is perhaps the most cherished possession of the Englishman'.[20] While Kerr's treatise dealt mainly with comfort from the point of view of architectural design and the organization of space, an increasing number of publications suggested that domestic management was fundamental to comfort. In 1866, for example, the advice writer Mrs Warren published *Comfort for Small Incomes*, a follow up to her previous book *How I Managed my House for £200 a Year*.[21] The implication of the book was that comfort was possible for the lower-middle classes, if wives and housekeepers were able to manage their resources effectively. Warren's manual was part of a growing body of domestic advice literature published in the second half of the nineteenth century that placed the responsibility for the provision of domestic comfort on the shoulders of Victorian women.[22] This link between women and domestic management was not new – but the growth in domestic advice manuals in this era articulated the notion more strongly and circulated it to a larger audience. As Deborah Cohen has shown, in the final decades of the nineteenth century, domestic and decorative advice literature was increasingly dominated by female writers, who used the genre to express a new professional identity.[23] This led to a more powerful statement of women's role as homemakers, and their importance. Mrs Arthur Stallard, for example, writing in the early twentieth century, began *The House as Home* with: 'Man never was, and never will be, a home-maker; that greatest of all powers, to my mind, is vested solely in woman.'[24]

How did advice writers relate women's role as domestic managers to the provision of comfort? According to some commentators the success or failure of a marriage could rest on the wife's ability to create the right kind of home for her husband. Mrs Haweis, another advice writer, offering advice 'to my daughter', sees the key reasons for marital failure to be dismay and distress, 'when the man finds that is idol does not know how to use his money to supervise his comfort'.[25] In this writer's view, the provision of comfort in the home was a service role performed by women, for men. There was a patriarchal expectation that a wife would perform as a domestic manager, and deliver comfort, largely for the benefit of her husband. However, quite often there was also an expectation that men and women would work together to create a comfortable home appropriate to their level of resources. John Kirton's *Cheerful Homes*, describes 'John and Mary' a typical lower-middle-class couple, who 'after meeting with what the circumstances of their position will enable them to pay for … spend their evenings in visiting different shops to purchase such articles of furniture, crockery, &c., as will be required to make them comfortable.'[26] As studies of the eighteenth century have shown, domestic cooperation was not specific to the nineteenth century – there seems to have been a longstanding expectation that the acquisition of goods for the home was a matter of negotiation between husbands and wives.[27] But comfort was not just about material provision and efficient organization. Emotional investment was viewed as essential – and this was seen as feminine. According to *Home Chat,* an ideal young wife was a good homemaker because of her emotional investment in her environment: 'Home – the sense of possession – that it is HER OWN HOUSE – appeals to her. She takes a delight in making it pretty and nice and comfortable. It is hers – to do with what she likes with … And Dick sees – and loves her ten times more for her dear housewifeliness.'[28] For this writer it was the individual personality of the wife, her emotional investment and her pleasure in the home that underlay the provision of comfort. Here, the provision of comfort is clearly not simply about material necessities but requires a feminine emotional investment as well as consensual cooperation between husband and wife. Creating comfort was about producing the right kind of marriage as much as a material space.

The growth in household management manuals was accompanied by an increase in books that gave instructions on home decoration. In the second half of the nineteenth century, the decorative excesses of the mid-Victorian home – its heavy furniture, crowded drawing rooms and parlours, and dark, dust catching drapery – were increasingly criticized by design reformers, who often wrote advice on home decoration.[29] In this new critical discourse the idea of comfort was often invoked – and used to express dismay at cluttered drawing rooms. Here, the word comfort was being used in a physical and material sense (although there was an underlying acknowledgement that physical discomfort led to emotional discomfort). Both female and male writers referred to the home in this way. For example, the advice writer Florence Caddy wrote of 'that truly English love of superfluous comforts that we mistake for civilisation'.[30] But it is noticeable that criticism often focused on drawing rooms and bedrooms – the spaces most strongly associated with women and femininity.[31] Some writers made a direct equation between women, femininity and the apparent discomforts of the mid-Victorian home. The architect and furniture designer Charles Locke Eastlake's book, *Hints on Household Taste,* was first published in 1868. For Eastlake, it was the uninformed woman, ignorant of the 'simplest and most elementary principles of decorative art'[32] who lay behind what he saw as the appalling decoration to be found in middle-class drawing rooms. He continued: 'Young ladies who may find this difficult to understand, should remember that they recognise the selfsame principle in a hundred different ways on matters of ordinary and even conventional taste.'[33] Eastlake drew on an older critique of female consumption, established in the early modern period – that portrayed female consumers as frivolous and wasteful.[34] Here this was rearticulated for the Victorian age – in response to the perceived decorative excesses of the nineteenth-century drawing room. Like the writers of domestic advice literature, Eastlake recognized the importance of women's role in creating the home – but rather than providing comfort, he believed that they undermined it.

Despite these critiques there is some evidence that mid-Victorian furnishings, dense decoration and heavily draped interiors persisted well into the early twentieth century.[35] Moreover, turning to different sources, it becomes clear that for some Victorians comfort lay not in artistic taste or even practical utility but was more strongly rooted in the emotional and personal meanings attached to their immediate environments. Mrs Orrinsmith, writing for the *Art at Home* series in the 1870s, singled out the 'ordinary lower middle-class drawing-room' for particular criticism as the epicentre of 'showy discomfort', overly formal and off-putting and cluttered with small tables and chairs with spindly legs.[36] However, for children who grew up in these homes, the emotional resonance of the domestic interior could override stylistic criticisms. Such recollections were often gendered. Philip Gibbs, the son of a civil servant with a large family, remembered his mother's drawing room in the 1870s was a haven of comfort, with both a physical and an emotional dimension:

> 'Yet somehow of other he and my mother fed us, clothed us – seven of us – and provided, by some miracle, a well-furnished home, in the comfortable mid-Victorian style. I can remember still the drawing room with its comfortable cabinets and what-nots, and a series of water-colours by a well-known artist of that time, and my mother's priceless possession, the grand piano, on which she played adorably.'[37]

Orrinsmith would have given the cabinets and what-nots short shrift. But for Gibbs it was precisely these things that constituted comfort – his memories of the drawing room created by his mother, in 'comfortable mid Victorian style' – had a great deal of emotional power, and had become a site of nostalgia, symbolising 'a world that has passed'.

Autobiographical writings tend to focus less on the qualities of the physical environment, but often used comfort to signify a feeling of emotional security arising from personal relationships. Male writers of middle-class autobiographies, recalling their Victorian childhoods, often referred to women as providing comfort in the home. While domestic advice manuals focused on the marital relationship, autobiographies celebrate a wider range of female comforters including mothers, sisters and even landladies. These women were praised for providing domestic order, sustenance and emotional support – comfort was created through the organization of the home and the provision of food but also through physical and emotional presence. Charles Reilly, the son of a Maida-Vale based architect, recalled the conventional gendered hierarchy and emotional order of his family in the 1870s, when he wrote about his father: 'My mother devoted herself to his comfort. He was very much the head of the family. Dinners kept waiting for him till 11 in evening – no one allowed to have anything first, youngsters barely allowed to speak to him'.[38] Motherless Methodist minister's son William Dawson found his main source of emotional support in his half-sister

Georgiana, who also did the bulk of household work in the family home in the 1860s: 'my half-sister Georgiana often sat beside my bed, comforting me after the mischances of the day'.[39] A.C. Deane, when recounting his time as a student at Clare College Cambridge in the 1880s, also notes: 'I was extremely comfortable in Bridge Street, with agreeable fellow-lodgers and an excellent and devoted land lady – specimens of whose accomplished needlework still ornament my hall here at Windsor'.[40] Comfort was secured by the landlady's good household management and care – materialized in hand-worked goods that the young man continued to treasure in later life. In these accounts the acts of female comforters were presented as important in the emotional lives of male writers. The emphasis was on female labour to provide comfort, but the result was a shared emotional world in which, ideally, both men and women felt secure and at ease.

Comfort in the drawing room

We will now return to the drawing room, which, according to Mrs Panton, was the central location for the creation of the marital relationship and the enactment and creation of comfort through the 'proper drawing room air'. Mark Girouard has pointed to the increased use of the drawing room in the country house at the late eighteenth and early nineteenth centuries. The name 'drawing room' came from the idea that the room would be used by the ladies of the house for 'withdrawing' after dinner, leaving the gentleman to enjoy their port and to air subjects considered unsuitable for ladies.[41] The room was thus associated with gendered use of space and certain expectations about moral and social behaviour. It is not clear at what point the drawing room became a fixture beyond the homes of the elite. Throughout the nineteenth century, middle-class homes were divided with increasing rigour. There was a shift towards greater segregation and specificity in house planning.[42] Late-seventeenth- and eighteenth-century inventories from middling sort London homes sometimes labelled dining rooms, drawing rooms and parlours, but many inventories did not distinguish between rooms, simply referring to them as 'chambers'.[43] By the mid-nineteenth century rooms were increasingly named after a specific function.[44] Advice manuals of all kinds tended to assume that the norm for middle-class homes was to have at least two reception rooms – which would be designated as the drawing and dining room.[45] In practice, the use of rooms and their naming could be quite diverse. And as Hoskins has shown, the term parlour was also often used to describe the main public living space in a diverse range of homes.[46] Approximately 67 per cent of the inventories and sale catalogues I've analysed included both these rooms. There was some variation within this, particularly on the borders of the middle-class group. Across the country, 'sitting room' was often used to describe rooms in the homes of farmers or shopkeepers.[47] However, the evidence suggests that across England the middle classes developed shared domestic practices for labelling and using these spaces. The shared cultural emphasis on the importance of the drawing room in the home is also borne out by the frequency with which it was photographed. Approximately 60 per cent of the images of domestic interiors from before 1910 held at the Greater Manchester Record Office show a drawing room or sitting room.[48]

The drawing room, the most public room in the house and often the most heavily decorated, was viewed as the wife's special responsibility.[49] Virtually all domestic manuals stress the middle-class femininity of this space. Mrs Haweis describes how even the most meagre sitting room can be given 'that indescribable "Lady's" look'.[50] Jennings writes that 'the whole atmosphere of the room is changed by the refinements of woman's subtle spell'.[51] Kerr describes it as 'entirely ladylike'.[52] In particular, the drawing room and dining room were designated feminine and masculine respectively.[53] The distinction reached its zenith in the 1880s and 1890s.[54] Advice writers viewed the dining room as a masculine space, to be decorated in dark colours and sombre oak. In the two illustrations shown in Figures 5.1 and 5.2, taken from H.R. Jennings' historical decorative advice manual *Our Homes* the delicate French furniture thought suitable for the drawing room is contrasted with the sombre massive oak of the ideal dining room suite. Inventories give us some sense that people were furnishing their homes according to these prescriptions – drawing room furniture tended to be rosewood or walnut, whereas dining room furniture was more often oak or mahogany.[55] Personal diaries also underscore the association of the drawing room with women, and with marriage – as they show us when people chose to create them. Drawing rooms were often absent from the homes of single men such as curates, who preferred to use the additional space for a study.[56] When the surveyor Edward Ryde converted his modest London bachelor quarters for his bride in the 1840s, the transformation was effected principally through the conversion of his work space into a drawing room.[57] In the 1880s, when London artist and his wife Andrew and Aggie Donaldson decorated their home, they too concentrated their efforts on the drawing room.[58]

In order to understand how the drawing room was imagined as a location for comfort and for the creation of relationships between men and women, it is useful to turn to advice writing and novels. Advice literature suggests that a

Figure 5.1 Illustration showing the ideal dining room, from H. J. Jennings, *Our Homes, and How to Beautify Them* (1902).

certain standard of etiquette and behaviour was expected in the drawing room, that contributed to relations between husbands and wives, and created the right kind of emotional atmosphere. Jennings discusses the atmosphere of the drawing room at length, taking a different tone to Panton but to a similar effect – stressing the emotional and behavioural qualities that went into creating comfort. Again, the room is represented as a polite space in which dress codes and certain rules of etiquette apply. Behaviour is thus conditioned by this atmosphere:

> It is thither that you adjourn from the dinner-table to listen to music, or indulge in the lighter intellectual *causeries* to which all can contribute their share. The inferior sex have cast off, for the time, the habiliments of their daily calling, and donned the dress jackets and polished boots of the masculine *demi-toilette*. The grace and elegancy of the surroundings, no less than the fact that it is the ladies' audience chamber, would exact this confession even if it were not convenient and comfortable in itself. You are in a room which expresses a quality *sui generis* – a quality of rest, sociability, and comfort in an artistic framework.[59]

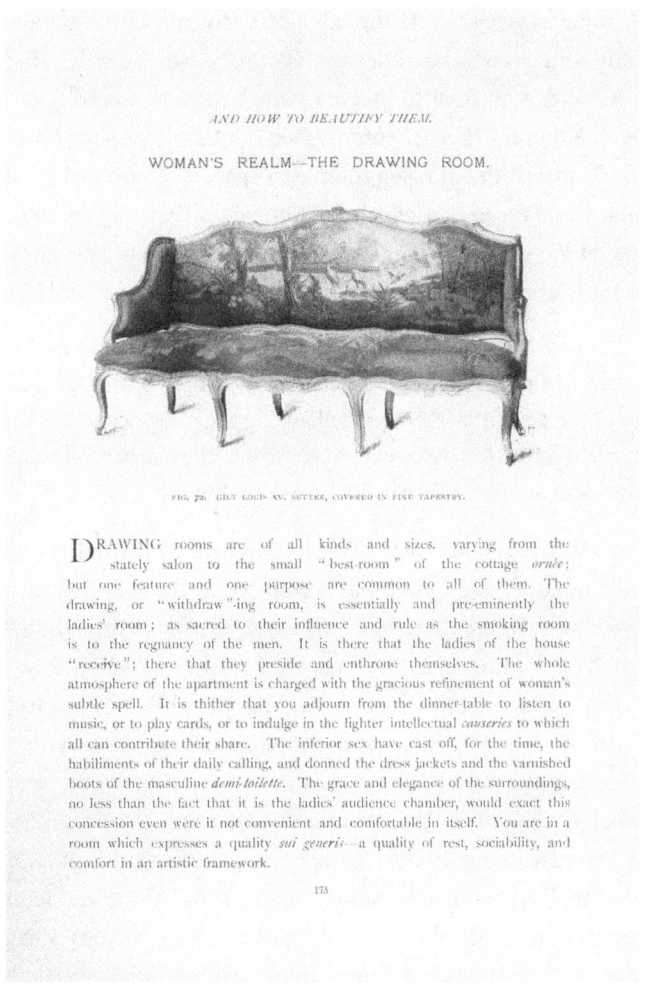

Figure 5.2 Illustration showing the ideal furnishing for the drawing room, from H. J. Jennings, *Our Homes, and How to Beautify Them* (1902).

Like Panton, Jennings was expressing a view of the social role of the drawing room, which had already been established in the mid-century novel. In this view, women are primarily responsible for creating the drawing room – femininity imbues it with 'grace and elegancy' and its special emotional atmosphere of 'rest, sociability and comfort.' Victorian novelists often described the drawing room and utilized the shared cultural expectation that it would be a feminine world. The gendering of comfort in the drawing room was imagined in a different way in Anthony Trollope's novel *Dr Thorne* (1858), however. Trollope depicts middle-aged bachelor Dr Thorne's creation of a drawing room for his niece. Trollope's description of the Thorne home as prepared, 'as though a Mrs. Thorne with a good fortune was coming home tomorrow', underlines the doctor's devotion to his niece.[60] It was customary for Victorian men to prepare their homes to receive their brides, so this statement reinforces Thorne's commitment. But Trollope also shows the reader Thorne's efforts to cast the drawing room as a space of emotional comfort. Using a very similar language to that which Panton would later employ to describe the 'small habits' of the drawing room, Trollope's description of this polite, intimate space is the foundation of a warm relationship between Thorne and his niece:

> He took her first into the shop, and then to the kitchen, thence to the dining-rooms, after that to his and to her bed-rooms, and so on till he came to the full glory of the new drawing-room, enhancing the pleasure by little jokes, and telling her that he should never dare to come into the last paradise without her permission, and not then till he had taken off his boots.[61]

Thorne's especial virtue and sensibility is highlighted by his ability to take on the feminine role of supplying emotional comfort – to the point of encouraging a gendered sociability in the drawing room that was usually thought to be created by the woman of the house. In the imagined world of Trollope's novel, we are presented with a situation in which it was also possible for men to participate in the culture of home making and the creation of comfort in the home, reminding us that the culture of comfort in the drawing room was dependent on consensual participation. The example also helps us to consider how comfort might have been created in homes made up of different kinds of families rather than conventional marital partnerships, and how masculine and feminine roles were sometimes more flexible than domestic advice writers imagined. But finding comfort in the drawing room could also be directly related to female autonomy and emotional security – an issue that I will now explore in relation to one particularly well documented individual.

Frederica Orlebar and her drawing room

Frederica Rouse Boughton, the daughter of a Shropshire gentleman, married Richard Orlebar, the son and heir of a Bedfordshire gentry family in 1861. Throughout her life, intermittently, she kept a detailed and reflective diary. The diary was written retrospectively and in places is more like a memoir than a daily journal – she probably wrote it in the expectation that it would be read by her descendants. The diary often describes Frederica's home and her material surroundings and expresses her notion of comfort in relation to her emotional state. Unlike the young middle-class women often described in domestic advice manuals, Frederica did not set up a brand new home. As a gentry wife, she moved into a pre-established household on a large family estate a long distance away from her friends and family. In her study of women in the country house in the long eighteenth century, Judith Lewis has shown how despite the fact that patriarchal property structures removed women from their family homes, and placed them in a temporary relationship with houses that they neither owned nor controlled, women were consistently able to use the world of goods to establish a sense of self and emotional security within the social space of the country house.[62] The Orlebar diaries demonstrate continuity in the emotional and material practices of elite women, as well as the use of the word 'comfort' to articulate a sense of emotional well-being in an apparently hostile material environment. Frederica's version of comfort is however embedded in the stylistic and social concerns of her age – her desire for a plethora of small objects, table coverings and 'modern elegancies' as well as her fixation with tea time can be seen as products of the mid-nineteenth century. The Orlebar marriage conformed to conventional Victorian expectations about male and female roles, but Frederica's investment in domestic decoration allowed her to assert her sense of self and to move towards a sense of emotional security in her home environment.

On her marriage, Frederica moved away from her family home, Larden Hall, and into Hinwick Hall – a country house on the Orlebar's estates (the main family house, Hinwick House, was occupied by Richard's father). Hinwick Hall was already occupied by Richard's elderly uncle and a body of servants managed by a housekeeper. When Frederica first visited in May 1861 she speculated that the furniture in the drawing room had not been altered in the past thirty years:

> The long stiff sofa with the white cover stretched right across the room, greeting the eye as you entered, and at the end of this by way of continuing the straight line, the tall backed Prie Dieu chair in faded worsted work ... it was also exceptionally stiff and proper in its lines – the effect was altogether too faded and washed out and pale – it wanted warming with rich red furniture and knick knacks – one never could live in such a precise room – it looked such a perfect essence of propriety that you could not but feel if you moved a chair out of its place, and omitted to put it back, it would of its own accord walk statelily [sic] home again and resume its place – back to the wall.[63]

The drawing room was arranged in an old-fashioned manner with chairs with their backs to the wall and sofa and chairs in a straight line – it was pale in colour and lacked the ornaments and decoration that Frederica expected to see in a drawing room. As we saw in the introduction to this book, complaints of this kind – about an overly formal arrangement of furniture – had been made since the turn of the century. So in the 1860s, Hinwick Hall was considerably behind the times. The stylistic solution Frederica proposed 'rich red furniture and knick knacks' – was specifically mid-Victorian (the kind of decoration that was to inspire the ire of decorative advice writers in the following decades). So too was her emphasis on the drawing room which was the first place she devoted her attention to on arrival: 'The first day we set hard to work altering the drawing room, and beginning the mighty change of furniture.'[64] Essential to this task was the support of her sister Frances, recently arrived from Larden, bringing with her furniture and objects from the family home: 'my writing table, my etagere &c all which were a great comfort to me.'[65] These goods were of practical value, but also – as Frederica indicates – an emotional consolation. Even these additions were not enough for these mid-Victorian young women who remained rather shocked by the bareness of the room and the 'wretched, clothless look of the table'.[66]

Eventually, a transformation was effected, which Frederica describes, retrospectively, in the early part of the 1861 diary:

> The drawing room is changed, it is true, and looks with the new pianoforte, (or rather the old friend from Larden) considerably more habitable than of yore – the blue (bird) screen of Aunt Fanny is a great addition, & our wedding writing table ornaments & all the wedding presents about the room give it a much more furnished effect – the three dear old cushions still hold the post of honour on the old sofa, but the sofa itself, being more useful than ornamental, has retired to a less conspicuous position than formerly – what a radical it must think me![67]

Although the diary makes light of the formal living arrangements she was confronted with, at times Frederica was clearly depressed and in low spirits during her first year at Hinwick Hall. In autumn 1861, she writes of a feeling of isolation: 'I felt a stranger among strangers, an inexplicably bitter feeling.'[68] These feelings manifested themselves in her reaction to the interior of her new home and in particular the 'general comfortless ugly look' of her marital bedroom which was eventually transformed.[69] Decorating and re-arranging the drawing room and bedroom allowed Frederica to stake her claim to these conventionally feminine territories and to assert her own comfort in the home.

The Orlebar diaries also allow us to see the relationship between creating a comfortable interior and marriage. Lewis' exploration of the life Frances Talbot, who married Viscount Boringdon and moved to Saltram in Devon in the early nineteenth century, demonstrates that Frances' strong emotional attachment to her new home was closely connected to the success of her marriage – the home became a site for building and expressing intimacy between herself and her husband.[70] The Orlebar home worked along similar lines – although here intimacy was built through the domestic rituals of the Victorian drawing room. Once set up, Frederica Orlebar's drawing room also allowed her to enact the intimacy of married life that she had imagined she would be able to achieve with her husband. During the evening when the husband had finished work or in the late afternoon for the five 'o' clock tea that the drawing room came into its own. Frederica portrayed such drawing-room exchanges as vital to the success of her marriage. Her diaries show her frustration with the formal family practice of eating in the dining room.[71] Later, when the dining room was being cleaned and her husband Richard's uncle was away for the day, she relished the opportunity to eat in the drawing room. Unlike the formal, distant set-up of the dining room, the smaller drawing-room table allowed a closer physical exchange between the couple. Of this arrangement Frederica wrote: 'I felt more brilliantly happy than I had done since the beginning of our wedding tour when I saw our own tea table pitched in the drawing room, with new bread and buns and coffee and eggs on the clean white cloth, instead of the stiff goodboy look of our regular everyday dinner.'[72] The joys of the tea table, and the importance of setting it out nicely, were often stressed by advice writers – Frederica's celebration of this particular meal chimes with a wider emphasis in Victorian culture.[73] John Tosh has argued that in the later part of the nineteenth century the 5 o'clock tea became an overly feminised ritual that men often found uncomfortable.[74] But for this couple, at this point in the century, the fireside tea was a joint emotional investment. Although Richard Orlebar did not keep a diary there is some evidence that he shared the domestic vision constructed by Frederica. Before their marriage, the couple exchanged letters, imagining the cosy fireside where they planned to spend their married lives together.[75] Richard was a consensual participant in these domestic rituals and it is clear that Frederica derived considerable emotional satisfaction from them.

A truly English love of comforts?

In the nineteenth century, creating comfort in English middle-class homes was dependent on a certain level of wealth and material resource. It was often associated with a new style of decoration found in middle and upper-class drawing rooms – furniture was draped with table cloths and antimacassars, mantel pieces were filled with ornaments. When comfort was discussed in relation to the home and domestic management it was understood that women were critical to its production – both in terms of domestic management and emotional labour. The expectation that women would create comfort by managing the home was not new in the nineteenth century. But the idea was articulated more widely and more clearly across a growing range of print media in which female voices were increasingly present. The drawing room was a key site for the creation of comfort through adherence to social etiquette and polite behaviour. A good emotional atmosphere in this space was an essential component of the right kind of marital relationship. The creation of comfort can be viewed as a female service role, but it could underpin female empowerment in the home. Women could use it to acclimatize to domestic space, especially if they were moving into their husband's familial home. As in the early modern period, women continued to use the material world around them to create emotional stability and a sense of comfort while existing within patriarchal property structures beyond their control. But the nineteenth century turn towards fuller domestic decoration, the creation of more overtly feminised spaces such as the drawing room, and rituals such as the 5 o'clock tea provided a new means for them to do so.

In the context of this volume, it is worth asking how far these ideas and domestic practices were specific to England – how far was the pursuit of comfort as a cultural as well as physical ideal, with a specific emotional resonance realised beyond the nation's borders? Some historians have argued for an increasingly homogeneous bourgeois culture in nineteenth-century Europe.[76] While a large-scale comparative study has yet to be undertaken, individual studies of England, Germany, Spain, Italy and Sweden reveal some broad similarities in cultural development. The celebration of virtuous domestic life, in which husband and wife adhered to gendered roles and brought up children in the Christian home, became the touchstone of middle-class families across vast geographical areas. Although this did take place on different timescales as the emergence of these ideals tended to be linked to industrialization.[77] We can certainly see a transnational emphasis on the female homemaker – the English 'Angel in the House' was known as the 'Femme de Foyer' in France while the Spanish middle classes celebrated the 'Angel del Hogar'.[78] While English and European homes were often structured and laid out differently (the English preferring houses to apartments), the English emphasis on the drawing room was paralleled by the celebration of public living spaces in European homes – in Spain a division developed between the gabinette (family room) and the sala principal (public room), while in Italy there was a new emphasis on the 'salotto' a room for entertaining that conveyed the family's social standing.[79] Increasingly, it was possible to buy similar or the same goods across the West. In industrialised nations there was a growth in the mass production of domestic goods as well as the development of networks required for their distribution.[80] A traveller who spent time in nineteenth-century English, French, German, or American homes of the middling sort would certainly have been struck by some similarities in how they were laid out and furnished. The densely furnished living room, that the English associated with comfort, was to be found across Europe.

Yet the specific emotional nuances of comfort and its creation through homemaking may have been distinctively English. Certainly English writers believed this was something unique about their own culture – as we saw in the introduction to this volume these ideas had a wide currency in the 1810s and 1820s, and were still strong in the 1860s.[81] Contemporary commentators also argued that the social practices of the drawing room were unique to Britain. In *House Architecture* (1880) the architect J. J. Stevenson writes: 'In accordance with our custom, which Continental nations consider barbarous, of the ladies retiring to it after dinner, and leaving the gentlemen to drink by themselves.'[82] Across Europe, an awareness of this cultural distinctiveness is evident in perceptions of different national styles. The practice of clustering things together was associated with an English idea of comfort.[83] The French also sometimes furnished their homes in what they perceived to be the English fashion. 'Le Hall' became a popular room in chateaux, apparently following an English form, yet the resulting room (primarily a sitting space that offered a more relaxed environment than the salon) actually bore little resemblance to the English room of the same name.[84] Gendered ideals were often subtly different – in France ideal womanhood was framed in the context of appropriate participation in the Republican state.[85] According to Mark Girouard, the French aristocracy were less obsessive about dividing up space between the sexes than the English.[86] Instead of being a separate male space, the 'salle de billiard' in the French chateau extended out from the salon.[87] The Spanish bourgeoisie also had gendered spaces – but invested more in male spaces such as studies (women's bedrooms were sparse in comparison).[88] From a range of new studies of inventories, we are beginning to have a sense of the different layouts, contents and cultural meanings of middle-class homes in different places – but we still know less about how contemporaries thought and felt about them, based on personal reflective sources such as diaries, letters and autobiographies.[89] Until we have a more comprehensive comparative study of women's responses to the home in nineteenth-century Europe it is difficult to draw firm conclusions – only at this point will we be able to say how far the ideal of comfort and its emotional domestic practices were 'truly English'.

Notes

1. J. E. Panton, *From Kitchen to Garret: Hints to Young Householders* (London: Ward & Downey, 1873), 86.
2. John Gloag, *Victorian Comfort: A Social History of Design from 1830-1900* (London: Adam and Charles Black, 1961), esp. 'The philosophy of comfort', xv–xvi.
3. John E. Crowley, *The Invention of Comfort: Sensibilities and Design in Early Modern Britain and Early America* (Baltimore: Johns Hopkins University Press, 2001); Joan DeJean, *The Age of Comfort: When Paris Discovered Casual – And the Modern Home Began* (London: Bloomsbury, 2009).
4. Annik Pardailhé-Galabrun, *The Birth of Intimacy: Private and Domestic Life in Early Modern Paris* (Cambridge: Polity Press, 1991), 215.
5. Katherine C. Grier, *Culture and Comfort: People, Parlors and Upholstery 1850-1930* (New York: The Strong Museum, 1988), 103, 105.
6. See Lesley Hoskins, 'Reading the inventory: Household goods, domestic cultures and difference in England and Wales, 1841-81' (Unpublished PhD thesis, QMUL 2011), 123, 140, 166 and Margaret Ponsonby, *Stories from Home: English Domestic Interiors, 1750-1850* (London: Routledge, 2006), 1, 3, 26, 46, 60, 63, 97, 106, 109, 116–17, 119, 124.
7. Hoskins, 'Reading the inventory', 268–70.
8. Crowley, *Invention of Comfort*, 260–89.
9. Judith S. Lewis, 'When a house is not a home: Elite English Women and the Eighteenth-Century Country House', *Journal of British Studies*, 48 (2009): 336–63.
10. For example, Patrica Branca, *Silent Sisterhood: Middle-Class Women in the Victorian Home* (London: Croom Helm, 1977).
11. Amanda Vickery, 'His and hers: Gender, consumption and household accounting in eighteenth-century England', *Past and Present*, 1 (supplement 1) (2006): 12–38.
12. Deborah Cohen, *Household Gods: The British and their Possessions* (London: Yale University Press, 2006), 89.
13. Amanda Vickery, 'Women and the world of goods: A Lancashire consumer and her possessions 1751-81', in J. Brewer and R. Porter (eds), *Consumption and the World of Goods* (London: Routledge, 1993), 274–301.

14 Lewis, 'When a house is not a home'.
15 Jane Hamlett, *Material Relations: Families and Middle-Class Domestic Interiors in England, 1850-1910* (Manchester: Manchester University Press, 2010), 'Chapter two: Material marriages'.
16 The original survey comprised a study of thirty-two decorative and domestic advice manuals, as well as supporting publications and magazines; c.200 autobiographies, mainly reflecting on Victorian childhood and published in the early-to-mid twentieth century, c.200 inventories and sale catalogues (sporadic, individual survivals drawn from a nationwide survey of local archives and record offices) and around thirty diaries and collections of personal papers and photographs. See Hamlett, *Material Relations,* 'Introduction'.
17 See for example Stephanie Olsen and Rob Boddice, 'Styling emotions history', *Journal of Social History*, 51, no. 3 (2017): 476–87.
18 *Cassell's Household Guide: Being a Complete Encyclopedia of Domestic and Social Economy and Forming a Guide to Every Department of Practical Life* (London, 1869–71), 110.
19 Lewis R. Farnell, *An Oxonian Looks Back* (London: Martin Hopkinson, 1934), 3.
20 Robert Kerr, *The Gentleman's House: Or, How to Plan English Residences, from the Parsonage to the Palace* (London: John Murray, 1864), 69.
21 Mrs Warren, *Comfort for Small Incomes by Mrs Warren, author or 'How I managed my house for £200 a year'* (London, 1866).
22 Hamlett, *Material Relations,* 84–90.
23 Cohen, *Household Gods,* 106–10.
24 Mrs Arthur Stallard, *The House as Home: Written for Those Who Really Matter in All Classes* (London: Andrew Melrose, 1913), 7.
25 *The Art of Housekeeping*, 3
26 John W. Kirton, *Cheerful Homes: How to Get and Keep them Or, Counsels to those about to Marry and Those Who Are Married* (London, 1882), 47.
27 For discussion see Vickery, 'His and hers', 12–38 and Amanda Vickery, *The Gentleman's Daughter: Women's Lives in Georgian England* (London: Yale, 1998), 72.
28 'Home Possession: An Article on Young Wives', *The Home,* xx, no. 251 (6 January 1900): 152.
29 Emma Ferry, 'Advice, Authorship and the Domestic Interior: An Interdisciplinary Study of Macmillan's 'Art at Home Series' 1876-1883 (Unpublished PhD thesis, Kingston University, 2004).
30 Florence Caddy, *Household Organisation* (London, 1877), 165–6.
31 Caddy, *Household Organisation;* Mrs Orrinsmith, *The Drawing Room: Its Decorations and Furniture* (London: Macmillan & Co., 1877); Charles L. Eastlake, *Hints on Household Taste in Furniture, Upholstery and other details* (London, 1878).
32 Eastlake, *Hints on Household Taste,* 9.

33 Ibid., 68.
34 Vickery, 'Women and the world of goods', 277.
35 Hamlett, *Material Relations*, 221–2.
36 Orrinsmith, *The Drawing Room*, 2.
37 Philip Gibbs, *England Speaks* (London: William Heinemann Ltd., 1935), 6.
38 C. H. Reilly, *Scaffolding in the Sky: A Semi-Architectural Autobiography* (London, 1938), 8.
39 W. J. Dawson, *The Autobiography of a Mind* (London, 1925), 31.
40 Anthony C. Deane, *Time Remembered* (London, 1945), 48.
41 This was originally an aristocratic practice. M. Girouard, *Life in the English Country House: A Social and Architectural History* (London: Yale University Press, 1978), 99–100.
42 Stefan Muthesius, *The English Terraced House* (London: Yale University Press, 1982), 45.
43 See J. Hamlett, Geffrye Museum report 3, July 2004 and J. Hamlett, Geffrye Museum report 4, August 2004.
44 Late-eighteenth-century inventories and sale catalogues tended to list rooms on a basis of their position in the house, '2 pairs of stairs right hand' etc, rather than naming them by function. See J. Hamlett, Geffrye Museum report 5, September 2004.
45 Jane Hamlett, '"The dining room should be a Man's Paradise, as the drawing room is a Woman's": Gender and middle-class domestic space in England, 1850-1910', *Gender and History*, 21, no. 3 (2009): 576–91.
46 For a discussion of the varied uses of rooms, especially in relation to different working roles, see Lesley Hoskins, 'Stories of home and work in the mid-nineteenth-century', *Home Cultures*, 8, no. 2 (2011): 151–69.
47 Valuation of the household furniture, plate, linen and other effects the property of the late Mr Joseph Beaumont of Brantingham Wold, 1860, East Riding of Yorkshire Archives, DDBD 8 45; Inventory of Thomas Hogget, Gilesgate, 1871, Durham Record Office, D/SJ C103; Inventory of furniture and effects at 17 Oakfield Terrace, Gosforth occupied by John Greenwell, 1907, Durham Record Office, D/Gw 43; Catalogue of sale of wheelwright's and carpenters equipment at Mottisford, Romsey, sold by Mr James Jenvey, on behalf of late Mr Alfred Jewel, 1904, Hampshire Record Office, 4M92/N/186/12; Poster advertising household furniture, property and effects of Mr Dumper of Hyde Street, Winchester, to be sold by auction 1862, Hampshire Record Office, 1M90/12; Sale poster for goods of Maria Pritchard of Winchester, spinster, 1888, Hampshire Record Office, 67M92W/19/18.
48 The Greater Manchester Record Office Documentary Photography Archive comprises the largest collection of family photographs in the UK, including 800,000 images.
49 The expectation that the drawing room would be the responsibility of the wife was repeatedly stated in publications across the period. J. C. Loudon, *The Suburban*

Gardener and Villa Companion (London: Longman, Orme, Brown, Green & Longmans, 1838), 101; Kerr, *The Gentleman's House*, 107; Robert Edis, *Decoration and Furniture of Town Houses* (London: Kegan Paul & Co., 1881), 193.
50 *The Art of Housekeeping*, 29.
51 H. J. Jennings, *Our Homes, and How to Beautify Them* (London: Harrison and Sons, 1902), 173.
52 Kerr, *The Gentleman's House*, 107.
53 Juliet Kinchin, 'Interiors: nineteenth-century essays on the 'masculine' and 'feminine' room', in Pat Kirkham (ed.) *The Gendered Object* (Manchester: Manchester University Press, 1996), 13–15.
54 Mrs Haweis, *The Art of Housekeeping: A Bridal Garland* (London: Sampson Low & Co., 1889), 29.
55 Hamlett, 'The dining room should be a Man's Paradise.'
56 Memorandum of Furniture at Curate's House, Pember, 1891, Berkshire Record Office, D/Eby Q 39.
57 Diaries of Edward Ryde, 11 January 1848, Surrey History Centre, 1262/5.
58 Diaries of Andrew and Aggie Donaldson, 4 September 1872, London Metropolitan Archives, F/DON/1; 27 August 1877, London Metropolitan Archives, F/DON/4.
59 Jennings, *Our Homes*, 173.
60 A. Trollope, *Doctor Thorne* (London: W Clowes and Sons, 1858), vol. 1, 61.
61 Ibid., 69.
62 Lewis, 'When a house is not a home.'
63 Diary of Frederica Orlebar, 28 May 1861, Bedford and Luton Archives and Local Studies Centre (B&L), OR2244/6.
64 17 October 1861 B&L, OR2244/6.
65 Ibid.
66 Ibid.
67 28 May 1861, B&L, OR2244/6.
68 17 October 1861, B&L, OR2244/6.
69 Ibid.
70 Lewis, 'When a house is not a home', 359.
71 17 October 1861, B&L, OR2244/6.
72 14 April 1862, B&L, OR2244/6.
73 Panton, *Kitchen to Garrett*, 89–90.
74 John Tosh, *A Man's Place: Masculinity and the Middle-Class Home in Victorian England* (London and New Haven: Yale, 1999), 170–94.
75 Hamlett, *Material Relations*, 92.
76 Jesus Cruz, *The Rise of Middle-Class Culture in Nineteenth-Century Spain* (Baton Rouge: Louisiana State University Press, 2011), 3.

77 See Ibid.; Leora Auslander, 'Reading German Jewry through Documentary Photography: From the Kaiserreich to the Third Reich', *Central European History*, 48 (2015): 300–34; Michelle Facos, 'The Ideal Swedish Home: Carl Larrson's Lilla Hytannäs', in Christopher Reed (ed.), *Not at Home: The Suppression of Domesticity in Modern Art and Architecture* (London: Thames and Hudson, 1996), 7–15; Ovrar Löfgren, 'The Sweetness of Home: Class, Culture and Family Life in Sweden', in Setha M. Low and Denise Lawrence-Zúñiga (eds), *The Anthropology of Space and Place: Locating Culture* (Oxford: Blackwell, 2003), 142–59; Ann Hallamore Caesar, 'Women and the Public/Private Divide: The Salotto, Home and Theatre in Late Nineteenth-Century Italy', in Perry Willson (ed.), *Gender, Family and Sexuality: The Private Sphere in Italy, 1860-1945* (Basingstoke: Palgrave Macmillan, 2004), 105–21.

78 Mary Nash, 'Un/Contested Identities: Motherhood, Sex Reform and the Modernization of Gender Identity in Early Twentieth-Century Spain', in Victoria Lorée Enders and Pamela Beth Radcliff (eds), *Constructing Spanish Womanhood: Female Identity in Modern Spain* (New York: State University of New York Press, 1999), 25–50, 28.

79 Cruz, *The Rise of Middle-Class Culture*, 73; Caesar, 'Women and the Public/Private Divide', 105.

80 John Benson, *The Rise of Consumer Society in Britain 1880-1980* (London: Longman, 1994); Grier, *Culture and Comfort*, 9.

81 Hoskins, 'Reading the inventory', 270.

82 John J. Stevenson, *House Architecture* (London: Macmillan & Co.), 57.

83 Cruz, *The Rise of Middle-Class Culture*, 60.

84 Mark Girouard, *Life in the French Country House* (London: Cassell & Co., 2000), 307–8; Also see Hermann Muthesius, *The English House Volume III: The Interior* (Frances Lincoln Ltd, London, 2007, first published in 1904, first published in English 1979), 169.

85 Lisa Tiersten, *Marianne in the Market: Envisioning Consumer Society in Fin-de-Siecle France* (London and Berkeley, University of California Press, 2001).

86 Girouard, *Life in the French Country House*, 309–11.

87 Ibid., 311.

88 Cruz, *The Rise of Middle-Class Culture*, 89.

89 For example, Marie Ulvang's recent research project on inventories in Sweden. https ://backdoorbroadcasting.net/2017/12/marie-ulvang-farmerfication-housing-and -the-housework-in-rural-sweden-1850-1910/

Object in focus 3:
The ideal home in 1732: The Uppark Dolls' House as a study in comfort

Patricia Ferguson

As an elite woman, Lady Sarah Fetherstonhaugh, née Lethieullier (1722–88) would have always known comfort, at least in material terms – how we often interpret it today. Her physical needs were served by the latest technology and a retinue of liveried domestic servants, but as to her emotional well-being, we can but speculate. She had one child, a son, and appeared very close to her Huguenot family, well-established members of London's mercantile elite. In 1746, at the age of twenty-four, Sarah married Sir Matthew Fetherstonhaugh (1714–74), of Fetherstone Castle, Northumberland, an investor in the East India Company and later an MP. The following year he was created a Baronet and purchased Uppark, West Sussex, which they immediately began remodelling, furnishing it with treasures acquired on a two-year Grand Tour. Sarah was one of the first female Grand Tourists.

Among the 'heirlooms', she brought to the marriage was a monumental toy house, known in the eighteenth century as a 'baby-house'. For many years it was displayed at their London home, Dover House in Whitehall, and since about 1774 it has been at Uppark. On the pediment of its façade is painted the Lethieullier coat of arms within a lozenge-shaped escutcheon. According to heraldic protocol, this was used by Sarah before marriage and she never repainted the arms to incorporate those of her husband. Dating to the 1730s, it is one of the most important doll's houses in Britain, the other is at Nostell Priory, Yorkshire.[1] Filled with miniature objects, these 'baby-houses' were made for the pleasure of adult women, but they were also used to teach children, especially girls, in preparation for their marriage and future, managing a grand household. Upper-class women often used them as a form of self-expression, personalizing and decorating their interiors over several generations. With their contents secured by a lock and key, a 'baby-house' was a private sanctuary with a controllable environment, a rare space of one's own in someone else's ancestral home. Role-playing dolls in artificial interactions simulated the social construction of homes, but the small structures are only ever described as 'houses'.

The standards of physical comfort available to the gentry are conveyed by diminutive familiar objects in varying degrees throughout the house. However, just as there is no paradigm for comfort, the notion of an 'ideal home' is also problematic.[2] With its façade recording a three-storied, nine-room Palladian mansion with a rusticated ground floor, the 'baby–house' is raised on an arcaded plinth.[3] The low-ceilinged public spaces on the ground floor include a working kitchen leading off the entrance or staircase hall, which opens into a 'parlour' or informal family room. The enfilade on the first floor, with the highest ceilings, includes a Saloon or withdrawing room, beside the dining room, leading on to a State Bedroom. This is now adapted as a lying-in room for postpartum confinement with a doll resting in the grand tester bed under a quilt and the new born in a wicker bassinet. The second or top floor has three bedrooms, differentiated by the colour of their silk bed-hangings. These are the private spaces. The interiors, a uniform stone colour, have not been repainted or wallpapered and there is very little evidence that the house was ever personalized by Sarah.

Figure 5a.1 The Uppark Dolls' House, c.1730. Dimensions: 964.5 x 215 x 925 cm. Uppark House, West Sussex (© National Trust Images/Nadia Mackenzie).

The Uppark 'baby-house' may not have been a bespoke commission, carefully filled with meaningful possessions selected or made with care to reflect Sarah's personality. Instead, it is possible that it was furnished as a set piece by an upholder acting as a decorator and ordering fashionable baby-sized objects from professional craftsmen. There is evidence that 'baby-houses' were often acquired fully furnished with the latest fashions and as such they may have appealed to aspirational parents as overt symbols of wealth and status, but also as an investment, especially as most elite girls were educated at home. The armigerous Lethieulliers although extremely cultured and wealthy were not members of the aristocracy and the 'baby-house' may have been part of their strategic and aspirational self-fashioning.

Alternatively, the house might have been bought second-hand. In 1732, two complete baby houses were advertised for sale by auction in London's broadsheets – a search of eighteenth-century British newspapers online revealed the term just three times – one of which, or both, may be the Uppark 'baby-house'. Firstly, in an anonymous sale of the contents of a large house in Putney, near the Church, 'a very neat Piece of Architecture in Wainscot of a regular elegant Design, being a small House (or Baby-House) furnish'd in a genteel, rich and beautiful Manner'; and secondly, sold on behalf of 'Mrs Savage', a London-based East India goods merchant, 'A Baby House in Wainscot, being a beautiful and large Piece of regular Architecture, consisting of several rooms furnished in an elegant Manner'.[4] Both were auctioned by Christopher Cock (d. 1748), the same auctioneer from whom Sarah's father, Christopher Lethieullier (1676-1736), a director of the Bank of England and the East India Company, purchased Belmont House, their family home in Uxbridge, along with its contents. If acquired second-hand from Cock, there would have been little need to furnish or personalize it, as Maria Edgeworth (1768-1849) observed in her 1798 *Practical Education*, completely furnished 'baby-houses' prove 'as tiresome to a child as a finished seat is to a young nobleman'.[5]

How the Uppark 'baby-house' contributed to Sarah's emotional comfort before and after her marriage is difficult to measure, but its architectural details and objects code the material culture of comfort that marked burgeoning improvements in upper-class daily life. Warmth being among the principle categories of physical comfort, the Uppark 'baby-house' has a decadent nine open hearths, one in each room.[6] These low-breast models, with very simple painted stone surrounds, are consistent in size. They are distinguished only by differently coloured marbling. This inefficient heating system drew the warm air (and in theory the smoke) up and out of the chimney, yet there are no chimney stacks on the roof to explain heating technology and ventilation. In most rooms, the hearth is fitted with a raised grate to improve airflow and a fireback, which radiates heat (see Jandot's contribution to this volume). None were improved with a cast-iron metal liner. Each hearth has its own set of shovels, pokers, and tongs, as if to authenticate the presence of heat. There are also two bed warmers, one in silver and the other ivory, both with turned wooden handles. As Ilmakunnas argues in her chapter in this volume, carpets and floor coverings added additional warmth and insulation to a room, yet only one survives in the 'baby-house' because, at mid-century, they were not yet commonplace. The large example in the Saloon offered comfort when sitting for extended periods.

The hearth fire also provided light. Here, it was enhanced by candles (heavily taxed from 1709 until 1831) with each room supplied with a pair of brass wall lights placed above the chimney. Their flames were reflected in the 'landskip glasses', long horizontal mirrors ensuite with overmantel paintings of landscapes; there are no ancestral portraits in the house. In the Saloon, there are six silver wall lights or sconces with shield-shaped backplates for reflection, c.1720–35, by David Clayton, a London silversmith; although, at the time such lighting would have been seen as slightly archaic. The light-coloured walls and ceilings were also easier to illuminate and the latter was protected from soot by glass shades suspended from the ceilings above the wall lights, suggesting the candles may on occasion have been lit. The display of silver in the dining room on the tiered marbled buffet-niche, a feature more commonly found in Scottish interiors, would have also reflected light from the fireplace, the two-branch chandelier and the windows. The façade is lavishly fenestrated with 21 sash windows, providing natural light for activities, ventilation and warmth when the sun came out. Commodious windows, like candles, were also an outward sign of wealth, when from 1696 any house with more than ten windows (and from 1766, more than seven) was subject to additional taxes per window.

Upholstered easy chairs and sofas offering comfort and informality are surprisingly absent from these interiors; they may have simply not survived or perhaps lounging was the antithesis of a perceived code of comportment.[7] A clear hierarchy of comfort is, however, apparent in the six sets of seating furniture, all side chairs, especially in the public area. The kitchen has two turned deal chairs with plank seats; the entrance hall – a waiting room for visitors, servants and workers from the estate, whose comfort was not a priority – has ten banister-back walnut chairs with uncomfortable cane seats (perhaps they originally had loose cushions); and the parlour, an informal sitting room (perhaps a breakfast room) where local gentry and others met with the family, has four chairs made in the same workshop with drop-in upholstered seats. Their degree of comfort provides evidence of the development in specialization in room use among various social strata. The tester beds, too, reveal a remarkable level of detail and added comfort, each having a tufted-mattress (hidden by the silk bed hangings) covered in gingham in imitation of adult-scaled examples.

The contents are far from encyclopaedic and what is absent is also informative. There are no servants' quarters, offices or bedrooms for the dolls masquerading as three liveried footmen, a cook, a housekeeper and a wet nurse; nor are there larders, laundries, storage rooms or a nursery. The needs of servants, who catered to the physical comfort of the family, are excluded from the narrative. There is no library, nor indeed any books for study, an obvious sign of erudition, no writing desks, nor any musical instruments; instead there are four dressing tables with mirrors. There are no chamber pots, commodes or closet stools that might introduce discussions of waste management, sewage disposal or sanitation.[8] The surviving contents therefore offer a very specific reading of comfort, omitting many aspects of what typically made a house comfortable, liveable and homely.

As an expression of the materiality of comfort, the Uppark 'baby-house' is an exquisite object, a luxurious toy, filled with small scale-copies of the fashionable 'necessities' of a comfortable home belonging to an elite woman of the 1730s. This small-scale assemblage also provided emotional comfort to adults (and the children in their care) willing to immerse themselves in its private and intimate world as a place of retreat and the freedom to construct their own personal ideals of home. However, Sarah Lethieullier's apparent lack of aesthetic engagement with the furnishing of the house hints that it did not offer her an outlet for creativity or emotional comfort. It was a doll's house and not her ideal home.

Notes

1. Gervase Jackson-Stops (ed.), *The Treasure Houses of Britain: Five Hundred Years of Private Patronage and Art Collecting* (New Haven and London: Yale University Press, 1985) cat. no. 590.
2. The term references the annual British commercial exhibition, the Ideal Home, which began in 1908, and was a 'demonstration of the best and latest products of the home-maker'.
3. Henry Avary Tipping, 'An Eighteenth Century Doll's House', *Country Life*, 28 December 1912, 936–8; and Christopher Hussey, 'Through the fourth wall: Scenes in a Georgian Dolls' Douse at Uppark', *Country Life*, 6 March 1942, 450–1. The later article used the same photographs.

4   *Daily Journal*, 31 May 1732 and *Daily Post*, 20 December 1732.
5   Maria Edgeworth and Richard Lovell Edgeworth, *Practical Education* (London, 1798), 4.
6   Jon Stobart and Cristina Prytz, 'Comfort in English and Swedish Country Houses, c. 1760–1820', *Social History*, 43, no. 2 (2018): 234–58 at 235 and Marilyn Palmer and Ian West, *Technology in the Country House* (Swindon: Historic England, 2016), see the 'Introduction: the background to technological change in country houses'.
7   Joan DeJean, *The Age of Comfort: When Paris Discovered Casual – and the Modern Home Began* (New York: Bloomsbury, 2009) Chapter 14.
8   There was water supply for closets and baths at Holkham Hall, Norfolk, from the 1730s and at Chatsworth in the 1690s.

Object in focus 4:
Comfort compromised? The 'bachelor box' in Finland at the turn of the twentieth century

Laika Nevalainen

In Finnish periodicals of the late nineteenth and early twentieth century, bachelors' apartments were often described as cold, bleak, lonely, sad, small, dark and empty.[1] Without a wife and a family, bachelors were essentially seen to be homeless. They were portrayed as lacking a home in terms of atmosphere and emotional meanings, but they were also seen to live without the more practical domestic comforts that were associated with a home such as meals or clean clothes. Here, I want to contrast these stereotypes with evidence from bachelors' probates and personal writings in order to discuss the extent to which the domestic comforts of bachelors were indeed limited or compromised. I will examine the different kinds of strategies and practices bachelors employed to achieve different forms of domestic comfort, focusing specifically on a form of bachelor housing called the 'bachelor box'. Domestic comfort functions as an analytical concept with which I refer to the fulfilling of domestic needs, such as eating, sleeping or cleanliness, as well as to feeling at ease and at home.[2]

In both public and personal writings, the term 'bachelor box', or just 'box', was used to refer to a room or a small one- to two-room apartment inhabited by a bachelor alone or together with one or several other bachelors. The room or apartment was either furnished by the bachelor himself or by his landlord. A box was most often associated with students and both male and female office workers. The term was also used by working-class men to refer to renting in contrast to living as a lodger, but here I will focus on more middle-class boxes.

In terms of furniture, a typical box would have contained a sofa or a sofa set, a bed in one form or another, a desk or table, and some form of storage. Despite representations often portraying the dwellings of bachelors as dismal places, evidence from probates demonstrates that bachelors living in box-sized apartments had a variety of items which would have provided them with visual pleasure, homeliness, comfort and warmth. For example, tailor Kalle K.'s probate listed a sofa and armchairs, a rocking chair, sofa cushions, a variety of bedclothes, rugs, pictures, a gramophone, lamps, curtains, a chandelier, crystal vases, a sculpture and a stuffed bird.[3]

Temporal and flexible use of space and material culture

The main problem boxes had was the limited amount of space. Bachelors could, however, employ different strategies to help them accommodate more domestic functions in their living spaces. One such strategy was to cluster items to form separate functional spaces within one room. For example, in Kalle K.'s apartment, the main room functioned both as a bedroom as well as a gentleman's room, which was a combination of a study and a living or drawing room for men. In this room, Kalle could use his sofa, desk and bed as the focal points of the separation of relaxing/entertainment from writing/working and from sleeping, and then centre the other relevant items around these points.[4]

Besides space, bachelors used furniture and other domestic items temporally and flexibly in order to achieve a higher degree of comfort. Different types of flexible beds are a good example of a piece of furniture which could be used temporally as well as flexibly to make way for other functions during the day or which could serve several different functions. Such flexible beds included foldable beds or trestle beds which could be set aside during the day.[5] Beds provided one of the easiest areas of domesticity upon which to implement flexibility, as sleeping was mostly temporally limited to a specific and undivided time period. Many bachelors seem to have slept permanently on different types of sofas or chaise lounges, as is apparent from the appearance in several of the probates of chaise longue quilts, pillows or bedclothes. This dual use added domestic comforts into small spaces as they made it possible for bachelors to have both a bed and a sofa. A sofa, in turn, provided a comfortable and relaxing place to sit both for the bachelor as well as his possible guests.

All in all, if we only focus on more 'traditional' items associated with hospitality we can only gain a limited picture of whether or not bachelors were able to host guests in their boxes. Very few of the bachelors who lived in boxes had, for example, a separate dining table, a dinner set or a coffee set, but they usually had at least some domestic items which allowed them to engage in at least some form of hospitality. The absence of an appropriate material culture for formal hospitality was no obstacle to inviting friends over and having a good time. Bachelors made use of whatever piece of furniture that provided comfortable seating, be it a sofa or a bed, or whatever vessel that could be used for drinking.[6] Box hospitality was hospitality which had to accommodate itself within the limits imposed by a smaller apartment without much differentiation possible within spaces or a large variety of different types of glasses, cups or serving ware.

Food and linen

Food and linen represent both domestic comforts (meals, clean sheets and shirts) and the domestic work (cooking and laundry) required to produce them. And exactly because of this two-sidedness, the comforts enjoyed by bachelors could be especially compromised in these respects. Bachelors themselves were not expected to take care of such domestic work, but bachelors living in boxes often had nobody to do this work for them or the material capacity to eat, much less cook at home. The domestic comforts of bachelors were enhanced through the packages of food and linen that their families sent them via the post. Common posted foodstuffs included bread, butter or jam and baked goods such as pies, pastries, cakes and biscuits. Female family members made, mended and washed clothes for their unmarried male relatives. Together with letters, these packages could alleviate homesickness, ease practical domestic problems and help to create a homely atmosphere.[7]

The food sent saved bachelors money but also provided them with foods that they would not otherwise have had: soft bread, pastries and other sweet treats. It gave them a treat or enabled them to provide hospitality to friends, as in the case of Julio R., who served a cake his mother hand sent him to his friends at an afternoon coffee at his apartment.[8] In addition, foods made according to familiar recipes or regional foods that were otherwise not necessarily available where the bachelor lived could physically ease a bachelor's homesickness.[9]

Bachelors, in turn, sent linen for washing or mending back to their parental home which could be hundreds of kilometres away. This exemplifies how domestic tasks were not only a question of money but also of knowhow – knowledge that bachelors often did not and were not even expected to have. Linen constituted the area of housekeeping in which bachelors were most lacking in domestic capital; Julio R. kept sending his laundry to be washed at his childhood home at least until he was thirty-three-years old.[10] Those that could not send their laundry to be washed by their female relatives had to resort to the services of laundry women. Laundry services together with public saunas and baths, different types of diners and restaurants, cafes and clubs, and different types of associations provided bachelors ways to outsource aspects of their domesticity as well as to enjoy comforts associated with home outside their dwellings.[11] In terms of food, bachelors ate at different types of diners, restaurants, bought their food from stalls at markets or from women selling meals from their homes.

Comfort from freedom

While the term box underlined that the dwelling in question was only temporary and not a home in the sense of a childhood or marital home, a box was especially in the case of students most strongly associated with the freedom to do what one wanted.[12] The main comfort of box living can be said to have been living alone and being free from the everyday control of parents or from the familial responsibilities of a married man. In a box, a bachelor was able to express and accommodate his personal interests and likes. He had the freedom to do what he wanted whenever he wanted. Living alone meant living without disturbances or the annoying habits (such as smoking) of a roommate, being able to sleep in peace, and not having to take any other person into consideration in one's domestic practices.[13] Domestic comfort therefore entailed not only experiencing physical comforts and satisfying one's physical needs, but also a mental feeling of being at ease and having one's *own* home.

Notes

1 See for example, Bor, 'Meidän lähimmäisiämme', *Oulun ilmoituslehti*, 8 February 1903, 2–3; Olli, 'Kirje Kuopiosta', *Uusi Savo*, 11 February 1899, 2–3; Adolf Paul, 'Sydämen halvaus', *Uusimaa*, 30 January 1899, 3–4; Don Ranunculo, 'Samhällsfördärf och visitkort', *Fyren*, 21 March 1903, 3; A. P., 'Kupiosta', *Päivälehti*, 6 January 1904, 2–3; Heinrich Wels, 'Löytöpaikka', *Tampereen Lehti*, 10 January 1899, 3; J., 'Anna', *Päijänne*, 2 June 1880, 2–3; 'Jatkokertomus', *Aura*, 20 June 1889, 3–4; Vanhapoika, 'Pien vihjaus Lahden likoill', *Lahden Lehti*, 12 August 1907, 2; Vanhapoika, 'Siihen se suli se minun rakkauteni', *Itä-Suomen Sanomat*, 11 January 1898, 3.

2 This article is based on research for my PhD thesis, 'Flexible Domesticities: Bachelorhood, Home and Everyday Practices in Finland from the 1880s to the 1930s' (European University Institute, 2018). The research was funded by the Academy of Finland.

3 National Archive of Finland (KA): Helsingin raastuvanoikeus, Ec:159, 28896.
4 KA: Helsingin raastuvanoikeus, Ec:159, 28896.
5 KA: Kalle Väisälän arkisto, 1 Biografinen aineisto, photo album; V. A. Koskenniemi, *Vuosisadanalun ylioppilas* (Helsinki: WSOY, 1947), 40.
6 The Photograph archive of the Helsinki City Museum: HKA/81, Vapaa-ajanviettoa 1, neg. no 65758.
7 KA: Kalle Väisälän arkisto, 2 Kirjeenvaihto, Kalle to his mother, 30 November 1913; KA: Uuno Pesosen arkisto, 1 Kirjeenvaihto, Uuno to his family, 30 September 1911; 10 October 1911; 23 January 1912; 20 February 1914; 28 October 1915; Åbo Akademi University (ÅA): Lofsdal-samlingen, Mapp 19, letters to Aline Reuter from Julio Reuter, 13 February 1882; 23 October 1884; 27 January 1894; 24 February 1894; 20 March 1894; 3 April 1894; 24 October 1894; 3 February 1895; 21 April 1896; 28 May 1896; The Society of Swedish Literature in Finland (SLS): A665, Mapp 30, Dagbok 5, 4 July 1909. See also Michael Roper, *The Secret Battle: Emotional Survival in the Great War* (Manchester: Manchester University Press, 2010), 10.
8 KA: Kalle Väisälän arkisto, Kalle to his mother, 6 October 1911; 17 November 1913; KA: Uuno Pesosen arkisto, Uuno to his family, 7 February 1912; ÅA: Lofsdal-samlingen, Mapp 20, letters to Aline Reuter from Julio Reuter, 20 March 1894.
9 KA: Uuno Pesosen arkisto, Uuno to his family, 30 September 1911; 21 October 1911; 11 November 1911; 23 January 1912; 7 February 1912; 26 February 1912; KA: Kalle Väisälän arkisto, Kalle to his mother, 29 October 1911; 30 November 1913.
10 KA: Kalle Väisälän arkisto, Kalle to his mother 9 March 1913; 24 October 1913; KA: Uuno Pesosen arkisto, Uuno to his family 19 October 1913; 1 April 1914; ÅA: Lofsdal-samlingen, Mapp 19, letters to Aline Reuter from Julio Reuter, 28 May 1896; Vickery, *Behind Closed Doors: At Home in Georgian England* (New Haven: Yale University Press, 2009), 120–2.
11 Vickery, *Behind Closed Doors*, 75.
12 For example, Ani, 'Fuksin päiväkirjasta: Oi Makarooooooooooni!!', *Ylioppilaslehti* 7B/1936, 123–4.
13 ÅA: Lofsdal-samlingen, Mapp 19, letters to Aline Reuter from Julio Reuter, 26 September 1881; National Library of Finland: Coll.433.2, Päiväkirja III, 22 September 1917; 26 October 1917; 3 November 1917; KA: V. J. Sukselaisen arkisto, Päiväkirja 5, 22 March 1930; 9 May 1930; Jane Hamlett, *Material Relations: Domestic Interiors and Middle-Class Families in England, 1850–1910* (Manchester: Manchester University Press, 2010), 158, 166; Lesley Hoskins, 'Stories of Work and Home in the Mid-Nineteenth Century', *Home Cultures*, 8, no. 2 (2011): 158; David Hussey and Margaret Ponsonby, *The Single Homemaker and Material Culture in the Long Eighteenth Century* (Burlington: Ashgate, 2012), 130, 138.

6

Feeling at home abroad:
Comfort, domesticity and social display on the Netherlandish Grand Tour, 1585–1815

Gerrit Verhoeven

Luxury and comfort feature largely in contemporary tourism. In hotels and B&B's all over the world, guest satisfaction surveys have become standard, with trite questions about the softness of the bed linen (Egyptian cotton obviously), the crispness of the croissants, the spotlessness of the bathroom, the politeness of the staff, and, last but not least, the stability of the Wi-Fi connection. For the Emirates, the Maldives, Turkey, and a series of other destinations, the brand of luxuriousness and comfort even serves as a major attraction to some tourists, who seem to prefer their five-star, all-in resort above tedious excursions to Efeze, scuba-diving in the Red Sea, or the umpteenth visit to a local pottery, tannery, or carpet weaver.[1] Given the importance of comfort in present-day tourism, it is rather puzzling that the subject has been hardly discussed in research on the Classical Grand Tour.[2] Most ink and paper has been spent on more spectacular features of the journey – including the cultural bliss of Roman ruins, Renaissance painting and baroque architecture, as well as salacious debauches such as gambling, carousing and sex – while the more mundane aspects have often been overlooked. Therefore, the everyday humdrum in hotels, inns and apartments was rarely if ever scrutinized in detail.[3] When the topic is broached, classic books on the Grand Tour tend to lapse into timeworn clichés about British nobles spending fortunes on luxurious apartments, exquisite food and rare wines. These gilded youths were escorted by large retinues of liveried footmen, cooks, coachmen and other servants.

Material features of the Grand Tour have often been analysed through the moral lens of aristocratic swaggering and conspicuous consumption.[4] Yet such stereotypes leave all sorts of questions unanswered. What services and facilities –

what level of comfort – did early modern travellers expect when they visited Rome, Paris or London on their Grand Tour? Were they dazzled by hotels and apartments with marble staircases, crackling fires, fine food, and other facilities or were they won over by the flawless service of the innkeeper and his maidservants? How did the yearning for luxury evolve through the ages? Which motives fuelled the quest for comfort? These and other questions are inspired by a surge in historical research on luxury and comfort in early modern Europe. Drawing upon lists of chattels and goods in post-mortem inventories, on receipts, and account books, on everyday entries in diaries and personal letters, and numerous other sources, experts have harvested some compelling evidence that the cry for comfort, domesticity and luxury was indeed becoming louder in the eighteenth century.

There seems to be an agreement that, at least among the upper classes, men and women were increasingly beguiled by cosy armchairs, swish mahogany tables, lush feather beds, smart mirrors, nifty stationary, high-tech mantle clocks, smart coffee sets, and a flood of other fashionable stuff. Furniture played a vital role in the refurbishment of eighteenth-century houses, but owners also hired painters, paperhangers, plumbers, plasterers and upholsters to obtain the most trendy, stylish and comfy interior. Even though the scale, impact and timing of the consumer (r)evolution are still under discussion, it is widely assumed that the lifestyle of (at least) the upper crust changed dramatically in the early modern period, as luxury and comfort were on the march. Furthermore, it has become clear that motivations should not be boiled down to social distinction and emulation alone; the craze for domestic comfort was also powered by a new passion for privacy, a craving for cleanliness, and a stronger emphasis on individual taste.[5]

These findings have unleashed a storm of new debates in consumption and retail history, yet they failed to make a dent in classic writing about the *Grand Tour*. To provide fresh perspective, a large sample of Dutch and Flemish travel accounts, personal letters, receipts and other sources – around 150 documents in total – have been analysed for this paper. Long-term evolutions can be traced, as these manuscripts date from the late sixteenth century to the end of the *Ancien Régime*.[6] Even in this sample, references to comfort, convenience and material well-being are relatively sparse; details about the everyday life in hotels and inns often being eclipsed by more serious matters. Moreover, *comfort(abel)* – in its modern sense of something that contributes to one's physical ease – only cropped up in Netherlandish speech in the nineteenth century, as it was derived from English (or French) around the 1840s. Dutch equivalents such as *gerieflijcke* [something that brings ease and benefit] or *ghemac* [a feeling of well-being] were more frequently used in the eighteenth century,[7] but they rarely if ever crop up in Netherlandish travel journals, as all to straightforward emotional expressions were shunned. Therefore, these sources have to be read against the grain whereby more common complaints about discomfort and unease have to be used as a benchmark to uncover unspoken ideas about luxury, convenience and comfort. Comfort is thus used as an analytical category to harvest ideas and opinions about physical and emotional well-being rather than as a descriptive concept that is found in the sources themselves. With these reservations in mind, Flemish and Dutch travel accounts provide rich detail on the material culture behind the Grand Tour and allow us to nuance the cliché of aristocratic squandering, extravagance and conspicuous consumption. First, the article sets out to examine the features and facilities – warmth, space, hygiene, privacy and elegance – of hotel rooms, inns and apartments, that were deemed essential by early modern travellers. Then the analysis looks into the services provided by footmen, innkeepers, travel guides and other staff. Last but not least, some slow-burn evolutions in the macro-geography of the classic Grand Tour will be traced. How did the quest for comfort and luxury shape early modern travel behaviour?

Facilities

Pieter de la Court, one of Leiden's leading textile barons, embarked on a trip to Paris in May 1700, together with his son and some other companions. They had barely crossed the French border when complaints about the filthy and uncomfortable inns poured in. In Arras, Pieter had to turn the sheets and blankets down, as they were teeming with fleas and other vermin. The inn in Bapaume was portrayed as 'more frowzy than a Dutch pigsty', while the lodgings in Péronne were deemed grimy and grubby (*bevinde in uijterste morsigkeijt*).[8] Travellers had been complaining bitterly about the lack of comfort and hygiene of roadside inns for ages, yet in the late seventeenth century the moaning and grumbling seemed to reach a new milestone. Dutch and Flemish travellers took more offence at dirty sheets, used cups and soiled liveries, as cleanliness turned into an inalienable feature of comfort.[9] New sensitivities percolated slowly but surely through early modern society, as Alain Corbin and others have shown. Cleaning and sanitation were increasingly used as a weapon to overcome the ubiquitous filth, foul odours and eternal grime. Especially in Holland, whose burghers were widely known for their obsession with cleaning, sweeping, mopping and scrubbing, luxury and comfort had virtually become synonymous with spotlessness.[10] No wonder that Dutch travellers exhibited the same sensitivities on the Grand Tour. Not all inns and hotels were lumped together in the same category: complaints about filth, stench and bedbugs were most bitter in isolated regions – the German woodland, the Spanish upcountry, the Apennine mountains, the Norwegian wilds – where accommodation was limited and often primitive, while travellers were much more satisfied about the facilities in large European towns.[11] Metropolises, such as London, Paris, Rome and Amsterdam, were more positively assessed: Pieter de la Court's lamentations about the rancidness of French inns came to an abrupt halt when he entered Paris. Together with his son Allard, he moved into some furnished rooms – *des chambres garnies* – which were labelled as sound and suitable.[12]

From the late seventeenth century onwards, Paris witnessed a boom in its hospitality industry, fuelled by a yearly influx of foreign and local travellers. Daniel Roche estimates that approximately 3,800 foreigners visited the metropolis annually in the late eighteenth century, and they were only the tip of the iceberg. Hotels, restaurants, inns, coffee houses and other venues catered for customers of every rank and station.[13] Top-notch were the *chambres garnies*. Flemish and Dutch travellers were eager to book this luxurious type of accommodation. Jan Teding van Berhout, scion of a wealthy regent family from Delft, checked into a lavish apartment at the *Hotel d'Orléans* in the midst of the pulsating *Faubourg Saint Germain*, where the most elegant *boutiques*, *cafés* and billiard rooms were located.[14] Convenience and satisfaction were, as it is still today, measured in terms of a favourable location.[15] When he was in Rome some months earlier, Berkhout had rented a similar accommodation, as these deluxe apartments popped up in most metropolises in eighteenth-century Europe.[16] Space and privacy were important features in making these furnished flats preferable to standard hotel rooms. In the letters to his uncle Paulus, Jan Teding van Berkhout bragged about the spacious layout of his multi-room *pied-à-terre* in Paris, where he had *une antichambre, une salle* [drawing room], and *une chambre à dormir* [bedroom] at his disposal; the icing on the cake was that Louis – Jan's Dutch personal manservant – had his own quarters.[17]

There is a touch of conspicuous consumption or aristocratic swagger (*adellijke snoeverijen*) in these descriptions, yet other motives should not be ruled out.[18] Domestic comfort was in the eighteenth century ever more equated with privacy.¹⁹ Mansions and manors were increasingly divided into all sort of rooms with a specific function and furnishing (including parlours, dining rooms, offices, libraries, billiard rooms and bedrooms) while the workspace of the servants (kitchens, sculleries, wine cellars, washhouses and the like) was increasingly separated from the master's living quarters by service staircases, entrances and passageways. These architectural developments were fuelled by new ideas about privacy and intimacy.²⁰ Teding van Berhout's letters – and other Netherlandish travel journals – evidence that hotelkeepers shrewdly rode the trend. Facilities had been markedly less luxurious a century before. François and Philippe Zoete de Laecke de Villers, two noble brothers from The Hague, stayed at the *Hotel de Montpellier* in Paris in 1657. They had one bedroom and a small *kabinet* (study) at their disposal. Apparently, there were no separate quarters for their personal footman *Le petit Frans*.²¹

Multi-room apartments not only met new requirements for privacy, but also provided the luxurious setting for socializing. In the eighteenth century, the social aspect of the Grand Tour – making new acquaintances and blending into local society life – became much more important.²² *Salons*, ballrooms, theatres, coffee houses, parks and pleasure gardens were ideal locales to befriend the cosmopolitan upper crust, yet luxurious lodgings served as an indispensable extension. On his classic Grand Tour to Rome in 1790, Louis Engelbert, the sixth duke of Arenberg, frequently hosted some powerful friends in his hotel rooms: princes, cardinals, earls, barons and other bigwigs were invited for dinner. The atmosphere was snug and stylish, as his rented apartment sported a spacious dining room with expensive furniture, silver candlesticks and other amenities. These quarters were also used to play cards in an intimate environment.²³ Luxury, elegance, and taste were no trifle in this matter, but served as admission ticket to the small circle of the rich and the famous.²⁴ On the other hand, these lush apartments functioned as a safe haven – a familiar yet makeshift home in a foreign environment. Each time he felt sick, tired or listless, Louis Engelbert locked himself up in his bedroom and enjoyed some reading.²⁵ When travel journals, personal letters and diaries are read against the grain, they evoke some warm feelings of domesticity and home comfort. Teding van Berkhout admitted to this brother Pieter that he loved nothing better than to settle in his armchair in the morning, sipping from his chocolate, before going out. Even though he does not exactly use words as *gerieffelijck* or *gemack*, material well-being is a much-discussed topic in his correspondence. Given the amount of paper and ink spent on the topic, these little luxuries might have been just as important to Berkhout as the classic sights on the Grand Tour.²⁶

Food was also a classic element to assess quality and excellence.[27] On his way to Paris, Pieter de la Court took a parsimonious meal in Senlis, where the warden served 'a tiny piece of veal and a withered salad'. Complaints were of little or no avail, but when he refused to pay the bill, the landlady threatened to remove the clean sheets from the bed.[28] These and similar incidents make clear that eighteenth-century travellers had a more or less precise idea of the quality they could expect for a certain price. Quality – or the lack of it in this particular case – was the sum of consumer expectations and the perception of the service(s).[29] For most inns and hotels in provincial Europe, the balance tipped to the negative side, as Flemish and Dutch city slickers were revolted by bad food, dirty sheets and other inconveniences. More positive sounds were heard in Europe's urban heartland and especially in the northern metropolises, although even there, complaints were not ruled out. François and Philippe Zoete de Laecke had to eat their meals in the *Hotel de Montpellier* in the communal dining room, where they rubbed shoulders with a taciturn bishop, a greedy almoner, a chatty merchant and a cavalryman. Apparently, the food was fine but overpriced, so François and Philippe moved to a new hotel at the Pont Neuf, where dinner was served in buffet-style, including no less than a dozen varieties of meat.[30] Barely a century later, a new standard had been set. Teding van Berkhout enjoyed his meals in privacy. *Traiteurs* brought the finest delicacies to his apartment. When the food did not please the palate, it was without further ado send back.[31] Later on, when Teding moved to London, he regretted that the high-quality service of *traiteurs*, *rôtisseurs* and other foodies was apparently missing in the British metropolis.[32]

There is obviously an element of aristocratic hedonism and extravagance in these descriptions, yet one has to very careful with moral judgements. Netherlandish elites had a clear-cut idea about the difference between luxury and swaggering. There was a narrow but well-defined line between reasonable comfort – fitting one's rank and station – and excessive profligacy.[33] For Pieter de la Court, the line was crossed when he booked a room in the vicinity of Versailles. Filled with disgust, he portrayed the excessive luxury of the silver tableware and other *folies*, while sourly recounting the exorbitant prices:

> A room for one guilder a night, with a silk blanket for 25 pennies. Wine is one guilder per bottle, while four pieces of beef or ham are sold for four guilders. Even some currants with sugar are one guilder. To make a long story short: we have spent 108 guilders – in words one hundred and eight guilders – today![34]

Even though Pieter ran several textile mills in Leiden and was – even in our terms – a millionaire, he was bewildered by the material overkill and the

Figure 6.1 Punt Jan (after Hubert Gravelot), *Sophia Strikes up a Conversation with the Innkeeper After Dinner Has Been Served* (1749) (Rijksmuseum, Amsterdam RP-P-1911-648).

outrageous prices. When reading between the lines, it is clear that he saw a correlation between the astronomical price level and the rising popularity of Versailles as a Tourist destination with streets packed with hotels, inns and restaurants.[35]

Warmth was also an important box on the checklist. Most inns and hotels were rather primitive in this regard, as hearths were usually situated in the bar or the common room, while bedrooms were unheated. Small wonder that early modern guidebooks, such as Ten Hoorn's *Reisboek door de Vereenigde Nederlandsche Provincien en der zelver aangrenzende landschappen* [*Guidebook for the United provinces and the neighbouring countries and kingdoms*] of 1700, began with some medical advice. Treatments for fleabites, diarrhoea, seasickness and other travel diseases were listed, yet most cures involved colds, sniffles and coughs from cold winds and draughts in coaches, barges and inns.[36] Stoves which would revolutionize domestic heating in the nineteenth century – were still rare in eighteenth-century western Europe, though more common in central and northern European countries (see Chapter 3).[37] Therefore, Corneille-Jean-Marie van den Branden, baron of Reeth [near Mechelen], was thrilled when he stumbled upon a wood stove in Bern, while he crossed Switzerland on his classic Grand Tour in 1715. Mesmerized, he wrote that 'it is warm, without all the drawbacks of an open fire. It felt like eternal spring'. Corneille even made a clumsy sketch of this piece of high-technology in his travel journal.[38] Warmth was also equated with comfort in Teding van Berkhout's journal. To his brother Pieter, he admitted that he spent a fortune on heating his homely apartment in de *Faubourg Saint Germain*.[39] Apparently, a crackling fire was considered a *sine qua non* for home comfort, even though a hearth was not always enough to banish the blistering cold. In the dead of winter, Paulus Teding van Berkhout wrote discontentedly to his favourite nephew that there was frost on his bedroom window when he awoke. Even in his stately home in Delft, freezing temperatures could not always be kept at bay.[40]

Furniture was a last important item to assess the quality of one's lodgings.[41] Unfortunately, most travellers were not very loquacious about the furnishings of their hotel rooms, inns and apartments. Even Jan Teding van Berkhout was short-winded, when he bragged about his studio to his brother Pieter. Although it was absolutely well-furnished and spacious (*le tout très joliment meublé et du grand air*), *Le grand fauteuil* – the large armchair – was the only piece of furniture which was put in the spotlight. Berkhout's choice was hardly surprising as upholstered armchairs were deemed the epitome of comfort in the eighteenth century.[42] Yet, there is a way to approximate what other furnishings were around in order to paint a less hazy still-life, for Teding van Berkhout was literally swamped by letters of family, friends and other acquaintances, who mobilized Jan for proxy-shopping in Paris. Teding ran to-and-fro to purchase a fashionable mirror for Pieter, a table for uncle Paulus, a hearthstone for a Mr Valencis, and a mass of other small merchandise [*emplettes*] which were bread and butter in a genteel lifestyle.[43] These and other letters evidence that Dutch and Flemish elites were already familiar with a deluxe material culture, as they fitted their stately mansions with smart furniture, fashionable wallpaper, heavy curtains and the like.[44] It would have been implausible if Jan Teding van Berkhout had settled for less when he dwelled in Paris on his Grand Tour through Europe. Therefore, it is likely, that the hazy sentence *le tout très joliment meublé* harboured an opulent and comfortable interior.

Services

In the eighteenth century, comfort was – as it still is today – more than the sum of facilities and material culture. Whether travellers were satisfied or felt frustrated about their hotels, inns and apartments also depended heavily on the service of the staff. Innkeepers and their personnel had to be friendly and polite, neatly dressed and helpful.[45] François and Philippe Zoete de Laecke were upset by the discourteous behaviour of their warden in the *Ville de Hambourg* in Paris. The hotel was run by a Regina de Hoeven, who, according to the noble brothers, unremittingly tried to rip them off. Discontented by her behaviour, they nicknamed her Regina de Hoere – *Regina the Whore* – and abruptly moved to the more luxurious *Hotel de Montpellier*.[46] Frequent complaints about the staff included drunkenness, stealing, impolite behaviour, swindle, laziness and other mischief.[47] On the other hand, obliging and efficient personnel added that little extra: they stirred the sense of well-being and ease of their guests and whetted their appetite to return one day. In 1740, the Leiden registrar Jan van Roijen sallied forth on a brief leisure trip (*plaijsier reijse*) to the Austrian Netherlands together with some friends. Apparently, the touring party had made a similar excursion some years before, as the publican in Kontich near Antwerp gave them a warm-hearted welcome, as if they were long-lost friends. In Mechelen, Roijen deplored that they had to stay in *De Keijserin* [the Empress] as their regular hangout was already taken. Friendliness, familiarity and intimacy fostered feelings of well-being and emotional comfort.[48]

Wardens, hotelkeepers, maids, and stable lads were vital to keep elite travellers satisfied, yet the importance of the personal staff was even larger. Flemish and Dutch *burghers* took their domestic servants along when they embarked on a classic Grand Tour or a *pleijsier-reijsje*, but unlike their British counterparts, their retinue was often small and unassuming. François and Philippe Zoete de Laecke relied on *Le petit Frans*, while Teding van Berkhout cherished Louis.[49] Jan van Roijen and his fellow travellers – six men in total – even shared one personal servant on their *reijsie* to the Austrian Netherlands in 1740.[50] Few in number, these footmen were hardly a token of social distinction and conspicuous consumption. Their value lay elsewhere. First of all, these manservants warranted a tailor-made quality standard for domestic service, as they were familiar with the fads and fancies of their masters. They were indispensable for everyday chores: warming the hot chocolate for breakfast, laying out the favourite attire for a ball, running small errands and other odd jobs. Moreover, they were in tune with the new passion of privacy. *Louis* ladled out the soup, decanted the wine and served the treats of the *traiteurs* in Tedings's tranquil and lush apartment, far away from the hustle and bustle of swarming dinner rooms, restaurants and other venues. Last but not least, these footmen were a familiar face in a foreign environment and therefore vital to create an *ersatz* home away from home. Domestic servants like Louis served as an emotional keepsake, which linked the Grand Tour traveller to his family back home. Warm feelings of happiness and satisfaction ooze from the letters of Jan Teding van Berkhout, who portrayed his morning ritual in soft – almost cloying – tones: Louis serving hot chocolate to his master, seated in his comfy armchair, while the *perruquier* [the hairdresser] and other servants did his bidding. *Voilà, comme [ça] vivent cent mille fainéants à Paris.*[51]

New research has evinced that some emotional attachment between masters and servants was not uncommon,[52] yet abroad these bonds tightened. On their long Grand Tour, youths were frequently overwhelmed by homesickness. Manservants such as Louis served as an antidote against these potentially dangerous and even unmanly sentiments. They provided instant emotional and psychological comfort.[53] In the autumn of 1646, Johannes Thijs, scion of a loaded Amsterdam merchant family, set off on a Grand Tour to Italy together with his tutor and servant Job Ludolf. Some months later, their ways parted in Paris, where Ludolf became secretary at the Swedish embassy. Thijs' letters are saturated with sadness and melancholy, as he missed his friendship and support. From Calais he wrote: 'I still have the memory of your presence and actions in my mind, which serves me as a sweet pastime. Yet these imaginings are not so strong that I would not regret the loss of your presence, which is made almost tangible by your letters.'[54]

These emotional bonds were no impediment whatsoever for a more business-like treatment. In the eyes of the masters, the contract with the servant was terminable at all times, when he – or she – failed to meet their (high) expectations. François and Philippe Zoete de Laecke dismissed *le petit Frans* without further ado for breaking the tableware, knocking of the wine and impolite behaviour.[55] Unruly behaviour and incompetence could not be tolerated, as they were incongruous with a yearning for well-being, security and exclusivity.[56]

Even though travellers had their own personal staff, their comfort and well-being were also guaranteed through a complex hire and fire strategy. Detailed bills and receipts bear witness of this commercial machinery behind a classic Grand Tour. Corneille van den Branden had to settle some accounts with the laundress, the barber, the linen maid and some other hirelings before he left Paris for Rome in 1713.[57] Virtually the same expenses were mentioned in the running account of Johan and Cornelis de Witt, who sallied forth on a Grand

Tour in 1645, besides some small fees for porters, seamstresses, stable lads, and more mysteriously, a *comediante* – literally *comedy actress*, which was, in all probability, a codeword for a prostitute.[58] These and other accounts evidence that European metropolises, such as Paris, London and Rome, already sported a fine-grained service industry, which was powered by a small army of occasional labourers and servants, whose main purpose was to fulfil the basic needs of local residents and moneyed travellers. Therefore, comfort was a complex sum of odd jobs, ranging from washing, bleaching and mending the linen to more specialized tasks such as shaving, hairdressing and powdering wigs. During the eighteenth century, the system was further fine tuned. Teding van Berkhout hired a lackey (a certain *Le Roy*) and a coachmen (*Bourguinon*), who could steer his luxurious, rented *berlingo* through Paris. A smart livery was ordered for them.[59] In a letter to Pieter, Jan admitted that he had doubted these expenses: 'And yet, when I see my elegant berlingo, my well-harnessed horses, my coachman in his beautiful attire and my fancy lackey, I believe that this move was absolutely necessary.'[60]

Obviously, there is a hint of debauchery and decadence in these words, yet more practical motives should not be ruled out. In the eighteenth century, Paris had become a whirligig of coaches, waggons, handcarts and other vehicles. For travellers such as Berkhout, who were relatively pressed for time, a rented *berlingo* was probably the fastest, easiest and most convenient option to see all the famous sights. On the other hand, the symbolical value of such liveried servants should not be underestimated. As a hallmark of exclusivity, these liveries opened the doors to the *salons*, balls, casinos and other happenings of the rich and the famous. Most likely, they were a *sine qua non* for foreigners, who tried to immerse themselves into local society life.[61]

On the highest rungs of the ladder, there were the most specialised servants. Teachers and tutors of all sorts were increasingly mentioned in account books, as travellers took private lessons in Italian and other modern languages – English was really a crackjaw – learned to play the cello, the flute or harpsichord, polished their dancing or fencing skills.[62] For Flemish and Dutch travellers, these private lessons turned into a sound and snug alternative for classic academic education. The famous *Academies* at the Loire had been teeming with pupils from the Low Countries in the early seventeenth century, yet their numbers decreased drastically in the later decades.[63] Among other reasons, a passion for privacy took its toll. During the eighteenth century, this new yearning slowly but surely remodelled the top-notch service industry in metropolises. *Traiteurs* and *rôtisseurs* introduced home delivery meals, while fancy *perruquiers* went door-to-door. Teding van Berkhout mentioned another exclusive service in the letters to his brother: 'Once in a while, I have some beautiful saleswomen coming over. I take a look at their merchandise and these girls entertain me for a couple of hours.⁶⁴ There is a dash of eroticism in these descriptions. Where these attractive *mademoiselles* upmarket prostitutes or rather exclusive salesgirls? Sex was a standard ingredient of the Grand Tour and the *modus operandi* was not uncommon – Sterne describes a similar encounter in his *Sentimental Journey* – but most evidence in Teding's letters points to the latter, although it seems likely, that these girls made the most of their sexual appeal to sell the most exclusive snuffboxes, stationery and other novelties without losing their morals. These exclusive services were the latest development in the Parisian retail industry, which – in the midst of the eighteenth century – also sported luxurious *boutiques* with large display windows, mahogany interiors, specialised salesmen and other amenities.⁶⁵

Travel guides were also a highly specialised service which materialized in the early eighteenth century. When he arrived in Paris in 1700, Pieter de la Court hired a Mr Pelt. According to his own account, he had accompanied more than a hundred guests in Versailles over the years, spoke several languages, and knew the ins-and-outs to enter every palace, church and museum in Paris.⁶⁶ These guides

Figure 6.2 John Pettit (after Frederick Byron), *The Amorous Traveller* (1789) (Rijksmuseum, Amsterdam RP-P-1985-49).

could be found in Rome, London and Paris, but also in other European hubs, which were part of the classic Grand Tour itinerary or developed into travel destinations in their own right. Even in the Austrian Netherlands, the service industry was thriving through a yearly influx of Dutch and other foreign travellers who were keen to see the baroque splendour of the Brabantine towns. On his *pleijsier-reijsje* to Brussels in the summer of 1732, the Leiden lawyer Pieter Cornelisz. van Dorp was approached by a Mr Smit. Barely arrived in Antwerp, this professional travel guide offered his services and presented a bottle of burgundy to Dorp and his companions.[67] For travellers who were unfamiliar with their destination, these 'hirelings' certified a flawless and comfortable stay, as they were – in theory – familiar with the most spectacular sights in town, knew the best hotels and inns, and were experienced in local fads and fashions. In times when tourist information was still hard to get – signposts were missing, while guidebooks only offered basic information – they provided instant psychological comfort.[68]

Spaces

Flemish and Dutch travel behaviour saw some fundamental changes in the early modern period. From the late sixteenth century onwards, the classic Grand Tour had been fashionable among upper-crust Netherlandish *burghers*, yet the tide was turning at the close of the seventeenth century. Travel became more seasonal, while shorter trips – tagged as *speelreijsje* [leisure trip], *somertogje* [summer trip] and even *vacance* [vacation] – became the latest vogue. These excursions appealed to men, women and even children; to younger, adult and elderly travellers, to the upper crust, but also to the well-heeled upper-middle class. New destinations emerged. London, Paris and Berlin were up-and-coming, while travellers also eagerly embarked on a *cours pittoresque* along the Rhine. Especially domestic travel – brief excursions in the Dutch Republic and the Austrian Netherlands – was on the rise in the eighteenth century.[69] There were still a few Dutch and Flemish travellers who embarked on the classic Grand Tour, yet their numbers fell, both in absolute and in relative terms. Meanwhile, the standard itinerary was gradually reshaped. Whereas Dutch and Flemish travellers had taken their time to visit a long list of (literally) hundreds of towns and cities in France, Italy and Switzerland in the seventeenth century, the Grand Tour was more and more restricted to a short list of metropolises in the eighteenth century. For example, Teding van Berkhout resided for months on end in Rome, Paris and London, while his stay in Naples, Venice and Florence was also lengthy. French and Italian provincial towns were, by contrast, dashed off in a tearing rush.[70] Louis Engelbert of Arenberg stayed for months in Rome, while a few days were sufficient to see Venice, Florence and Bologna.[71]

Experts have identified a multitude of causes behind this shift. Itineraries and destinations were gradually reshuffled by a new rationale behind the Grand Tour (education gave way to leisure and art), by a landslide in the social profile of travellers (the influx of female, older and middle-class travellers), by a transport (r)evolution (North-West Europe became more accessible through stone-slab paved roads and barge canals), by an upgrade in the cultural hardware (Louis' XIV large-scale investments in urban renewal, flag-ship architecture, painting, music and other arts), and various other aspects.[72] Luxury and comfort have rarely if ever been taken into account, although it is likely, that the yearning for material ease may well have shaped travellers' preferences and choices. It is plausible, that the cry for comfort had some ramifications on the spatial blueprint of early modern travel behaviour. Due to their highly developed service industry, metropolises such as London, Paris, Amsterdam and Rome were able to satisfy these desires and demands, while provincial towns and rural backwaters increasingly fell short of the mark. Eighteenth-century travellers were increasingly drawn to destinations with a hallmark for quality and comfort.

It remains a moot question as to where travellers obtained their information on material comfort. Occasionally, early modern guidebooks provided details on accommodation. Ten Hoorn's 1700 *Reisboek* listed all the inns and hotels in Paris and provided details on price and quality, yet such down-to-earth information was usually missing in early modern manuals.[73] It is more likely, that most travellers relied on word of mouth and referrals by local travel guides, ambassadors, business relations and – even more important – family members and friends, who had made the same trip years before.[74] Travellers like Teding van Berkhout, who painted a vivid picture of the luxurious setting of hotels, inns and apartments in London, Paris and Rome in his letters home, endorsed and fuelled the image of comfort, exclusiveness and material *savoir vivre*, which was inextricably bound to European metropolises. Likely, they acted as a beacon, steering the travel preferences of future generations.[75]

Conclusion: Comfort on the move

What did quality and comfort mean for early modern travellers? Which facilities and services were considered a *sine qua non*? How did the desire for well-being evolve through the ages? These are the questions that this chapter has sought to address. Even if comfort – or its eighteenth-century equivalents such as *ghemack* or *gerieffelijck* – is not explicitly mentioned in the sources, its meaning can be inferred from travel journals, letters and ego-documents by reading them against the grain. First of all, these sources seem to evidence that the need for luxury and comfort on the Grand Tour was definitely on the rise in the late seventeenth and eighteenth century. Fuelled by a series of consumer changes in their domestic environment, Netherlandish travellers became more fussy and fastidious about the facilities and services of hotels, inns and apartments. They were looking for clean, well-heated and spacious, multi-room apartments with luxurious furniture, situated in a central and/or chic district of town. Letters and diaries illustrate that eighteenth-century travellers had well-defined ideas about the basic comfort and amenities they desired and expected, but also knew the price for these luxuries. Yet, comfort was – as it still is today – not only the sum of physical conveniences; physiological and psychological features were at least of equal importance. Comfort and convenience were also influenced by the efficiency of services of personal staff, wardens, innkeepers and hotel managers, and a small army of 'hirelings'. For eighteenth-century travellers, it was clear that the highest level of quality and comfort was to be found in metropolises, such as London, Paris, Rome and Amsterdam, while more provincial towns increasingly fell short in this regard. Due to their well-developed service and hospitality industry, Europe's urban core could easily respond to the newest fads and fashions in home comfort. No wonder that the spatial blueprint of early modern travel behaviour was reshaped accordingly.

This research also provides some valuable insights about the rationale and motives behind the quest for luxury and comfort. Conspicuous consumption and hedonism should not be ruled out completely, yet most travellers had a more complex set of reasons. Moreover, Flemish and Dutch travellers were rather thrifty in this regard. In their search for luxurious apartments, fine food and experienced staff, they relentlessly guarded the thin line between proper comfort and immoral profligacy. Even if they were immensely rich, these *burghers* frowned upon excessive aristocratic swaggering. Alternative motives should not be downplayed. Eighteenth-century travellers were pushed to a new level of comfort by a new passion for privacy, which made multi-room apartments, personal staff and home delivery almost a *sine qua non*. New requirements – in particular the growing importance of the social dimension of the Grand Tour – fuelled the quest for material well-being, as well-furnished apartments and liveried footmen served as an admission ticket to the exclusive circle of local noblemen, officials and other bigwigs. Finally, emotions should not be disregarded. Eighteenth-century travellers dwelled for months on end in foreign metropolises. Hence, they were frequently overcome by home sickness. Comfort – wrapped up in homely apartments with snug furniture, as well as familiar faces of manservants – served as a valuable antidote against these negative, and even unmanly, sentiments, and guaranteed the travellers' psychological well-being. Luxuries and comfort were essential in creating a makeshift home away from home.

Notes

1 From the '80s onwards, guest satisfaction has become a major research item in the interdisciplinary field of the *Tourism Studies*. Interesting reads are: Tijana Radojevic, Nemanja Stanisic and Nemad Stanic, 'Ensuring positive feedback: Factors that influence customer satisfaction in the contemporary hospitality industry', *Tourism Management*, 51 (2015): 13–21; Ibrahim Dortyol, Inci Varinli and Olgun Kitapci, 'How do international tourists perceive hotel quality?: An exploratory study of service quality in Antalya tourism region', *International Journal of Contemporary Hospitality Management*, 26, no. 3 (2014): 470–95.

2 Although much is known about nineteenth-century *Grand Hotels & Palaces*, early modern antecedents have often been overlooked. Some examples: Derek Taylor, *Ritzy: British Hotels, 1837-1987* (London: The Millman Press, 2003); David Bowie, 'Pure diffusion? The great English hotel charges debate in The Times, 1853', *Business History*, 58, no. 2 (2016): 159–78.

3 (Dis)Comfort on the *Grand Tour* is rarely analysed in detail: Jeremy Black, *Italy and the Grand Tour* (New Haven: YUP, 2003), 68–85; Matthis Leibetseder, *Die Kavalierstour. Adlige Erziehungsreisen in 17. Und 18. Jahrhunderts* (Köln: Böhlau, 2004), 54–80.

4 Anthony Burgess, 'The Grand Tour', in Anthony Burgess and Francis Haskell (eds), *The Age of the Grand Tour* (London: Harper-Collins, 1967), 13–32; John Stoye, 'The Grand Tour in the Seventeenth Century', *Journal of Anglo-Italian Studies*, 1 (1991): 62–74; Christopher Hibbert, *The Grand Tour* (London: Methuen, 1987), 32–3; Cesare De Seta, 'Grand Tour: The Lure of Italy in the eighteenth century', in Ilaria Bignamini and Andrew Wilton (eds), *Grand Tour: The Lure of Italy in the Eighteenth Century* (London: Tate Gallery, 1996), 13–19.

5 Frank Trentman, *Empire of Things: How We became a World of Consumers from the Fifteenth Century to the Twenty-First* (London: Penguin, 2016), 22–3, 55–9; Clive Edwards, *Turning Houses into Homes. A History of the Retailing and Consumption of Domestic Furnishings* (Aldershot: Ashgate 2005); Joan DeJean, *The Age of Comfort*.

When Paris Discovered Casual and the Modern Home Began (London: Bloomsburry, 2009), 1–4; Rafaella Sarti, *Europe at Home: Family and Material Culture, 1500-1800* (New Haven: YUP, 2002); Amanda Vickery, *Behind Closed Doors: At Home in Georgian England* (New Haven: YUP, 2009); Marie-Odile Bernez, 'Comfort, the acceptable face of luxury: An eighteenth-century cultural etymology', *Journal for Early Modern Cultural Studies*, 14, no. 2 (2014): 3–21; Bruno Blondé and Ilja Van Damme, 'Retail growth and consumer changes in a declining urban economy: Antwerp (1650-1750)', *Economic History Review*, 63, no. 3 (2010): 638–63. For a more critical interpretation of the rise of comfort: John Crowley, *The Invention of Comfort. Sensibilities & Design in Early Modern Britain & Early America* (Baltimore: Johns Hopkins University Press, 2001), ix–x.

6 More information about the original sample in: Gerrit Verhoeven, *Europe within Reach: Netherlandish Travellers on the Grand Tour and Beyond (1585-1750)* (Leiden: Brill 2015), 1–28; Gerrit Verhoeven, 'Foreshadowing tourism? Looking for modern and obsolete features – or a missing link – in early modern travel behaviour (1600-1750)', *Annals of Tourism Research*, 42 (2013): 262–83.

7 A Dutch conceptual history of comfort remains to be written. More about the etymology: http://gtb.inl.nl/iWDB/search?actie=article&wdb=MNW&id=11782&lemmodern=gemak&domein=0&conc=true

8 Pieter de la Court, *Brieven van Pieter de la Court van der Voort aan Sara Poelaert tijdens zijn reis naar Parijs* (1700) [Leiden City Archives, FA de la Court 64], 8 August 1700.

9 Today, cleanliness and hygiene are key on guest satisfaction surveys: Radojevi, Stanisic and Stanic, 'Ensuring positive feedback', 14; Dortyol, Varinli and Kitapci, 'How do international tourists perceive quality?', 483.

10 Classics are: Alain Corbin, *The Foul and the Fragrant: Odor and the French Social Imagination* (Harvard: Harvard University Press, 1988); Simon Schama, *The Embarrassment of Riches. An Interpretation of Dutch Culture in the Golden Age* (London: Random House, 1997). For a similar evolution in Britain: Edwards, *Turning Houses into Homes*, 90.

11 Some illustrative examples in: Jacobus Gronovius, *Dagverhaal eener reis naar Spanje en Italien* (1672-473) [Leiden University Library, Ltk 859] 14, 19; Abraham van der Meersch, *Reisverhaal* (1672) [Amsterdam University Library, coll. Hss. W. 75] 24-25; Johannes Samuel Cassa, *Journaal van het geene mij voorgekomen is, so op mijn reis na Aaken* (1748) [City Archive The Hague, Ov. Verz. Hs. 161] 28, 36.

12 De la Court, *Brieven*, 15 August 1700.

13 Daniel Roche, *La Ville Promise* (Paris: Fayard, 2000), 236, 238.

14 Jan Teding van Berkhout, *Correspondentie met Paulus Teding van Berkhout* (1739-41) [National Archives The Hague, FA Teding van Berkhout 3.20.59:267] 29 December 1740.

15 Favourable locations also played a part in: Radojevic, Stanisic and Stanic, 'Ensuring positive feedback', 14.
16 Teding van Berkhout, *Correspondentie met Paulus*, 12 December 1739. See also: Corneille van den Branden, *Notes du voyage en France, Italie, partie de la Suisse et de l'Allemagne* (1713-'15) [National Archives Brussels, FA van den Branden I 196: 15b], 393.
17 Teding van Berkhout, *Correspondentie met Paulus*, 29 December 1740.
18 Veblen's *conspicuous consumption* model has been questioned in several recent studies in luxury hospitality services: Wan Yang and Anne Mattila, 'Why do we buy luxury experiences? Measuring value perceptions of luxury hospitality services', *International Journal of Contemporary Hospitality Management*, 28, no. 9 (2016): 1848-67. Crowley reverses the argument: most consumption items were initially rather bought to express status and gentility than to take away physical discomfort. Crowley, *The Invention of Comfort*, 143-7.
19 Dejean, *The Age of Comfort*, 47-57.
20 More on privacy: Sarti, *Europe at Home*, 135-45; Edwards, *Turning Houses into Homes*, 90-3; Hannah Greig and Giorgio Riello, 'Eighteenth-century interiors: Redesigning the Georgian', *Journal of Design History*, 20, no. 4 (2007): 280-1; Christoph Heyl, *A Passion for Privacy: Untersuchungen zur Genese der bürgerlichen Privatsphäre in London* (München : De Gruyter, 2004), 160-220.
21 Philippe Zoete van Laecke, *Memoires de ce que nous avons vue et appris de plus remarquable en nos voyages* (1656) [National Library The Hague, 75 J 51] 9r.
22 Sarah Goldsmith, 'The social challenge: Northern and Central European Societies on the eighteenth-century aristocratic grand tour', in Sarah Goldsmith, Rosemary Sweet and Gerrit Verhoeven (eds), *Beyond the Grand Tour: Northern Metropolises and Early Modern Travel Behaviour* (London: Routledge, 2017).
23 Xavier Duquenne, *Le Voyage du Duc d'Arenberg en Italie en 1791* (Brussels: Arenberg Foundation, 2013), 79, 90.
24 More about the link between taste and comfort: Edwards, *Turning Houses into Homes*, 37, 79.
25 Duquenne, *Le Voyage*, 58, 90.
26 Teding van Berkhout, *Correspondentie met Pieter*, 26 January 1741.
27 Today, food quality still ranks high in guest satisfaction surveys. Dortyol, Varinli and Kitapci, 'How do interational tourists perceive hotel quality?', 481.
28 De la Court, *Brieven*, 8 August 1700.
29 Dortyol, Varinli and Kitapci, 'How do interational tourists perceive hotel quality?', 481.
30 Zoete de Laecke, *Memoires*, 65v.
31 Teding van Berkhout, *Correspondentie met Pieter*, 26 January 1741.
32 Teding van Berkhout, *Correspondentie met Paulus*, 12 May 1741.

33 Jan de Vries, 'Luxury in the Dutch Golden Age in theory and practice', in Maxine Berg and Elizabeth Eger (eds), *Luxury in the Eighteenth Century: Debates, Desires, and Delectable Goods* (Basingstoke: Palgrave, 2003), 41–56. There was as similar debate about the difference between necessities and luxuries in Britain: Crowley, *The Invention of Comfort*, 142–3; Edwards, *Turning Houses into Homes*, 87–9; Bernez, 'Comfort', 3–21; Vickery, *Behind Closed Doors*, 180.

34 De la Court, *Brieven*, 21 August 1700.

35 Ibid.

36 Anonymous, *Reis-boek door de Vereenigde Nederlandsche Provincien en der zelver aangrenzende landschappen en koningrijken* (Amsterdam: Ten Hoorn, 1700). See chapter: *Reys medicijn-boek*.

37 Sarti, *Europe at Home*, 93–4; Edwards, *Turning Houses into Homes*, 90; Dejean, *The Age of Comfort*, 101–2; Crowley, *The Invention of Comfort*, 187–8.

38 Van den Branden, *Notes du voyage*, 513.

39 Teding van Berkhout, *Correspondentie met Pieter*, 26 January 1741.

40 Teding van Berhout, *Correspondentie met Paulus*, 13 January 1741.

41 Furniture is still an important aspect of comfort. Dortyol, Varinli and Kitapci, 'How do international tourists perceive hotel quality?', 481.

42 Bernez, 'Comfort', 9; DeJean, *The Age of Comfort*, 103–4. For a more critical interpretation: Crowley, *The Invention of Comfort*, 146.

43 Teding van Berkhout, *Correspondentie met Pieter*, 29 December 1740; Teding van Berkhout, *Correspondentie met Paulus*, 6 February 1741.

44 De Vries, 'Luxury in the Dutch Golden Age', 41–56.

45 Friendliness, helpfulness and appearance of the staff are still very important categories in guest satisfaction surveys. See: Dortyol, Varinli, Kitapci, 'How do international tourists perceive hotel quality?', 481.

46 Zoete de Laecke, *Memoires*, 8v–9r.

47 Ibid., 31r, 62r.

48 Jan van Royen, *Journael gehouden van reijsie van Leijden over Rotterdam, Breda, Antwerpen, Bruxel, Namen, Huij, Luijk, Maastrigt, 's Hertogenbosch* (1740) [Regional Archives Leiden, LB 62250], 12–14.

49 Zoete de Laecke, *Memoires*, 62r; Teding van Berkhout, *Correspondentie met Pieter*, 26 January 1741.

50 Van Royen, *Journael van reijsie*, 1–2.

51 Teding van Berkhout, *Correspondentie met Pieter*, 26 January 1741.

52 Tim Meldrum, *Domestic Service and Gender, 1660-1750* (Harlow: Pearson, 2000), 89–90.

53 Susan Matt, *Homesickness. An American History* (Oxford: Oxford University Press, 2011); Sarah Goldsmith, 'Nostalgia, homesickness, and emotional formation on the eighteenth-century Grand Tour', *Cultural and Social History*, 15, no. 3 (2018): 333–60.

54 Johannes Thijs, *Vervolgh van Copije van mijne brieven* (1646-'49) [Leiden University Library, Thys. 102: B1], 19 April 1648 and 20 December 1648.
55 Zoete van Laecke, *Memoires*, 62r.
56 Nowadays, efficiency and friendliness of the hotel staff is still an important aspect of guest satisfaction surveys: Radojevic, Stanisic and Stanic, 'Ensuring positive feedback', 14; Dortyol, Varinli and Kitapci, 'How do international tourists perceive quality?', 485.
57 Van den Branden, *Notes du voyage*, Account book.
58 Johan de Wit, *Journaal van zijn reis naar Frankrijk en Engeland* (1645-'47) [National Archive The Hague, FA De Wit-Beyerman 3.20.66.01:1[19]], Account book.
59 Teding van Berkhout, *Correspondentie met Pieter*, 29 December 1740.
60 Teding van Berkhout, *Correspondentie met Pieter*, 26 January 1741.
61 About livries and their symbolic meaning: Thorstein Veblen, *The Theory of the Leisure Class. An economic study of institutions* (London: Allen & Unwin, 1970), 54-7; Jean Hecht, *The Domestic Servant Class in Eighteenth-Century England* (London: Routledge, 1956), 2-6.
62 Some examples: Duquenne, *Le Voyage*, 79; Teding van Berkhout, *Correspondentie met Coenraad*, 9 March 1741; Van den Branden, *Notes du voyage*, Account book.
63 Verhoeven, *Europe within reach*, 61-70.
64 Teding van Berkhout, *Correspondentie met Pieter*, 26 January 1741.
65 Claire Walsh, 'Shopping et Tourisme. L'attrait des boutiques Parisiennes au XVIIIe siècle', in Natacha Coquery(ed.), *La boutique et la ville. Commerces, commerçants, espaces et clientèles, XVIe-XXe siècle* (Tours: Belin, 2000), 223-37; Carolyn Sargentson, 'The manufacture and marketing of luxury goods: The marchands merciers of late 17th- and 18th-century Paris', in Robert Fox and Anthony Turner, *Luxury Trades and Consumerism in Ancien Régime Paris* (Aldershot: Routledge, 1998), 99-137.
66 De la Court, *Brieven*, 15 August 1700.
67 Pieter van Dorp, *Kort verhaal van het divertissant somertogje en pleijsier-reijsje* (1732) [Central Bureau for Genealogy, The Hague, FA Mispelblom Beijer 47] 6v.
68 Even in the nineteenth century, tourist information was often hard to get. See: Anne Geurts, 'Modern travel: A personal affair', in Alison Martin, Lut Missine and Beatrix van Dam (eds), *Travel Writing in Dutch and German, 1790-1930. Modernity, Regionality, Mobility* (London: Routledge, 2017), 214-34.
69 More about on these evolutions: Verhoeven, 'Foreshadowing tourism?', 262-83; Roey Sweet, Gerrit Verhoeven and Sarah Goldsmith, 'Introduction', in Goldsmith, Sweet and Verhoeven, *Beyond the Grand Tour*, 1-24.
70 Teding stayed six months in Rome, five in Paris, and two in London, while the long trek from Rome to Paris was made in barely six months. Teding van Berkhout, *Correspondentie met Paulus*.

71 Gerrit Verhoeven, 'Tangible beauty. Louis Engelbert's Grand Tour', in Mark Derez, Soetkin Vanhauwaert and Anne Verbrugge (eds), *Arenberg. Portrait of a Family, Story of a Collection* (Turnhout: Brepols, 2018), 312–19.

72 Gerrit Verhoeven, 'In search of the New Rome? Creative cities and early modern travel behaviour', in Ilja Van Damme, Bert De Munck and Andrew Miles (eds), *Cities and Creativity from the Renaissance to the Present* (London: Routledge, 2017), 65–84.

73 *Reis-boek*, 412–14.

74 Word-of-mouth recommendations are still extremely important in guest satisfaction. See: Radojevic, Stanisic and Stanic, 'Ensuring positive feedback', 14–15.

75 Radojevic, Stanisic and Stanic, 'Ensuring positive feedback', 14–15.

People in focus 3:
Moving house: Comfort disrupted in the domestic and emotional life of an eighteenth-century bachelor

Helen Metcalfe

In 1821 the essayist and poet Charles Lamb discussed his relationship and residence with his sister, Mary, in mutually supportive terms that reflect how a shared investment in the running of the household and common interests or values reinforced family connections.[1] In the essay 'Mackery End', Charles presented these domestic arrangements as a source of comfort because their 'double singleness' allowed them to maintain their individual 'tastes and habits':

> We house together, old bachelor and maid, in a sort of double singleness; with such tolerable comfort [...]. We agree pretty well in our tastes and habits – yet so, as 'with a difference'. We are generally in harmony, with occasional bickerings – as *it should be among near relations*.[2]

For Lamb, interactions between family members resulted in related states of emotion being accessed, albeit not always harmoniously. Thus the home was a site where communities of feelings could co-exist, with a broad range of emotions being experienced within its walls. Lamb's emotional household is the focus of this case study, as it underscores the importance of sibling attachments to some unmarried men in their pursuit of domestic comfort. Indeed, Lamb's feelings of comfort were a direct result of his relationship with Mary, whom he later referred to as his 'truest comforter'.[3] Unconfined by the model of the nuptial familial household, siblinghood offered single men and women access to a household organised around principles of unity, affection and friendship, based on bonds of common heritage.[4] These relationships, maintains Amy Harris, served as 'bridges to adulthood and as necessary supports for lifelong social, financial, and material success'.[5] The strategies for managing the emotional household, then, contrast with those required by practical management, since affective bonds were shaped much less by the structures and prescriptions of wider society.

The co-residence of Charles and Mary Lamb exemplifies the life-long bonds of siblinghood, but their relationship was one also dominated by narratives of loss and loneliness, with Lamb's reflections on his emotional and physical domestic comfort being a constant feature of his letters. Interrogating Charles's letters for his experience of the domestic culture of comfort – which for this bachelor were shaped by affective sibling bonds and domestic disruption – offers a tantalizing view of the emotional household, but also takes into account changing attitudes towards comfort during the late-Georgian period. Looking beyond John E. Crowley's assessment of the material culture of domestic comfort and the use of improved facilities for achieving physical comfort during this period, this study evaluates Charles's descriptions of comfort to reveal the vital role of emotional and material, familial and physical domestic comforts combined.

The Lambs' living arrangements were frequently in flux as a result of Mary's recurring mental health problems. Mary had killed their mother in what has been described as a 'violent fit of insanity' in 1796, after which Lamb opted to

Figure 6a.1 Charles Lamb. English essayist (1775–1834). After the portrait by William Hazlitt (1754).

care for his sister rather than commit her to an asylum.[6] Charles's commitment to Mary's health despite, or perhaps because of, public criticism, resulted in several domestic relocations. In the shadow of Mary's illness, the Lambs moved lodgings no fewer than eight times between 1799 and 1833 – and, while this was a flexible lifestyle choice it was also one that, at times, afforded less than commodious surroundings. Charles and Mary often found themselves lodging in the garret rooms which, in common with the basement, were available to lodgers at the lower end of the rental market. These rooms were generally cheaper than all other floors because conditions were often unpleasant with damp rooms that were poorly lit and cramped.[7] While lodging was a persistent feature of this bachelor's lifestyle, it was frequently met with enthusiasm and good humour yet the emotional comfort Lamb drew from his sister's companionship remained the priority – without which Charles's domestic contentment and feelings of emotional and physical comfort were disrupted.

Co-residence figured prominently in Charles's life, albeit interrupted by periods of convalescence for Mary. These relapses were frequently followed by Mary's removal from the home and in an 1827 letter to his friend, the poet Bernard Barton, Lamb displayed his characteristically despondent tone in consequence:

> Nine weeks are completed, and Mary does not get any better. It is perfectly exhausting [...] every thing is very gloomy. But for long experience, I should fear her ever getting well. [...] Here is a comfortable house but no servants. One does not make a household.[8]

Lamb's concerns in the letter alert us to some of the ways in which contemporaries understood and applied definitions of both comfort and family – particularly as this passage also shows that for Lamb the two were directly related. It was not unusual for brothers and sisters to live together in this period, yet accounts of never-married women are only marginally more visible in the historical record than their male counterparts, and are usually examined through their status as dependents in the homes of their more affluent (and frequently older) male relatives. The sibling relationship between the Lambs, and Charles's narratives of loss, disrupt these assessments and locates sibling solidarity and single status as the principal component of Charles's notion of emotional and domestic comfort. 'It is no new thing for me to be left by my sister', Lamb observed to a family friend in 1834 that 'when she is not violent her rambling chat is better to me than the sense and sanity of this world [...] I could be nowhere happier than under the same roof with her'.[9] Charles's loneliness without Mary identifies their relationship as one based on love and companionship. More unexpectedly, this extract underscores that Charles's happiness was almost completely reliant upon Mary's company – without which, his experience of emotional domestic comfort remained unfulfilled.

Despite his living arrangements being born out of such emotional upheaval, Lamb's enthusiasm rarely faltered when the time came to move to new lodgings. In March 1801, in a letter to the traveller and writer Thomas Manning, Lamb recorded his thoughts on the forthcoming move to Mitre Court Building, Inner Temple, with typically dry humour:

> I am going to change my Lodgings, having received a hint that it would be agreeable [...] I have partly fixed upon most delectable Rooms, which look out (when you stand a Tip toe) over the Thames & Surrey Hills [...]. – There I shall have all the privacy of a house without the encumbrance, and shall be able to lock my friends out as often as I desire [...] for my present lodgings resemble a minister's levee.[10]

Lamb wrote to Manning again in April to invite him to view his new lodgings, observing cheerfully that, 'I prefer the attic story for the air'.[11] Being housed in the garret offered rooms with a view, albeit on 'tip toe', but importantly for Lamb they also offered accommodation that was 'agreeable' and free from the responsibilities of running a household. This extract reveals that privacy was an important feature in Lamb's choice of accommodation and reflects the way in which domestic space in its most basic form could provide comfort and protection in times of emotional distress. Indeed, Amanda Vickery asserts that, without the vestiges of privacy, life 'was understood to be a most sorry degradation, which stripped away the defences of the spirit'.[12] Notwithstanding the emotional comfort Charles derived from Mary's companionship, his jurisdiction over the physical domestic environment (and the management and organization of his domestic interior boundaries) went hand in hand with how this bachelor experienced comfort within the home.

The Lambs moved lodgings with increasing frequency and while Charles's devotion to his sister's emotional needs remained constant, relocating was met with occasional frustration from Lamb. 'What a dislocation of comfort is comprised in that word moving!' he declaimed, 'such a heap of little nasty things, after you think all is got into the cart [...] Then you can find nothing you want for many days'.[13] Indeed, a later move to Inner Temple Lane was not an immediate success because, while 'the rooms are delicious', and 'I try to persuade myself it is much pleasanter than Mitre Court', recorded Lamb to Samuel Coleridge, 'alas! the Household Gods are slow to come in a new Mansion, They are in their infancy to me, I do not feel them yet—no hearth has blazed to them yet—. How I hate and dread New Places!'[14] Lamb's discontent at the prospect of another move reveals that he derived great comfort from his personal space and domestic material objects combined, and is indicative of Lamb's continued pursuit of domesticity. Moreover, Lamb associated the disruption of his domesticity with the loss of comfort and stability – physically and emotionally. Nevertheless, these extracts show that, although domestic comforts were at times slow in coming for Lamb, they were not neglected. Apprehension and doubt unsettled this serial lodger, but he was reassured in equal measure by the anticipation that, despite not feeling them yet, his domestic comforts and subsequent happiness would eventually follow – both of which he prized highly.

The frequency with which Mary's relapses occurred (and her subsequent removal from the home) were a source of great sorrow for Charles, and resulted in his subsequent emotional and physical disorientation at the loss of his companion – concerns which Lamb frequently returned to in his letters: 'Mary has been ill and gone from home these five weeks yesterday. She has left me very lonely and very miserable', he confided to a friend in October 1815; 'I stroll about, but there is no rest but at ones [sic] own fireside, and there is no rest for me there now'.[15] The trope of the home and hearth, and its association with domestic comfort and contentment, was explicit in Lamb's depiction of the fireside, but the true source of domestic contentment for Charles was Mary, without whom he remained restless. The affective bonds between these siblings united the qualities of paternal and maternal support and provided Lamb with a sense of belonging that underpinned his notion of the emotional landscape of the home. Yet key to Lamb's model of, and subsequent feelings he attributed to, domestic comfort was a mutual sibling attachment formed through a genuine devotion that offered companionship, comfort and solidarity for them both.

Notes

1 Barbara Rosenwein, *Emotional Communities in the Early Middle Ages* (London: Cornell University Press, 2007), 24; Susan Broomhall, 'Emotions in the household', in Susan Broomhall (ed.), *Emotions in the Household, 1200–1900* (Houndmills: Palgrave, 2008), 1–37.
2 Charles Lamb, 'Mackery End, in Hertfordshire', *London Journal*, 4, no. 19 (1821): 28–30 (28). Original emphasis.

3 Ibid., 29.
4 Amy Harris, *Siblinghood and Social Relations in Georgian England: Share and Share Alike* (Manchester: Manchester University Press, 2012), 56, 57.
5 Ibid., 18.
6 Jane Aaron, 'Lamb, Mary Anne (1764–1847)', *Oxford Dictionary of National Biography* (Oxford: Oxford University Press, 2004), http://www.oxforddnb.com/view/article/15918 (accessed 5 April 2015).
7 Joanne McEwan, 'The lodging exchange: Space, authority and knowledge in eighteenth-century London', in Joanne McEwan and Pamela Sharpe (eds), *Accommodating Poverty: The Housing and Living Arrangements of the English Poor, c. 1600–1850* (Houndmills: Palgrave Macmillan, 2011), 50–68 (54); Dan Cruikshank and Neil Burton, *Life in the Georgian City* (London: Viking, 1990), 62.
8 c. December 1827, Charles to Bernard Barton, BL, *Letters of Charles Lamb to Bernard Barton,* Add. MS: 35256, ff. 69.
9 14 February 1834, Charles to Maria Fryer, *The Complete Letters of Charles and Mary Lamb*, ed., E. V. Lucas, 3 vols (London: J. M. Dent, 1935), vol. III, 401, ff. 993.
10 26 or 27 February 1800, Lamb to Thomas Manning, *The Letters of Charles and Mary Anne Lamb*, ed., Marrs, Jr., Edwin, W., 3 vols (London: Cornell University Press, 1975), vol. 1, 277.
11 April 1801, Lamb to Manning, *Letters*, ed., Marrs, vol. 2, 3.
12 Amanda Vickery, 'An Englishman's home is his castle? Thresholds, boundaries and privacies in the eighteenth-century London house', *Past & Present*, 199, no. 1 (2008): 147–73 (152).
13 28 or 29 March 1809, Lamb to Manning, *Letters*, ed., Marrs, vol. 3, 4.
14 7 June 1809, Lamb to Samuel Coleridge, *Letters*, ed., Marrs, vol. 3, 13.
15 19 October 1815, Charles to Sara Hutchinson, *Letters*, ed., Marrs, vol. 3, 202, 203, ff. 309.

7

Home from home? Making life comfortable in the Victorian barracks

Rowena Willard-Wright

A search of nineteenth-century newspapers in the British Newspaper Archives, using the term 'Home Comforts', elicits hundreds of articles and adverts describing this as being offered in places that are definitively not home, such as boarding houses, private schools and furnished apartments for 'commercial gentlemen'. By the mid-nineteenth century, it begins to be applied to military life, home comforts being described as honourably given up, to 'follow the drum'. Later in the nineteenth century, as improvements to the regular soldier's accommodation become politically necessary, home comforts were instead seen as essential to enhancing the soldier's lifestyle.[1] That said, military barracks were not designed to be like home, the army controlled personal effects and expression, in order to create a hierarchical and conforming fighting body of men, the regular soldier and officer living in very different spaces in barracks, in order to cement the hierarchies. Likewise, what was considered to be, or not be, a personal possession was strictly controlled. It is within such an institutional environment that a focused, more distinct, idea of what home comforts were and their importance, might be gained.

I have been influenced in my approach by Daniel Miller's social and anthropological book, *The Comfort of things*, in particular by his use of close assessment of material culture in the home, in order to reveal the history and character of individuals.[2] However, I am unable to fully replicate his methods, as he was able to talk to his subjects and check his assumptions. Even so, I am using the curation of items around the soldiers' beds to analyse their biographies and possessions, in an attempt to identify what represented making a 'home' within barracks.

The barracks

An inability to recruit soldiers for service in the second-half of the nineteenth century meant that it was in the army's interest to change the public's idea of the soldier. He was no longer the 'Scum of the earth', as described by the Duke of Wellington,[3] and a career in the army was as respectable as any other labour. Poor recruitment was driven in part by the perceived failure of the British to efficiently manage war and in part by concerns about pollution, disease and the quality of life of the soldier in barracks.[4] When a rebuild of accommodation at Aldershot was mooted in 1855, a Barrack Accommodation Committee was set up expressly to better balance the 'considerations of economy' against 'the comfort and convenience of the soldiers'.[5] By the end of the 1880s, after a particularly bad outbreak of enteric fever in the Dublin barracks, there was an increase in barrack building, engendering a standard design for the new localization depots.[6] Soldiers were to be housed in large and long barrack rooms, well ventilated, with bed spaces evenly spaced out, running along on either side, with communal movable benches and tables in the centre. The ordinary soldier thus had no privacy; only the NCO had a room of his own, usually to one end of the main room. It was a form known to work well, as it ensured that all would witness the misdemeanours of any single soldier. Thus, if an officer caught you out, the whole of the barrack room would be punished, as a way of making soldiers self-policing.[7] Reform fostered closer control of living spaces, to ensure a similar standard was kept to. This led to standardization, not only of the layout of buildings, but of the wider barrack fixtures and fittings. Designs for standard fireplaces, stables, latrines, washrooms and kitchen equipment were provided by War Office pattern books, with clear demarcation of equipment made to be used by the officers, NCOs and regular soldiers.[8]

To ensure wide and quick uptake of War Office regulations, schedules of barrack furniture were instituted by the Cardwell reforms of 1872 and from then on any changes to them were disseminated via numbered Army Circulars which prescribed what each recruit was provided with. This way a large army could calculate its costs, control consumption and enforce hygiene standards. This list of provisions was similar to that of the early nineteenth century, but more comprehensive, covering cleaning equipment and kitchen utensils (see below). It is striking that not only were the requirements for each man described, so too were variant circumstances, indicating an understanding and attempt to deal with shortage issues and availability of different types of fuel and facilities in barracks, both abroad and at home. An inventory board is included, which would have listed what was in each room, so that loss and destruction could be identified, and no doubt punished, but also to help with identifying procurement requirements, the costs of which were intended to be standardized.[9] And the designs for furniture were themselves standardized: the bases of the iron beds were telescoping, so that they could serve as seats during the daytime. The bed had a coir mattress, blankets, a bolster and sheets, folded neatly then strapped together, often with a cotton towel draped over the headboard, like an antimacassar.[10]

Circular dated 1887: for Non Commissioned Officer's and Privates' Rooms[11]

A quart soup basin (to each man)
A barrack bedstead (to each man)
Bellows (where turf or wood is issued as fuel)
Two blankets (to each man)
An inventory board
A coal box
A variety of scrubbing brushes: a hand scrubbing brush, a long handled brush, a long sweeping brush
A galvanised Iron candlestick (where gas and oil is not supplied)
A 3-gallon soup can
Barrack bolster and pillowcase (to each man)
A round meat tin (to each man)
A fender for each fireplace
6ft and 4ft soldiers' forms for each table
A hammer for breaking coal (where inland coal is used)
A hanging barrack lamp (where paraffin is used by War Office authority)
A mop with a handle
Earthen ware dinner plates to each man
A soldier's poker for each fireplace
A barrack rug (or third blanket when stock of rugs is depleted - to each man)
2 barrack linen sheets
A shovel to each fireplace
A sergeants' stool to each table
Bed straps to each man
6 or 4ft tables to every 8 or 6 men
Wood tub or iron galvanised coal tray
Urine tub

An 8-gallon washing tub of galvanised iron and wood
- When meals are necessarily cooked in barrack-rooms issues of cooking utensils may be made if necessary, in accordance with schedule 412.
- Hair beds, bolsters and slipcases will be issued at authorised foreign stations.
- A second urine tub may be issued to each room of more than 14 men.

Different brigades had different kit and therefore different methods of displaying the kit in the barracks, but in general the overall effect was the same. The iron shelf over the bed, along with a pegboard for hats and other articles, the iron barrack bed and wooden trunk, were fixtures of the barracks. However, the kit itself was the soldier's to look after, clean and arrange with great precision, before being examined at kit inspection. The effect of this was to subsume his personality into the greater being of the company. Like the uniform, his furnishings were part of his identity as a soldier. One of the attractions of joining the army was that as a new recruit you were given your 'free kit',[12] but the uniform remained the property of the state.[13]

A visual and functional comparison can be made with hospital interiors and barrack rooms. The Army Sanitary Committee reforms (1861–2), post the Crimean war, had been driven by members of the medical profession, including Florence Nightingale. It was also believed that in order to support the improvements in the 'class of society' from which the rank and file were to be recruited, greater 'demands of [a] sanitary and moral character' would be required in the lifestyle of the regular soldier.[14] By the 1880s cleanliness was most definitely seen as akin to godliness in the British army, and its achievement was a major part of the soldier's day. After reveille, at 6 o'clock, there was a short wash and the soldier's bed was made up before parade, the regiment breakfasted at about 7:45, and then orderly room business was completed, including the polishing of kit, the cleaning of barrack rooms and the latrines. After another parade at 9:30, for an hour, and another parade at 11:30, dinner was served at 1 o'clock. Recruits were drilled from 14:30 and after that there was tea at 16:30. The ranks enjoyed free time until 21:30, when the roll call was taken, followed either by guard duty, or lights out at 22:15.[15] The only change to that routine occurred at weekends, when church attendance might be included, or a period of free time on Saturdays 'which a soldier generally counts as his own'.[16] Thus, in the drive to improve the quality of accommodation in barracks, a more controlled and controlling system of furnishings and routine was created, continuing the tight institutional grip on the day-to-day life of the regular soldier, in contrast to the freedom of personal choice he might have had at home.

Life in the ranks of the English army – published in 1888 – describes a barrack room for the new recruit, in which is the first and only written mention of a specific phenomenon: 'a piece of the wall is also at his disposal so that if he likes he can hang up any small pictures or photographs'.[17] This enlivened what was an institutionally impersonal environment. Some images were communal;[18] others were personal and hung up alongside their beds as the only material display of self-expression the soldiers were allowed to have.[19]

There are many photographs of decorated bed spaces from different regiments, the earliest dated to 1864, continuing up to the beginning of the Second World War.[20] Some show the barrack room as a whole, some simply a single bed. There is no evidence of these photographs being sent to families, although the family sometimes colluded in the displays by sending the photographs and postcards, and as such represent a continuing link to home. Surviving within regimental archives, for the most part, these photographs appear to have been officially sanctioned by the army, some being used by the War Office for training in kit layout.[21] In the case of some from the Gloucestershire regiment, this not only included the neatness of the kit, but also appears to have included the neatness and 'curation' of the personal displays, as the number of images and their innovative methods of display indicate.

The soldier

A photograph taken in the Horfield Barracks in Bristol in 1904 shows the bed spaces of two ordinary soldiers: Thomas King and William Sayer (Figure 7.1).[22] Thomas King (1879–1930) was born in Gloucester and joined his local regiment, the Gloucestershire, in 1903.[23] Most of the images that he had above his bed were fixed on boards with photographic corners, as if in a photograph album. This is a very particular allusion; other bed displays show photographs placed in fan shapes around the bed, or hanging in frames, referencing shop and public celebratory displays, or the domestic interior.[24] The photograph album is visually representative of the collecting of personal memories, using images of places, events, friends and family. From King's army records and the census, we know that he came from a large family – the eldest son in a family of ten.[25] He lists two of his siblings as being in the navy and another in the Hussars. This is reflected in the photographs to the left of his bed, a number of which show young couples; one where the courting male is in naval uniform

Figure 7.1 The bed spaces in Horfield Barracks of Lance Corporal Thomas King and private William T. Sayer of the Gloucestershire Regiment, 1904.

and others in army uniform. Although they are too small to identify particular individuals, there is a large oval portrait of a Hussar standing alongside his horse, which we might assume is his brother or at least alludes to him. From this we can see there is pride in their roles in the military as a family. The shelf over King's bed has also been adapted for photographic display. *Cartes de visite* or studio portraits dominate, one in particular shows a woman surrounded by lilies, a symbol of mourning. Thomas King's mother died before he entered the service, so this may be a portrait of her.

The images around the bed also indicate different types of mass-market leisure activities. Music hall or variety was one of the most popular forms of public entertainment by the 1900s, Bristol having at least eight theatres specializing in this entertainment by 1904.[26] Some of the portrait photographs displayed by King are in a costume or pose that suggest that they are of actors and actresses. A head and shoulders portrait of a girl on the far bottom right of his display is posed in a manner popular among actresses of the time; these were a form of pin-up. To her left are a fashionably dressed couple within a staged set, in poses that suggest performance. Then to the far left, on the level of his water bottle, is a man in a top hat and tails, appearing to exaggeratedly creep towards an opening. This is likely to represent a comedy actor or actress, male impersonators, like Vesta Tilley, being popular with the military; in the 1900s she created the character of Burlington Bertie, a young aristocratic idler.

Also among the images are postcards of places, some are local to Bristol: two show the twin chimneys of a local Bristol Brewery; two depict ships in the port and another is of a local landmark called the Dutch House. By the early 1900s, seaside holidays were commonplace, so it is unsurprising that Thomas has postcards of beaches and the sea; one in particular shows Durdle Dor in Dorset and another the Blackpool Tower.[27] There are also more cultural and urban landmarks depicted: a cathedral overlooking a river; a stone bridge across a wide river; the dome of the National Gallery and another of Threadneedle Street in London. We cannot know if King ever visited these places or if some were postcards sent by friends or family. However, they show the role of leisure time as an indicator of personal and group status, as well as the importance to King of keeping in touch with family and friends. Even if he did not personally participate in all of these events, the photographs and postcards, and any text written on them, involve him as an onlooker, the objects standing in as collective memories, linking him to home.

Above King's shelf are colour prints of paintings, some bought specifically and others cut from illustrated magazines. The easiest to identify is the painting *When did you last see your father?* by William Frederick Yeames. Painted in 1878 and subsequently bought by the Walker Art Gallery in Liverpool, it rapidly became well known and was the subject of a popular ballad in the 1890s.[28] Ballads were still an important disseminator of culture, sung in pubs and on the musical hall stage; they were also associated with solders as a pastime, hence Kipling's series of poems called the 'Barrack Room Ballads'.[29]. The subject of the painting was the dilemma of the young child in a time of war, bought up to tell the truth, but telling the truth would betray his father. The child as a potential hero was ubiquitous in the narrative of children's literature, in particular, stories written for boys concentrated on delineating the ideal English hero of the Empire and the military, whose heroism at heart was an act of protection of family and friends.[30] Yeames' painting also refers to the fragility of family at a time of war.

Of course, without talking to the soldier, we cannot know what it meant to him personally or how he knew the painting.

The short service soldier – a product of late nineteenth-century reforms to recruitment – had a flexible career, staying in for as little as three years before becoming a reserve, and had access to a library in the barracks during his leisure time. There are books in the kits of both of our soldiers, and we know that Thomas King had attained a third- and second-class certificate of education while in the army.[31] Literature was a way of escaping the confines of the barracks. John Pindar, a self-described 'ordinary soldier' writes in his autobiography of 1877.[32]

> I have felt more pleasure in my barrack room pouring over the inspired pages of Milton ... than I would ad mists the attractions of all the gin palaces in the world. Still I must admit I often felt a sense of loneliness creeping over me whenever my thoughts would revert to home, which they often did ... . Often on a Foreign shore the word home has cheered my lonely heart.

Pindar's sentiments of homesickness would appear to be materialized in Thomas King's displays of photographs, transforming monolithic army culture by including his family and their life events in his personal space. This, as well as the wider jingoistic promotion of the military and in particular rooting the regiment in local depots, encouraged and created military families, thus making their actual home and family status, military.

William Thomas Sayer (1881–1916), born in a workhouse in St Pancras, London, was around 24 when the photograph was taken. Sayers' photographic portraits appear to be mostly of the same person, probably himself. One shows him standing by his bed, indicating pride in his personal space. Of the other pictures, there are few of identifiable events or locations; instead they are mostly purchased pictures and prints. The pictures Sayer chose are surprisingly sentimental. One is a picture of kittens, a genre popular enough at this time for artists to specialize in cat paintings. Kittens, however, were usually associated with women's taste, as alluded to in another of Sayer's pictures, this time of two children, a boy and a girl, the boy passing a puppy to the girl, who is next to a cat. The complexity of communal narrative and variety see in Thomas King's display that is completely missing in Sayer's, whose only picture with a military subject is a photograph of a row of ammunition shells; again no individual is depicted. From this one might assume Sayer was the more solitary of the two men, with few friends or family. The photograph certainly appears to show two very different personalities, so how does this fit with what we know of their lives?

King reached the rank of Sergeant some time between 1911 and 1913, after which he was discharged, missing the First World War.[33] In the census of 1911, Sayer is listed alongside King in the barracks in Bristol, but he has only attained the rank of Lance Corporal. However, unlike King, he is married – to a woman called Emily Lily who is listed in the census as living in barracks, most likely in married quarters with Sayer.[34] Just before the outbreak of the First World War, their son Denis was born in Romford, where Emily's parents were living. William was mobilized with his regiment on the 11th of August 1914 and killed in action near Loos, on the 29th of March 1916, where he was buried.

King died unmarried in the Westbury-on-Severn workhouse on 14th of October 1930, at the age of fifty-one. A short extract from a local newspaper describes how earlier that year he had been in the workhouse infirmary, as a man of no fixed abode, suffering from a cold. He was discharged and in an effort to re-enter, he threw stones at the workhouse windows, for which he was charged and sent to prison for seven days.[35] By this time, his personal possessions amounted to in a single bag, as described in the newspaper report. It is likely that these included the photograph of his barrack room bed space, a photograph of himself as a sergeant, and seven items of army paper work, as well as two badges for his skills at sharp shooting and his sergeant's sash. All of these are held together as a collection in the Regimental Museum in Gloucester and it is possible that he requested they be returned to the regiment on his death. King's death in the workhouse is indeed a sad end, we know that one soldier on being re-recruited from a workhouse at the beginning of the First World War, confessed to his recruiting officer, 'I didn't want them to know me here by the name they knew me then … for the old regiment's sake.'[36]

The continuing narrative of the lives of these two men might seem contradictory to the evidence of their bed spaces, the more outgoing and successful, in terms of his army career, died alone – while the more sentimental, least visibly demonstrative and seemingly solitary, married and had a child. That Sayer had no images of his family around his bed is perhaps because his childhood which was complicated by illegitimacy, and by being born in the workhouse to a single mother, so he may not have kept in touch with or indeed had a secure family home. He was also not born in Gloucestershire and was in effect an outsider, so making friends or keeping in touch with friends would have been harder. King had strong family ties in 1904 and apparently a good army life from his promotions, but clearly found life outside the army difficult. This may have been compounded by the war; he was thirty-four years old when he left the army and 37 in 1916, when conscription commenced for men between the ages of eighteen to forty. His previous army service should have made him an attractive recruit, so he cannot have been fit enough physically, or mentally, to join up. This alone could have been shaming. Likewise, after the war and into the 1920s, finding work during the depression was difficult maybe explaining why he was homeless when he died.

The officer

Over the course of the nineteenth century, officers bought and furnished their spaces with campaign furniture, which by the 1880–90s was thoroughly embedded in the homes of the upper and colonial middle-classes, both at home and abroad. In the same 1887 circular, which described the furnishings of a soldier's barracks, the officer's rooms are listed thus:[37]

> Bellows (where turf or wood is issued as fuel)
> Inventory board
> Two officer's chairs (or Windsor)
> A pair of officer's firedogs (if necessary, where turf or wood is issued as fuel)
> Officer's poker
> Coal scuttle
> Officer's fire shovel
> Officers room table
> Officer's fire tongs
> - The furniture will be issued to each room for which the officer is entitled under Army regulations.
> - Globes for gas will also be supplied for bed-rooms, sitting rooms and passages at special quarters where such quarters are fitted with gas.

Not least among the things that differed from the furnishings given to the soldier is that he occupies a bed-sitting room on his own. Thus the officer had a level of privacy and personal possessions not permitted to the ordinary soldier. Although a non commissioned officer like a sergeant would also be given a single room to himself, the circulars still list similar furnishings to that of the regular soldier, although very occasionally names painted onto campaign furniture link their ownership to a sergeant.[38]

For the officer, the military was not merely a career; it confirmed his social position as a gentleman. The officer or his parents bought the commission and any promotions thereafter, his pay barely covering the cost of the uniform. Therefore everything the officer possessed was his own, and thus reflected upon his status and the status of his regiment. The Cardwell reforms were meant to relax some of these class rigidities, the officer no longer bought their commission and in theory promotion was for merit, but in reality the importance of social class remained. A typical late-nineteenth-century officer would have spent most of his childhood in a boarding school, some of which had cadet classes specifically for those intending to go into the army. Following school, the officer cadet attended Woolwich or Sandhurst for his final training and after passing out he would then go on to join his regiment as an officer. Most came from the landed gentry, so their family home would have been in the country; he might also have had a town house in London, or more likely, used one of the many clubs that catered for officers. Army officers enjoyed lengthy periods of leave; unmarried officers were expected to take part in the season, especially debutant's balls, as they were deemed eminently marriageable. Partly because of this, many of their clubs were located around St James's Palace, the more prestigious, like the Army and Navy Club, being found in Pall Mall.

Unsurprisingly, it was on the edges of Pall Mall, Trafalgar square, Piccadilly and the Strand that the furnishers of campaign furniture could be found.[39] John W. Allen was one such manufacturer, with premises on the western side of the Strand. Described in advertisements as being founded in 1798, they were one of the longest trading barrack and camp equipage makers. Catering for both civil and military customers, their advertising became both more inclusive of other markets and more targeted in the *Post Office Directory* of 1890, where the same company is mentioned three times: as a dressing bag & dressing case maker; a manufacturer of barrack furniture and military outfitter, and a portmanteau and travelling bag manufacturer.

The Napoleonic Wars had brought many gentlemen into the military, increasing the demand for campaign furniture. The officer occupied spaces in barracks that were not convenient for the numerous items of elegant and fragile furniture he would have had at home, and in the field his furniture required structural strength and to be capable of being easily 'knocked-down' and packed into trunks for transportation. Making such equipage was, at most, a sideline for cabinetmakers of note; those that specialized in campaign furniture often came from a different trade altogether. Allen, like other makers, started as a portmanteau or a trunk maker, but began to include camp equipage among his stock. By the 1830s, they had grown to such an extent that they also had a factory and retailer in Whitechapel. An advert of 1878 in the Army List carries the Royal Coat of Arms of the Prince of Wales, indicating that they enjoyed his patronage.[40]

Word of mouth and association with royalty was important for status, which is illustrated by a surviving album of letters entitled *Testimonials of Barrack Furniture*, dated from 1868 to 1873. It contains 39 letters sent to Allen by officers of various British regiments. One in particular identifies why movable furniture that you could easily take with you was important, Captain Gibb of the Royal Artillery writing:[41]

> The mahogany round table & six (6) drawing room chairs, indeed everything with which you supplied me a year ago are of the very best material and very moderately charged for. The travelling chiffonier or sideboard & the round table & chairs has been of the greatest use in change of quarters, which I have to make 4 times within the year.

These frequent changes in location meant that embodied in the officer's furnishings was a personal sense of stability and thus home. A good example of this is the camp bed belonging to the Duke of Wellington, which still survives at Walmer Castle in Kent. A man of Wellington's wealth and status could well afford a new and elegant bed but he chose instead to sleep in his camp bed, with its simple chamois covered bolster and army blanket, albeit one covered in a fine greenish-blue taffeta silk. This was striking because he also provided himself with the new and rarefied comforts of central heating and an ensuite flushing water closet. Wellington's attachment to his campaign bed was seen as representative of a personal character trait, the cartoonist William Heath drew Wellington carrying his bed, as a way of illustrating his unpopular continuing martial character, despite his now civilian role as head of His Majesty's Government.[42]

An idea of what might be considered a standard set of furnishings for a junior officer is supplied by Allen's adverts. One from *The Army and Navy List Advertiser* of 1878, describes a 'Barrack room outfit' as comprising a: 'Bedstead and bedding, in Chest and Valise; Mahogany Drawers, in Chest to form a Wardrobe; Easy chair in chest to form a dressing table; Mahogany wash-hand stand and fittings in Oak tub.' When this 'outfit' is compared to that of the standard furnishings provided for an officer in the Army circular of 1887, it is clear that it provides what was missing: namely the bed, a comfortable chair, a private bath and washstand, a dressing table and draws for clothing – items that offered convenience and comfort and enabled personal hygiene and dress. The utility of such furniture is apparent from their ability to serve several functions, for example the chest or trunk for transport, which contains the easy chair, also acts as a dressing table.

In total there are only four packed chests which together contain eight items. Another advertisement by Allen from the *The Army and Navy List Advertiser* of 1891[43] states that the whole ensemble costs just £25, which in 1881 is about half the annual wage of a general labourer, but easily purchased within the £625 annual wage of a surgeon or medical officer.[44] Variations and customisations of campaign furniture designs could be requested according to the taste and budget of the officer. Some were made in satinwood and others in oak; the padded seat might be of good leather or made from a stiff oilcloth, to imitate leather. Officers from regiments considered to be of greater prestige, such as the household cavalry, tended to choose the more expensive materials and designs. Allen advertised another 'outfit' for cavalry officers in 1860, which cost £83 2 s 6 d, £24 10s of which was the cost of a canteen to cater for the needs of three persons, indicating the importance of private dining in confirming status on the officer.[45]

Unlike the regular soldier's bed space, the interiors of officers' room were rarely photographed. However, a few officers with time on their hands and a talent for art have depicted their rooms. A watercolour by Lieutenant Edward Hovell Thurlow (1839–1925) of the Royal Artillery[46] shows his barrack room at Landguard Fort (Figure 7.2). He was 17 when he painted this picture, which he describes as 'done in bed, Nov 27th 1856'.[47] The major difference between this interior and that shown in the photograph of the ordinary soldiers' bed space,

Figure 7.2 The barrack room of Lieutenant Edward Hovell Thurlow at Landguard Fort, 1856.

is that the officer is able to compose the furniture in any way he chooses and so he can made it more like a domestic interior. The fixtures and fittings provided for him also lent themselves to this. For example, the officer had a carpet, rather than bare floors, and a fireplace, adding warmth to the small room. Likewise the built-in cupboards, to the left of the fireplace and within the alcove, provide personal privacy for belongings.

The officer's own furniture assists with this domestication; to the right is a campaign chest of drawers, with removable galleried shelves. To the left of the fireplace is a leather padded armchair known as a Douro chair.[48] The bed, that we cannot see, is likely to be a campaign bed, as is the chaise longue to the far left of the watercolour. The table and the Windsor chair behind it would have been part of the barrack furniture described in the regulations, as was the coalscuttle. The two deep-buttoned armchairs could also be part of the barracks furnishings, but it is also possible that the officer owned these. On top of the alcove cupboard to the right of the fireplace, is a selection of travelling boxes: a circular hatbox and lockable document or dispatch boxes, which gave the officer a degree of privacy for his correspondence. On the mantle piece are inkbottles and quills for writing, along with a collection of small personal items. There are two diminutive framed pictures immediately above; being in a landscape format they are likely to be illustrations of scenes rather than portraits, although it is possible that they are framed group photographs. The table and the galleried shelves of the chest of drawers hold numerous books, alluding to the greater education, wealth and leisure time the officer. The largest box, on the top shelf of the chest of drawers, is likely to be a travelling writing slope. Whereas the regular soldiers' photographs included images of pets, this officer has painted company into his room, with a cat seated on the top rail of an armchair. The cat is likely to have belonged to the Fort, but officers sometimes owned dogs. A Landguard Fort ghost story of 1857, gives an atmospheric description of an officer's life in barracks, including his ownership of a friendly bulldog. The officer, an Ensign, was also assigned a private as a manservant. Both the pet and the servant enhanced the officer's day-to-day life, making it more comfortable and emotionally secure.[49]

A rare survival describing the life of the officer exists in a set of Albums called *Camp sketches*. These contain photographs of 122 sketches, created as a humorous reminder of life in camp at Somerford Park, where the 5th Cheshire Rifle Volunteers took their annual drill. Dated 1872 to 1890, one depicts a woman drawing at a table opposite her officer husband, and it is possible that she may have been the artist.[50] In one of the cartoons, entitled 'The adjutant's Idea: "Always like to have all my home comforts with me!"' (Figure 7.3), the officer

Home from Home?

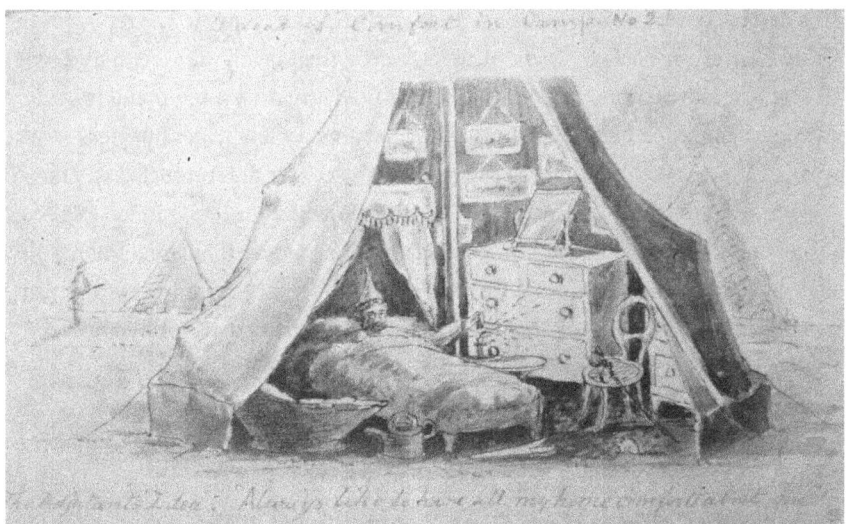

Figure 7.3 The adjutant's idea: 'Always like to have all my home comforts with me!' pencil sketch, c. 1872–90.

in question has made no concessions to luxury and comfort just because he is under canvas, recreating his bedroom as if it were at home. He has a campaign bed with an angel tester, a hip bath and a can for hot water, a chest of drawers and mirror, a cane bottomed balloon backed chair and another smaller chest of drawers, a small side table and six framed pictures. All of this clearly crammed uncomfortably into his tent. The artist sees the humour in this situation, but the soldier himself is simply following normal practice. Although published for civil service officers and their families, the advice of *The Complete Indian Housekeeper and Cook*, published in 1890, would read just as well for the military; 'the first axiom for camp is not to do without comfort'. It then goes on to describe how that is best achieved: 'do not make yourself uncomfortable for want of things to which you are accustomed'.[51] In other words, comfort is related to precisely reproducing your home – just as the adjutant attempts.[52]

This lavish recreation of home also represented the divide between officer and the regular soldier. The latter could only take what he could carry in to war, whereas an officer had his furnishings carried for him. A decrease in the weight of equipment ordinary soldiers had to carry took place after the 1870s, the infantry pack reducing to 41 pounds in transit, with 18 pounds carried separately in a personal valise within the baggage train.[53] In contrast, there were no limits on the weight an officer could take, apart from his own fiscal circumstances, as he paid for the mules and local servants to carry his luggage while on campaign.

This had become a serious issue by the late nineteenth century. The report of the *Kabul Committee on Equipment* of 1882 lists in great detail the weight and types of baggage allowed on the mule train required to carry a regiment from one location to another, describing how it had become an inefficient business for the army. Much less furniture is seen as being 'necessary for the comfort of an officer': just a bed, a table and a chair, and it recommends that officers purchase specific designs made by Ross of Dublin, choosing them because they are lighter.[54] This attempt to standardise officers' furniture indicates that the culture of the army was changing. In furniture terms this was embodied in the Roorkhee chair, named after a garrison town in India. Using stretched canvas for the seating and leather straps for the arm rest, they could be taken apart and rolled up, making them much lighter and smaller in transport, they were first designed and sold by the Army and Navy Stores in 1898.[55] Changes in economy of design and cost continued, so that by the First World War most traditional manufacturers, like Allen, were no longer trading; even Ross of Dublin went out of business in 1907. These companies were in the main replaced by the Army and Navy Co-operative Society (later known as the Army and Navy Stores), which originally started as a club to reduce costs for the officer through group purchasing.[56]

Such furnishings survived their travels only to end up back home and out of place in the country or London house. Like Wellington's bed, they might for a while be used by their owner out of nostalgia or practicality; the wounded or ill found a campaign bed's movability useful and manufacturers of campaign furniture also advertised invalid furniture in their catalogues.[57] But it is usual in inventories to find these pieces stored away or used by servants: what had once been essential for the status of the Victorian officer was unnecessary at home.

Conclusions: Regulating comfort

Those aspects of daily life and material comfort which simulated home, such as personal space, personal furnishings and privacy, were denied to the regular soldier – unless he had a wife, which itself was an inducement to good behaviour, as the commanding officer gave permission for marriage. Much like the inmate of the workhouse, or public school, the individual's lack of power within the institution was represented by his lack of control over material comfort and privacy. Being allowed to display personally owned images did not actually increase either of these for the regular soldier, but it did allow for controlled personal expression and the creation/illusion of joint memories with loved ones outside barracks. The cultural significance of this communication, not only for the soldier, but also for family at home, reached its height during the First World War, when the term 'home comforts' became synonymous with personal correspondence and homemade gifts for soldiers.[58]

The late-nineteenth-century postcard and photograph were part of a much wider societal growth in literacy, leisure time and non-essential, status driven, consumption. Likewise, the move away from buying customised campaign furniture, from specialist shops, was part of wider changes in consumption and in imperial and military organization.[59] The military reforms of Cardwell and Haldane recognized that empires and armies could not be efficiently run or maintained by individualistic officers funding their accommodation and equipment. As Sir George Otto Trevelyan stated in the 1872 parliamentary debate on Cardwell's reforms.

> As long as they had a bad system it was impossible to economize, and for the first time in his experience of Parliament they had had within the last two years proposals as to the military expenditure by which, he must repeat, they would get their money's worth for their money.[60]

So it was inevitable that the army would control the consumption of all it employed, even officers. By the beginning of the twentieth century, just as department stores sold western consumer goods across the world, the British army had barracks and permanent bases from which to maintain the Empire. The officer and soldier no longer had to bring their home comforts with them, either the army provided them physically or via its postal service, or they could purchase them. The world was now their home and being an officer in the army of the British Empire was status enough.

Notes

1 British Newspaper Archive search (30 December 2018); using the terms 'soldiers' and 'home comforts', the earliest example is from the *Morning Post* of Tuesday 13 May 1856 called 'Embodied or disembodied militia' (p. 2) describing the country squire giving up his home comforts to 'follow the drum'. From the 1860s home comforts relates to improving the life of the soldier. *Bridport News* - Friday 23 May in 1884 p. 4. The Soldiers' Institute in Portland barracks is described as

being 'replete with home comforts and amusements'. (From the 1860s Regimental Institutes provided improving pastimes, such as reading and singing, in English barracks. They often had Christian charitable links, and as such the term 'home comforts' becomes a signifier of a moralising influence on the solder).
2. Daniel Miller, *The Comfort of Things* (Polity Press, 2009).
3. The Duke of Wellington wrote to the Secretary of War, Lord Bathurst, on the 29th June 1813: 'It is quite impossible for me or any other man to command a British Army under the existing system. We have in the service the scum of the earth as common soldiers.'
4. Edward P. J. Gosling, *Tommy Atkins, War Office Reform and the Social and Cultural Presence of the Late-Victorian Army in Britain*, c.1868 – 1899, a PhD thesis submitted to Plymouth, July 2015, 1–33.
5. Allan Ramsay Skelley, *The Victorian Army at Home: The Recruitment and Terms and Conditions of the British Regular, 1859-1899* [Hereafter, *Victorian Army at Home*], 28–9.
6. *Victorian Army at Home*, 63.
7. James Douet, *British Barracks 1600-1914: Their Architecture and Role in Society*, H.M.S.O., 1988, 170.
8. *War Office Pattern Book, List and Drawings of Pattern Articles to be adopted in War Department works and buildings*, 1898 (English Heritage – Dover Castle)
9. *Priced Vocabulary of All Stores Used in Her Majesty's Service and Provided by Control Department* (Woolwich, 1875).
10. Barrack beds were made of wood, until c.1825 when a folding iron bedstead was introduced (early example in Dover Castle collection, English Heritage). By the 1870s a telescoping form known as the Macdonald was in common usage.
11. *Army circulars*, War Office (London: H.M.S.O., 1887) [Hereafter: *Army Circulars*], 18–19.
12. John Pindar, *Autobiography of a Private Soldier* (1877, Edinburgh: Menzies) [Hereafter: *Autobiography of a Private Soldier*], 162. The kit was in fact not free, as a standard charge for it was taken out of your pay as stoppages, along with the cost of your our uniform, your food, wear and tear on barracks equipment, as well as the cost of hair cutting. All of which left the soldier with very little actual money. *Victorian Army at Home*, 182.
13. *Victorian Army at Home*, 184.
14. Ibid., 29.
15. Trevor May, *Military Barracks* (Shire Publications, 2002), 22. As described by J. E. A. Troyte, September 1873.
16. *Autobiography of a Private Soldier*, 110.
17. *Life in the Ranks of the English Army*, Reprinted from 'Cassel's Magazine' (London: Stationery Office, 1883).

18 A Gloucestershire barrack room, taken in 1904, shows postcards displayed neatly around the frame of a window on an end wall, including individually framed official portraits of Edward VII and Queen Alexandra, as part of a communal display. Soldiers of Gloucestershire museum: GLRRM: 04109.
19 Personal possessions were normally kept in the soldier's trunk.
20 'A private of the Royal Fusiliers standing by his kit layout', *Weapons and Equipment*, fig. 84, 110.
21 'Kit layout in Barracks, first battalion the Suffolk regiment c. 1900'. From Featherstone, Donald, *Weapons and Equipment of the Victorian Soldier* (Blandford Press, 1978) [Hereafter: *Weapons and Equipment*] Fig. 99, 124.
22 The Bristol barracks were first opened around 1845, having been built after the 1831 political riots in Bristol. Horfield Barracks were refurbished after Caldwell's reforms in 1873, in order to serve as a local Military Centre.
23 Thomas King's short service attestation papers, which he signed upon joining the army, are dated 1903. The 'Certificate of Qualification for Promotion to corporal' was awarded to 7111 Lance Corporal Thomas King, 2nd Battalion, The Gloucestershire Regiment on the 21 October 1904. GLRRM: 07118.4.
24 'A barrack room, the Gloucestershire Regiment, 1904.' Soldiers of Gloucestershire museum: GLRRM: 04109.
25 Soldiers of Gloucestershire Museum - GLRRM: 07118.1.
26 https://en.wikipedia.org/wiki/List_of_theatres_in_Bristol
27 John Storey, *The Making of English Popular Culture* (London: Routledge, 2016) [Hereafter: *English Popular Culture*], 104.
28 http://www.liverpoolmuseums.org.uk/walker/collections/paintings/19c/item-23 8802.aspx
29 Ballad pubs, or 'convivials' were the predecessors of Music Hall, and had lasted longer in Bristol than in many other cities. Dr Nick Nource, post doctoral research associate at the University of Bristol, from a talk given at M-Shed, 17 May 2018.
30 Jochen Petzold, 'Inventing the Victorian Boy: S.O.Beeton's The Boy's own magazine', *The Making of English Popular Culture*, ed., John Storey (London: Routledge, 2016), 76–89.
31 Soldiers of Gloucestershire Museum. GLRRM: 07118.2 and GLRRM: 07118.3. In 1861 three levels or standards were set out and were linked with promotion in the ranks. The third-class certificate specified the standard for promotion to the rank of corporal. From *The Victorian army At Home*, 311.
32 *Autobiography of a Private Soldier*, 23.
33 Thomas King's army service appears to have been for 10 years. This would have been long enough for his discharge may have been agreed, he may also have been invalided out of the army, but as yet I have found no documentation identifying

34 Provision of purpose built accommodation for married soldiers is first suggested in the 1855 Barrack Accommodation Report. *British Barracks*, 128.
35 *The Gloucestershire Citizen*, Friday 28 February 1930 (front page article under the column title 'scenes at the workhouse').
36 *Victorian Army at Home*, 304.
37 *Army Circulars*, 6.
38 Ibid., 21–2. An example of a sergeant's campaign is a box table with an engraved metal plate identifying its owner as 'C.R. Sargent J. Moorhouse of the Royal Engineers'. *My Barrack room: A Catalogue of 18th, 19th & Early 20th Century Campaign Furniture & Travel Equipment* (published by Christopher Clarke (Antiques) Ltd. 2012), [Hereafter: *My Barrack Room*], 4.
39 There were, of course, manufacturers of campaign furnishings in military towns, such as the Seagrove family of Portsmouth, based opposite the dockyard, on the Hard in Portsea. Likewise colonial equipment could be supplied many foreign makers abroad, such as the camphor wood trunks made in Hong Kong, whose wood acted as a repellant to insects.
40 http://www.campaignfurniture.com/antiques/j-w-allen-advert
41 http://www.campaignfurniture.com/antiques/testimonial-of-barrack-furniture
42 Cartoon by William Heath, '*Take up your bed – and walk!!!*' dated 1 October 1829 - V&A museum: 1233:93-1882.
43 Nicholas A. Brawer, *British Campaign Furniture: Elegance under Canvas, 1740-1914*, Harry N. Abrams, 2001 [Hereafter: *British Campaign Furniture*], 161.
44 Williamson, 'The structure of pay in Britain, 1710-1911', *Research in Economic History*, 7, 1982. http://www.wirksworth.org.uk/a04value.htm#Williamson
45 *British Campaign Furniture*, 62.
46 J. H. Leslie, *The History of Landguard Fort, in Suffolk*, Eyre and Spottiswoode, 1898, 80–1. Hovell Thurlow's room was in the Officer's barracks on the first floor, adjacent to, and over looking over the guardroom and chapel.
47 *My Barrack Room*, 6.
48 Named after the Duke of Wellington, whose titles included the Marquess of Douro.
49 Lieutenant Colonel Garland Matthews, 'The Ghost of Landguard Fort', *Essex Standard* - Saturday, 28 December 1889, 6.
50 *The Baggage Elephant: Eighteenth, Nineteenth an Early Twentieth Century Campaign Furniture & Travel Equipment* (Christopher Clarke (Antiques) Ltd., 2015), 59.
51 Flora Annie Webster Steel, *The Complete Indian Housekeeper and Cook* (Heineman, 1890), 148 and 152.
52 *British Campaign Furniture*, 94.
53 *Victorian Army at Home*, 63.

54 *The Report of the Kabul Committee on Equipment* (Calcutta, 1882), 22.
55 *British Campaign Furniture*, 70–2.
56 Ibid., 69.
57 Ibid., 103.
58 British Newspaper Archive search (30 December 2018); using the terms 'Soldiers' and 'Home Comforts'.
59 Frank Trentmann, *Empire of Things* (Penguin History, 2016), 202 and 204.
60 Hansard, *Military Forces Localisation (Expenses) Bill—Bill 222*, 29 July 1872, Volume 213. Second Reading Adjourned Debate. Comments of Mr Trevellyan.

Object in focus 5:
A wallpaper sandwich: Comfort in the student room in nineteenth-century Cambridge

Serena Dyer

During renovations in the late 1990s, a 'wallpaper sandwich', made up of twelve preserved layers of wallpaper, was removed from the wall of a student room at Peterhouse College at the University of Cambridge.[1] This sandwich, now in the collection of the Museum of Domestic Design and Architecture at Middlesex University, provides a tangible connection to the temporary domestic spaces created by the students at the college. Unique within the museum's collections, these wallpapers were chosen, hung and lived with by generation after generation of students. The wallpapers salvaged from this discovery had been hung between 1795 and the twentieth century, and their designs are diverse. Together, these papers provide a microcosmic view of the tastes and domestic priorities of Cambridge students over two hundred years.[2]

These wallpapers reveal a complex system of masculine identities which were inherently connected with material constructions of domestic comfort. No longer tied to parents, tutors or school-masters, young men entering the college were creating a new identity for themselves, both metaphorically and materially, through the decoration and material culture of their rooms.[3] Some aspects of a room – such as furniture – were occasionally assimilated by each generation of students, for example by buying furniture from the previous occupant.[4] However, these inherited objects were integrated into broader, personalized domestic schemes. The transitory and impermanent nature of wallpaper meant that it was easy to replace and overwrite the identity articulated by the previous occupants of these college rooms. Comfort – both physical and psychological – offers a fruitful lens through which to reassess this masculine refashioning of a small interior space. Using a selection of the papers from the Peterhouse College wallpaper sandwich as a framework, this study examines the how wallpaper enabled students to create a comfortable domestic haven within the college.

Students at Peterhouse, as with many of the other historic colleges, were intensely aware that they were only the most recent young men to occupy these 'hallowed' college rooms.[5] In his 1909 history of the University of Oxford, Ralph Durand explicitly wrote that 'so long as Oxford's stately colleges preserve even a semblance of their ancient form, they will have power to bring us in some degree into communion with those who lived and worked, thought and played within their walls'.[6] This sense, both metaphysical and material, of ancient inheritance and institutional identity seeped into the domestic experience of living in the college. The wallpaper sandwich provides a tangible means of accessing these layers of student inheritance, its palimpsest-like nature allows us to strip back through each superimposed layer of student taste.[7]

The decision to separate the wallpaper sandwich into its individual layers has allowed the identification of each wallpaper by its printing techniques, paper-manufacturing methods, the quality of the paper used, and its style and aesthetic. The bottom layer of the sandwich (Figure 7a.1) dates from the final years of the eighteenth century. It is a handmade laid paper, of relatively poor quality. This fragment of domestic ephemerality is symptomatic of the growing popularity of wallpaper in the eighteenth century and acts as a prelude to the more active use of wallpaper in the room as the nineteenth century progressed.[8] It was only in the eighteenth century that wallpaper came into regular use as an alternative to expensive textile wallcoverings or the hanging of heavy tapestries.[9] During this period, wallpaper was primarily used to decorate private spaces, such as bedrooms and dressing rooms, and had close links with notions of privacy and comfort.[10] This initial use of wallpaper in the student room marks this space as a sanctum and a domestic refuge within the institutional formality of the wider college, highlighting the equivalency of the student room and the private spaces of the bedroom, dressing room or closet.

Despite the relative ephemerality of wallpaper and its increased affordability in the late eighteenth and early nineteenth centuries, it would take another fifty years for one of the occupants of the student room at Peterhouse to take it upon themselves to repaper the walls. The second paper in the sandwich is machine printed, rather than hand block printed, and is of extremely poor quality – something which is immediately evident as the coloured blocked are misaligned and the design has not transferred cleanly the paper. The design features a white ground, with lattice detailing in gold, with a ruddy-brown motif inside each. There are hints of the popular gothic, reminiscent of the Puginesque motifs popular at the time (see Study 3), but this is a poor imitation of a fashionable aesthetic. It is likely that the 50 years of wear and tear endured by the paper

Figure 7a.1 Bottom layer of the wallpaper sandwich, 1795, Museum of Domestic Design and Architecture, BADDA 4869.

beneath had led it to become too dirty and tired for this latest occupant to endure.

The large, fifty-year gap between the hanging of the first and second papers is in accordance with contemporary depictions of student rooms in contemporary literature. *The Adventures of Mr Verdant Green: An Oxford Freshman* was published in 1853 and contains numerous descriptions of the social and material life of a university undergraduate of the mid-century. The protagonist, when first introduced to his own room, noted that:

> The once white-washed walls were coated with the uncleansed dust of the three past terms; and where the plaster had not been chipped off by flying porter-bottles or the heels of Wellington boots, its surface had afforded an irresistible temptation to those imaginative undergraduates who displayed their artistic genius in candle-smoke cartoons of the heads of the University, and other popular and unpopular characters.[11]

This description of a shabby, rough domestic space reflects none of the neatness and politeness assumed of Vickery's eighteenth-century wallpaper consumers.

However, it does depict and intensely masculine material environment, constructed through use, reuse, wear and tear. Masculine domestic comfort in the university college of the 1850s was generated not through the careful maintenance of a pristine domestic space, but rather through the intentional display of crafted neglect.

In order to fashion a semblance of domestic comfort, male students were avid consumers, often consuming unwanted items from each other.[12] The acquisition of these objects not only reflected taste and character, but also frugality and resourcefulness. Cambridge undergraduate Nugent-Bankes recorded how he and he fellow undergraduates would visit second-hand shops scattered through the city. From these he acquired 'an armchair, a bookcase and a writing table, all undeniable bargains and all capable of being put into good working order after a little judicious exercise of the hinges, drawer-handles and other component parts'.[13] This mismatched paraphernalia of youth was an articulation of multiple influences upon student identity and a material expression of the attributes of the independent young man.

From the late 1870s onwards, an intriguing change in attitude towards the decorating of college domestic space seems to have occurred. Within the room in Peterhouse, wallpapers, once a shabby backdrop to an ever-changing material landscape, were changed with a remarkable increase in frequency. By 1874 Britian produced over thirty-two million rolls of wallpaper each year, compared with only 1.2 million roles in 1834.[14] The mass production of wallpapers significantly lowered their cost and – even among the relatively wealthy students of Cambridge – this economic shift appears to have resulted in a new enthusiasm for decorating the domestic college space. While there was a fifty-year gap between the first two papers, now the papers were changed every three to five years. The first layer from within this period of increased frequency of new hangs was placed on the wall around 1879 and was the Mallow design produced by Morris and Co. The choice of this Morris wallpaper demonstrates a more intense interest in fashionable style than was articulated in the earlier wallpaper choices. Similarly, an awareness of, and conformity to, institutional college style is potentially at play. In 1868 – 1874, William Morris, along with Edward Burne-Jones and Ford Madox Brown, were heavily involved in the redevelopment of the public spaces within Peterhouse College, focusing on the Hall and Combination Room.[15] Mallow was a mid-range paper, costing around 20 shillings per roll in 1890.[16] Mallow's busy, quintessentially Victorian aesthetic continued through the remainder of the nineteenth-century papers and indicates a sense of conformity and conservativism in the domestic identity constructed by these students. As relatively expensive and fashionable as Mallow was, its life on the student room wall was short lived. In less than a decade, two more layers of wallpaper had been added. The final layers of paper, scattered throughout the twentieth century, reveal a plainer aesthetic, governed by function, and providing a backdrop to the posters and trinkets of successive generations of students.

These wallpapers played a crucial role in constructing comfort within the domestic space inhabited by undergraduate students at Oxford and Cambridge in the nineteenth century. Significantly, gender does not seem to have dictated the domestic choices of these men. Instead, thoughtful aesthetic reflection, homosocial cultures and popular interests and associations seem to have dominated the plurality of masculinities evident in these spaces and contributed to a specifically student-centred culture of both physical and physiological comfort. The importance of wallpaper as the backdrop for this youthful exploration of selfhood increased as wallpaper itself became cheaper and more disposable. The resultant transitory, impermanent attitude to domestic design articulated in the wallpaper sandwich highlights that these layers of wallpaper were conceived as temporary aesthetic experiments, allowing students to define their own domestic experience. The students who inhabited these rooms crafted their own individual selfhood, temporary domestic comfort and masculine identities within these spaces.

Notes

1 A portion of this chapter has previously been published in Serena Dyer, 'Masculinities, wallpaper, and crafting domestic space within the University, 1795–1914', *Nineteenth-Century Gender Studies*, 14, no. 2 (2018). It is reproduced by kind permission of the editors of *Nineteenth-Century Gender Studies*.
2 Women were not admitted to Peterhouse College, Cambridge until the late twentieth century.
3 College records imply that students have autonomy over the decoration of their rooms.
4 Jane Hamlett, '"Nicely Feminine, yet Learned": Student Rooms at Royal Holloway and the Oxford and Cambridge Colleges in Late Nineteenth-Century Britain', *Women's History Review*, 15, no. 1 (2006): 143.
5 Paul R. Deslandes, *Oxbridge Men: British Masculinity and the Undergraduate Experience, 1850–1920* (Bloomington: Indiana University Press, 2005), 20.
6 Ralph Durand, *Oxford: Its Buildings and Gardens* (London: Grant Richards, 1909), 2.
7 The exact location of the room within the college from which the sandwich was removed was not recorded by the contractors undertaking the construction work.

While records of past student occupants do exist within the college archive, it is not possible to accurately align these with the wallpapers.
8 The first record of paper used to decorate an interior wall dates from 1509 and was recovered from another of the University of Cambridge's colleges, Christs College. See Amanda Vickery, *Behind Closed Doors: At Home in Georgian England* (London: Yale University Press, 2009), 167.
9 Lesley Hoskins, *The Papered Wall: The History, Patterns and Techniques of Wallpaper* (London: Thames & Hudson, 2005); Treve Rosoman, *London Wallpapers: Their Manufacture and Use, 1690–1840* (Swindon: English Heritage, 2009); Karen Lipsedge, *Domestic Space in Eighteenth-Century British Novels* (Basingstoke: Palgrave Macmillan, 2012), 46–7.
10 Amanda Vickery, '"Neat and not too showy": Words and wallpaper in Regency England', in John Styles and Amanda Vickery (eds), *Gender, Taste, and Material Culture in Britain and North America, 1700–1830* (London: Yale University Press, 2006), 201.
11 Cuthbert Bede, *The Adventures of Mr. Verdant Green, an Oxford Freshman* (London: Nathaniel Cooke, 1853), 30.
12 Margot Finn, 'Men's things: Masculine possession in the consumer revolution', *Social History*, 25, no. 2 (2000): 133–55.
13 George Nugent-Bankes, *Cambridge Trifles; or, Splutterings from an Undergraduate Pen* (London: G. P. Putnam, 1881), 18–19.
14 Zoe Hendon, *Wallpaper* (London: Bloomsbury, 2018), 14.
15 Charles Harvey and Jon Press, *William Morris: Design and Enterprise in Victorian Britain* (Manchester: Manchester University Press, 1991), 76; A. F. Kersting and David Watkin, *Peterhouse 1284–1984: An Architectural Record* (Cambridge: Master and Fellows of Peterhouse, 1984).
16 Harvey and Press, *William Morris*, 174.

8

Making a home:
Family, memory and domestic objects in England, c.1750–1830

Jon Stobart

In Northanger Abbey, Catherine Morland is fascinated by the suite of rooms that nobody ever enters, preserved in the memory of the long dead Mrs Tilney. The General having hurried her from the door when she was being shown round the house by Eleanor Tilney, Catherine quizzes her companion:

> 'It remains as it was, I suppose?' said she, in a tone of feeling.
> 'Yes, entirely.'
> 'And how long ago may it be that your mother died?'
> 'She has been dead these nine years.'

Imaging that the room held some dark secret, she returns later, on her own, only to be intensely disappointed to find a 'large well-proportioned apartment, an handsome dimity bed ... a bright Bath stove, mahogany wardrobes and neatly-painted chairs'.[1] While this is a parodic reference to a similarly 'monumentalised' suite of rooms in Ann Radcliffe's *The Mysteries of Udolpho* (1794), the incident also serves to highlight the ways in which domestic spaces and the things they contained could form an important and tangible link to the past. Tara Hamling notes that material objects were 'good for thinking and feeling with', but they were also good for remembering with.[2] Indeed, Marius Kwint has argued that objects serve memory in three ways: they furnish memory by constituting an often very vivid picture of the past (memories of a mother's dress or a favourite toy); they stimulate memory by bringing back dormant or forgotten experiences (a particular food transporting the person back to an earlier time), and they form records of memory that go beyond individual experience, linking people across time and space (a photograph album or a door frame marked with children's heights).[3]

Many of the most memory-laden objects are everyday domestic items that constitute a home both in a practical, liveable sense and in terms of emotional attachment. For Judith Lewis, it was the link between emotion/memory and object/space that allowed at least some women to feel 'at home' in what might otherwise be luxurious but uncomfortable country houses.[4] To achieve this function, however, things and spaces needed to develop associations with people. This might be achieved through making or gifting. Amanda Vickery, for instance, has noted the emotional significance of women's handicrafts and their incorporation into the domestic interior and, while Lena Cowen Orlin cautions that the scope for individuals to sentimentalize objects through bequests was conditioned by the conventions of will making, bequeathing was a key mechanism for imparting memorial significance onto an object.[5] Yet it was owning and using objects that did more than anything to develop person–object relationships and memories, a process which Amber Epp and Linda Price describe in terms of 'warming up' the item, most often through regular use and its location in a room that was frequently occupied by the family.[6]

My purpose in this chapter is to examine some of the ways in which family and memory were bound up with specific objects and domestic spaces, helping to shape their meaning and use, and contributing to the construction of home and the comfort it might afford. In doing this, I depart radically from eighteenth-century ideas of architectural association,[7] which focused on the power of the exterior to evoke historical, epochal and political associations in the mind of the viewer, and instead explore interiors spaces and personal and private associations with objects. In this, I draw implicitly on Gaston Bachelard's notion of 'home' as a palimpsest of personal memories, at once comprising and spatially organizing recollections of events, people and objects.[8] Moving down through different spatial scales, I commence with the house as a whole, examining how older properties in particular were consciously memorialized as symbols of familial status and identity. Next, I examine the use of particular rooms as vehicles for recording family history, but also as places in which everyday life was played out and which thus became containers of individual memories. Lastly, I arrive at specific objects where the focus falls initially on family pictures and their role in communicating both lineage and kinship, and in capturing memories of loved ones separated by time or space. I then turn to household objects and consider the ways in which they tied together family and home through sentiment and memory. Overall, I argue that family was just as important in the (collective) memory as it was in real life in its power to make a house into a home.

The house as family memorial

Partly because its association with Shakespeare (who was reputedly caught poaching in its grounds), Charlecote Park in Warwickshire exemplifies the way in which national history became increasingly entangled with the country house.[9] In April 1765, the then owner, George Lucy, wrote 'but what have I to do (who am happy to have a good old house) but make it decent and to content myself with that'.[10] What he did, in fact, was to erase much of whatever was left of the original interiors with little regard 'either to Shakespeare or to his own ancestors'.[11] Yet these improvements did not affect the exterior appearance of the house; neither did they eradicate its symbolic importance as a link to the past. As her father noted when the newly married Mary Elizabeth Lucy moved into the house in 1823: 'any man with money can build a new house but money will not build an old respectable Mansion like Charlecote'.[12] An ancient house spoke of an equally ancient lineage, both in its overall appearance and through the detail of its decoration. An American visitor in 1820 remarked on the great hall, which 'still retains much of the appearance it must have had in the days of Shakespeare', but also the stained glass in the windows emblazoned with the Lucy arms, which traced the family line back to medieval times.[13] Not satisfied with this evocation of the past, John Hammond Lucy (Mary's husband) set about re-edifying the interiors in a broadly Jacobean style, with new ceilings, fireplaces and a range of Elizabethan and Jacobean furniture – either original or reproduction.[14]

Such decorative schemes were in keeping with the prevailing taste of the 1820s and 1830s, but Lucy was constructing more than simply a fashionable house. He was fascinated with heraldry and with tracing the history of his family. He commissioned a pedigree book from the Heralds' College, had the stained glass in the hall repaired and reset (with meticulous care being taken about colours and dates), and commissioned from Thomas Willement a whole new set of armorial glass which traced 'the descent of Sir John Lucy Knight who built Charlecote House in the reign of Queen Elizabeth'.[15] Together with carefully chosen furniture, his aim was to create a house with a Jacobean spirit but also one that memorialized both the Lucy family and the historic associations of Charlecote. In 1837, he bought a suite of ebony furniture that was reputed to have been a present from Queen Elizabeth to Robert Dudley, Earl of Leicester, and had originally been at nearby Kenilworth Castle. This made them of particular interest because Elizabeth had visited Charlecote when staying with Dudley at Kenilworth; they were given an additional layer of meaning because the needlework upholstery was worked by Mary Elizabeth. Past and present were thus stitched together in the fabric of the house.[16]

Audley End in Essex was also caught up in the growing taste for Jacobean interiors. Originally built as a prodigy house and with associations with Stuart royalty, the house went into a period of decline before being inherited in 1762 by Sir John Griffin Griffin who undertook a range of improvements, including the creation a small suite of rooms by Robert Adam. Linked to his acquisition of the revived title of Baron de Walden, he decorated the first-floor saloon with a series of ancestral portraits that traced his decent from Thomas, Lord Audley of Walden, who had originally been granted the monastic estate on which Audley was built. As Hannah Chavasse argues, this asserted both his lineage and his connection to the house itself.[17] This connection between family and house was redefined and strengthened by John's successor, Richard Neville, third Lord Braybrooke.[18] Like George Hammond Lucy, he was an antiquarian intent on remodelling his house in an authentic manner. Rather than looking elsewhere for 'genuine' Jacobean objects, though, Neville took inspiration from surviving aspects of the house itself, restoring original features and reproducing extant decorative schemes elsewhere in the house. Yet this search for authenticity was tempered with a respect for the changes made by his predecessor: the Adam rooms remained untouched as did a new suite of first-floor rooms fitted out after John's peerage was granted (Figure 8.1).[19]

This challenges John Cornforth's assertion that the inspiration of the past became 'less strongly personal' in the late eighteenth and early nineteenth century, and more part of a general move to romanticism.[20] Richard Neville clearly made a close association between the house and his ancestors: it was a memorial to their endeavours and achievements. In this, the materiality of the house was underpinned through the pages of Neville's *History of Audley End*, published in 1836. As well as detailing the development of the house, this told the story of its owners; a critical tone was struck when discussing the misdemeanours of early owners, but was largely celebratory when it came to his immediate predecessors. Chavasse rightly stresses that Neville was actively managing the family image, but he was also memorializing family and its link to the house. On occasions, this was rendered through detailed biographies of particular objects: two volumes of Pliny, for example, bore the autograph of Sir Henry Neville (Ambassador to France, d.1615), while the south library contained curtains made from Florentine damask given to another Henry Neville by the third Grand Duke of Tuscany 'with whom, from letters still extant in the family,

Figure 8.1 Great Hall, Audley End, mid-nineteenth century (unknown artist), © English Heritage.

he appears to have lived in habits of intimacy'.[21] Family papers and objects as heirlooms are drawn together both in the surviving materiality of the house and the pages of Neville's history. Audley End, like Charlecote Park, thus shows how family could be consciously constructed and memorialized in the house. Elsewhere, a similar process of memorialization can be seen in particular parts of the house, but particular rooms could also hold more personal memories of family.

Rooms, memorials and memories

State apartments were a common feature of English country houses throughout the eighteenth century. Their original function as rooms in which visiting royalty would stay became redundant as Hanoverian monarchs eschewed tours of their kingdom and they increasingly became vested as symbols of rank and lineage.[22] At Stoneleigh Abbey in Warwickshire, Edward, third Lord Leigh, had a large extension built onto a house that largely comprised buildings that were part of the former Cistercian monastery. The Great Apartment – comprising a drawing room, parlour and state bedchamber – was decorated in what Andor Gomme has called 'conservative but still swagger taste': the stylar wainscoting and heavy Corinthian pilasters were complemented by walnut and guilt furniture and crimson velvet drapery.[23] As was typical of such apartments, Edward wrote his family status into the fabric of the rooms, his coronet and arms being carved into the capitals of the pilasters. He also commissioned a set of seven walnut chairs embroidered with scenes from classical mythology and again with his coronet and arms painted in full colour in a gilded panel at the top of the chair backs – as was common for hall chairs at this time. The arm chair also includes a panel at the base of the backrest with the monograms of Edward and his wife Mary Holbech. In this way, the traditional badges of rank and pedigree are given a personal touch, linking husband and wife to their linear family. What is perhaps most striking about these rooms is the way that they were preserved, largely unaltered, through successive improvements

Figure 8.2 Armchair: Walnut veneer and gilt gesso frames, painted coats of arms and embroidered covers, c.1725 (Stoneleigh Abbey)

made by subsequent generations of the Leighs. Other rooms demonstrated their fashionable taste and sociability; the Great Apartment was preserved as a marker of family lineage (Figure 8.2).

At Canons Ashby in Northamptonshire, the improvements made by Edward Dryden in the first decade of the eighteenth century included placing the family coats of arms over a new grandiose entrance, despite the fact that Edward had inherited the estate, but not the title. Elsewhere he retained the impressive but very old-fashionable Jacobean overmantel in the former Great Chamber, emblazoned with the coats of arms of various Dryden ancestors. To this, he added a new family motto: 'Antient as the Druids'. In the great hall, he created the impression of a medieval hall by assembling and hanging a wide array of weapons. In one room, then, he retained emblems and memorials of family and in another he created lineage afresh through assemblages of appropriate artefacts. When Edward died in 1717, an inventory was taken of the contents of the house, itemized room by room. Each was identified either by its name or location, with several given the names of people.[24] 'Mr Wyche's Room', 'Joseph Garner's Room', 'Thomas Garner's Room' and 'Christopher's Room' were named for the servants who occupied them, but two were identified by reference to family members. 'Sir E. Dryden's Room' was named for Edward's father, Erasmus (who had inherited the family title and periodically lived at Canons Ashby, looking after the house and estate for his son) and may have been the room in which he slept when at the house. 'Late Sir Robert's Room' referred to the third baronet, who had bequeathed the estate to Edward in 1708, and may again reflect the former use of the room as Sir Robert's bed chamber – the silk damask bed hangings certainly suggest that it had been a room of note, although there is nothing to suggest the kind of shrine to a dead relative that Catherine Morland found at Northanger Abbey. What is more telling than these carry-overs from a previous generation is that, while any association with Erasmus is quickly dropped, Sir Robert's name remained attached to his room through three subsequent owners. It was by no means an exceptional room in terms of its furniture (an unremarkable bed, a few chairs and tables and, in 1770, 42 gooseberry bottles) yet the name remained as a link to the individual who had given the estate to this branch of the family.

It seems unlikely that this naming indicated a sustained emotional memory of Sir Robert; rather it was a memorial, much as the gauntlets sword, spurs, tabard helm, pennants and standard placed in the church at Canons Ashby by Edward Dryden to commemorate his benefactor.[25] A deeper attachment to rooms and family can be found in the pages of Mary Elizabeth Lucy's memoirs.

These often situate the unfolding story of her life and family in the interior spaces of Charlecote Park, particularly the bed chambers where her children were born and where she watched several of them die. She sometimes noted her place by their side in a little bed placed there especially. In this way, the family home resembled Bachelard's imagining of a dwelling in which 'a great many of our memories are housed, and if the house is a bit elaborate, if it has a cellar and a garret, nooks and corridors, our memories have refuges that are more clearly delineated'.[26]

For Mary Elizabeth, the space in which her memories were most sharply delineated was the church in the grounds of the estate. At one level, this was a straightforward memorial to the Lucy pedigree as it contained the funerary monuments of the builder of the house, his son and grandson. Her decision to rebuild it as a memorial to her dead husband followed a similar practice of memorialization, as did the windows inserted into the new structure, one for each her children. Wider family was also commemorated, with Mary Elizabeth's sister and brother-in-law, Lord Willoughby de Brooke, donating a new stone font.[27] Yet the great irony in all this is that the old church held so many memories of family and its destruction stimulated remembering:

> The last Sunday that Divine Service was performed in the old church I could not help feeling very sorrowful as it contained memories dear to my very soul. How many times since I had been a wife and a mother (now 26 years) with husband and children I had prayed in that old family pew with its large oak desk around which we dealt together, there in the plain ancient Norman font all our children had been Christened. Before that Altar we had received 'the bread of life', and the old church bell had rung its remorseless toll four different times and the burial service had been read for my beloved husband and three beloved sons, and once had rung merrily and the marriage service had been read for my dearest Emily. The recollection of these things kindled at my heart and caused my tears to fall fast on the old building as it fell to the ground and there was not one stone left upon another.[28]

Weekly routines and the most significant events in her family life were held in fabric of the church and all are recalled as the building is pulled down. The loss of the building prompts remembering but perhaps also signals a loss of those memories. In this way, we see how the rooms making up a house could stimulate memory, but were also crucial in holding and shaping memories of family and past events that helped to make the house into a home and to offer the comfort of family remembered.

Family trees and family albums

Just as rooms contained memories, they also contained objects which themselves were memorials, prompts for memory and bringers of comfort. Among the most potent things in this respect are family portraits. These were often deployed in explicitly dynastic terms, sometimes to trace the decent of title (as at Audley End) and sometimes to map out a broader family tree of connections. This was a key part of any visit to a country house; visitors expected to see portraits of ancestors and to be able to use these to trace the pedigree of the family. Mrs Lybbe Powys invariably commented on such things, noting at Knole House, for instance, the 'portraits of family for many generations'.[29] Perhaps the most famous attempt to orchestrate family portraits in this way was undertaken by Henrietta Cavendish at Wellbeck Abbey in Nottinghamshire.[30] After the death of her husband, Edward Harley, second Earl of Oxford, she set about assembling and organizing over 200 portraits of her and her husband's family lines. They were hung in different rooms at Wellbeck, primarily according to the branch of the family they depicted. Some were annotated with inscriptions to clarify the identity of the person depicted and their relationship to Henrietta or Edward, or to underline great deeds or royal connections. This huge display of portraits formed what Kate Retford has termed a 'pictorial family tree' which left the visitor with no doubt about the pedigree and good connections of the Cavendish family: it memorialized and celebrated family.[31] Some found the effect a little overbearing, Mrs Delany noting that 'everything displays the antiquity of the noble race from whence the owners are descended … but there is a glare of grandeur'.[32] Certainly, there was little room here for personal memories or emotional attachment.

Such sentiments were perhaps not what family portraits were meant for, but there is evidence elsewhere that they were deployed in a rather different manner. The collection of family portraits at Stoneleigh Abbey was assembled by Thomas, fourth Lord Leigh, in the 1730s and 1740s with a substantial number also coming to Stoneleigh from the house of his uncle, Charles Leigh, who died just a few months prior to Thomas in 1749.[33] The collection included paintings of Sir Thomas Leigh (d.1571), who acquired the estate when the original monastery was dissolved, and his wife Alice. But the majority depicted more recent descendants and various branches of the synchronic family, including the Honourable Lady Rockingham, the mother of Eleanor, wife of the second Lord Leigh; Thomas Holbech, the father of the third Lord Leigh's wife, Mary;

the Honourable Miss Verney, an aunt of the fourth Lord Leigh, and Mary Isham, a cousin who married into the Ishams of Lamport Hall in Northamptonshire. Numbering about thirty pictures in total, these portraits were listed in the 1749 inventory as hanging in the Picture Gallery. The separate collections of Charles and Thomas had been amalgamated into a single assemblage that demonstrated both the Leigh's family lineage and their broader kinship networks.

Upon Thomas's death, the house was unoccupied for the next fifteen years until his son, Edward, came of age and began an extensive programme of refurbishment. This included a reorganization of his pictures, partly prompted by his own purchases, partly through further additions from Leighton Buzzard, but mostly as a result of a rather different set of curation practices. Edward relocated 15 family pictures to the Breakfast and Dining Parlour (which formed the main rooms for informal entertaining in the house); he also hung four in the Brown Parlour and one in the Drawing Room (both within the Great Apartment), and a further five in private family rooms at the back of the house; two were placed in his own dressing room.[34] This redistribution seems to have reflected personal choices rather than dynastic posturing. The 'family pictures' in the breakfast and dining rooms were hung alongside landscapes and historical pieces; those in the private family rooms were put in the place of a series of racing prints bought by his father, which Edward rehung in the picture gallery. Dispersed in this way, the portraits could no longer constitute a meaningful family tree; a better analogy might be the family album, with different rooms forming different pages in the book. In the absence of information about which portraits were located in which rooms, it is impossible to know for certain, but Edward may well have been grouping pictures in a manner that reflected his emotional rather than dynastic association with family.

This is certainly the case with Mary Elizabeth Lucy's collection of miniatures. Here, of course, the medium as well as the subject of the painting is significant: miniatures might be displayed on the wall, but could equally be kept in a drawer or box; they could be handled and were sometimes worn as lockets, bringing memories of their subject physically close. Mary Elizabeth had eight miniatures painted by the Liverpool-based artist Thomas Hargreaves when she married and left the family home in 1824. There was one of herself, one of each of her parents and four sisters, and one of her old nurse, Catherine Hughes. Looking at these pictures brought back vivid memories of the person depicted. Writing of the time when Catherine has recently died, she recalled having commissioned the miniature and noted that 'I always look at it with the most affectionate pleasure, and almost fancy I can hear her speak, it is such an admirable likeness'.[35] Object, person and memory were thus intertwined in a way that offered solace and linked Mary Elizabeth back to an earlier time, but also took her to a different place. Looking at the miniatures, her memory of Catherine is so vivid that the old lady almost comes alive. This carries Mary Elizabeth back in time and links her present marital home at Charlecote with her past childhood home in north Wales. No doubt similar emotions and memories were prompted when she gazed at the tiny paintings of her mother, father and sisters; keeping a similar picture of herself within her collection of miniatures may have helped symbolically to lock herself in her family; if so, it is notable that this was a partial reconstruction, her three brothers apparently being omitted from the virtual family group (Figure 8.3).

This reminds us that family, as well as family pictures, could be curated in different ways: as dynasty or as a family of current kinship ties. It also shows that blood was just as potent as cohabitation in creating and maintaining emotional bonds, and that conceptions of the family home did not simply change over the life course as a person moved from parental to marital home.[36] Mary Elizabeth was surely not alone in maintaining an emotional bond to – and finding comfort in – several different homes, built up over her life and remembered through the aid of mementoes. In her case, these were paintings, but a range of household objects also had the power to hold memories of family and shape ideas of home.

Figure 8.3 Portrait miniature, watercolour on ivory, Catherine Hughes (c.1750–after 1824) by George Hargreaves (1797-1870), CHA/D/17. Courtesy of National Trust.

Household objects: Remembering family and friends

Sarah Churchill, wife of the Duke of Marlborough, was given a life interest in Blenheim Palace and the freedom to dispose of her own property. This prompted her to make an inventory of the palace, distinguishing goods belonging to her from those that were heirlooms of the estate. One mechanism that she used in doing this was to note the biographies of certain objects. In one room, there was a 'yellow Damask Bed lined with white Sattin Embroidered and a very old suit of tapestry hangings which the Queen gave me to furnish part of my lodgings at Windsor Castle which afterwards I sent to St. Albans and afterwards to Blenheim'. In her own bed chamber, she identified a valance 'of a very rich embroidery which was made of the duchess of Marlborough's clothes'.[37] These biographies were not only a reflection of her ability to remember the provenance and life story of household objects, they also showed the power of these things to carry and perhaps prompt memories. And their stories were interwoven with her own: goods coming from the Queen and taken along as she moved from house to house. What is striking, though, is that the emotional and memorial significance of these objects did not rub off onto Blenheim. She felt no affection for the house and it never became home – a site of memory or a place of comfort – in the same way as Holywell, her childhood home where she had lived when first married. While Richard Neville linked his object biographies firmly into the story of the family and the house at Audley End, Sarah Churchill was more detached.

Further down the social scale, we can see a similar concern with the biography of things. Elizabeth Forth was the daughter of a wealthy Yorkshire grocer, Robert Woodhouse, and married the Reverend John Forth in 1791.[38] They inherited a wide array of household goods from both sets of parents as well as acquiring pieces of their own. An inventory taken in 1806 notes the provenance of many of these objects, the contents of a cupboard being especially rich in biographical detail:

1 large silver sauce boat marked EW which belonged to Mrs Forth's mother, the gift of Mrs Williamson

1 small silver cream or sauce boat marked REW – which belonged to the same & the gift of the same

One silver soup ladle the gift of Mrs Wright

1 compleat set of white and Gold tea China the gift of Mrs Woodhouse

2 Foreign Blue and White China tea pots and one Cream pot, one of the tea pots and Cream Pot the gift of Mrs Woodhouse and the Tea pot the Gift of Mrs Wright[39]

This itemization of gifts and family connections underlines the importance of objects, associations and memories in the construction of home. The Forth's house, like the one imagined by Bachelard, was stuffed with reminders of dead friends and relatives, the importance of which is apparent from their careful itemization on the inventory.[40] Perhaps the appraisers were being followed round the rooms by Mrs Forth, telling them the biography of each object and urging them to write them down; or perhaps Mrs Forth herself had the pen in her hand and recorded the personal provenance of each thing she listed. Whatever the precise mechanism, the inventory is remarkable because it carries the web of person-object relationships beyond the recollections of an individual and onto the written pages of what might otherwise be a dry and impersonal inventory. Text and object thus went together in carrying memories of previous ownership and family ties on to subsequent generations.

Communicating to the next generation the memories contained in household objects was also in the mind of Ellen Weeton when writing in 1824 to Mary, her nine-year-old daughter.[41] Ellen was a governess, living away from the family home, and her letter accompanied a parcel of textiles that she was passing on to the little girl. As Ellen explained:

> I have inclosed 4 different kinds of Gimp, of 4 and 2 yds length as you may perceive when you measure it (my mother once had gowns trimmed with it – perhaps 60 years ago) [...] The Green ribbon is part of a box-full my mother (your grandmother Weeton) once had; they were taken in a prize, which my father captured during the American war.[42]

These items are accompanied by their respective biographies that tied them and by extension the girl to her grandparents. Memories were kept alive through the objects and through narrating their stories. Indeed, Ellen is quite clear about her purpose:

> I am thus minute, my Mary, that you might know something of the history of your mother's family [...] the piece of patchwork is of an old quilt, I made it above 20 years ago [...] the Hexagon in the middle was a shred of our best bed hangings, they were chintz, from the East Indies which my father brought home with him[43]

She wanted to keep her daughter connected with her maternal family and chose to do this through material objects, no doubt hoping that, in touching these textiles, her daughter would remember these stories and come closer to her family.

Ellen Weeton was consciously deploying household objects as records of memory that could then serve to stimulate remembering of family and home. Not everyone was so deliberate, but the power of household objects to store memories could impinge on people almost despite themselves. Mrs Delany, writing to Anne Dewes shortly before departing for Dublin, informed her sister that 'I have got an old broken Indian chest for you, some scrub chairs, a sofa and couch – (the couch is precious because covered with a gift of my mother's, but it is so lumbering a thing I can't take it with me) – a clock, and a few pictures'.[44] Only the couch is singled out as holding any particular significance among these assorted objects because it was a link back to their mother. Although the connection is made in an aside and almost brushed off with a dismissal of the couch as large and unwieldy, Mary perhaps hoped to pass on a loyalty to the piece as a family heirloom.

No such sentiment can be detected in the actions and writings of Elizabeth Dryden. In an inventory drawn up in 1819, Elizabeth went through the house, distinguishing things that were hers from those that were 'Heir Looms of the Mansion of Canons Ashby' – much as Sarah Churchill had done 100 years earlier.[45] The circumstances in which she found herself must have shaped Elizabeth's feelings towards these belongings. She was being pursued by her dead husband's creditors and had a fractious relationship with her children, especially her second son Henry, who had inherited the estate the previous year. She therefore had an interest in downplaying the monetary value of the estate as opposed to her own property, but may also have viewed objects with particular familial associations with a somewhat jaundiced eye. Whatever the cause, Elizabeth made few emotional links with the contents of what had been her home for over sixty years as daughter, wife and now dowager. Her disconnect from family seems particularly strong when it came to the family papers. Two years earlier, she noted in a letter that 'all the family writings which I have are in a long box bound with Hair with my Grandfathers initials, sometimes in the Brown Gallery & sometimes in the Storeroom, but ought to be in Sir Edward Drydens custody, as he has the greatest interest in them, not having any myself'.[46] This, of course, reflected her eldest son's then ownership of the estate, but it also suggests a disregard for family history that is remarkable in itself. Bachelard might write about the significance of a cask that 'contains the things that are unforgettable', but Elizabeth apparently had little desire to know or remember the things contained in this box.[47] Only once does she betray any notion that the contents of the house held any memories of family. In the same letter she dismisses the family papers, she notes, 'Two small Cabinet Pictures purchased by my Uncle are in good preservation & hang on each side of the best Cabinet in the Drawing Room.'[48] Quality and location are all noted, but it is the association with her uncle (and adoptive father) which makes these pictures stand out. They formed a link with a previous generation and had, perhaps, been specifically gifted to Elizabeth.

Sentimentalizing and memorializing through bequests

Although bequeathing often served to sentimentalize and memorialize objects, Elizabeth Dryden again largely eschewed the opportunity.[49] Most of her bequests were small cash gifts, the only personal items being gifted to Caroline her daughter, Mr Fladgate her executor, and the wife of her long-serving steward, William Peacock. Perhaps again reflecting her indifferent relationship with her children, it was Mrs Peacock who was to receive 'my gold watch and seal and gold key and rings attached to it', whereas Caroline got Elizabeth's 'wearing apparel, work baskets & boxes with stores of thread &c &c &c … together with all the tea and sugar in the storeroom'.[50] Might this be read as a touching gift of the most personal of items in the hope that Caroline would remember her mother when wearing the clothes or using the work baskets? Perhaps, but it seems more likely that this was a calculated slight as Elizabeth added that 'if my daughter declines taking the legacy herein mentioned, I then desire it may be given to Miss Anne Phelps the present eldest daughter of Mrs Phelps' – a family friend.

Although there is little to suggest that Elizabeth was concerned with passing on family associations and memories through her bequests, other women were anxious to preserve and mark bonds of kinship and household community, as noted by Maxine Berg.[51] The goods were not necessarily of high monetary value, but they marked and carried important sentimental associations. Phillipa Hayes had been the housekeeper, correspondent and confidante of the life-long bachelor George Lucy of Charlecote Park for about 30 years when she died in 1772. By this time, she constituted the closest thing that Lucy had to family.[52] She appointed him as her executor and gave him 'out of the great regard I have for him, my cornelian seal, and desire he will accept my buff tabby to cover his easy chair'.[53] These two objects have particular significance. Cornelian seals were often held on a ring, so Mrs Hayes may have worn hers as an item of jewellery and most likely used it to seal her letters. It was thus a potent symbol of their long epistolary relationship and a reminder to Lucy of their correspondence and the enjoyment that he had in reading her letters. The buff tabby had probably covered her own chair; passing it on to be used in the same manner would again have encouraged Lucy to remember his old friend. Every time he sat in his easy chair, he would have come into contact with her cloth and through it with memories of her. Through everyday material objects that were loaded with personal associations, Mrs Hayes thus offered George Lucy ways of remembering their friendship in much the same way that Sarah Churchill recalled past relationships via a range of material objects.[54]

Mary Leigh used bequests in a similar way, reinforcing familial relationships through material objects. In the absence of any close family, she made dozens of cash bequests and marked particular friendships and kinship bonds with gifts of rings and brooches bought especially from William Makepeace, the London silversmith. These were more than the simple mourning rings typically distributed after funerals, some being fitted with gemstones or pearls. Most cost 5 guineas, but four brooches decorated with brilliants cost £50 apiece.[55] Such jewellery could have been worn by the recipient and, as with Mrs Hayes's cornelian seal, act as a reminder to the wearer of their relationship with Mary. More potent still were things that Mary herself had owned. She noted that 'I desire all the legacys I have received may be returned to the familys from when I had them'.[56] Specifically, this meant returning to Mrs Yorke's family an amber egg and gold spoon, to Lady Howard a painting of Tintern Abbey by Turner, and to the Dolben family a silver model of St Paul's. That Mary could recall who these things were from suggests that they held some emotional importance for her; giving them back would have added another layer of significance: memories of Mary as well as the person who had originally gifted the egg, painting or model to her. But the most poignant reminders of Mary's relationship with family contained in her will are the picture of Admiral Craven – which she desired to be hung up at the Craven's house, Coombe Abbey – and the 'miniature picture of William, Lord Craven, dated 1786' which she gave to William's daughter Mary Craven.[57] William Craven was her cousin and had been responsible, along with Mary, for the maintenance of the Stoneleigh estate during the long period mental illness that prevented her brother, Edward, from managing his own affairs. 1786 was the year in which Edward died. Moreover, family tradition has it that she had tender feelings for William, so the miniature would have held layers of complex emotional resonance for Mary; passing it to his daughter served to continue the memory of this close relationship onto the next generation, much as Berg argues.[58]

Edward Leigh also made a post-mortem gift to his cousin that again had particular personal significance. He was a talented musician and his violins went with him when he was taken to London and then Lincolnshire for treatment.[59] Three of these were given to William Craven and formed another reminder of the close bond between the two families.[60] This transfer of gifts between people was also a movement of material objects across space, taking part of one home into another. As well as locking memories into place, the mobility of objects thus helped to bring together different homes in ways that parallel Mary Elizabeth Lucy's imagining of another home when she gazed at the miniatures of her family.

Conclusions: Family, memory and home

If home is a place of emotional attachment to objects and family, then we must be mindful that these associations could be diachronic as well as synchronic. Memory was important in making a home and bringing comfort. Neither Henrietta Cavendish's pictorial family tree nor George Hammond Lucy's armorial stained glass turned their houses into homes, but the Leighs' collection of portraits may have done more to link them with their immediate ancestors and Mary Elizabeth Lucy's collection of miniatures were certainly charged with emotional memories of family and home. Memory imbued in everyday objects underpinned the role of diachronic as well as wider kin in building emotional bonds. The association of things and people was often powerful and enduring, especially when object biographies were retold to self and others. Household objects could be kept 'warm' through repeated narration of their familial significance as well their everyday use. At the same time, objects could help to carry memory across time and space, especially as they were gifted or bequeathed. They stimulated remembering, but also went beyond the individual: memory, like the goods themselves, passing down generations and tying one home to another.

Things, family and memory thus combined, but it is in their association with or collection in a particular place that they helped to produce feelings of home. This links to Bachelard's assertion that the house and its various spaces formed containers of memories. Ellen Weeton's work basket, Mrs Forth's cupboard, the old church at Charlecote or the material and written house created by Richard Neville were all receptacles holding memories of family in the material objects they contained. Catherine Morland may have been disappointed in the mundanity of the rooms that she found, but they nonetheless formed a material link to a family member long since dead. As such, they were a constant reminder of Mrs Tilney's place in the family and in the home.

Notes

1. Jane Austen, *Northanger Abbey* (1818; Oxford: Oxford World's Classics edition, 1980), 149, 155.
2. Tara Hamling, 'Household objects', in Susan Broomhall (ed.), *Early Modern Emotions: An Introduction* (London: Routledge, 2017), 135.
3. Marius Kwint, 'Introduction: The physical past', in Marius Kwint, Christopher Breward and Jeremy Aynsley (eds), *Material Memories* (Oxford: Oxford University Press, 1999), 2. See also Stephanie Downes, Sally Holloway and Sarah Randles, 'A feeling for things, past and present', in Stephanie Downes, Sally Holloway and Sarah Randles (eds), *Feeling Things: Objects and Emotions through History* (Oxford: Oxford University Press, 2018), 8–23.
4. Judith Lewis, 'When a house is not a home: Elite English women and the eighteenth-century country house', *Journal of British Studies*, 48 (2009): 336–63.
5. Amanda Vickery, *Behind Closed Doors: At Home in Georgian England* (New Haven: Yale University Press, 2009), 231–57; Lena Cowen Orlin, 'Empty vessels', in Tara Hamling and Catherine Richardson (eds), *Everyday Objects: Medieval and Early Modern Material Culture and Its Meanings* (Farnham: Ashgate, 2010), 299–308.
6. Amber Epp and Linda Price, 'The storied life of singularized objects: Forces of agency and network transformation', *Journal of Consumer Research*, 36 (2010): 820–37.
7. See John Archer, 'The beginnings of association in British architectural esthetics', *Eighteenth-Century Studies*, 16, no. 3 (1983): 241–64.
8. Gaston Bachelard, *The Poetics of Space* (London: Penguin, 1964).
9. Adrian Tinniswood, *The Polite Tourist* (London: The National Trust, 1998), 128–30.
10. Warwickshire Record Office (WRO), L6/1473 letter to Mrs Hayes, 14 April 1765.
11. Clive Wainwright, *The Romantic Interior: The British Collector at Home, 1750-1850* (New Haven: Yale University Press, 1989), 211.
12. WRO, L6/1538, Sir John Williams to Mary Elizabeth Lucy, no date, c.1823.
13. Quoted in Wainwright, *Romantic Interior*, 213.
14. Wainwright, *Romantic Interiors*, 225–40.
15. See Ibid., 225.
16. Ibid., 228–9. In reality, they were seventeenth-century products of Indian workshops, but this does little to detract from their ability to memorialize past events.
17. Hannah Chavasse, 'Material culture and the country house: Fashion, comfort and lineage' (unpublished PhD thesis, University of Northampton, 2015), 77.
18. Sir John, by then first Lord Braybrooke, was succeeded by Richard, Second Lord Braybrooke in 1797 and then by his son, Richard, third Lord Braybrooke in 1825.
19. Chavasse, 'Material culture', 200–9.

20 John Cornforth, 'The backward look', in G. Jackson-Stops (ed.), *The Treasure Houses of Britain: Five Hundred Years of Private Patronage and Art Collecting* (New Haven: Yale Univeristy Press, 1985), 68.
21 Braybrooke, *History of Audley End*, 117–18. Quoted in Chavasse, 'Material culture', 217.
22 John Cornforth, *Early Georgian Interiors* (New Haven, 2004), 13–19.
23 Andor Gomme, 'Abbey into palace: A lesser Wilton?' in Robert Bearman (ed.), *Stoneleigh Abbey: The House, Its Owners, Its Land* (Stratford-upon-Avon: The Shakespeare Birthplace Trust, 2004), 87.
24 Northamptonshire Record Office (NRO), D(CA)901: inventory of 1717.
25 See Jon Stobart and Mark Rothery, *Consumption and the Country House* (Oxford: Oxford University Press, 2016), 180–1.
26 Bachelard, *Poetics of Space*, 30.
27 Alice Fairfax-Lucy, *Charlecote and the Lucys* (London: Victor Gollancz, 1990), 286. The author is quite scathing about the new chapel, describing it as a pastiche replacing a genuinely old structure and meaningful structure.
28 Elise Donald (ed.), *Mistress of Charlecote: The Memoirs of Mary Elizabeth Lucy, 1803-1889* (London: Victor Gollancz, 1983), 81–2.
29 E. J. Climenson (ed.), *Passages form the Diaries of Mrs Philip Lybbe Powys* (London, 1899), 54.
30 Kate Retford, 'Patrilineal portraiture? Gender and genealogy in the eighteenth-century English country house', in John Styles and Amanda Vickery (eds), *Gender, Taste and Material Culture in Britain and North America 1700-1830* (New Haven: Yale University Press, 2006), 315–44.
31 Ibid., 327.
32 S. Woolsey (ed.), *The Autobiography and Correspondence of Mrs Delany* (Boston, MA: 1879), Vol. 1, Letter to Mrs Dewes, 7 September 1756.
33 Shakespeare Central Library and Archive (SCLA), DR18/31/903 Inventory of Leighton Buzzard, 1749; DR18/4/27 Inventory of Stoneleigh Abbey, 1749.
34 SCLA, DR18/4/43, Inventory of Stoneleigh Abbey 1774, with amendments in 1806.
35 Donald, *Mistress of Charlecote*, 56.
36 Katie Barclay, 'Family and household', in Susan Broomhall, *Early Modern Emotions* (London: Routledge, 2017), 244–6
37 Quoted in Lewis, 'When a house is not a home', 347.
38 Vickery, *Behind Closed Doors*, 224–5.
39 Quoted in Vickery, *Behind Closed Doors*, 225.
40 Bachelard, *Poetics of Space*, 30.
41 Discussed in Ariane Fennetaux, 'Sentimental economics: Recycling textiles in eighteenth-century Britain', in Ariane Fennetaux, Amelie Junqua and Sophie Vasset (eds), *The Afterlife of Used Things: Recycling in the Long Eighteenth Century* (London: Routledge, 2015), 134.

42 Ellen Weeton, *Miss Weeton's Journal of a Governess, 1807-1825* (Oxford: Oxford University Press, 1939), vol. 2, 325.
43 Ibid.
44 Woolsey, *Correspondence of Mrs Delany*, vol. 1, 465: letter to Anne Dewes, 10 March 1744.
45 NRO, D(CA) 904, Inventory of Canons Ashby, 1819
46 NRO, D(CA) 903b, Letter, 13 January 1817.
47 Bachelard, *Poetics of Space*, 105.
48 NRO, D(CA) 903b, Letter, 13 January 1817.
49 Orlin, 'Empty vessels'.
50 The National Archives (TNA), Prob11/1691: will of Elizabeth Dryden.
51 Maxine Berg, 'Women's consumption and the industrial classes of eighteenth-century England', *Journal of Social History*, 30 (1996): 415-34.
52 Jon Stobart, 'Housekeeper, correspondent and confidante: The under-told story of Mrs Hayes of Charlecote Park', *Family and Community History*, 21, no. 2 (2018): 96-111.
53 Fairfax-Lucy, *Charlecote and the Lucys*, 221.
54 Lewis, 'When a house is not a home'.
55 SCLA, DR 671 56 List of rings and brooches given by Mary Leigh.
56 TNA, Prob11/1448: will of Mary Leigh.
57 Ibid.
58 Berg, 'Women's consumption'.
59 Mairi Macdonald, 'Not unmarked by some eccentricities: The Leigh family of Stoneleigh Abbey', in Robert Bearman (ed.), *Stoneleigh Abbey: The House, Its Owners, Its Lands* (Stratford-upon-Avon: The Shakespeare Birthplace Trust, 2004), 150-1.
60 SCLA, DR18/13/9/24 copy of the will of Edward, Lord Leigh.

Object in focus 6:
The comfort of animal 'things' in late-Victorian Britain

Julie-Marie Strange

Histories of the emotional and material comforts of home tend to overlook animals.[1] The 'comfort of things' has an established scholarship but the 'things' in question are almost entirely inanimate.[2] 'Pets' occupied a liminal position in late-Victorian thought, caught between being a thing of property (dogs were legally defined as a chattel) with plastic materiality and a sentient companion.[3] This interlude, focusing on late-Victorian author George R Sims, situates animals in the material comfort of home. 'Comfort' might well describe the objects (animate and inanimate) with which Sims furnished his home to facilitate and reflect his career as a successful author but it is primarily used here in a more abstract sense to convey the relationships and feelings that constituted Sims's emotional and subjective self at home. For Sims, the 'comfort' of animal things was firstly in how they reflected his distinctive attributes and interests, the place where he was most 'at home', and secondly in how animals made home comforting by offering unique styles of companionship that were not available or valued in the world beyond home.

Sims's celebrity and wealth by the late nineteenth century were phenomenal. He was the subject of multiple biographical sketches across a range of magazines. These features interviewed celebrities at home and were accompanied by description and photographs of the domestic interior. In almost all the sketches of Sims at home, animals (alive and representational) were placed centre stage. Focusing on these features, the interlude illuminates how Sims's animal 'things' were intrinsic to fashioning his selfhood.

Sims at home

George Robert Sims (born 1847) was a prolific dramatist, novelist and journalist. Born into a well-connected family, he trained for business but aspired to be a writer. By the early 1880s, he enjoyed commercial success across multiple genres and had a reputation as a keen social commentator. Sims's energies were not confined to writing: he invented a 'cure' for baldness, dabbled in the occult, bred and showed dogs, campaigned tirelessly across a range of social causes and liked to gamble.[4] Sims reputedly loved three things: 'children, horses and dogs, particularly dogs'.[5] Intrinsic to Sims's authorial output was compassion. He was a friend of the poor and a 'lover of all dumb animals'.[6] Unashamedly populist, he was shunned by the literati as facile and sentimental.

By the late 1880s Sims's address on Clarence Terrace, overlooking Regents Park, declared his financial success. The house, likened to a 'museum', teemed with curios, 'Chinese gods and other household ones dear to memory'.[7] An 'oriental' room boasted rich Turkish rugs and wall hangings, elaborately carved woodwork and an array of slippers, smoking apparatus, bronze and gold. Other rooms sported collections of 'dolls of the world', tin soldiers, tea sets, lava cats, glassware and porcelain. Widowed twice between the 1880s and 1900, his domestic companions were animal: he lived with up to 14 dogs, numerous cats and multiple birds. Sims bred pedigree bulldogs and Dalmatians (his third wife bred Pomeranians) but most of his cats were strays (although he did have at least one pedigree named Flash).

Visiting journalists immediately encountered Sims's pets. One 'at home' noted the 'very lively intelligent pets, who make friends with one's boot', and sized up guests for approval (or not).[8] Dogs 'bounced' and 'scrambled' about the house, were present during interviews and photographed, licked interviewers, and demonstrated distinctive personalities.[9] Despite his collections of curiosities and relics, Sims seemingly allowed dogs and cats free movement across the house. Pets were portrayed as domestic companions rather than ornaments. Sims claimed to habitually dine with his cats and dogs (they were 'exceptionally well mannered animals'); cats slept on his desk; and Christmas cards featured Sims and his pets sharing Christmas dinner, the archetypal 'family' occasion (Figure 8a.1).[10]

Sims's home displayed an extensive range of inanimate animals too. As one journalist commented, 'Love of dogs, and dog life, is written all over the room in print and oil, china and composition'.[11] Sims's animal things reflected his tastes and interests to generate comfort as feeling (they rendered home a peculiarly personal space) and the journalists that visited him knew that this home was particular to Sims. The *New Penny Magazine* noted 'portraits of past and present canines in every material, models and pictures in various sizes' while numerous trophies testified to the prize-winning pedigree of several dogs.[12] The

Christmas Day with his favourite companions.

Figure 8a.1 Christmas Day with his Favourite Companions, *The Idler*, December 1897, 686.

Daily News Weekly noted the drawing-room portrait of Sims's bulldog Barney Barnato (named after the financier) with the inscription: 'For never man had friend,/ More enduring to the end,/ Truer mate, in every/ Turn of time and tide.'[13] Animal things supported the idea of the broader 'animal' family: decorative cards announced a bull pup's 'christening' and two Immortelles decorated the wall of Sims's study to commemorate 'Dinkie' & 'Pickle', 'devoted' and faithful canine friends for fifteen and fourteen years respectively.[14] Other much-loved animals became *objet d'art* in death: the hoof of Sims's pony 'Beauty' was an inkwell, a memento no doubt but also a neat motif for how his pets provided an income stream though his writing. Sims tended to blur the boundaries between animal as companion and as object, between comfort as representation and relationship, between 'animal' and 'human'. Sims's writing regularly featured animal companions while some of his dogs were attributed authorial voices in their own right and fronted fundraising campaigns for other dependents, notably widows and orphans of the Boer War. Sims commodified his pets, invested them with political opinions and made commercial capital from them, including endorsing pet products in his journalism. His animals helped constitute Sims's subjective comfort at home but were vital to generating the income that facilitated a more literal material comfort too.

Animal comforts of home

There is little doubt that Sims's home declared his fondness for animals ('Evidence of Mr. Sims' love of dogs meet one at every turn'), or that his pets reciprocated (they 'follow him like a shadow').[15] Of one bulldog, Sims said 'He's my constant companion', 'a real, downright chum'.[16] Elsewhere, 'I'm not a dog fancier, but a dog lover. I want my dogs to be here, my companions'.[17] Many journalists commented on his widower status, the absence of children, and the underlying sadness of the man who proclaimed jollity too loudly: 'His is the laughter which was ever akin to tears'.[18] The implication was that Sims had substituted human love for that of animals but, to observers at least, canine love did not quite compensate.

For his critics, Sims's animal things were often a source of discomfort. In placing animals at the centre of his domestic environment, Sims staked a claim for feeling outside the currencies of market value (he did not care if valuable relics were damaged by animals) and orthodox, human-centred affective hierarchies. Sims was a keen advocate for animal welfare and campaigned against the introduction of the dog licence, a tax that penalized working-class dog lovers.[19] Much of his writing politicized animals by seeking to speak for them but also, even in his anthropocentric silliness, by staking a claim for taking seriously the emotional and material comfort they brought.

In a context where debates about animal welfare (particularly vivisection) were crudely divided between heart (animal welfare) and head (science), Sims's detractors took his sympathy with animals as evidence of his emotional immaturity (even sympathetic sketches likened him to a whimsical child). For Sims, animal things and their place in his home – chaotic, excessive, unorthodox – were intrinsic to his public persona: irreverent and gregarious, eccentric and fun, defender of the weak and vulnerable. They were also, seemingly, the relationships that supported his emotional well-being, his sense of home as family space, and supported his capacity to empathize with others for whom animal companionship constituted joy and happiness. Animals have often been considered peripheral to human histories, including those of the home. George R. Sims was, perhaps, especially fulsome concerning the domestic and emotional comfort of animals in his life. But the example reminds us just how important animals were in mediating human identity and how, for some humans at least, animal comfort in its material and emotional forms was what made home.

Notes

1. Hilda Kean, *The Cat and Dog Massacre: The Real Story of World War II's Unknown Tragedy* (Chicago: Chicago University Press, 2017), 10–15.
2. Daniel Miller, *The Comfort of Things* (Cambridge: Polity, 2008).
3. Harriet Ritvo, *The Animal Estate: The English and Other Creatures in the Victorian Age* (Cambridge: Harvard University Press, 1987); Kathleen Kete, *The Beast in the Boudoir: Pet-Keeping in Nineteenth-Century Paris* (Berkeley: University of California Press, 1994); and Michael Worboys, Julie-Marie Strange and Neil Pemberton, *The Invention of the Modern Dog: Breed and Blood in Victorian Britain* (Baltimore: Johns Hopkins University Press, 2018).
4. 'George Robert Sims', Philip Waller, *Oxford Dictionary of National Biography*, https://doi.org/10.1093/ref:odnb/37964
5. 'Our Character Sketch', no publication details, The George R. Sims Collection, John Rylands Special Collections, University of Manchester (JRL), GB 133 GRS/10-2-1, Newscuttings.
6. 'Mr G. R. Sims Interviewed', *Illustrated Sporting and Dramatic News*, 6 February 1897, 896–8 and J. Pearce, 'House and home: Biographical sketch of George R Sims', *House and Home*, 19 May 1882, reprinted as *Popular Biographies*, no. 1 (London: House and Home, 1882).
7. 'Mr G. R. Sims at Home', *The Bookseller's Supplement*, 7 September 1895, 38–40.
8. 'Our Character Sketch'.
9. '"Dagonet" at Home', *The Princess*, 9 November 1895, 2-5 [Dagonet was a pen name]; 'A notable "dispatch" contributor', *The Weekly Dispatch*, no date, GB 133 GRS/10-3-1 (JRL); 'A Morning with Mr G. R. Sims and his Bulldog', *Chums*, no date, GB 133 GRS/10-10-3-1 (JRL).
10. 'Christmas: Then, and Now!', *The Idler*, no date, GB 133 GRS/10-2-1 (JRL); 'Mr G. R. Sims Interviewed'; 'Quaint George Sims', *Sunday Advertiser*, 29 April 1894.
11. 'Our Character Sketch'.
12. 'An Hour with George R. Sims', *The New Penny Magazine*, no date, GB 133 GRS/10-2-1 (JRL).
13. 'The Dogs of England', *The Daily News Weekly*, no date, c.1898. GB 133 GRS/10-2-1 (JRL).
14. 'Our Character Sketch'. 'Journalists of Today', *The Sketch*, 24 July 1895, p. 703, and ephemera in GB 133 GRS/10-3-1 (JRL).
15. 'Quaint George Sims'.
16. '"Dagonet" at Home'; 'A notable "dispatch" contributor'.
17. 'An Hour with George R. Sims'.
18. 'Journalists of Today'.
19. Sims's poem 'Told to the Missionary' addressed this issue directly. In George R. Sims, *The Dagonet Ballads* (London: J. P. Fuller, 1881).

Afterthoughts: The comforts of home

Jon Stobart

In March 2017, the Bloomberg Consumer Comfort Index hit its highest point in a decade.[1] Around the same time, Airbus reported that it was testing the passenger comfort of its new A350–1000. Both of these news stories use comfort in a particular way – in relation to our material and physical well-being. This same idea of comfort is picked up by furniture retailers and home improvement companies when naming their businesses 'Home Comforts'. As the contributions to this volume have made very clear, these ideas were as important in the eighteenth and nineteenth centuries as they are today. Building on the work of John Crowley, Joan DeJean and others, the essays assembled here have highlighted the ways in which householders became ever more concerned with the physical comfort of their domestic surroundings and increasingly interested in enhancing those qualities that made them comfortable.

Reflecting upon the arguments made in individual chapters, two broad findings relating to physical comfort merit particular emphasis. The first is the complexity of the task facing a householder in the eighteenth or nineteenth century who wished to make their dwelling more comfortable. This was true in terms of what comfort meant (that is, what it was that the householder was trying to improve) and how this improvement could be achieved. In relation to the former, considerable emphasis was placed on enhancing thermal comfort, but ideas of privacy and convenience – and the liveability of the house – were also important. Thermal comfort can be seen as an essentially technological issue: improved designs for hearths and stoves lie at the heart of the analysis offered by Jandot and Denis, and in the specific case studies examined by Prytz and Boccini. Read at one level, then, the story is one of progressive if not always seamless improvement, with better technology (itself arising from the desire for enhanced thermal comfort) eventually leading to warmer and more comfortable rooms – a process especially apparent in the efforts of Sir John Soane. Less immediately obvious, but just as profound in its implications for domestic life, is the way that better heating technology also impacted upon the use of rooms, a point raised by Denis in particular. If more rooms could be heated efficiently and effectively, then it allowed more of the house to be used on a regular basis: people had less need to be cooped up in the only warm room in the house. But this link between warmth and room-use also worked the other way around: as Ilmakunnas notes, smaller and single-function rooms could be more easily warmed when in use and closed off (and left cold) when they were not needed. Moving down a spatial scale, importance also attached to the assemblage of furniture and the arrangement of the room itself – being close to the fire or stove remained important, as Denis and Jandot make clear. Privacy and convenience, by contrast, are less technological issues and might be thought of primarily in terms of the arrangement of rooms. As Davrius argues in his case study of Blondel's idealization of the *maison de plaisance*, it was corridors and back stairs that allowed movement around the house that did not bring master and servant into contact unnecessarily. Privacy was also engineered through the creation of specialist rooms that helped to segregate different household functions and – to an extent – gendered practices, a set of changes seen in a range of contexts across Europe. But privacy was not simply the concern of architects; it was also a product of technological improvements: water closets were important in this regard, as Lucey demonstrates in his study, but so too were stoves that required refuelling less frequently.

There is, therefore, much in these essays and case studies to support the well-established arguments about the link between comfort and changing domestic material culture. However, the second key finding to emerge from this collection serves to challenge any easy assumptions that we might make about the progressive nature of improved comfort. There is a streak of celebratory teleology in Joan DeJean's analysis, in particular, that needs to be questioned. Many of the contributions to this volume emphasize the non-linear nature of causation that linked motivation, preference and improved bodily comfort. Motivations were rarely simple. Taking the organization of rooms, for example, we have already seen that this might be read in terms of thermal efficiency or as a way of creating privacy and facilitating new modes of living that were more informal and comfortable. Understanding what drove change in each instance is therefore complex and generalizations are difficult to sustain. Moreover, the ways in which motivation led to changing domestic arrangements and material culture was by no means straightforward. In terms of heating technology, Jandot observes a clear cultural divide between western (fires) and the rest of Europe (stoves) with a mutual rejection and even incomprehension of the merits of alternative technologies. Cultural (and climatic) specificities might also impact on architectural designs, as Ilmakunnas shows in her discussion of the translocation of French designs to Swedish contexts. This underlines the importance of the kind of comparative approach embodied in this volume: it takes us beyond cultural-specific arguments and reveals what is 'universal' and what is not. Even within a particular cultural milieu, improvements to physical comfort were by no means linear and progressive. Boccini's study of Sir John Soane makes clear that there could be numerous failures along the way, and Denis shows how older and less-efficient technologies might be retained, even in the face of alternatives that offered greater comfort. Aesthetics, status and tradition all played a part in shaping people's perceptions of comfort and choices in terms of how to achieve this. John Crowley argues that comfort replaced gentility and fashion as the key driver in shaping domestic environments, but this was far from a smooth or complete process, and it perhaps mistakenly assumes that the two were in conflict. More profoundly, we need to recognize that technological change was not always driven by the desire for greater comfort. Improvements to stoves in Sweden and hearths in France were a product of fuel scarcity as much as the search for warmer rooms, as Prytz and Jandot make clear. This reminds us that we need to avoid teleological arguments and recognize that change was sometimes non-linear and always contingent.

What this collection has also made abundantly clear is that home was much more than a warm and convenient house. In rejecting more efficient heating systems, for example, householders in nineteenth-century Antwerp reasserted the importance of the hearth as a symbol of hospitality and home. Comfort came in many guises, three aspects of which can be drawn out from the contributions to the second section of the book, in particular. The first is that home and comfort were ideas and practices to be learned and ideals to be promoted. We can see this most explicitly in didactic devices such as the conduct literature and growing array of journals discussed by Hamlett and in architectural treatises which, as Townshend demonstrates, became increasingly concerned with notions of convenience and later comfort – both for the elite and for the ordinary household. However, there were other, more visceral mechanisms through which idealizations of home were also spread, most notably the baby houses highlighted in Ferguson's study; and home comforts could also be learned through daily practices, like those of young Finnish men in their bachelor boxes. At one level, all this lends support to John Crowley's idea that comfort became a leitmotif for the age, and yet the daily practices discussed by Nevalainen and Metcalfe in their respective studies involved many compromises: the ideals learned in the parental home or promoted in journals and treatises could rarely be attained in full. Again, comfort was contingent and partial.

The second key aspect is that home and especially home comforts were by no means fixed in time and space. This is true in terms of changes over the longue durée in what constituted comfort and how it might be achieved. As already noted, higher room temperatures were expected; so too were a growing array of easy chairs and the convenience of better lighting and private rooms. It is also apparent in the distinctions and connections in levels and types of comfort afforded in the parental or marital home outlined by Stobart and in the ways that lifecycle changes impacted on what was possible and desirable, be that the student rooms studied by Dyer or the barracks explored in more detail by Willard-Wright. Through all of these studies, it is apparent that material objects were fundamentally important in shaping homes and ideas of home. There were key objects that rendered homes comfortable in a physical and emotional sense. Some of these were linked to particular ways of living – Hamlett's cosy Victorian parlour or the comfortable beds and familiar food sought out by Verhoeven's Grand Tourists. Others, however, were of a more sentimental variety. These include pets which, as Strange makes clear, offered companionship and a focus for emotions; but they might also be things that acted as reminders of family members separated by time or space, such as the miniatures examined by Stobart or the photographs over soldier's barrack room beds discussed by Willard-Wright. Moreover, and as these same contributions make clear, home comforts were mobile and could be substituted with surrogates. Travellers could seek out the comfort of home in hotels and lodgings, students and bachelors could recreate them in their rooms, and young men could carry reminders and some of the comforts of home with them into their military lives.

The implications of this are profound: home was neither fixed nor permanent. In part, this was down to the mobility of goods; in part it was due to the importance of links with other people as well as with objects. This is my third point: that emotional attachments between people were fundamental in making the home and in keeping alive the ideal of home in the face of spatial and temporal dislocation. As Metcalfe demonstrates in her study, the companionship of family could create and sustain feelings of home despite a peripatetic existence, and in the absence of many of the expected material trappings. Equally, Stobart shows that memories of family could make a house into a home as objects and rooms were mentally and emotionally populated with family members, sometimes distant and sometimes long deceased.

So, where does all this leave our understanding of comfort and home? Both are, of course, complex and multifaceted. As historians and the writers of a host of contemporary architectural treatises, pamphlets on improved fireplaces, conduct literature and the like insist, the physical comfort of the domestic environment was important. Anyone with the scope to choose was increasingly aiming to be being warm in a house that was convenient and liveable, with easy furniture and a measure of privacy from servants, guests and other family members. But it was emotional ties that made a house into a home. This not only meant ties with particular objects – which Judith Lewis has emphasized – but also bonds with people, sometimes in a direct sense and sometimes mediated through things. Home was thus spatially bounded, yet permeable and mobile. Most people referred to home in terms of a particular place and it was generally represented in the form of a house or rooms; but feelings of home and especially home comforts could be recreated away from home as a specific spatial location. Perhaps most importantly, we need to suspend, interrogate and revise the idea that there was a single model or even a single ideal of home. This is something that becomes particularly clear by comparing different places, times and experiences, and underlines the value of this kind of comparative volume. Home could be an aristocratic country house, a bachelor pad, or a barrack room; it could be centred on a cosy parlour, a fire or stove, pet dogs, or memory-laden pictures; and it might be articulated through things or people, objects or emotions. Home comprised any and sometimes all of these things; above all, it was a place where people felt contented.

Note

1 https://www.bloomberg.com/news/articles/2017-03-09/u-s-consumer-comfort-reaches-decade-high-on-economic-optimism (accessed 6 February 2019).

Bibliography

Abad, Reynald. (2016), 'L'Ancien Régime à la recherche d'une transition énergétique ? La France du XVIIIe siècle face au bois', in Yves Bouvier and Léonard Laborie (eds), *L'Europe en transitions: Énergie, mobilité, communication XVIIIe–XIXe siècles*, 23–84, Paris: Nouveau Monde éditions.

Adams, Christine. (2000), *A Taste for Comfort and Status: A Bourgeois Family in Eighteenth-Century France*, Philadelphia: Penn State University Press.

Archer, John. (1985), *The Literature of British Domestic Architecture*, 1715–1842, Cambridge, MA and London: MIT Press.

Archer, John. (1983), 'The Beginnings of Association in British Architectural Esthetics', *Eighteenth-Century Studies*, 16 (3): 241–64.

Auslander, Leora. (2015), 'Reading German Jewry through Documentary Photography: From the Kaiserreich to the Third Reich', *Central European History*, 48: 300–334.

Auslander, Leora. (1996), *Taste and Power: Furnishing Modern France*, Berkeley: University of California Press.

Baatsen, Inneke, Bruno Blondé, Sofie De Caigny and Britt Denis. (2016), 'In de keuken', in Leen Beyers and Ilja Van Damme (eds), *Antwerpen à la carte: eten en de stad, van de Middeleeuwen tot vandaag*, 98–127, Antwerpen: BAI.

Bachelard, Gaston. (1964), *The Poetics of Space* (1958), Harmondsworth: Penguin.

Barclay, Katie. (2017), 'Family and Household', in Susan Broomhall (ed), *Early Modern Emotions*, London: Routledge.

Barnaby, Alice. (2002), 'Light Touches: Cultural Practices of Illumination, London 1780–1840', 244–7, Unpublished PhD thesis, University of Exeter.

Barnwell, P.S. and Palmer, Marylin (eds). (2012), *Country House Technology*, Donington: Shaun Tyas.

Bedoire, Fredric. (2001), *Guldålder: Slott och politik i 1600-talets Sverige*, Stockholm: Bonnier.

Belhoste, Bruno. (2018), *Paris Savant: Capital of Science in the Age of Enlightenment*, trad. Susan Emanuel, New York: Oxford University Press.

Benson, John. (1994), *The Rise of Consumer Society in Britain* 1880–1980, London: Longman.

Berg, Maxine and Elizabeth Eger (eds). (2003), *Luxury in the Eighteenth Century: Debates, Desires and Delectable Goods*, Basingstoke: Palgrave Macmillan.

Berg, Maxine. (1996), 'Women's Consumption and the Industrial Classes of Eighteenth-Century England', *Journal of Social History*, 30: 415–34.

Berg, Maxine. (2005), *Luxury and Pleasure in Eighteenth-Century Britain*, Oxford: Oxford University Press.

Bergmans, Anna, Jan De Maeyer, Wim Denslagen and Wies van Leeuwen. (2002), 'Inleiding. Een pleidooi voor goede manieren', in Anna Bergmans, Jan De Maeyer, Wim Denslagen en Wies van Leeuwen (eds), *Neostijlen in de negentiende eeuw. Zorg geboden? Handelingen van het twee Vlaams-Nederlands restauratiesymposium*, 7–12, Leuven: Universitaire Pers Leuven.

Bernez, Marie-Odile. (2014), 'Comfort, the Acceptable Face of Luxury: An Eighteenth-Century Cultural Etymology', *Journal for Early Modern Cultural Studies*, 14 (2): 3–21.

Berry, Christopher. (1999), *The Idea of Luxury: A Conceptual and Historical Investigation*, Cambridge: Cambridge University Press.

Black, Jeremy. (2003), *Italy and the Grand Tour*, New Haven: Yale University Press.

Blondé, Bruno and Ilja Van Damme. (2010), 'Retail Growth and Consumer Changes in a Declining Urban Economy: Antwerp (1650–1750)', *Economic History Review*, 63 (3): 638–63.

Bowie, David. (2016), 'Pure Diffusion? The Great English Hotel Charges Debate in *The Times*, 1853', *Business History*, 58 (2): 159–78.

Bradbury, O. (2015), *Sir John Soane's Influence on Architecture from 1791: A Continuing Legacy*, Farnham, Surrey: Ashgate Publishing Limited.

Branca, Patricia. (1977), *Silent Sisterhood: Middle-Class Women in the Victorian Home*, London: Croom Helm.

Brawer, Nicholas A. (2001), *British Campaign Furniture: Elegance Under Canvas, 1740–1914*, New York: Harry N. Abrams.

Broomhall, Susan (ed). (2008), *Emotions in the Household, 1200–1900*, Basingstoke: Palgrave.

Broomhall, Susan. (2008), 'Emotions in the Household', in Susan Broomhall (ed), *Emotions in the Household, 1200–1900*, 1–37, Basingstoke: Palgrave.

Burgess, Anthony. (1967), 'The Grand Tour', in Anthony Burgess and Francis Haskell (eds), *The Age of the Grand Tour*, 13–32, London: Harper-Collins.

Caesar, Ann Hallamore. (2004), 'Women and the Public/Private Divide: The Salotto, Home and Theatre in Late Nineteenth-Century Italy', in Perry Willson (ed), *Gender, Family and Sexuality: The Private Sphere in Italy, 1860–1945*, 105–21, Basingstoke: Palgrave Macmillan.

Caradonna, Jeremy. (2012), *The Enlightenment in Practice: Academic Prize Contests and Intellectual Culture in France, 1670–1794*, Ithaca: Cornell University Press.

Charpy, Manuel. (2010), 'Le théâtre des objets. Espaces privés, culture matérielle et identité bourgeoise, Paris, 1830–1914', Doctorat d'histoire contemporaine de l'Université François Rabelais de Tours.

Chavasse, Hannah. (2015), 'Material Culture and the Country House: Fashion, Comfort and Lineage', unpublished PhD thesis, University of Northampton.

Cieraad, Irene. (2006), 'Van haardscherm tot beeldscherm. Over de relatie tussen meubelschikking, sociabiliteit en woontechniek', in Clara H. Mulder and Fenne M. Pinkster (eds), *Onderscheid in wonen. Het sociale van binnen en buiten*, 27–47, Amsterdam: Amsterdam University Press.

Cohen, Deborah. (2006), *Household Gods: The British and Their Possessions*, New Haven: Yale University Press.
Corbin, Alain. (1988), *The Foul and the Fragrant: Odor and the French Social Imagination*, Harvard: Harard University Press.
Corcoran, Michael. (2005), *Our Good Health: A History of Dublin's Water and Drainage*, 60–69, Dublin: Dublin City Council.
Cornforth, John (1985), 'The Backward Look', in G. Jackson-Stops (ed), *The Treasure Houses of Britain: Five Hundred Years of Private Patronage and Art Collecting*, New Haven: Yale University Press.
Cornforth, John. (1978), *English Interiors 1790–1848: The Quest for Comfort*, London: Barrie and Jenkins.
Cowen Orlin, Lena. (2010), 'Empty Vessels', in Tara Hamling and Catherine Richardson (eds), *Everyday Objects: Medieval and Early Modern Material Culture and Its Meanings*, 299–308, Farnham: Ashgate.
Cramér, Margareta. (1991), *Den Verkliga Kakelugnen: Fabrikstillverkade Kakelugnar i Stockholm 1846–1926*, Stockholm: Kommittén för stockholmsforskning.
Crowley, John E. (2001), *The Invention of Comfort: Sensibilities and Design in Early Modern Britain and Early America*, Baltimore: Johns Hopkins University Press.
Crowley, John. (2003), 'From Luxury to Comfort and Back Again: Landscape Architecture and the Cottage in Britain and America', in M. Berg and E. Eger (eds), *Luxury in the Eighteenth Century: Debates, Desires and Delectable Goods*, 135–50, Basingstoke: Palgrave Macmillan.
Cruikshank, Dan and Neil Burton. (1990), *Life in the Georgian City*, London: Viking.
Cruz, Jesus. (2011), *The Rise of Middle-Class Culture in Nineteenth-Century Spain*, Baton Rouge: Louisiana State University Press.
Daunton, Martin J. (1983), *House and Home in the Victorian City: Working-class Housing 1850–1914*, London: Edward Arnold.
Davidoff, Leonore and Catherine Hall. (1987), *Family Fortunes. Men and Women of the English Middle Class 1780–1850*, Chicago: Chicago Univresity Press.
Davrius, Aurélien. (2018), *Jacques-François Blondel, architecte des Lumières*, Paris: Classiques Garnier.
Davrius, Aurélien. (2016), *Jacques-François Blondel, un architecte dans la 'République des Arts'*, Genève: Droz.
De Caigny, Sofie. (2010), *Bouwen aan een nieuwe thuis. Wooncultuur in Vlaanderen tijdens het interbellum*, Leuven: Universitaire Pers Leuven.
De Seta, Cesare. (1996), 'Grand Tour: The Lure of Italy in the Eighteenth Century', in Ilaria Bignamini and Andrew Wilton (eds), *Grand Tour. The Lure of Italy in the Eighteenth Century*, 13–19, London: Tate Gallery.
de Vries, Jan. (2003), 'Luxury in the Dutch Golden Age in Theory and Practice', in Maxine Berg and Elizabeth Eger (eds), *Luxury in the Eighteenth Century. Debates, Desires, and Delectable Goods*, 41–56, Basingstoke: Palgrave.

de Vries, Jan. (2008), *The Industrious Revolution: Consumer Behavior and the Household Economy, 1650 to the Present*, New York: Cambridge University Press.

DeJean, Joan. (2009), *The Age of Comfort: When Paris Discovered Casual – and the Modern Home Began*, New York: Bloomsbury.

Denis, Britt. (2016), 'In Search of Material Practices: The Nineteenth-Century European Domestic Interior Rehabilitated', *History of Retailing and Consumption*, 2 (2): 97–112.

Denison, Edward and Guand Yu Ren. (2012), *The Life of the British Home: An Architectural History*, Chichester: John Wiley and Sons.

Dennis, Richard. (2008), *Cities in modernity. Representations and Productions of Metropolitan Space, 1840–1930*, Cambridge: Cambridge University Press.

Deslandes, Paul R. (2005), *Oxbridge Men: British Masculinity and the Undergraduate Experience, 1850–1920*, Bloomington: Indiana University Press.

Dibbits, Hester. (2001), *Vertrouwd bezit, Materiële cultuur in Doesburg en Maassluis, 1650–1800*, Nijmegen: Uitgeverij SUN.

Flanders, Judith. (2014), *The Making of Home: The 500-year Story of How Our Houses Became Homes*, London: Atlantic Books.

Dickson, David. (2001), 'Death of a Capital? Dublin and the Consequences of Union', in Peter Clark and Raymond Gillespie (eds), Two Capitals: London and Dublin, 1500–1840, 111–31, Oxford: Oxford University Press.

Dortyol, Ibrahim, Inci Varinli and Olgun Kitapci. (2014), 'How do International Tourists Perceive Hotel Quality?: An Exploratory Study of Service Quality in Antalya Tourism Region', *International Journal of Contemporary Hospitality Management*, 26 (3): 470–95.

Douet, James. (1988), *British Barracks 1600–1914: Their Architecture and Role in Society*, London: H.M.S.O.

Downes, Stephanie, Sally Holloway and Sarah Randles. (2018), 'A Feeling for Things, Past and Present', in Sephanie Downs, Sally Holloway and Sarah Randles (eds), *Feeling Things: Objects and Emotions through History*, 8–23, Oxford: Oxford University Press.

Dubbini, R. (1989), *Nascita dell'idea di comfort*, in "Storia del disegno industriale", 1, Electa, Milan.

Durand, Ralph. (1909), *Oxford: Its Buildings and Gardens*, London: Grant Richards.

Dyer, Serena. (2018), 'Masculinities, Wallpaper, and Crafting Domestic Space within the University, 1795–1914', *Nineteenth-Century Gender Studies*, 14 (2).

Edwards, Clive. (2005), *Turning Houses into Homes. A History of the Retailing and Consumption of Domestic Furnishings*, Adershot: Ashgate.

Eibach, Joachim and Inken Schmidt-Voges (ed). (2015), *Das Haus in der Geschichte Europas: Ein Handbuch*, Oldenburg: De Gruyter.

Epp, Amber and Linda Price. (2010), 'The Storied Life of Singularized Objects: Forces of Agency and Network Transformation', *Journal of Consumer Research*, 36: 820–37.

Eriksdotter, Gunhild. (2013), 'Did the Little Ice Age Affect Indoor Climate and Comfort? Re-Theorizing Climate History and Architecture from the Early Modern Period', *The Journal for Early Modern Cultural Studies*, 13 (2): 24–42.

Eriksdotter, Gunhild and Mattias Legnér. (2015), 'Indoor Climate and Thermal Comfort from a Long-Term Perspective: Burmeister House in Visby, c. 1650–1900', *Home Cultures*, 12 (1): 29–53.

Facos, Michelle. (1996), 'The Ideal Swedish Home: Carl Larrson's Lilla Hytannäs', in Christopher Reed (ed), *Not at Home: The Suppression of Domesticity in Modern Art and Architecture*, 7–15, London: Thames and Hudson.

Fairfax-Lucy, Alice. (1990), *Charlecote and the Lucys*, London: Victor Gollancz.

Featherstone, Donald. (1978), *Weapons and Equipment of the Victorian Soldier*, London: Blandford Press.

Fennetaux, Arianne. (2015), 'Sentimental Economics: Recycling Textiles in Eighteenth-Century Britain', in Ariane Fennetaux, Amelie Junqua and Sophie Vasset (eds), *The Afterlife of Used Things: Recycling in the Long Eighteenth Century*, 122–41, London: Routledge.

Ferry, Emma. (2004), 'Advice, Authorship and the Domestic Interior: An Interdisciplinary Study of Macmillan's "Art at Home Series" 1876–1883', Unpublished PhD thesis, Kingston University.

Figeac, Michel. (2001), *La douceur des Lumières: Noblesse et art de vivre en Guyenne au XVIIIe siècle*, Bordeaux: Mollat Éditions.

Finn, Margot and Kate Smith (ed). (2018), *The East India Company at Home, 1757–1857*, London: University College London Press.

Finn, Margot. (2000), 'Men's Things: Masculine Possession in the Consumer Revolution', *Social History*, 25 (2): 133–55.

French, Henry and Mark Rothery. (2013), *Man's Estate: Landed Gentry Masculinities, 1660–1900*, Oxford: Oxford University Press.

Galavan, Susan. (2017), *Dublin's Bourgeois Homes: Building the Victorian Suburbs, 1850–1901*, London and New York: Routledge.

Gay, Peter. (1984), *The Bourgeois Experience. Victoria to Freud. Volume One: Education of the Senses*, New York: Oxford University Press.

Gere, Charlotte. (1989), *Nineteenth-Century Decoration: The Art of the Interior*, New York: Harry N. Abrams.

Geurts, Anne. (2017), 'Modern Travel: A Personal Affair', in Alison Martin, Lut Missine and Beatrix van Dam (eds), *Travel Writing in Dutch and German, 1790–1930. Modernity, Regionality, Mobility*, 214–34, London: Routledge.

Girling-Budd, Amanda. (2004), 'Comfort and Gentility: Furnishings by Gillows, Lancaster, 1840–55', in Susie McKellar and Penny Sparke (eds), *Interior Design and Identity*, 27–47, Manchester & New York: Manchester University Press.

Girouard, Mark. (1978), *Life in the English Country House*, New Haven: Yale University Press.

Girouard, Mark. (2000), *Life in the French Country House*, London: Cassell & Co.

Gloag, John. (1961), *Victorian Comfort: A Social History of Design from 1830 to 1900*, London: Adam and Charles Black.

Goldsmith, Sarah. (2018), 'Nostalgia, Homesickness, and Emotional Formation on the Eighteenth-Century Grand Tour', *Cultural and Social History*, 15 (3): 333–60.

Goldsmith, Sarah. (2017), 'The Social Challenge: Northern and Central European Societies on the Eighteenth-Century Aristocratic Grand Tour', in Sarah Goldsmith, Rosemary Sweet and Gerrit Verhoeven (eds), *Beyond the Grand Tour. Northern Metropolises and Early Modern Travel Behaviour*, 65–82, London: Routledge.

Gomme, Andor. (2004), 'Abbey into Palace: A Lesser Wilton?', in Robert Bearman (ed), *Stoneleigh Abbey: The House, Its Owners, Its Land*, 82–115, Stratford-upon-Avon: The Shakespeare Birthplace Trust.

Gooday, Graeme. (2008), *Domesticating Electricity: Technology, Uncertainty and Gender*, 1880–1914, London: Pickering & Chatto.

Goodman, Dena and Kathryn Nordberg (eds). (2007), *Furnishing the Eighteenth Century: What Furniture Can Tell Us about the European and American Past*, London: Routledge.

Gosling, Edward P. J. (2015), '*Tommy Atkins, War Office Reform and the Social and Cultural Presence of the Late-Victorian Army in Britain, c.1868–1899*', Unpublished PhD thesis, University of Plymouth.

Goubert, Jean-Pierre. (1988), *Du luxe au confort*. Paris: Berlin.

Greig, Hannah and Giorgio Riello. (2007), 'Eighteenth-Century Interiors: Redesigning the Georgian', *Journal of Design History*, 20 (4), 273–289.

Grier, Katherine C. (2010), *Culture and Comfort. Parlor Making and Middle-Class Identity*, 1850–1930, Washington and London: Smithsonian Institution Press.

Grier, Katherine. (1988), *Culture and Comfort: People, Parlors and Upholstery* 1850–1930, New York: Strong Museum.

Griffin, David. (1996/1997), 'The Building and Furnishing of a Dublin Townhouse in the 18th Century', *Bulletin of the Irish Georgian Society*, 37: 24–39.

Guillerme, André. (1992), 'Chaleur et chauffage: l'introduction du Confort à Paris sous la Restauration', *History of Technology*, 14: 16–53.

Hamlett, Jane (2009), '"The Dining Room should be a Man's Paradise, as the Drawing Room is a Woman's": Gender and Middle-Class Domestic Space in England, 1850–1910', *Gender and History*, 21 (3): 576–91.

Hamlett, Jane. (2006), '"Nicely Feminine, yet Learned': Student Rooms at Royal Holloway and the Oxford and Cambridge Colleges in Late Nineteenth-Century Britain', *Women's History Review*, 15 (1): 137–61.

Hamlett, Jane. (2004), Geffrye Museum reports 3–5, unpublished research reports, Geffrye Museum of the Home.

Hamlett, Jane. (2010), *Material Relations: Domestic Interiors and Middle-Class Families in England*, 1850–1910, Manchester: Manchester University Press.

Hamling, Tara. (2017), 'Household Objects', in Susan Broomhall (ed), *Early Modern Emotions: An Introduction*, 135, London: Routledge.

Hansson, Joakim. (2015), *Komfort framför allt, men även till Nytta och Nöje: Teknik, Apparater och Redskap i Byggnader före andra Världskriget*, Helsinki.

Hardyment, Christina. (1992), *Home Comfort. A History of Domestic Arrangements*, London: Viking and the National Trust.

Harris, Amy. (2012), *Siblinghood and Social Relations in Georgian England: Share and Share Alike*, Manchester: Manchester University Press.

Harvey, Charles and Jon Press. (1991), *William Morris: Design and Enterprise in Victorian Britain*, Manchester: Manchester University Press.

Harvey, Karen. (2009), 'Men Making Home: Masculinity and Domesticity in Eighteenth-Century Britain', *Gender and History*, 21 (3), 520–40.

Harvey, Karen. (2012), *The Little Republic: Masculinity and Domestic Authority in Eighteenth-Century Britain*, Oxford: Oxford University Press.

Hauge, Stephen. (2016), *The Gentleman's House in the British Atlantic World, 1680–1780*, Basingstoke: Palgrave Macmillan.

Hecht, Jean. (1956), *The Domestic Servant Class in Eighteenth-Century England*, London: Routledge.

Hendon, Zoe. (2018), *Wallpaper*, London: Bloomsbury.

Heyl, Christoph. (2004), *A Passion for Privacy. Untersuchungen zur Genese der bürgerlichen Privatsphäre in London*, München: De Gruyter.

Heyman, Vincent. (1994), 'Architecture et habitants: les intérieurs privés de la bourgeoisie à la fin du XIXe siècle: Bruxelles, quartier Léopold-extension nord-est', Thèse de doctorat, Université Libre de Bruxelles, Faculté de Philosophie et Lettres.

Hibbert, Christopher. (1987), *The Grand Tour*, London: Methuen.

Hilaire-Pérez, Liliane. (2000), *L'invention technique au siècle des Lumières*, Paris: Albin Michel.

Hoskins, Lesley. (2011), 'Reading the Inventory: Household Goods, Domestic Cultures and difference in England and Wales, 1841–1881', Unpublished PhD thesis, QMUL.

Hoskins, Lesley. (2011), 'Stories of Home and Work in the Mid-Nineteenth-Century', *Home Cultures*, 8 (2): 151–69.

Hoskins, Lesley. (2005), *The Papered Wall: The History, Patterns and Techniques of Wallpaper*, London: Thames & Hudson.

https://backdoorbroadcasting.net/2017/12/marie-ulvang-farmerfication-housing-and-the-housework-in-rural-sweden-1850-1910/.

https://www.bloomberg.com/news/articles/2017-03-09/u-s-consumer-comfort-reaches-decade-high-on-economic-optimism (accessed 6 February 2019).

Hunt, Margaret. (1996), *The Middling Sort: Commerce, Gender and the Family in England, 1680–1780*, Berkeley: University of California Press, 1996

Hussey, Christopher. (1942), 'Through the Fourth Wall: Scenes in a Georgian dolls' House at Uppark', *Country Life*, 6 March: 450–51.

Hussey, David E. and Margaret Ponsonby. (2012), *The Single Homemaker and Material Culture in the Long Eighteenth Century*, Burlington, VT: Ashgate.

Ilmakunnas, Johanna. (2017), 'French Fashions: Aspects of Elite Lifestyle in Eighteenth-Century', in Johanna Ilmakunnas and Jon Stobart (eds), *A Taste for Luxury in Early Modern Europe: Display, Acquisition and Boundaries*, 243–63, London: Bloomsbury Academic.

Ilmakunnas, Johanna. (2019), 'Aristocratic Townhouse as Urban Space: The Fersen Palace in Eighteenth-Century Stockholm', in Elaine Chalus and Marjo Kaartinen (eds), *Gendering Spaces in European Towns, 1500–1914*, 15–31, New York and London: Routledge.

Ilmakunnas, Johanna. (2016), 'To Build According to One's Status: A Country House in late 18th-Century Sweden', in Jon Stobart and Andrew Hann (eds), *The Country House: Material Culture and Consumption*, 33–41, Swindon: English Heritage.

Ilmakunnas, Johanna. (2012), *Ett ståndsmässigt liv: Familjen von Fersens livsstil på 1700-talet*, Helsingfors and Stockholm: Svenska litteratursällskapet i Finland and Atlantis.

Jackson-Stops, Gervase (ed). (1985), *The Treasure Houses of Britain: Five Hundred Years of Private Patronage and Art Collecting*, Washington, New Haven and London: Yale University Press.

Jackson, Lee. (2014), *Dirty Old London: The Victorian Fight Against Filth*, New Haven and London: Yale University Press.

Jandot, Olivier. (2017), *Les délices du feu: l'homme, le chaud et le froid à l'époque moderne*, Ceyzérieu: Champ Vallon.

Kean, Hilda. (2017), *The Cat and Dog Massacre: The Real Story of World War II's Unknown Tragedy*, Chicago: Chicago University Press.

Kelley, Victoria. (2010), *Soap and Water. Cleanliness, Dirt and the Working Classes in Victorian and Edwardian Britain*, London and New York: I.B. Tauris.

Kersting, A. F. and David Watkin. (1984), *Peterhouse 1284–1984: An Architectural Record*, Cambridge: Master and Fellows of Peterhouse.

Kete, Kathleen. (1994), *The Beast in the Boudoir: Pet-Keeping in Nineteenth-Century Paris*, Berkeley: University of California Press.

Knox, T. and H. Dorey. (2012), *Thoroughly Modern Soane*, London: Sir John Soane's Museum.

Kwint, Marius. (1999), 'Introduction: The Physical Past', in Marius Kwint, Christopher Breward and Jeremy Aynsley (eds), *Material Memories*, 1–16, Oxford: Oxford University Press.

Le Goff, Olivier. (1994), *L'invention du confort: naissance d'une forme sociale*, Lyon: Presses universitaires de Lyon.

Leibetseder, Matthis. (2004), *Die Kavalierstour. Adlige Erziehungsreisen in 17. Und 18. Jahrhunderts*, Köln: Böhlau.

Lemay, Joseph A. Leo. (2006), *The Life of Benjamin Franklin*, Philadelphia: University of Pennsylvania Press.

Lewallen, Nina. (2009/2010), 'Architecture and Performance at the Hôtel du Maine in Eighteenth-Century Paris', *Studies in the Decorative Arts*, 17 (1): 2–32.

Lewis, Judith S. (2009), 'When a House is not a Home: Elite English Women and the Eighteenth-Century Country House', *Journal of British Studies*, 48: 336–63.

Lindfield, Peter N. (2016), *Georgian Gothic: Medievalist Architecture, Furniture and Interiors, 1730–1840*, Woodbridge: Boydell.

Lintsen, H. W. (ed). (1992), *Geschiedenis van de techniek in Nederland. De wording van een moderne samenleving 1800–1890. Deel IV*, Zutphen: Walburg Pers.

Lipsedge, Karen. (2012), *Domestic Space in Eighteenth-Century British Novels*, Basingstoke: Palgrave Macmillan.

Lobel, Cindy R. (2014), *Urban Appetites. Food and Culture in Nineteenth-Century New York*, Chicago and London: The University of Chicago Press.

Locqueneux, Robert. (1996), *Préhistoire et histoire de la thermodynamique classique: une histoire de la chaleur*, Paris: Société Française d'Histoire des Sciences et des Techniques.

Locqueneux, Robert. (2014), *Sur la nature du feu aux siècles classiques: réflexion des physiciens et des chimistes*, Paris: L'Harmattan.

Löfgren, Ovrar. (2003), 'The Sweetness of Home: Class, Culture and Family Life in Sweden', in Setha M. Low and Denise Lawrence-Zúñiga (eds), *The Anthropology of Space and Place: Locating Culture*, 142–59, Oxford: Blackwell.

Logan, Thad. (2006), *The Victorian Parlour. A Cultural Study*, Cambridge: Cambridge University Press.

Macdonald, Mairi. (2004), 'Not Unmarked by Some Eccentricities: The Leigh Family of Stoneleigh Abbey', in Robert Bearman (ed), Stoneleigh Abbey: *The House, Its Owners, Its Lands*, 131–62, Stratford-upon-Avon: The Shakespeare Birthplace Trust.

Maldonado, Tomas (transl. John Cullars). (1991), 'The Idea of Comfort', *Design Issues*, 8 (1): 35–43.

Matt, Susan. (2011), *Homesickness. An American History*, Oxford: Oxford University Press.

May, Trevor. (2002), *Military Barracks*, Oxford and New York: Shire Publications.

McCarthy, Patricia. (2016), *Life in the Country House in Georgian Ireland*, New Haven and London: Yale University Press.

McEwan, Joanne and Pamela Sharpe (eds). (2011), *Accommodating Poverty: The Housing and Living Arrangements of the English Poor, c.1600–1850*, Basingstoke: Palgrave Macmillan.

McEwan, Joanne. (2011), 'The Lodging Exchange: Space, Authority and Knowledge in Eighteenth-Century London', in Joanne McEwan and Pamela Sharpe (eds), *Accommodating Poverty: The Housing and Living Arrangements of the English Poor, c. 1600–1850*, 50–68, Basingstoke: Palgrave Macmillan.

Meldrum, Tim. (2000), *Domestic Service and Gender*, 1660–1750, Harlow: Pearson.

Metcalfe, Helen. (2017), 'The Social Experience of Bachelorhood in Late-Georgian England, c.1760–1830', Unpublished PhD thesis, University of Manchester.

Miller, Daniel. (2008), *The Comfort of Things*, Cambridge: Polity.

Mitchell, David M. (2009), '"My Purple will be too sad for that Melancholy Room": Furnishings for Interiors in London and Paris, 1660–1735', *Textile History*, 40 (1): 3–28.

Montijn, Ileen. (1998), *Leven op Stand 1890–1940*, Amsterdam: Thomas Rap.

Muthesius, Stefan. (1982), *The English Terraced House*, New Haven: Yale University Press.

Muthesius, Stefan. (2009), *A Poetic Home: Designing the 19th-century Domestic Interior*, New York: Thames & Hudson.

Nagengast, Bernard. (1995), 'An Early History of Comfort Heating', in Barry Donaldson, Bernard Nagengast and Gershon Meckler (eds), *Heat & Cold: Mastering the Great Indoors, a Selective History of Heating, Ventilation, Refrigeration and Air Conditioning*, Sydney, OH: ASHRAE.

Nash, Mary. (1999), 'Un/Contested Identities: Motherhood, Sex Reform and the Modernization of Gender Identity in Early Twentieth-Century Spain', in Victoria Lorée Enders and Pamela Beth Radcliff (eds), *Constructing Spanish Womanhood: Female Identity in Modern Spain*, 25–50, New York: State University of New York Press.

Nordin, Jonas. (2013), *Versailles: Slottet, Parken, Livet*, Stockholm: Norstedts.

Ó Gráda, Diarmuid. (2015), *Georgian Dublin: The Forces That Shaped the City*, Cork: Cork University Press.

Olsen, Stephanie and Rob Boddice. (2017), 'Styling Emotions History', *Journal of Social History*, 51 (3): 476–87.

Otter, Christopher. (2013), 'Locating Matter: The Place of Materiality in Urban History', in Tony Bennett and Patrick Joyce (eds), *Material Powers: Cultural Studies, History and the Material Turn*, 38–59, New York: Routledge.

Oudshoorn, Nelly and Trevor Pinch (eds). (2003), *How Users Matter. The Co-construction of Users and Technology*, Cambridge: MIT Press.

Overton, Mark, Jane Whittle, Darron Dean and Andrew Hann. (2004), *Production and Consumption in English Households, 1600–1750*, London: Routledge.

Page, Norman. (1972), *The Language of Jane Austen*, Oxford: Oxford University Press.

Palmer, S. (1997), *The Soanes at Home: Domestic Life at Lincoln's Inn Fields*, London: Sir John Soane's Museum.

Palmer, Marilyn and Ian West. (2013), 'Nineteenth-century Technical Innovations in British Country Houses and their Estates', *Engineering History and Heritage*, 166 (1): 36–44.

Palmer, Marilyn and Ian West. (2016), *Technology in the Country House*, London: Historic England.

Pardailhé-Galabrun, Annick. (1988), *La naissance de l'intime: 3 000 foyers parisiens, XVIIe–XVIIIe siècles*, Paris: Presses Universitaires de France.

Pardailhé-Galabrun, Annik. (1991), *The Birth of Intimacy: Private and Domestic Life in Early Modern Paris*, Cambridge: Polity Press.

Petzold, Jochen. (2016), 'Inventing the Victorian Boy: S.O.Beeton's The Boy's Own Magazine', in John Storey (ed), *The Making of English Popular Culture*, 76–89, London: Routledge.

Phillipps, Kenneth. (1970), *Jane Austen's English*, London: Duetsch.

Ponsonby, Margaret. (2007), *Stories from Home: English Domestic Interiors*, 1750–1850, Farnham: Ashgate.

Radojevic, Tijana, Nemanja Stanisic and Nemad Stanic. (2015), 'Ensuring Positive Feedback: Factors that Influence Customer Satisfaction in the Contemporary Hospitality Industry', *Tourism Management*, 51: 13–21.

Retford, Kate. (2006), 'Patrilineal Portraiture? Gender and Genealogy in the Eighteenth-Century English Country House', in John Styles and Amanda Vickery (eds), *Gender, Taste and Material Culture in Britain and North America 1700–1830*, 315–44, New Haven: Yale University Press.

Ritvo, Harriet. (1987), *The Animal Estate: The English and Other Creatures in the Victorian Age*, Cambridge, MA: Harvard University Press.

Roche, Daniel. (transl. Brian Pearce), (2000), *A History of Everyday Things: The Birth of Consumption in France*, 1600–1800, Cambridge: Cambridge University Press.

Roche, Daniel. (2000), *La Ville Promise*, Paris: Fayard.

Rollenhagen, Tilly (2017), *Carl Johan Cronstedt: Arkitekt och Organisatör*, Stockholm: Balkong Forlag.

Roper, Michael. (2010), *The Secret Battle. Emotional Survival in the Great War*, Manchester: Manchester University Press.

Rose, Mark. (1995), *Cities of Light and Heat: Domesticating Gas and Electricity in Urban America*, University Park: Pennsylvania State University Press.

Rosoman, Treve. (2009), *London Wallpapers: Their Manufacture and Use*, 1690–1840, Swindon: English Heritage.

Rothery, Mark and Henry French. (2012), *Making Men: The Formation of Masculine Identities in England, c.1660–1900 – A Sourcebook*, Basingstoke: Macmillan.

Runefelt, Leif. (2015), *Att hasta mot undergången: Anspråk, flyktighet, förställning i debatten om konsumtion i Sverige 1730–1830*, Lund: Nordic Academic Press.

Rybczynzki, Witold. (1988), *Home: A Short History of an Idea*, London: William Heinemann.

Sargentson, Carolyn. (1998), 'The Manufacture and Marketing of Luxury Goods : The Marchands Merciers of late 17th- and 18th-century Paris', in Robert Fox and Anthony Turner (eds), *Luxury Trades and Consumerism in Ancien Régime Paris*, 99–137, Aldershot: Ashgate.

Sarti Raffaella. (2004), *Europe at Home. Family and Material Culture 1500–1800*, New Haven: Yale University Press.

Schama, Simon. (1997), *The Embarrassment of Riches. An Interpretation of Dutch Culture in the Golden Age*, London: Random House.

Scheire, Willem. (2012), 'Geschiedschrijving van het evidente: het verhaal van de koelkast', *Volkskunde*, 113 (2): 129–51.

Scherman, Susanna. (2007a), *Den Svenska Kakelugnen: 1700-talets Tillverkning från Marieberg till Rörstrand*, Stockholm.

Scherman, Susanna. (2007b), *Den Svenska Kakelungnen: 1700-talets Tillverkning från Marieberg och Rörstrand*, Stockholm: Wahlström & Wistrand.

Schivelbusch, Wolfgang. (1995), *Disenchanted Night. The Industrialization of Light in the Nineteenth Century*, Berkely: University of California Press.

Schuurman, Anton. (1997), 'Aards Geluk. Consumptie en de moderne samenleving', in Anton Schuurman, Jan de Vries, Ad Van der Woude (eds), *Aards geluk. De Nederlanders en hun spullen, 1550-1850*, 11-28, Amsterdam: Balans.

Schuurman, Anton. (1989), *Materiële cultuur en levensstijl, Een onderzoek naar de taal der dingen op het Nederlandse platteland in de 19^e eeuw:de Zaanstreek, Oost-Groningen, Oost-Brabant*, Utrecht: HES Uitgevers.

Schwartz Cowan, Ruth. (1989), 'The Consumption Junction: A Proposal for Research Strategies in the Sociology of Technology', in Wiebe E. Bijker and Trevor Pinch (eds), *The Social Construction of Technological Systems: New Directions in the Sociology and History of Technology*, 261-80, Cambridge: MIT Press.

Schwartz Cowan, Ruth. (1983), *More Work for Mother. The Ironies of Household Technology from the Open Hearth to the Microwave*, New York: Basic Books.

Segers, Yves. (2003), *Economische groei en levensstandaard. Particuliere consumptie en voedselverbruik in België, 1800-1913*, Leuven: Universitaire Pers Leuven.

Selling, Gösta (1967), 'Den Svenska Kakelugnens Tvåhundraårsjubileum', *Saga och Sed*, 75-101.

Sir John Soane's Museum. (2007), *A New Description of Sir John Soane's Museum*, London.

Skelley, Allan Ramsay. (1977), *The Victorian Army at Home: The Recruitment and Terms and Conditions of the British Regular, 1859-1899*, Montreal: McGill-Queen's University Press.

Slack, Paul. (2015), *The Invention of Improvement*, Oxford: Oxford University Press.

Stewart, Rachel. (2009), *The Town House in Georgian London*, New Haven and London: Yale University Press.

Stobart, Jon and Cristina Prytz. (2018), 'Comfort in English and Swedish Country Houses, c.1760-1820', *Social History*, 43 (2): 234-58.

Stobart, Jon and Mark Rothery. (2016), *Consumption and the Country House*, Oxford: Oxford University Press.

Stobart, Jon. (2018), 'Housekeeper, Correspondent and Confidante: The Under-told Story of Mrs Hayes of Charlecote Park', *Family and Community History*, 21 (2): 96-111.

Stokroos, Meindert. (2001), *Verwarmen en verlichten in de negentiende eeuw*, Zutphen: Walburg Pers.

Storey, John. (2016), *The making of English Popular Culture*, London: Routledge.

Stoye, John. (1991), 'The Grand Tour in the Seventeenth Century', *Journal of Anglo-Italian Studies*, 1: 62-74.

Taylor, Derek. (2003), *Ritzy: British Hotels, 1837-1987*, London: The Millman Press.

Taylor, Vanessa and Frank Trentmann. (2011), 'Liquid Politics. Water and the Politics of Everyday Life in the Modern City', *Past & Present*, 211 (1): 199-241.

Thornton, Peter. (2000), *Authentic Décor: The Domestic Interior 1620-1920*, London: Seven Dials, Cassell & Co.

Tiersten, Lisa. (2001), *Marianne in the Market: Envisioning Consumer Society in Fin-de-Siecle France*, Berkeley: University of California Press.

Tinniswood, Adrian. (1995), *Life in the English Country Cottage*, London: Weidenfeld Nicholson.

Tinniswood, Adrian. (1998), *The Polite Tourist*, London: The National Trust.

Tipping, Henry Avary. (1912), 'An Eighteenth Century Doll's House', *Country Life*, 28 December: 936–8.

Tosh, John. (1999), *A Man's Place: Masculinity and the Middle-Class Home in Victorian England*, London and New Haven: Yale University Press.

Trentmann, Frank. (2016), *Empire of Things. How we became a World of Consumers from the Fifteenth Century to the Twenty-First*, London: Penguin.

Ulväng, Göran. (2008), *Herrgårdarnas historia: Arbete, liv och bebyggelse på uppländska herrgårdar*, Hedemora: Hallgren & Björklund Förlag.

Ulvang, Marie. (2017), 'Farmerification Housing and Housework in Rural Sweden', Podcast.

Veblen, Thorstein. (1970), *The Theory of the Leisure Class. An Economic Study of Institutions*, London: Allen & Unwin.

Verhoeven, Gerrit. (2013), 'Foreshadowing Tourism? Looking for Modern and Obsolete Features – or a Missing Link – in Early Modern Travel Behaviour (1600–1750)', *Annals of Tourism Research*, 42: 262–83.

Verhoeven, Gerrit. (2017), 'In Search of the New Rome? Creative Cities and early Modern Travel Behaviour', in Ilja Van Damme, Bert De Munck and Andrew Miles (eds), *Cities and Creativity from the Renaissance to the Present*, 65–84, London: Routledge.

Verhoeven, Gerrit. (2018), 'Tangible Beauty. Louis Engelbert's Grand Tour', in Mark Derez, Soetkin Vanhauwaert and Anne Verbrugge (eds), *Arenberg. Portrait of a Family, Story of a Collection*, 312–19, Turnhout: Brepols.

Verhoeven, Gerrit. (2015), *Europe within Reach. Netherlandish Travellers on the Grand Tour and Beyond (1585–1750)*, Leiden: Brill.

Vickery, Amanda. (2009), *Behind Closed Doors. At Home in Georgian England*, New Haven: Yale University Press.

Vickery, Amanda. (2008), 'An Englishman's Home is His Castle? Thresholds, Boundaries and Privacies in the Eighteenth-Century London House', *Past & Present*, 199 (1): 147–73.

Vickery, Amanda. (2006), 'His and Hers: Gender, Consumption and Household Accounting in Eighteenth-Century England', *Past and Present*, 197 (1): 12–38.

Vickery, Amanda. (1993), 'Women and the World of Goods: A Lancashire Consumer and her Possessions 1751–1781', in John Brewer and Roy Porter (eds), *Consumption and the World of Goods*, 274–301, London: Routledge.

Vickery, Amanda. (2006), '"Neat and Not Too Showy": Words and Wallpaper in Regency England," in John Styles and Amanda Vickery (eds), *Gender, Taste, and Material Culture in Britain and North America, 1700–1830*, 201–24, London: Yale University Press.

Voskuil, J. J. (1987), "Boedelsbeschrijvingen als bron voor groepsvorming en groepsgedrag", Volkskundig Bulletin, 13 (1): 30–58.

Wainwright, Clive. (1989), *The Romantic Interior. The British Collector at Home, 1750–1850*, New Haven: Yale University Press.

Waller, Philip. 'George Robert Sims', *Oxford Dictionary of National Biography*.

Walsh, Claire. (2000), 'Shopping et Tourisme. L'attrait des boutiques Parisiennes au XVIIIe siècle', in Natacha Coquery (ed), *La boutique et la ville. Commerces, commerçants, espaces et clientèles, XVIe–XXe siècle*, 223–37, Tours: Belin.

Watkin, D. (1996), *Sir John Soane: Enlightenment, thought and the Royal Academy Lectures*, Cambridge: Cambridge University Press.

Weber, Eugen. (1977), *Peasants into Frenchmen: The Modernization of Rural France, 1870–1914*, London: Chatto and Windus.

Whitfield, Carol. (1982), 'Barracks Life in the Nineteenth Century; or, How and Why Tommy's Lot Improved', *Material Culture Review*, 15: 49–52.

Willmert, T. (1993), 'Heating Methods and their Impact on Soane's Work: Lincoln's Inn Fields and Dulwich Picture Gallery', *Journal of Society of Architectural Historians*, LII, 26–58.

Wolff, Charlotta. (2005), *Vänskap och makt: Den svenska politiska eliten och upplysningstidens Frankrike*, Helsingfors and Stockholm: Svenska litteratursällskapet i Finland and Atlantis.

Worboys, Michael, Julie-Marie Strange and Neil Pemberton, *The Invention of the Modern Dog: Breed and Blood in Victorian Britain*, Baltimore, MD: Johns Hopkins University Press.

Wright, Lawrence. (1964), *Home Fires Burning. The History of Domestic Heating and Cooking*, London: Routledge and Kegan Paul.

Wright, Lawrence. (1960), *Clean and Decent: The Fascinating History of the Bathroom and the Water Closet*, London: Routledge and Kegan Paul.

Wylie, Laurence. (1957), *Village in the Vaucluse*, Cambridge: Harvard University Press.

Yang, Wan and Anne Mattila. (2016), 'Why do we buy Luxury Experiences? Measuring Value Perceptions of Luxury Hospitality Services', *International Journal of Contemporary Hospitality Management*, 28 (9): 1848–67.

Index

Note: Page numbers in italics refer to figures.

Abbot Baudeau   82
Adam, James   32
Adam, Robert   32, 68, 217
Adams, Christine   26
Adventures of Mr Verdant Green, The   210
advice literature   105, 109, 111, 113–15, 127, 128, 130–6, 139–41, 145 n.16
Ahlund, Mikael   66 n.55
Åkerö house design   55–6
Allen, John W.   197–9
American Dictionary of the English Language (Webster)   3
Amorous Traveller, The   171
animal things, in late-Victorian Britain   234–7
Archer, John   19, 37 n.25
architectural 'fitness'   31
architectural convenience   20–1
architectural treatises   11, 39, 46, 67, 100, 101, *102*, 130, 241, 242
armchairs   46, 53, 54, 56, 61, 74, 156, 161, 164, 167, 169, 200, 211, *219*
Armfelt, Gustaf Mauritz   97
Army and Navy list advertiser (1878, 1891)   198, 199
Army Sanitary Committee reforms (1861–2)   190
Arrowsmith, John   2
Art at Home series   133
Audley End (Essex)   217–18, *218*
Austen, Jane   4, 5, 7, 8, 15 nn.19–20, 15 n.26, 16 nn.43–4, 22, 35, 38 n.51, 231 n.1
autobiographies   133

baby-house   149–50
Bachelard, Gaston   9, 215, 227, 230
bachelor box, in Finland   155–6
  comfort from freedom and   158
  food and linen and   157–8
  and space and material culture temporal, temporal and flexible use of   156–7

bachelorhood   12, 13, 16 n.46, 135, 137, 155–8, 181–5, 228, 241, 242
ballad pubs   205 n.29
Bankes, Nugent   211
Barrack Accommodation Committee (1855)   188
barrack beds   204 n.10
barracks   187–91, *192*, 194–7, 200, 203–4 n.1, 204 n.12, 205 n.22, 206 n.46, 242
Barrett, Thomas   25
Barton, Bernard   183
bed chambers   35, 56, 61, 67–71, 218, 220–1, 225
bedrooms   3, 35, 42, 49, 54, 56, 61, 68, 69, 71, 73, 75, 84, 88, 96, 129, 132, 140, 143, 150, 156, 164, 166, 167, 201, 209
  in Duchess of Orleans' apartment at Palais-Royal   75
beds   53, 54, 61, 74, 85, 153, 156, 161, 187, 189, 191, *192*, 204 n.10, 242
Belgian homes   104–6
  domestic comfort and   106–9
  light and   109–12
  reasoned resilience and   114–16
  spatial arrangements and household organization and   112–14
bequests, sentimentalizing and memorializing through   228–30
Berg, Maxine   37 n.24, 228, 229
Bergmans, Anna   121 n.62
Berkhout, Jan Teding van   163, 164, 165, 167–72, 179 n.70
Berkhout, Paulus Teding van   167
Bernez, Marie-Odile   4, 7, 46
Berry, Christopher J.   37 n.24
Black, Jeremy   175 n.3
Blondel, Jacques-François   39–43, 46, 50
Bloomberg Consumer Comfort Index   239

bourgeois home comforts 32–5
Bowie, David 175 n.2
Bramah, Joseph 68, 69
Branden, Corneille-Jean-Marie van den 167, 169
Briseux, Charles Étienne 46, 50
Bristol barracks 205 n.22
Brooke, Willoughby de 221
Brown, Ford Madox 211
Brown, Lancelot 'Capability' 30
Brown, Richard 35
Burne-Jones, Edward 211
Burney, Fanny 8
Buxton, Juliana Mary 10

Caddy, Florence 132
Caminologie, ou Traité des cheminées (Caminology, or Treaty of Fireplaces) 78
Campbell, Colen 21
Camp sketches 200
campaign furniture 13, 196, 197, 199, 202, 203, 206 n.39
candles 109, 110, 113, 152
Canons Ashby (Northamptonshire) 220
canopy beds 54, 56, 61
Carcel lamp 110
Cardwell reforms (1872) 188, 197, 203, 205 n.22
Cassa, Johannes Samuel 176 n.11
Cassell's Household Guide 130
'Castle Gothic' style 31
Cavendish, Henrietta 222, 230
central heating 99–101, 198
Chain of Principles (Arrowsmith) 2
chairs 3, 8, 9, 10, 23, 46, 50, 53–4, 56, 58–61, 74, 133, 139, 152, 156, 161, 164, 167, 169, 198, 200–2, 211, 214, 219, 227–9, 242
Chambers, William 22, 26
Charlecote Park (Warwickshire) 216, 221, 224
Charpy, Manuel 119 n.29
Chavasse, Hannah 217
Cheerful Homes (Kirton) 131
chimneys 3, 21, 78, 80, 83, 93–6, 100, 151, 152, 193
'Church Gothic' style 31
Churchill, Sarah 225, 227, 229

Cieraad, Irene 115, 121 n.62
Classical style 22, 24–5, 30–3
Clayton, David 152
climate and architecture 24, 49, 59, 61–2, 74, 76, 88, 93, 96
closets 19, 42, 49, 153, 209. *See also* water closets
Coade, Eleanor 103 n.2
Coade stone 100, 103 n.2
coal 67, 85, 94, 96, 100, 109, 200
Cock, Christopher 151
Cohen, Deborah 129, 131
Cointeraux, François 86
cold 10, 24, 28, 35, 40, 48–50, 59, 61, 93, 95, 96, 101, 102, 105, 106, 119 n.28, 167
  impossible fight against 73–6
  thermal comfort and 77, 79, 81, 84–8
colonnade 24
column stove 108, 119 n.30
comfort, origin and early views of 2–7
comfortable home
  for labouring poor 25–32
  through objects 53–7
Comfort for Small Incomes (Warren) 130
Comfort of things, The (Miller) 187
Comforts of Matrimony (Sayer) 7, 8, 9
Complete and Universal English Dictionary (Barclay) 3
Complete Body of Architecture, A (Ware) 20, 21, 67
Complete Indian Housekeeper and Cook, The 201
Conolly, Louisa 68
consolation 1, 2, 3, 6, 7, 25, 140
conspicuous consumption model 160–1, 163, 168, 174, 177 n.18
contentment 7, 9, 19, 68, 183, 185, 216, 243
convenience
  comparison with beautiful and proportional facades 23
  domestic architecture 20
  of inhabitant, comparison with architectural design 20–1
Convenient and Ornamental Architecture, Consisting of Original Designs, for Plans, Elevations, and Sections (Crunden) 26

Corbin, Alain   162, 176 n.10
Corcoran, Michael   72 n.17
Cornforth, John   3, 5, 71 n.1, 217, 241
corridors   12, 96, 240
cottages   5, 7, 27–30, *29*, 33, *34*, 39, 75, 77
　with four rooms, elevation and plans for   *29*
　idealisation of   15 n.26
　inconveniences of   28
country houses   3, 5, 6, 21, 24, 25, 27, 29, 32, 35, 39–40, 129, 134, 139, 215, 216, 218, 222, 243. *See also* Swedish country houses
countryside   40, 42, 84, 87–8
　countryside, French   88
Court, Pieter de la   162, 165, 167, 171
Cowan, Ruth Schwartz   105, 118 n.8
Craven, William   229, 230
creature comforts   2, 20
Cronstedt, Carl Johan   94
Crowley, John   3, 4, 15 n.26, 30, 45, 128, 177 n.18, 178 n.33, 239, 241
Crunden, John   26
Cumming, Alexander   68
Cursory Notes of Building (North)   20

Daily News Weekly   236
darkness   50, 105, 106, 155
d'Aulnay, Dupré   79
Dawson, William   133
Deane, A. C.   134
decoration of rooms   13, 25, 41, 46, 48–9, 74, 95, 110, 149, 151, 191, 216–18, 229, 236
　home making and   127, 128, 130–2, 135, 139, 140, 142, 145 n.16
　in Swedish country houses   52–60
　wallpaper sandwich and   208, 209, 211, 212 n.3, 213 n.8
Defoe, Daniel   8
DeJean, Joan   3, 4, 5, 26, 37 n.25, 46, 239, 240
De la distribution des maisons de plaisance (Blondel)   40, *41*
democratization, of comfort   122 n.72
Denison, Edward   21
Desaguliers, John Theophilus   78
Désarnod, Charles-François   85
Description of the Villa of Mr Horace Walpole, A (Walpole)   25

Designs for Elegant Cottages and Small Villas, Calculated for the Comfort and Convenience of Persons of Moderate and of Ample Fortune (Gyfford)   32, *34*
de Villers, François Zoete de Laecke   164, 168, 169
de Villers, Philippe Zoete de Laecke   164, 168, 169
Dewes, Anne   227
dialogue conteinyng the nomber in effect of all the prouerbes in the Englishe tongue, A (Heywood)   8
diaries   6, 58, 62, 135, 138–41, 144, 145 n.16, 161, 164, 174
Dictionary of Human Conservation (Macquart)   87
Dictionary of the English Language (Johnson)   2, 20
dining room   33, 47, 49, 51, 53, 61, 97, 101, 108, 109, 134, 138, 141, 150, 152, 156, 164, 165, 199, 223
　ideal   135, *136*
discomfort   6, 7, 30, 46, 53, 62, 76, 77, 109, 115, 132–3, 162, 177 n.18, 237
　comfort and   57–61
divans   53
dogs   13, 61, 200, 234–7
Domestic Architecture (Brown)   35
domestic comforts   4, 12, 21, 28, 30, 35, 39, 43, 68, 78, 104, 106, 110, 112–13, 114, 117, 131, 155–8, 161, 163–4, 181–5, 208, 211–12
　and home comfort, comparison of   27
domestic convenience   24, 68
domestic heat   86, 107. *See also* thermal comfort
domestic material culture   3, 12, 49, 240. *See also* material culture
Donaldson, Aggie   135
Donaldson, Andrew   135
Dorp, Pieter Cornelisz van   172
Dortyol, Ibrahim   175 n.1, 176 n.9, 177 n.27, 178 nn.41, 45, 179 n.56
double glazing   96
Douro chair   200
drawing room   6, 12, 33, 35, 49, 51–4, 62, 67, 74, 75, 75, 156, 163, 198, 218, 223, 228, 236

drawing rooms, Victorian middle-class   127–30, 146 n.49
  comfort in   134–8
  English love of comforts and   141–4
  Orlebar and   138–41
  women and comfort in home and   130–4
dressing rooms   62, 67–71, 129, 209, 223
Dr Thorne (Trollope)   137
Dryden, Edward   220
Dryden, Elizabeth   227, 228
Duke of Wellington   188, 198, 204 n.3
Durand, Ralph   209

Eastlake, Charles Locke   132
economy, compactness, and regularity, principles of   34
Edgeworth, Maria   151
Edward, Mary Holbech   219
Edward, third Lord Leigh   218, 219
Edwards, Clive   176 n.10, 177 nn.20, 33, 178 n.33
Eger, Elizabeth   37 n.24
Ekeblad, Brita Horn   56, 57, 96, 97
Ekeblad, Clas Julius   56–7, 96
elegance   5–7, 21–4, 29, 31, 35, 42, 69, 108, 136, 137, 139, 151, 162–4, 170, 197, 198
  utility and   33
Elements of Criticism (Home and Kames)   23, 24
Elsam, Richard   69
Emma (Austen)   8, 35–6
emotions   2, 7, 9–13, 39, 62, 93, 100, 103, 106, 155, 200, 234, 237, 242–3
  bachelorhood and   181–5
  family, memory, and domestic objects and   215, 220, 222–5, 227, 229, 230
  the Netherlandish Grand Tour and   162, 168, 169, 175
  Uppark Doll's House and   149, 151, 153
  Victorian middle-class drawing rooms and   127–34, 136–43
Engelbert, Louis   164, 173
English comfort   4, 6
Epp, Amber   215
Eriksdotter, Gulhild   49

Essay on Taste, An (Gerard)   22
Essay on the Principle of Population (Malthus)   9
external regularity and internal convenience   23, 24

Fairfax-Lucy, Alice   232 n.27
family, objects and memory   214–15
  family trees and family albums and   222–4
  house as family memorial and   216–18
  household objects and   225–8
  rooms and memorials and   218–21
  sentimentalizing and memorializing through bequests and   228–30
family and friends   7, 8, 25, 39, 42, 50, 57, 62, 115, 139, 157, 167, 168, 173, 181, 191, 193–5, 225–9
Febvre, Lucien   76
Feetham, William   101, 103 n.4
Ferrars, Robert   5
Fersen, Axel von   48, 49, 52, 54, 64 n.17, 65 n.41
Fetherstonhaugh, Matthew   149
Fetherstonhaugh, Sarah   149, 153
fireplaces   74, 75–6, 80–1, 108. *See also* thermal comfort
fires   3, 5, 6, 9, 10, 16 n.50, 50, 59, 94–6, 152, 167, 240
  in Belgian homes   106, 108–9, 113–15, 120 n.33
  thermal comfort in France and   75–81, 84, 85
Fitzgerald, William   10
Flexible Domesticities   155
floorplans and designs   50, 51, 72 n.28, 96, 152, 217
Fois-Mie, H.   119 n.26
food   2, 27, 40, 58, 133, 165, 177 n.27, 204 n.12, 242
food and linen, and bachelor boxes   157–8
Forth, Elizabeth   225, 230
Forth, John   225
Four Books of Andrea Palladio's Architecture, A (Ware)   21
Fourier, Jean-Baptiste Joseph   80
Franklin, Benjamin   78

Franklin stove   80
French aristocracy   143
Fridsberg, Olof   55
From Kitchen to Garrett (Panton)   127
fuel   12, 84, 94, 108, *111*, 113, 240, 241. *See also* coal; wood
fuel efficiency   52, 79, 81, 85, 107, 188
furniture   3, 5, 6, 13, 19, 46, 49, 53, 54, 56, 60, 100, 127, 139–40, 142, 146 n.47, 152, 156, 161, 167, 178 n.33, 188–9, 196, 198, 200–2, 206 nn.38–9, 216

Gachard, M.   120 n.39
Galavan, Susan   72 n.17
Gardie, Hedvig De la   59
Gaskell, Elizabeth   3, 7
gas lighting   110
Gauger, Nicolas   77–8, 85
Gay, Peter   122 n.72
Geijer, Erik Gustaf   6
gender   109, 112, 117, 127–9, 133, 134, 137, 138, 142, 143, 212, 240
Genneté, Léopold de   78
genre painting   59–60
Gerard, Alexander   22, 26
Geurts, Anne   179 n.68
Gibbons, Edward   86
Gibbs, Philip   133
Gilpin, William   24–5
Girouard, Mark   5, 71 n.1, 134, 143
Gloag, John   128
Gloucestershire barrack   205 n.18
Goff, Olivier le   86, 114, 115
Goldsmith, Sarah   10, 179 n.69
Gomme, Andor   218
Gore, William   67
Gothic style, of building   24
Gothic-style interiors   30, 31
Grand Tour   10, 12, 149, 242
    the Netherlandish   160–75
Granhammar country estate (Sweden)   48, 50–2
    plans of   51
Grant, Anne   22
Greater Manchester Record Office Documentary Photography Archive   146 n.48
Greig, Hannah   177 n.20

Grier, Katherine   128
Griffin, John Griffin   217
Gronovius, Jacobus   176 n.11
Guang Yu Ren   21
guest satisfaction   175 n.1, 176 n.9, 178 n.45, 179 n.56, 180 n.74
Gyfford, Edward   32–3, 34
Gyllenborg, Carl Johan   58
Gyllenborg, Sara   58

Hamling, Tara   214
Hardyment, Christina   104
Hargreaves, Thomas   223
Hårleman, Carl   47–8, 49, 50
Harley, Edward   222, 223
Harris, Amy   181
Harvey, Karen   16 n.36, 129
Haussmann buildings   43
Haweis, Mrs.   131, 135
Hawksmoor, Nicholas   32
Hayes, Phillipa   228
hearth   75, 79, 81, 88, 95, 115, 116, 119 n.26, 151–2, 166, 167, 185, 239, 241
    comfortable   106–9
Heath, William   198
heating   20, 21, 27, 35, 48, 49, 52, 74, 76–80, 82, 84–8, 95, 97, 99–102, 104–9, 112–17, 118 n.10, 119 nn.21, 28, 120 n.33, 151–2, 167, 198, 240, 241
    devices   *107*, 119 n.28
Hébrard, Pierre   78
Heidenstam, Verner von   93, 97, 97 n.1
Heyl, Christoph   177 n.20
Heywood, John   8
Hilleström, Pehr   59–61
Hints for Dwellings (Laing)   32, 33
Hints on Household Taste (Eastlake)   132
Hints to Gentlemen of Landed Property (Kent)   26
Hinwick Hall   139–40
History of Audley End (Neville)   217
History of Rasselas (Johnson)   2
home   7–10. *See also individual entries*
    abroad and at   9–10
    and house compared   7, 9, 93
Home, Henry   23
Home Chat   131
'Home Comfort' (Hardyment)   104

home comforts   1, 11–13, 19, 22, 23, 26,
    27, 30, 36, 93, 164, 167, 174, 187,
    200, 203–4 n.1, 234, 241–3
  bourgeois   32–5
  comparison with domestic
    comfort   27
homesickness   194
Hoorn, Ten   166, 173
Horfield Barracks   205 n.22
Hoskins, Lesley   113, 128, 134, 146 n.46
house, as family memorial   216–18
House Architecture (Stevenson)   143
'House Gothic' style   31
household objects and memory   225–8
house-museum and heating system
    99–103
  basement rooms plan at   *102*
How I Managed my House for £200 a Year
    (Warren)   130
Huddleston, Richard   10
Hughes, Catherine   223, 224
Hume, David   20, 33
Hussey, Christopher   153 n.3
hygiene   109, 113, 162, 176 n.9,
    188, 198

Ideal Home exhibition   153 n.2
inconveniences   6, 22, 25, 28, 30, 33, 77,
    79, 80, 102, 105, 165
  physical   23, 24
indoor temperature   74–5
informality and physical comfort, linking
    of   5
Inquiry into the Nature and Causes of the
    Wealth of Nations, An (Smith)   27
internal convenience   23
intimacy   5, 9, 10, 127, 138, 141, 153,
    164, 168, 218. *See also* privacy
Ivanhoe (Scott)   4

Jacobean interiors   216, 217
Jennings, H. R.   135, 136
Johnson, Samuel   2, 20
Journal des Luxus und der Moden   6
Journal oeconomique   79
journals   6, 79, 138, 162, 164, 167, 174, 241

Kabul Committee on Equipment
    (1882)   202
Kalle, K.   156

Kames, Lord   23–4, 26
Kent, Nathaniel   26–8
Kerr, Robert   130, 135
Kersey, John   2, 7
King, Thomas   191, 192, 194–6,
    205 nn.23, 33
Kirton, John   131
Kitapci, Olgun   175 n.1, 176 n.9,
    177 n.27, 178 nn.41, 45, 179 n.56
kitchen   33, 35, 40, 51–2, 94, 100, 112,
    138, 150, 152, 188
  impacting thermal comfort   51–2
Knight, John Lucy   216
Knight, Richard Payne   25, 30
Kwint, Marius   214

Laing, David   32, 33, 34
Lamb, Charles   181–5, *182*
Lamb, Mary   181, 182–5
La Mécanique du Feu (The Mechanics of
    Fire) (Gauger)   77
lamps   3, 106, 109, 110
Lantingshausen, Jacob Albrect von   50
laundry services and bachelor
    boxes   157–8
Leeuwen, Wim Denslagen en Wies
    van   121 n.62
Legnér, Mattias   49
Leibetseder, Matthis   175 n.3
Leigh, Charles   222
Leigh, Edward, fifth Lord Leigh   229–30
Leigh, Mary   229
Leigh, Thomas, fourth Lord Leigh
    222
Leslie, J. H.   206 n.46
Lethieullier, Christopher   151
letters   6, 12, 58, 59, 62, 73, 141, 144,
    157, 161, 163, 164, 167, 169–71,
    173, 174, 182–5, 198, 217,
    226–8
Letters from the Mountains (Grant)   22
Lewis, Judith   9, 129, 139, 215, 243
light/lighting   5, 20, 23, 45, 49, 50, 52,
    61, 62, 77–8, 93, 100, 102, 103–6,
    108–17, 152, 242. *See also* candles;
    lamps
  artificial   49, 50, 54
  devices, by fuel   110–11, *111*
  natural   60, 111
Ljung country house   54

Löfstad country house 54
Logan, Thad 129
Loudon, J. C. 146 n.49
Lucy, George 216, 228, 229
Lucy, George Hammond 217, 230
Lucy, John Hammond 216
Lucy, Mary Elizabeth 216, 220–1, 223, 224, 230
Ludolf, Job 169
luxury, studies of 37 n.24

'Mackery End' (Charles) 181
Macquart, Louis-Charles-Henri 87
Maeyer, Jan De 121 n.62
maison de plaisance models 40, 42–3
Makepeace, William 229
Mälsåker country estate (Sweden) 48–50
Malthus, Thomas 9
Manning, Thomas 184
Mariette, Jean 39
Marquis of Montalembert 80
Mary Barton (Gaskell) 3
masculinities 51, 129, 135, 136, 138, 208, 211, 212
master–servant relationship 12, 39–43, 52, 61, 97, 108, 109, 112–15, 117, 121 n.62, 153, 163, 164, 168–70, 200, 240, 243
material culture 3, 12, 49, 106, 151, 162, 167, 168, 182, 187, 208, 240
  and consumption 54
  temporal and flexible use of space and 156–7
Mattila, Anne 177 n.18
Meersch, Abraham van der 176 n.11
Memoirs of the Royal Academy of Sciences 80
memorials 9, 222–30, 231 n.16
  bequests and 228–30
  house as family 216–18
  rooms, memories and 218–21
memory 13, 133, 191, 193, 169, 203, 214, 215, 235, 242. See also memorials
Mercier, Louis-Sébastien 84
Milistina 10
Miller, Daniel 187
miniatures 223, *224*, 229
mirrors 49, 50, 54, 55, 62, 101, 152, 153, 167, 201

Moll Flanders 2
Montagu, Elizabeth 25
Montesquieu 86
Moore, Hannah 8
Morland, Catherine 214, 220, 230
Morris, William 211
Morris wallpaper 211–12
moving house and bachelors 181–5
Mr Bragwell and his two daughters (Moore) 8
Museum of Domestic Design and Architecture (Middlesex University) 208
Muthesius, Stefan 117 n.3
Mysteries of Udolpho, The (Radcliffe) 214

Neo-Classical style 25, 35
Netherlandish Grand Tour 160–2
  facilities 162–7
  services 168–72
  spaces 172–3
Neville, Richard 217, 225, 230
Neville, Sir Henry 217
New Designs in Architecture, Consisting of Plans, Elevations, and Sections for Various Buildings (Richardson) 28
New Dictionary of the English Language (Richardson) 3, 7
New English Dictionary (Kersey) 2
New Penny Magazine 235
New World of Words (Phillips) 7
Noldus Badeloch Vera 64 n.15
Norrby, Göran 64 n.17
North, Roger 20, 34
Northanger Abbey (Austen) 4
Nource, Nick 205 n.29

Observations on the Theory and Practice of Landscape Gardening (Repton) 30, 31
Ó Gráda, Diarmuid 72 n.17
On Planning a Country House (North) 20
open fire technology 108–9
Orlebar, Frederica 138
Orlin, Lena Cowen 215
Orrinsmith, Mrs. 133
Our Homes (Jennings) 135, *136*
Oxenstierna, Johan Gabriel 6, 58

paintings 5, 53–6, 58–62, 66 n.55, 152, 160, 193–4, 222–4, 229
Palladianism 21
Pamela (Richardson) 2
Panton, Jane Ellen 127, 134, 136, 138
Peacock, William 228
Pemberton, William 68
Pennsylvania fireplace. *See* Franklin stove
people and objects, relationship between 9–12. *See also individual entries*
Perkins, A. M. 101
petrol (paraffin) lamps 110
Phillips, Edward 7
photographs 135, 145 n.16, 146 n.48, 153 n.3, 159 n.5, 214, 234, 235
  Victorian barracks and 191–5, 199, 200, 203
physical comfort 4, 5, 10, 12, 19, 45, 46, 54, 56, 102, 109, 115, 150, 151, 153, 158, 182, 183, 239, 241, 243
pictorial family tree 222
pictures 6, 57–61, 106, 173, 214, 215, 223–4, 227–9, 235, 243
  Victorian barracks and 191, 194, 199, 200, 201
picturesque aesthetic 5, 6, 24, 30, 32
Pindar, John 194, 204 n.12
Plans et Élevations des Bâtiments de Suède (Hårleman) 50
Political, Economic and Philosophical Essays (Rumford) 80
powdering room 68–71
Powys, Lybbe 222
Practical Education (Edgeworth) 151
Price, H. C. 101
Price, Linda 215
Price, Uvedale 30, 32
Pride and Prejudice (Austen) 4
privacy 3, 5, 7, 12, 20, 26, 27, 61, 100, 105, 161–5, 168–70, 177 n.20, 184, 188, 196, 200, 202, 209, 239, 240, 243. *See also* intimacy
Puckler-Muskau, Prince 6, 7, 15 n.27

Queen Marie Antoinette 95
Quinquet lamps 110

Radcliffe, Ann 214

Radojevic, Tijana 175 n.1, 176 n.9, 177 n.15, 179 n.56, 180 n.74
Ramel, Hans 50
Regimental Museum (Gloucester) 195
Rehn, Jean Eric *51*, 54, 61
Reilly, Charles 133
Reisboek (*Guidebook for the United provinces and the neighbouring countries and kingdoms*) (Hoorn) 166, 173
Repton, Humphry 30–2
Retford, Kate 222
Richardson, Charles 3, 7
Richardson, Charles James 100, 101
Richardson, George 28
Richardson, Samuel 2, 7
Riello, Giorgio 177 n.20
Roche, Daniel 105, 163
Roijen, Jan van 168
room arrangement 5, 23, 28, 35, 43, 61, 67, 81, 112–14, 116, 127, 130, 139–40, 181–4, 240
room use 26, 30, 40, 49, 112, 153, 240. *See also individual entries*
rooms and memorials 218–21
Ross of Dublin 202
Rumford, Comte de 80–1
Rumford stove 81
Rybczynzki, Witold 9, 26, 37 n.25
Ryde, Edward 135

Sarti, Rafaella 116, 177 n.20
Sayer, Robert 7
Sayer, William Thomas 191, 194–5
Schama, Simon 176 n.10
Scheire, Willem 117
Schivelbusch, Wolfgang 110
Schuurman, Anton 120 n.37
Scott, Walter 4
Selling, Gösta 52, 53
Sense and Sensibility (Austen) 4, 5, 8
Series of Plans, for Cottages or Habitations of the Labourer, Either in Husbandry, or the Mechanic Arts, Adapted as well to Towns, as to the Country (Wood) 28
Serlio, Sebastiano 39
servants 52, 61, 67, 71, 139, 149, 153, 200, 201, 202, 220, 243

in Belgian homes 108, 109, 112–15, 117, 121 n.62
the Netherlandish Grand Tour and 160, 163–4, 168–70, 175
showy discomfort 115
Sims, George R. 234–7
Sketches and Hints on Landscape Gardening (Repton) 30
Sketches in Architecture (Soane) 29
Smith, Adam 27, 33
Soane, John 12, 29, 32, 99–103, 239, 241
Société libre d'émulation (Free Society of Emulation) 82
Société royale d'Agriculture de Lyon (Royal Agricultural Society of Lyon) 82
sofas 3, 6, 9, 53, 54, 61, 139, 140, 152, 155, 156, 157, 227
Soldiers' Institute (Portland barracks) 203 n.1
Soop, Gustaf 48
Sophia Strikes up a Conversation with the Innkeeper After Dinner Has Been Served 166
Southey, Robert 109
spaces 11, 12, 13, 39, 40, 42, 74, 85, 101–3, 149, 150, 156–7, 163, 172–4, 184, 185, 235, 237, 240, 242, 243
in Belgian homes 105, 106, 107, 110–17
convenience, utility, and comfort and 23, 27, 28, 32–5
family, memory and domestic objects and 214, 215, 221, 230
Georgian Dublin and 67–71
student rooms and 208–12
in Swedish country houses 45–9, 53–5, 58, 61–2
Victorian barracks and 187, 188, 191, 192, 194–7, 199, 202
in Victorian middle-class drawing rooms 127–30, 132, 134–6, 138, 139, 142–3
Sparre, Ulla 55
Sparrgren, Lorentz Svensson 56
spatial arrangements and household organization 112–14
staircases 30, 40, 43, 47, 50, 68, 100, 102, 150, 161, 164
Stallard, Arthur 131
Stanic, Nemad 175 n.1, 176 n.9, 177 n.15, 179 n.56, 180 n.74

Stanisic, Nemanja 175 n.1, 176 n.9, 177 n.15, 179 n.56, 180 n.74
state apartments 218–19
Stevenson, J. J. 143
Stokroos, Meindert 119 n.30
Stola house (Sweden) 96–7
Stoneleigh Abbey (Warwickshire) 218–19, 222
stoves 82, 83, 85, 87, 88, 100, 101, 106–9, 116, 119 nn.21, 26, 120 nn.33, 39, 167, 239–41
column 108, 119 n.30
Franklin 80
Rumford 81
specialized kitchen 114
tiled 12, 49, 52–4, 59, 61, 76, 93–7
student rooms 155, 158, 208–12, 242
Swedish country houses 45–6
architecture, technology, and comfort and 46–53
comfortable, creation in northern climate 61–2
comfortable home, through objects 53–7
comfort and discomfort and 57–61
Dutch influences in 64 n.15
Sweet, Roey 179 n.69
symmetry, shortcomings of 31
sympathy 20, 33, 237

Tableau de Paris (Mercier) 84
Taylor, Derek 175 n.2
Tessin, Carl Gustaf 50, 55
Tessin, Nicodemus 48
Testimonials of Barrack Furniture 198
thermal comfort 49, 52–4, 61, 73–6, 239. *See also* central heating; fires; stoves
complexities of improving 87–8
eighteenth century domestic heating scientific and technical reflections 76–9
invention of 83–7
kitchen impacting 51–2
Soane Museum and 99–103
technical reflection levels 79–83
Thijs, Johannes 169
Thurlow, Edward Hovell 199–200, *199*, 206 n.46

tiled stoves. *See under* stoves
Tilley, Vesta   193
Tilney, Eleanor   214
Tinniswood, Adrian   15 n.26
Tipping, Henry Avary   153 n.3
Tosh, John   141
travel and comfort   10, 75, 76, 93, 143, 160, 184, 202, 242
    feeling at home abroad and   161–75
Travel Diaries (Montaigne)   76
Treatise of Human Nature, A (Hume)   20
Treatise on Civil Architecture, A (Chambers)   22
Trevelyan, George Otto   203
Trollope, Anthony   137–8

Ulvang, Marie   148 n.89
Uppark Dolls' House   149–53, *150*
utility   21, 22–4, 26, 31, 33, 35–6, 42, 69, 132, 198

Varinli, Inci   175 n.1, 176 n.9, 177 n.27, 178 nn.41, 45, 179 n.56
ventilation   3, 96, 100, 101, 152, 188
vertical flues   94
Vickery, Amanda   8, 129, 184, 213 n.8, 215
Victorian Army At Home   205 n.31, 205–6 n.33
Victorian barracks   187–91
    comfort regulation   202–3
    officers and   196–202
    photographs, images, postcards, and paintings and   191–6, 205 n.18
    sketches   200–1, *201*
Vitruvius Britannicus (Campbell)   21
Vries, Jan de   104, 113
Vuylsteke, Jozef   120 n.33

Wainwright, Clive   231 n.16
Walker Art Gallery (Liverpool)   193
wallpaper sandwich and student room   208–12, *210*
Walpole, Horace   25
Walsh, J. H.   110
Wan Yang   177 n.18
Ware, Isaac   20–1, 23, 26, 67, 68
warmth   12, 27, 30, 45, 49, 52, 54, 59, 61, 75, 84, 86, 95, 103, 106, 119 n.21, 151, 152, 156, 162, 166, 167, 200, 240
water closets   3, 11, 12, 21, 33, 35, 67–71, 154 n.8, 198, 240
    valve   40–1
weather, effects on daily life   59
Webster, Noah   3
Webster, Thomas   121 n.62
Weeton, Ellen   226–7, 230
Wellbeck Abbey (Nottinghamshire)   222
well-being   19, 43, 78, 79, 99, 162, 164, 168, 169, 175
    emotional   9, 45, 103, 106, 139, 149, 162
    material   46, 84, 161, 164, 174, 239
    mental   46, 58
    physical   45, 46, 58, 97, 103, 106, 162, 239
When did you last see your father? (Yeames)   193
Wijnblad, Carl   47
Willement Thomas   216
windows   23, 30, 49, 51, 54, 59–62, 76, 96, 100, 102, 111, 152, 167, 171, 195, 205 n.18, 216, 221
wood, as fuel   74, 76, 95
wood shortage   79, 83–4, 94
Wood, John   28
Woodhouse, Robert   225
Wool Winder, The (painting)   *60*, 60–1
working-class houses   29–30
Wrede, Fabian Casimir   94
Wright, Lawrence   96
Wyatt, James   25
Wylie, Laurence   88
Wynn, Watkin Williams   68

Yeames, William Frederick   193

www.ingramcontent.com/pod-product-compliance
Lightning Source LLC
Chambersburg PA
CBHW070021010526
44117CB00011B/1670